ANCIENT ANGER

Anger is found everywhere in the ancient world, starting with the very first word of the *Iliad* and continuing through all literary genres and every aspect of public and private life. Yet it is only very recently, as a variety of disciplines start to devote attention to the history and nature of the emotions, that classicists, ancient historians, and ancient philosophers have begun to study anger in antiquity with the seriousness and attention it deserves. This volume brings together a number of significant new studies, by authors from different disciplines and countries, on literary, philosophical, medical, and political aspects of ancient anger from Homer until the Roman imperial period. It studies some of the most important ancient sources and provides a paradigmatic selection of approaches to them, and should stimulate further research on this important subject in a number of fields.

SUSANNA BRAUND is Professor of Classics at Yale University. She has authored books and articles on Roman satire, Roman epic and other aspects of Roman literature, including *Beyond Anger: a Study of Juvenal's Third Book of Satires* (1988) and *Latin Literature* (2002). With Christopher Gill, she co-edited *The Passions in Roman Thought and Literature* (1997). Her current major ongoing project is a commentary on Seneca's *De Clementia*.

GLENN W. MOST is Professor of Greek Philology at the Scuola Normale Superiore di Pisa, and Professor in the Committee on Social Thought, University of Chicago. He is the author of *The Measures of Praise: Structure and Function in Pindar's Second Pythian and Seventh Nemean Odes* (1985) and editor and co-editor of numerous books on classical studies, literary theory and philosophy.

VOLUME XXXII
ANCIENT ANGER

Perspectives from Homer to Galen

BY

SUSANNA BRAUND

Professor of Classics, Yale University

AND

GLENN W. MOST

Professor of Greek Philology, Scuola Normale Superiore di Pisa and
Professor in the Committee on Social Thought, University of Chicago

YALE CLASSICAL STUDIES

EDITED FOR THE DEPARTMENT OF CLASSICS

CAMBRIDGE
UNIVERSITY PRESS

PUBLISHED BY THE PRESS SYNDICATE OF THE UNIVERSITY OF CAMBRIDGE
The Pitt Building, Trumpington Street, Cambridge, United Kingdom

CAMBRIDGE UNIVERSITY PRESS
The Edinburgh Building, Cambridge, CB2 2RU, UK
40 West 20th Street, New York, NY 10011–4211, USA
477 Williamstown Road, Port Melbourne, VIC 3207, Australia
Ruiz de Alarcón 13, 28014 Madrid, Spain
Dock House, The Waterfront, Cape Town 8001, South Africa

http://www.cambridge.org

First published 2003
Reprinted 2004

Printed in the United Kingdom at the University Press, Cambridge

Typeface Adobe Garamond 11/12.5 pt.   *System* LATEX 2ε [TB]

A catalogue record for this book is available from the British Library

Library of Congress cataloguing in publication data
Ancient anger: perspectives from Homer to Galen / edited by Susanna Braund, Glenn W. Most.
p.   cm.   (Yale Classical Studies; v. 32)
Includes bibliographical references and indexes.
ISBN 0 521 82625 X (hardback)
1. Classical literature – History and criticism.   2. Anger in literature.   3. Anger – Greece.
4. Anger – Rome.   I. Braund, Susanna.   II. Most, Glenn W.   III. Series.
PA3015.A58A88   2003
880′.09 – dc21   2003051550 CIP

ISBN 0 521 82625 X hardback

Contents

Notes on contributors   *page* vii
Acknowledgments   ix
List of abbreviations   x

Introduction   1
Susanna Braund and Glenn W. Most

1   Ethics, ethology, terminology: Iliadic anger
    and the cross-cultural study of emotion   11
    D. L. Cairns

2   Anger and pity in Homer's *Iliad*   50
    Glenn W. Most

3   Angry bees, wasps, and jurors: the symbolic politics
    of ὀργή in Athens   76
    D. S. Allen

4   Aristotle on anger and the emotions: the strategies
    of status   99
    David Konstan

5   The rage of women   121
    W. V. Harris

6   *Thumos* as masculine ideal and social pathology in ancient
    Greek magical spells   144
    Christopher A. Faraone

7   Anger and gender in Chariton's *Chaereas and Callirhoe*   163
    J. H. D. Scourfield

8 "Your mother nursed you with bile": anger in babies
   and small children   185
   Ann Ellis Hanson

9 Reactive and objective attitudes: anger in Virgil's *Aeneid*
   and Hellenistic philosophy   208
   Christopher Gill

10 The angry poet and the angry gods: problems of theodicy
    in Lucan's epic of defeat   229
    Elaine Fantham

11 An ABC of epic *ira*: anger, beasts, and cannibalism   250
    Susanna Braund and Giles Gilbert

References   286
Index of passages cited   306
Index of proper names   314
Index of topics   321

Notes on contributors

DANIELLE ALLEN is Associate Professor in the Departments of Classics and Political Science and the Committee on Social Thought at the University of Chicago. In the spring of 2002 she was awarded a MacArthur Prize.

SUSANNA MORTON BRAUND is Professor of Classics at Yale University and previously taught at the Universities of Exeter, Bristol, and London. She has published extensively on Roman satire and epic and with Chris Gill co-edited *The Passions in Roman Thought and Literature* (Cambridge, 1997). Her latest book is *Latin Literature* (London and New York, 2002).

DOUGLAS CAIRNS has taught at the Universities of St. Andrews, Otago, and Leeds, and is now Senior Lecturer and Head of the Department of Classics, University of Glasgow. He is author of *Aidos: the Psychology and Ethics of Honour and Shame in Ancient Greek Literature* (Oxford, 1993) and editor of *Oxford Readings in Homer's* Iliad (Oxford, 2001). He takes up the Chair of Classics at the University of Edinburgh in 2004.

ELAINE FANTHAM was educated at Oxford and taught at the University of Toronto, Canada from 1968–86 before moving to Princeton University, where she was Giger Professor of Latin from 1986–2000. She is the author of commentaries on Seneca's *Trojan Women* (Princeton, 1982), Lucan *de Bello Civili* Book 2 (Cambridge, 1992) and Ovid *Fasti* Book 4 (Cambridge, 1998) as well as numerous articles on Lucan and other Roman authors.

CHRISTOPHER A. FARAONE is Professor of Classics at the University of Chicago. He is co-editor (with T. Carpenter) of *Masks of Dionysus* (Ithaca, NY, 1993) and author of *Ancient Greek Love Magic* (Cambridge, MA, 1999) and a number of articles on early Greek poetry, religion, and magic.

GILES GILBERT wrote his dissertation on the depiction of battle in imperial Latin epic at Royal Holloway, University of London; he was awarded the Ph.D. in 2001 and is now teaching Classics at Bancroft's School in Essex, UK.

CHRISTOPHER GILL is Professor of Ancient Thought at the University of Exeter. He is the author of *Personality in Greek Epic, Tragedy and Philosophy: the Self in Dialogue* (Oxford, 1996) and has edited or co-edited six volumes of essays, including, with Susanna Braund, *The Passions in Roman Thought and Literature* (Cambridge, 1997).

ANN ELLIS HANSON teaches in the Classics Department, Yale University, and is a MacArthur Fellow (1992–97). She is the author of some ninety articles in the fields of papyrology and Greek and Roman medicine.

W. V. HARRIS received his D.Phil. from Oxford University; he writes about Greek and Roman History, and also about Italian politics. He is Shepherd Professor of History at Columbia University. His book *Restraining Rage: the Ideology of Anger Control in Classical Antiquity* was published by Harvard at the beginning of 2002.

DAVID KONSTAN is John Rowe Workman Distinguished Professor of Classics and Professor of Comparative Literature at Brown University and he was President of the American Philological Association in 1999. Among his recent publications are *Friendship in the Classical World* (Cambridge, 1997) and *Pity Transformed* (London, 2001). He is currently working on a book on *The Emotions of the Ancient Greeks*.

GLENN W. MOST is Professor of Greek Philology at the Scuola Normale Superiore di Pisa and Professor in the Committee on Social Thought at the University of Chicago. He has written widely on ancient and modern literature, philosophy, scholarship, and art.

J. H. D. SCOURFIELD is Professor of Classics at the National University of Ireland, Maynooth, and author of *Consoling Heliodorus: a Commentary on Jerome, Letter 60* (Oxford, 1993). His research interests include bereavement and grief in the ancient world, and the ancient novel.

Acknowledgments

At the conclusion of what has been a pleasant and stimulating collaboration, we wish to thank all those who have made it possible. The expenses of the original Heidelberg colloquium were borne by a Gottfried Wilhelm Leibniz Preis of the Deutsche Forschungsgemeinschaft. We would also like to thank Giancarlo Abbamonte (Naples), Victor Bers and John Matthews (Yale), Peter Toohey (Calgary), Michael Sharp at Cambridge University Press and Jan Chapman, the copy-editor, and above all Ingeborg von Appen (Heidelberg), who organized the practicalities of the colloquium, and Peter Mazur (Yale), who compiled the indexes and prepared the volume for publication.

Abbreviations

ARV²   J. D. Beazley (1963) *Attic Red-Figure Vase-Painters*, 2nd edn. Oxford.

DT   A. Audollent (1904) *Defixionum Tabellae*. Paris.

DTA   R. Wünsch (1987) *Defixionum Tabellae Atticae*, Appendix to *Inscriptiones Graecae* III. Berlin.

GMA   R. Kotansky (1994) *Greek Magical Amulets: the Inscribed Gold, Silver, Copper, and Bronze Lamellae*, part I : *Published Texts of Known Provenance*, Papyrologica Coloniensia 22.1. Opladen.

GMPT   Betz, H. D. (ed.) (1986) *The Greek Magical Papyri in Translation*. Chicago.

KAR   E. Ebeling. (1915–23) *Keilschrifturkunden aus Assur religiösen Inhalts*, 2 vols. Leipzig.

Lfgr E   B. Snell et al. (eds.) (1979–) *Lexicon des frühgriechischen Epos*. Göttingen.

PGM   K. Preisendanz [and A. Henrichs] (1973–74) *Papyri Graecae Magicae: Die Griechischen Zauberpapyri*, second edn. Stuttgart.

PGM Hymn   E. Heitsch, apud *PGM* pp. 237–66.

SGD   D. Jordan (1985) "A survey of Greek defixiones not included in the special corpora," *GRBS* 26: 151–97.

SM   R. Daniel and F. Maltomini (1990–1) *Supplementum Magicum*, 2 vols., Papyrologica Coloniensia 16.1 and 2. Opladen.

Introduction

Susanna Braund and Glenn W. Most

These days, the emotions are hot stuff. No doubt they always have been, and in more ways than one. For, however often and drastically they interfere with our thinking, the fact remains that the emotions are good tools for thought – not only for thought about the similarities and differences between humans and animals,[1] but even more for reflection upon the similarities and differences between humans and humans. Attributing to other human beings the same kinds of emotional states as those we attribute to ourselves is one of the fundamental strategies in all attempts at understanding across the gulfs that separate one culture from another, one age from another, one person from another. Astonishingly, such attempts seem often to succeed; but the questions of why they do, and how they fail, have provided conundra for anthropology, hermeneutics, historical studies, lexicography, and a host of other disciplines.[2] For at first glance emotions may well seem universal, and indispensable to anything we would wish to count as being human, and it is certain that in the end we cannot do without them as an explanatory category in our dealings with other humans and their works; yet by the same token it does not take much reflection or experience to see that what has been understood as an emotion and what has been thought proper to do with it, in private and in public, vary and have varied widely across all possible sets of parameters. How many ancient Greeks would have agreed with Adam Smith that "[t]he expression of anger towards anybody present, if it exceeds a bare intimation that we are sensible to ill usage, is regarded not only as an insult to that particular person, but as a rudeness to the whole company"?[3] How many Inuit? How many Maoris? How many New Yorkers?

[1] Darwin (1998) remains an unsurpassed starting-point.
[2] The wider interest in the passions on the part of recent historians is now reflected in a review essay by medievalist Barbara Rosenwein (2002).
[3] A. Smith (1976) 35.

I

In recent years the emotions have migrated from the peripheries into the center of attention of a number of fields of scholarship which had previously scorned them as unscientific, ignored them as trivial, or repressed them as perilous. Over the past decade or so, for example, many psychologists, who a generation ago might have been studying the mechanisms of perception, the patterns of behavior, and the development of children, have been doing intensive research into the physiological basis and the conscious experience of various states of emotion. Armed not only with a new paradigm of what makes humans humans but also with an array of expensive new technologies and intimidatingly acronymic instrumentation – CAT (a.k.a. CT), fMRI (a.k.a. MRI or NMR), PET – they have already made a number of important discoveries about the processes and functions of emotional states *in situ, in vivo*, and in real time.[4] And the recent tendency of philosophers to study not only language, epistemology, and the natural sciences, but also ethics, political theory, and the identity of the self, has led to a reawakening of interest in the role of the emotions in the construction of our sense of ourselves and of our world and in our dealings with other persons. An older philosophical tradition, going back in modern times to Descartes[5] and Hume[6] but more recently overshadowed by analytic and rationalistic tendencies, has thereby been revitalized by being brought into contact with contemporary developments in philosophical research, by stimulus from other disciplines, and by the experience of the savage irrationalities of the twentieth century and the insistent longings of our own times.[7]

Of course, this tradition goes back ultimately to ancient philosophy; Plato, Aristotle, Epicurus, and the Stoa all took strong and very different stands about the place of emotion in a happy life (or, more often, in an unhappy one). Moreover, few accounts of the role of emotions in human life have etched themselves as ineradicably into the collective memory of the Western tradition as have those to be found in Greek and Roman epic,

---

[4] For a representative panorama of recent approaches and results see, for example, Plutchik (1980, 1994); Heilman and Satz (1983); Scherer and Ekman (1984); Plutchik and Kellerman (1986); Lazarus (1991); Birbaumer (1993); Lewis and Haviland (1993); Damasio (1994); Ekman and Davidson (1994); Power and Dalgleish (1997); R. Carter (1998); LeDoux (1998); Panksepp (1998); Dalgleish and Power (1999); Borod (2000); Lane and Nadel (2000); Lewis and Haviland-Jones (2000); and Scherer, Schorr, and Johnstone (2001). For social perspectives on emotions, see also Harré (1986) and Harré and Parrott (1996).

[5] Descartes (1985).   [6] Hume (1978).

[7] For representative recent examples, and some important older ones, see Sartre (1962); Kenny (1963); S. Williams (1973); Rorty (1980); Calhoun and Solomon (1984); Taylor (1985); de Sousa (1987); Gordon (1987); Platts (1991); Oakley (1992); R. Solomon (1993); Davies and Stone (1995); Stocker and Hegeman (1996); Griffiths (1997); Hjort and Laver (1997); Hornsby (1997); Blackburn (1998); O'Hear (1998); Wollheim (1999); and Goldie (2000). For a helpful orientation on non-philosophical usages, see Russell, Fernandez-Dols, Manstead, and Wellenkamp (1995).

lyric, tragedy, and other genres. So it is hardly surprising that the fashion for passion has increasingly invested classical studies within the past years. The current debate about the passions in antiquity took root among classicists in the 1990s in the work of scholars such as Martha Nussbaum,[8] Douglas Cairns,[9] David Konstan,[10] and Richard Sorabji,[11] among others. The passions in Roman culture were the subject of a conference which resulted in a volume published in 1997 by Susanna Braund and Christopher Gill.[12] The present volume continues the work of these scholars, as of others, and focuses upon one emotion, anger, in particular. It is thus complementary to William Harris' *Restraining Rage: the Ideology of Anger Control in Classical Antiquity* (Cambridge, MA, 2002). It is our hope that our publication, taken together with that of Harris, will set a new agenda for the study of ancient anger and will provoke and inspire work by many other scholars both within and beyond the field of classics.

This volume is an outcome of a colloquium on "Anger in Antiquity" organized by the present co-editors and held at Heidelberg University in September 1999; it consists of eleven of the papers delivered on that occasion, modified for publication in the light of our discussions. Although there are inevitably numerous gaps in our coverage – for example, Greek and Roman iamb, satire, and comedy, Jewish and Christian literature, and the archaeological record receive no discussion at all, or much too little[13] – the eleven chapters nonetheless cohere closely and take the debate forward significantly in the areas of the cultural specificity of anger, anger and philosophy, anger and gender, and anger in epic poetry.

Anger and epic seem to go hand in hand. If different genres are particularly associated with different emotions, then epic surely lays claim to anger. The "wrath of Achilles" in the *Iliad* famously makes anger the first word in Western literature, and the debate about the anger of Aeneas at the end of the *Aeneid* continues to rage. We therefore make no apologies for the unabashed focus upon epic in this volume. Of the eleven chapters here, the first two and last three investigate many aspects of rage in Greek and Latin epic poetry; Homeric epic remains a point of reference too for many of the rest. The other recurring text is Aristotle's account of anger in the *Rhetoric*, which receives detailed discussion in one chapter and informs many others. But the phenomenon of anger is by no means confined to epic and philosophical prose. This volume finds anger everywhere – in

---

[8] Nussbaum (1994, 2001).   [9] Cairns (1993).   [10] Konstan (1994, 1997, 2001).
[11] Sorabji (2000).   [12] Braund and Gill (1997).
[13] So too, there is no specific discussion of Seneca's *De ira*, though the chapter by Braund and Gilbert covers in an appendix some of that material.

the Athenian law courts, in drama, comic and tragic, in magic spells, in the Greek novel, and in the medical writer Galen. We do not claim that this volume presents a comprehensive or exhaustive treatment of ancient anger, but we do hope that by raising new questions about anger as it appears in both familiar and unfamiliar contexts in ancient culture it will make a substantial contribution to the current debate about the passions in antiquity.

We decided to organize the chapters in this volume in a broadly chronological sequence, although other principles of arrangement informed the colloquium and there are many possible collecting-points that could be used to organize a discussion of anger – for example, the terminology, psychology, physiology, ethics, politics, and aesthetics of anger. All these topics are discussed at various points in the volume and several general questions relating to anger and its spheres of operation recur. To what extent is anger culturally specific or universal? Is it better to see anger as a psychological phenomenon, as an emotional state open above all to our own introspection, or rather as a sociological one, as a form of behavior manifested by specific individuals so that specific audiences can note and appreciate it? How can we analyze the vocabulary of anger? How do ancient constructions of ethics and politics map onto modern assumptions about anger? Does anger belong in the public or the private domain? How is anger connected with issues of status and with issues of gender and age? In the outline of the eleven chapters which follows we attempt to highlight the central problems they consider and the rich interconnections between them.

The first chapter in the volume raises many issues central to the study of ancient anger. In "Ethics, ethology, terminology: Iliadic anger and the cross-cultural study of emotion", Douglas Cairns argues that emotions have universal and culture-specific aspects and that dialogue between ancient cultures and our own is possible. Emotions have evolved to help to promote social co-operation. In the case of anger, which is a human universal with specific neurophysiological changes, it is usefully seen as "a response to a breach of co-operation which . . . guarantees and makes credible the threat inherent in the offended party's reaction . . ." But, as with other emotions, the taxonomy of terms for anger differs from culture to culture. Cairns' focus is the construction of anger in the Homeric worldview. After his justification for the study of Homeric anger, Cairns maps it against Aristotle's definition to find an overall coherence. He analyzes in detail the Homeric terminology for anger, including *mēnis*, *cholos*, and *nemesis*, concluding that "Homeric anger-terms clearly demonstrate the location of the emotion of anger in the ethics of reciprocity." This requires a slight revision of Aristotle's definition, while retaining his association between anger and *timē*. Cairns concludes with a discussion of the centrality of *timē* to Greek notions of selfhood and identity as social phenomena, with a focus especially upon the eyes, the gaze, and the look as deployed and as withheld.

The second chapter in the volume, by Glenn Most, shares with Cairns' study a focus upon anger in the *Iliad* but illuminates Iliadic anger through an examination of Iliadic pity. In Most's reading of the *Iliad*, "Anger and pity in Homer's *Iliad*," the central question raised is, what does it mean for an epic of wrath, which starts with "anger" and which offers so many manifestations of anger, to culminate in episode of pity? Rather than accept the opening words of the poem as essentially programmatic, Most sees the structure of the poem as an invitation to explore the relationship between anger and pity, including self-pity. His central argument is that in the poem's incidents of what characters take to be undeserved suffering, the anger inspired by the perpetrator and the pity inspired by the sufferer, so different from Christian concepts, are not mutually exclusive but intimately interconnected: "a Homeric character cannot ever feel pity . . . without at the same time actually or potentially feeling some degree of anger at the agent or agents who caused this suffering." In Homer "pity and anger are two sides of the very same coin." Most proposes that the *Iliad* is structured in three stages: (1) Achilles' pity for himself and anger at Agamemnon; (2) his pity for Patroklos and his anger at Hector and the Trojans; (3) his pity for Priam; and he offers an analysis of salient elements of the poem to support his reading, culminating in Achilles' evolution of character which enables him to begin, too late, to master his own anger.

In the chapter by Danielle Allen, "Angry bees, wasps, and jurors: the symbolic politics of ὀργή in Athens," we meet a non-Homeric term for anger, *orgē*. Allen explores the significance of *orgē* in democratic Athens as instantiated in tragedy, comedy (Aristophanes' *Wasps*), and especially forensic oratory. She starts from a passage in Demosthenes to suggest that "the job of law . . . was to determine how much anger ought to be applied to particular types of wrongdoing" and proceeds to argue that *orgē* was "a central term in the ethical discourses that produced Athenian definitions of the good citizen, justice, and just behavior." She shows how in the public sphere, that is, for men, hot-blooded anger was seen as appropriate or even necessary. By contrast, for women anger was out of bounds: the problems caused by the intrusion of anger into the household are explored in tragedy. Allen goes on to suggest that this binary opposition illuminates the phenomenon of sycophancy at Athens. After discussing the erotic and iretic signification of figs, she states that "the rhetoric of sycophancy established an ethics for the male use of anger that kept aggressive competition from doing damage to the public sphere, just as the ethics for the female use of anger kept the Athenian valorization of *orgē* from doing damage to the private sphere." In other words, Athenian constructions of *orgē* supported the designation of men but not women as political agents, capable of acting legitimately on anger.

All three of these chapters take Aristotle's definition of anger as a point of reference; and the fourth contribution to the volume, David Konstan's "Aristotle on anger and the emotions: the strategies of status," presents a detailed examination of Aristotle's account of anger in the *Rhetoric*. In his close analysis Konstan situates Aristotle's treatment of anger in the context of his framework of the passions (including pity) in general, arguing for the relevance of cognitive as well as physiological theories of emotion. He sees Aristotle's distinction between anger and hatred as crucial: anger is a personal matter, "the impulse to right a wrong done to oneself, in regard to opinion or reputation," in contrast with hatred, which can be directed against a group. He concludes that Aristotle's view of anger "as an attack upon one's social standing or honor" which creates a desire for "a compensating act of retribution" illuminates the role of anger more generally in the classical period. Konstan situates the characteristic pattern – the slight is offered, there is pain at the slight, then revenge for the slight and pleasure in the revenge – thoroughly in the context of social life, thus linking with ideas about honor and public image explored by Cairns and Allen. This chapter makes a strong case for the difficulty of analyzing in modern terms the ideological construction of the emotions in Greek antiquity.

William Harris takes up the same point at the beginning of his contribution to this volume, "The rage of women," which develops further several points made in the relevant chapter of his book *Restraining Rage*. Starting (again) from Aristotle, Harris associates rage with action in order to distinguish it from mere irritation, and he notes the frequent association of rage with madness. He offers an overview of ancient ideas, from Homer through the Hellenistic period and into the Roman period, about the reining in of anger which still allowed for legitimate anger on the part of men and then turns to his main topic – women and anger. Harris' focus makes a shift into the domestic sphere which complements the civic emphasis of previous chapters in the volume. He tracks the negative stereotype of women as especially susceptible to anger from Homer onwards, including tragedy, Herodotus, Aristophanes, Plato, oratory, and Herodas into Greek literature of the Roman period, including Philodemus and Plutarch. He demonstrates that the stereotype "implies that there was almost no legitimate place for women's anger in the classical city" and asks why Greek men wanted "to reserve anger for their own use." This delegitimization of female anger he sees as an essential element in male psychological control. The chapter concludes with an examination of four tragedies in which the stereotype is subjected to scrutiny, Euripides' *Medea, Hecuba*, and *Electra* and Sophocles' *Electra*. These exceptions to the general rule seem only to confirm the stereotype that excluded women from political life and deprived them of what Harris styles "the right to rage."

In the next chapter, "*Thumos* as masculine ideal and social pathology in ancient Greek magical spells," Christopher Faraone explores women's experience of the anger of men in Greek culture, using the evidence afforded by spells designed to restrain the *thumos*. This chapter distinguishes between "black magic" curses and "white magic" amulets: the former traditionally operate between social equals while the latter are typically used by social subordinates (wives against their husbands, petitioners against rulers). Faraone finds a tension between constructions of masculinity and the role of anger. In the curses, the aim is to bind one's rivals' anger, competitive drive, or erotic passion, designated by *thumos* or *orgē* (cf. Allen's chapter in this volume), which are seen as integral to the male psyche. But in the amulets and closely related love potions deployed by women and other social subordinates, the superior male's *thumos* is viewed negatively as a pathology or disease in need of cure. Faraone comes to the conclusion that "using magic to bind a man's *thumos* not only controls his anger; it also involves a much more diffuse attack on a man's will, courage, and sexual desire – character traits and faculties that are very closely tied to his masculinity" – his *machismo*. This chapter thus offers a rare glimpse of the female experience of male passions.

The chapter by David Scourfield, "Anger and gender in Chariton's *Chaereas and Callirhoe*," picks up issues about anger and gender already raised by Allen, Harris, and Faraone. Scourfield demonstrates the centrality of anger in Chariton's narrative and highlights the complex intertextualities whereby the novel reworks important moments of anger from earlier Greek literature, including Homer, Euripides, and Menander. He focuses first upon the character of Chaereas who, he argues, develops from a youth who is unable to restrain his anger into a man who shows proper self-control (cf. Most's chapter in this volume). Then he turns the spotlight upon the lack of anger shown by the heroine Callirhoe. Scourfield argues not that she is incapable of anger but that she can control it through her rationality: "Chariton shuns the standard view of women as weak emotional creatures," challenging the stereotype (which is depicted in Harris' chapter). He concludes that the novel creates two potential readerships, depending on how the relation between gender and anger is construed.

The next chapter, " 'Your mother nursed you with bile': anger in babies and small children," by Ann Ellis Hanson, offers an exploration of the experience of anger in infancy and childhood. Starting from the assertion in *Iliad* 16 that Achilles was nursed on bile (*cholos*), Hanson focuses upon ancient views of the formation and suppression of anger in babies and children. Her chapter uses texts of philosophers and medical writers, including Plato and Galen, to examine the shaping of character in the very young through their physiological and psychological treatment. She discusses the practice of swaddling newborn babies, toddlers' first attempts at locomotion, teething and socialization in play, and at every point indicates the ways in which the Homeric poems map onto later theories. The central issue emerges as the advisability of avoiding prolonged frustration to the infant "lest angry responses become habitual." She concludes that although Achilles' angry temperament was acquired, "the child-rearing practices imagined for epic . . . offer no encouragement to the notion that Achilles was allowed to practice anger at home."

Continuing the focus upon anger in epic poetry, Christopher Gill offers a new examination of the vexed question of the relationship between Hellenistic philosophical ideas about anger and Virgil's *Aeneid* in "Reactive and objective attitudes: anger in Virgil's *Aeneid* and Hellenistic philosophy." He sets out "to sharpen our conceptual and critical means" for defining the complexity of this text "by the distinction between reactive and objective attitudes and by linking this distinction with various ancient philosophical approaches." Accordingly, he takes as his starting-point the philosopher Strawson's distinction between "reactive" and "objective" attitudes in interpersonal relations, a distinction which hinges upon the relationship of the two individuals as being either one of equals or asymmetrical. He then analyzes the Aristotelian, Stoic, and Epicurean attitudes to anger in those terms, concluding that the Aristotelian attitude is essentially "reactive" and the Stoic essentially "objective," with the Epicurean attitude falling in between. Turning his attention to the *Aeneid*, Gill first resists critical attempts to find in such a complex poem a single approach to anger. He proposes that the poem offers "a coherent synthesis" of the reactive and objective strands and through a close reading of the most salient episodes he demonstrates its philosophical complexities. He proposes that "there is a relatively systematic attempt to associate Aeneas with a more objective attitude" but that at times, including at the poem's finale, Aeneas is deflected from the high ethical standards to which he aspires.

The focus upon epic anger continues in the next chapter, "The angry poet and the angry gods: problems of theodicy in Lucan's epic of defeat," by Elaine Fantham. Fantham expands the discussion of anger to include the anger of supernatural agencies – the gods and Fortuna – and the anger of the superhuman figure of Caesar in Lucan's epic poem about the civil war. The paper starts with an overview of the motif of divine retribution (*ira deorum*) in earlier Latin literature, especially Livy and Virgil, both important intertexts for Lucan. Fantham then draws attention to the dominance of anger at the start of Lucan's epic, in the forms of the divine hostility to Rome implicit in Lucan's statement *uictrix causa deis placuit* ("the gods favored the conquering side") and of Caesar's anger. She observes that though the gods do not intervene in the action, Lucan implies their active hostility. While noting the shift of focus from the gods to Fortuna after Pharsalus, she concludes that "Lucan does not see Fortuna as a causality distinct from the gods." Fantham also examines the authorial anger expressed in the apostrophes that protest against Pompey's defeat and death. She ends by arguing that Caesar, who is characterized by anger, enacts divine anger against Rome: she links Caesar, "the human thunderbolt," with the traditional weapon of the angry Jupiter, "not just as analogue, but as the actual representative and embodiment of the divine anger which overthrew the Roman Republic." Given the degree to which the question of anger dominates discussion of the *Aeneid*, it seems surprising that no one before Fantham has so carefully analyzed the role of anger in the *Bellum Ciuile*.

The final chapter in the volume, by Susanna Braund and Giles Gilbert, is "An ABC of epic *ira*: anger, beasts, and cannibalism." This is an examination of the psychopathology of the warrior on the battlefield as presented in Roman epic poetry from Virgil to the Flavians. Braund and Gilbert conduct a close examination of *ira* in the texts of Virgil, Lucan, Statius, and Silius Italicus, which reveals a strong tendency to depict the epic warrior's anger not directly but indirectly, through the medium of similes which liken the warrior to a fierce beast. The chapter includes an analysis of these similes, similes whose significance has not been fully appreciated: some depict anger as a positive and indeed necessary element for the warrior, while others suggest a negative moral interpretation of epic *ira*. Braund and Gilbert make a connection between Statius' depiction of the young Achilles' diet of raw and still-living animals (*Achilleid* 2: their starting-point, and cf. Hanson's chapter in this volume) and his depiction of Tydeus' act of cannibalism on the battlefield (*Thebaid* 8: their finishing-point), which is clearly a case of *ira* beyond bounds. They conclude that anger has to have its limits.

The variety and range of the issues raised in this volume might well seem daunting. But let us suggest in conclusion that one convenient and engaging way of focusing many of them is to consider in the light of the contributions collected here the Hellenistic mosaic signed by the artist Dioskourides of Samos, which is in the collection of the National Archaeological Museum of Naples and of which an illustration graces the front cover of this book. It seems to show an angry old woman captured in a private moment with two other women and a boy; and, in fact, conventionally anger is very often associated in antiquity with the old, and with privacy, and above all with women. Yet of course it is not an old woman we see represented here, but a male actor wearing the mask of an old woman in the stage production of a comedy. What seems to be a woman is a man's (the actor's, the author's) representation of a woman; what seems to be private is a public representation of the private domain taking place within an institutionalized civic space devoted to that very purpose; what seems to be anger is a dramatic representation of anger, tactically deploying the well-established and thoroughly familiar symptomatology of that emotion in order to convince spectators (the other three on the stage, the audience of the comedy) that s/he is in its grip. Was s/he really angry? If so, how and why was she angry, and how did the ancients know she was, and how do we know she is? How much can we finally know about what angry ancient women, or for that matter angry ancient men, really felt in the privacy of their homes, and of their minds? Can we hope to penetrate through all the levels of play-acting, one after another, to reach some core of authenticity that would not be play-acting? Or is it not better to inquire into the profound truths revealed about ourselves and our cultures by what we choose to enact and how we choose to do so? The complexities of what might at first seem to be a very straightforward scene begin to exfoliate in layers of increasing richness as soon as we start to reflect upon it.

The articles collected here raise questions and make suggestions that, taken seriously and followed through thoughtfully, promise ultimately to help us better to understand at least some of these complexities: those of that character, an angry old woman – but also those of the actor who played her, the author who invented her, the artist who depicted her, the audiences of the play who laughed at her and the spectators of the mosaic who decorated their home with her – and, perhaps, in the end, those of ourselves as well.

CHAPTER I

Ethics, ethology, terminology: Iliadic anger and the cross-cultural study of emotion

D. L. Cairns

To study the emotional language of another culture is to enter into the most significant questions raised by the study of emotion, since it raises the fundamental issues of the universality or cultural specificity of the emotions and of the contribution made by linguistic labels and categories to the construction of emotions as cultural phenomena. It is thus the responsibility of the classicist who would study the emotional terminology of the Greeks or the Romans also to become familiar with current research on the nature of emotion in other disciplines and to situate the study of ancient terminology in a wider context in which full account is taken of aspects of emotion other than the sense and reference of particular linguistic markers.[1] It has to be said that this is a responsibility that, more often than not, is shirked by the cultural determinists who currently dominate both classical studies and the humanities in general.[2] Their approach assumes that all significant features of a culture are products of conditions specific

This chapter was initially submitted for publication in the summer of 2000; I have been able in a few places to update and revise, but its shape remains as it originally was. I should like to thank the organizers of the Heidelberg colloquium for inviting me to contribute and for the intellectual stimulation afforded by the colloquium itself; I am grateful also to my fellow-participants for discussion during the colloquium, which has, I hope, sharpened my thinking about anger. While preparing the paper I was fortunate enough to be invited to preside over a series of seminars on anger in the *Iliad* at the University of Leiden in May–June 1999. I must thank my hosts, Dr. Ilja Leonard Pfeijffer, Adriaan Rademaker, Chiara Robbiano, and Professor Ineke Sluiter for the warmth of their welcome; and I am very grateful to Christiaan Caspers, Susannah Herman, Casper de Jonge, Daan Link, Joris Stolwijk, and Lina van't Wout for the quality of their contributions. I must also record my gratitude to Professor Norman Austin for allowing me to see in advance of publication the paper which appeared as Austin (1999).

[1] These other factors will be both non-linguistic and linguistic; on the importance of aspects of emotion-language other than the labels that a culture attaches to the emotions it recognizes, see Kövecses (2000), esp. 2–6, 139–40, 184, 188–9; on the need for cross-cultural studies of the full range of emotion-language, see Lakoff and Kövecses (1987) 220; Kövecses (2000) 1, 139–63; cf. Russell (1991) 434.

[2] A case in point is Muellner (1996), who claims without argument that "there is no reason to assume that the metaphors, the rules, and therefore the emotions that they represent and that we tend to experience as inherent in human nature are actually universal" (p. 1), and argues that Homeric *mēnis* is "a far cry from any shared, secular notion of anger specific [*sic*] to contemporary Western culture"

to that culture; and since this holds both of the culture under investigation and of the investigator's own, it requires the investigator somehow to seek access to phenomena wholly specific to a society that is alien to his/her own experience. Thankfully, however, we do not have to strive for such an impossible goal: all cultures exhibit points of overlap and contact that make them mutually intelligible; and all cultures have been formed and inhabited by a species which evolved its capacity for the creation of culture under a broadly uniform set of environmental pressures. The possibility for dialogue between ancient cultures and our own exists; we must attempt it in a way which avoids both the naive assumption of shared humanity and unsustainable strategies of alienation.

Emotions involve judgments and evaluations about states of affairs in the world; but they are not solely ways of seeing the world. They also encompass physical aspects in the form of their typical neurophysiological and visceral changes, and these, since they depend on the evolved organic nature of the species, cannot be entirely given by culture.[3] Detailed studies have demonstrated that the facial expression of emotion is largely a matter of phylogenetic adaptation: infants in all cultures, even deaf-blind infants, exhibit the same range of facial expressions in their early development; and though cultures differ both in what they regard as an appropriate elicitor for a given facial expression and in the degree to which they authorize or deprecate different forms of expression, nevertheless individuals in one society generally have no difficulty in correctly interpreting the facial expressions of members of another.[4] Associated with the physical aspects of emotion just mentioned will be many characteristic symptoms and behavior patterns; many of these will also be instinctive or cultural elaborations of the instinctive.

This leaves all the many aspects of emotion or emotional scenarios which can vary from culture to culture: the eliciting conditions (if disgust and its

---

(p. 133), because "[f]or us emotions are primarily individualized and internal, and their social dimensions are semantically secondary" (p. 138). Cf. his apology for the use of the word "humanly" at p. 174, n. 86. For a similarly motivated denial of the universality of anger, see Fowler (1997) 16–17. Fowler argues: "Anger is . . . very far from being a cultural universal, even if the only people who are said to have nothing that could be called anger at all are the Utku of Canada" (p. 17); even if it were true that the Utku "have nothing that could be called anger," surely this would make anger all but, rather than "very far from" universal? In fact, the supposed absence of anger among this Inuit people seems to rest on a misidentification of strong cultural prohibitions on the expression of an emotion with the absence of the emotion as such: see Russell (1991) 444; Pinker (1997) 364–8; Harris (2002) 34.

[3] For an excellent account, see de Sousa (1987) 47–106.

[4] This is a field, pioneered by Darwin, that Paul Ekman (together with his several collaborators, and in publications too numerous to cite) has made his own; the development of facial-expression studies may now be most conveniently traced in Ekman's edition of Darwin (1998), with copious references to modern research (esp. pp. 445–8). See also Eibl-Eibesfeldt (1989) 425–547 passim.

facial expression are universal, what is occasion for disgust in one society is clearly not in all);[5] the valorization of different emotions (cultural differences in the valorization of anger are a pertinent consideration here);[6] the forms of expression which are and are not culturally approved for different categories of individual (e.g. the rather different cultural expectations of men and in women in our society with regard to the expression of anger);[7] the imagery of emotion; and, of course, emotion-words. These aspects are not negligible. But this enumeration of universal and variable factors would be misleading if it suggested a sharp distinction between the two categories; for (on the one hand) all aspects of emotion are subject to construction through their incorporation in the complex syndromes of factors that constitute emotions. The cognitive-evaluative aspect of emotion as a response to states of affairs in the world will always presuppose an element of constructionism – the typical scenarios in which emotions are deployed and to which emotion-words are attached must be understood within the practices of a particular culture, and thus all aspects of the total emotional experience will be subject to construction and interpretation in terms which may be particular to a specific culture.[8] On the other hand, there are aspects of the cultural construction of emotion that will be firmly rooted in our physical nature as human beings: as George Lakoff and his collaborators have shown, the cultural models and folk theories that structure a culture's emotional life and the metaphors and metonymies that structure our emotion-concepts derive to a very large extent from our experiences as physically embodied beings in the world.[9] Thus there will remain fundamental and substantial

---

[5] Discussion and references in Pinker (1997) 378–85.

[6] Pertinent considerations with regard to anger in Homer in van Wees (1992) 126–38, 154; for studies of the general issues involved, see Oatley, Jenkins, and Stein (1998) 240.

[7] Again, there are numerous relevant studies by Ekman; see (e.g.) Ekman (1980); cf. (more recently) his "Afterword" to Darwin (1998) 383–5. See also (with specific reference to the importance of cultural permission in the expression of anger) de Sousa (1987) 256, 259.

[8] This is not to say that emotions so constructed are not themselves neurophysiologically encoded; the biological basis of human emotion is not limited to its phylogenetic components (see n. 12 below).

[9] See in general Lakoff and Johnson (1980); Johnson (1987); specifically on emotion, see Kövecses (2000); and specifically on anger, see Lakoff and Kövecses (1987); Kövecses (2000) 21–3, 142–63. The important point is that the ways in which folk theories of anger and other emotions are structured via metaphors and metonymies rooted in the physiological functioning of the body place certain constraints upon the concepts of those emotions that can emerge in a particular culture (Lakoff and Kövecses [1987] 219–20; Kövecses [2000] 177, 183, 185). With the approach of Lakoff and Kövecses to the search for universal aspects of emotion-language and concepts one might contrast that of Anna Wierzbicka, who has, in a number of publications over several years (see most recently Wierzbicka [1999]), sought to analyze culturally specific emotion-terms into universal semantically primitive components. This procedure is much less rich and rewarding than that of Lakoff et al., for (a) it concentrates on labels to the exclusion of other aspects of emotion-language and (b) it shows only that these labels can be analyzed in terms which might be familiar to members of other cultures,

aspects of any genuine emotional scenario, and thus of any one individual's emotional repertoire, which are not determined by culture but rather depend on biological factors; and "biology versus culture" is a false antithesis when the biological must be experienced and constructed in a cultural context and when shared cultural categories draw on our nature as a physically embodied, social species. Therefore, if it is proper for us to pay particular attention to the ways in which the construction of emotion varies from culture to culture, it is also necessary for us to accept that we cannot expect that variation to be free and unconstrained.

Thus studies of emotional terminology will always be necessary – it is in the labeling of emotion and its location within the semantic categories of the culture that we can expect the greatest degree of variation in the way that cultures map out their emotional lives[10] – but they will never be sufficient. We do need to start with the terms that the Greeks themselves used to describe their emotional experience, and we should certainly not foist our own preconceptions about particular emotions on to our data; but philological study must not stop with the investigation of the sense and reference of particular linguistic labels, and the resources of the philologist, even of the classicist in general, will not suffice for the study of ancient emotion; for the right methodological principles, for the proper interpretative categories, we also need to look to the insights of other disciplines; and we need to supplement our studies of the semantics of ancient terms with such data as we can recover about other aspects (both linguistic and non-linguistic) of emotional experience. The goal of this chapter will be to attempt such an approach with particular reference to the terminology, ethics, and nonverbal expression of anger in Homer's *Iliad*.

Recent research on the neurophysiology of emotion suggests that, in neural and in evolutionary terms, emotions are complex phenomena involving the interaction of several distinct brain regions, both cortical and subcortical, evolutionarily "old" and evolutionarily "new," in such a way that emotion forms part of an integrated system which includes both higher cognitive functions and basic systems of body regulation.[11] In the light of these studies, emotions emerge as mechanisms which link brain, nervous

---

not that the clusters of semantic primitives of which emotion-terms consist play any significant role in a culture's representation of its own emotional concepts. As a strategy for the translation and mutual understanding of cultures' emotion-labels it has its utility, but the basis for cross-cultural understanding of emotional concepts and experience is much wider than this approach suggests.

[10] For a detailed study, see Russell (1991); cf. Elster (1999a) 417.

[11] See Damasio (1994); LeDoux (1996); Lane and Nadel (1999); Rolls (1999); Borod (2000); see also the discussion (of the implications of some of this work for the Stoic cognitive-evaluative view of emotion) in Sorabji (2000) 144–55.

system, and body and which (in different degrees) draw both on basic, pre-organized (innate) dispositions and on higher-order dispositions that are fine-tuned or calibrated in each individual according to the history of his or her interactions with the physical and social environment.[12] Such a picture suggests that there will be an evolutionary rationale for emotion (for how else might such a complicated set of mechanisms be explained if not by natural selection?);[13] but it also suggests, perhaps, that any such rationale may have to exhibit a greater degree of detail, nuance, and complexity than anything that has so far been put forward as an explanation of that sort.

These remarks are prefatory to a brief consideration of accounts of the evolution of emotion offered by the emerging discipline of evolutionary psychology. This approach roots emotions in the evolution of co-operation, as mechanisms "designed" (to use a common metaphor of evolutionary theory, rooted in what Daniel Dennett calls the "intentional stance")[14] to demonstrate commitment in co-operative social relationships which bring significant long-term benefit to their participants. The first step toward an explanation here is Robert Axelrod's demonstration (based on game-theory and computer models of interaction) of how simple reciprocity ("tit-for-tat," i.e. "at first co-operate, then respond in kind to your part-ner's response") might establish itself as an evolutionarily stable strategy, benefiting its practitioners mutually and establishing ascendancy over its alternatives.[15] The strategy of tit-for-tat answers in the natural world to one studied in several species and labeled "reciprocal altruism" by Robert Trivers, who argues that the evolution of such a strategy might be corre-lated with that of emotion in humans (and primates); emotions such as guilt or anger serve the needs of reciprocal altruism by promoting behav-ior in accordance with its rules, by conveying one's willingness to resume co-operation or demonstrating one's determination to punish defectors.[16] Robert Frank has pointed out, however, (first) that reciprocal altruism might more economically be supported by psychological mechanisms of much greater simplicity than the emotions (the very fact that "tit-for-tat" flourishes in computer simulations shows that it need not be sustained by emotion; why should natural selection provide such an expensive solution to a relatively simple problem?) and (second) that human emotions sustain not only reciprocal altruism (co-operation that is clearly in the individual's

[12] Damasio (1994) 110–12, 131–8, 149–51 (and 285, n. 16), 177, 180–1, 190–1, 260, 264.
[13] See Rolls (1999) 266–76.   [14] (1995) 229–38.
[15] See Axelrod (1984); cf. Dawkins (1989) 202–33; Ridley (1996) 53–66.
[16] Trivers (1971, repr. 1994), esp. 85 on anger; (1985) 386–9; cf. R. Wright (1995) 189–209, Pinker (1997) 402–5.

own interest), but genuine altruism (acceptance of an obvious cost that out-
weighs any probable benefit to oneself).[17] Frank's answer is what he calls
the "commitment model" – emotions serve co-operation (which is in the
ultimate interest of the individual) not on a case-by-case but on a dispositional basis, in the sense that those who can display a disposition toward the
requisite emotion establish for themselves an advantage in co-operation *in
general* rather than in any single transaction or series of transactions; emotions solve the "commitment problem" by ensuring that the dispositions
which can bring long-term rewards are manifested even where the material
disadvantage to the individual is high.[18] In this scheme, anger is a response
to a breach of co-operation which, by its character as an affective reaction
liable to evade rational control, guarantees and makes credible the threat
inherent in the offended party's reaction, even where to carry out such a
threat would be costly for its agent.[19] The adaptiveness of anger lies in the
ability of those who possess a recognized disposition to be angry to deter
others' attempts to exploit them.

The power and attractions of such an approach, it seems to me, lie first
in the fact that the answer is being sought in the right place – given all
the aspects of emotion that are rooted in biology, natural selection is the
only mechanism which can plausibly explain their origins – and second
in the relatively close fit between this account of what emotions are for
and our ordinary intuitions as to what they actually do. The legitimate
emphasis which such approaches place on the selective pressure exerted
by the environment locates emotion firmly in the development of human
sociality; they also therefore stress the communicative function of emotion
in social interaction; and in emphasizing the fact that emotion is an aspect
of group, not just of individual life, they break away importantly from
the Western tradition from Descartes to Freud. Emotions, on this view,
are adaptive because they influence our social behavior and because they
communicate our commitment to others. In the emotions which support
co-operation the evolutionary rationale sees the roots of our "moral" sense,
but this is a moral sense that is thoroughly embedded not only in the
affective and desiderative capacities of individuals, but also in the structures
and practices of group life. That this is true of Greek ethical notions has
been noted;[20] but the evolutionary perspective suggests that what some feel

---

[17] Frank (1988) 35–7; cf. G. Miller (2000) 303–18, 335–7.
[18] Frank (1988) *passim*; cf. Ridley (1996) 131–47; Pinker (1997) 406–16; E. O. Wilson (1998) 125–6;
    G. Miller (2000) 306. For criticism, see Elster (1990) 881–3, 885; (1999a) 287–98, 301–6.
[19] See Frank (1988) 53–5, 83.
[20] For a stimulating exposition of the Greeks' "participant" ethical framework, see Gill (1996).

they have discovered as a specific feature of Greek culture is in fact of much wider, indeed universal, application. Muellner's remarks[21] on the primacy of the social dimension of emotion in Homer *versus* "our" supposedly individualized and internalized conception construct an "us" *versus* "them" antithesis that errs, as such constructs often do, not in its understanding of ancient sources, but in its unreflective definition of a modernity that has to be the polar opposite of antiquity if cultural determinist assumptions are to be maintained. If nothing else, the crucial importance of emotional signals, especially facial expressions, in "our" culture (as in all cultures) should have inhibited the formulation of this antithesis, for if visible expression is important in the emotional scenarios of all cultures, then sociality is a universal attribute of emotion.[22]

Ancient definitions of anger, in so far as they locate that concept very firmly in reciprocal or hierarchical structures of honor (i.e. in structures which depend upon publicly observable forms of social interaction), have much in common with the evolutionary approach.[23] Aristotle defines anger as "a desire accompanied by pain, for a perceived revenge for a perceived slight upon oneself or one of one's own, the slight being unwarranted";[24] thus he accommodates anger's affective, evaluative, and desiderative aspects and locates it in relationships in which others' respect is a legitimate expectation. Aristotle thus agrees with our modern biologically oriented theorists that anger is a fundamental strategy in maintaining the ties which bind our social and ethical lives. This contrasts markedly with the ethical status of anger not only in the post-Enlightenment tradition, but also in the Stoic and Christian ethics that are its antecedents, for which anger is to be eliminated, suppressed, or at best transformed from a "natural" to a "moral" sentiment.[25]

---

[21] (1996) 138 (cf. n. 2 above). Muellner's antithesis has a pedigree in contemporary ethnology: see (e.g.) Rosaldo (1980); Lutz (1988).

[22] The universality of the Aristotelian insight that "emotions are rooted not only in individual psychology, but also in social interaction" is of central importance in the study of Elster (1999a) (quotation p. 50); cf. Averill (1990) 126.

[23] See [Plato] *Def.* 415e11; Arist. *Rh.* 2.2.1378a30–2; *Top.* 4.6.127b30–1, 6.13.151a15–16, 6.13.156a32–3; cf. *De an.* 1.1.403a30–1.

[24] On the text and its translation, see Harris (1997), (2002) 57, and in this volume (ch. 5); Konstan (this volume, ch. 4); I originally contemplated the translation "conspicuous revenge for a perceived slight," taking the subject of the *phantasia* as different in the two cases – the victim perceives the offense, but the revenge is perceived by all; but Konstan has convinced me that the *phantasia* is better taken as that of the victim in both cases – a prospective *phantasia* of revenge and a retrospective *phantasia* that a slight has been received.

[25] On Stoic and Christian theories, see now Sorabji (2000); Harris (2002). For a characteristic statement of anger's lack of moral significance, see Rawls (1973) 488, with 479–90 in general on "moral" and "non-moral" sentiments.

Aristotle's definition of anger also accords with the "prototypical scenario" of anger established by Lakoff and Kövecses in their study of that
concept in contemporary American English, in so far as that scenario is one
in which the painful emotion of anger is elicited by offense and assuaged by
revenge.[26] That concept, however, is fleshed out by a range of metaphors
and metonymies which present anger as an ontological entity, a force exerted on the self, a hot fluid in a container, an opponent against which
one can struggle, a fire, a dangerous and aggressive animal, and suchlike.
To a very large extent these metaphors and metonymies are rooted in the
phenomenology of anger as an observable psychophysical experience with
a typical range of physiological symptoms, signs, and expressions. Kövecses
has recently taken these studies further and verified through studies of the
imagery of anger in other languages that there is indeed a considerable
degree of cross-cultural commonality in the conceptualization of anger
through its metaphors and metonymies and that the prototypical scenario
is not prototypical in American English alone.[27] We shall see below (first)
that the prototypical scenario (which is also Aristotle's paradigm) holds (for
the most part) for the presentation of anger in the *Iliad* too, and (second)
that this scenario in Homer is similarly elaborated by means of metaphors
and metonymies comparable to those used in English and other modern
languages.

It is no surprise that the evolutionary account of anger overlaps with that
of Lakoff and Kövecses. Both take their cue from the observed fact that
anger is an embodied psychophysical mechanism; the evolutionary account
seeks a rationale for this in adaptation, and Lakoff and Kövecses establish
the fundamental significance of embodiment in the conceptualization of
the emotion. Since physical embodiment limits the possibilities for the
conceptualization of anger within cultures, it must be taken seriously in
any cross-cultural study of anger.[28]

No one engaged in the study of emotion in ancient Greek society can afford to ignore the evolutionary dimension. The degree of common ground
which this approach establishes between cultures can assist us, as classicists,
to bring our understanding of ancient culture into meaningful relation

[26] See Lakoff and Kövecses (1987) 211–19 on the prototypical scenario and its focal relation to a wide
range of non-prototypical cases. Lakoff and Kövecses explicitly acknowledge the similarity between
their notion of the prototypical scenario and de Sousa's of "paradigm scenarios"; cf. n. 121 below.
For the important observation that Aristotle's definition is also to be taken as a prototype, see Harris
(2002) 58–9.

[27] Kövecses (2000) 142–61 (on English, Hungarian, Chinese, Japanese, and – more briefly – other
languages).

[28] Lakoff and Kövecses (1987) 219–20.

with an informed understanding of our own and other societies. To criticize an evolutionary rationale for the existence of a particular emotion on
the grounds that it does not account for every individual's experience of
the emotion is simply to confuse levels of explanation; the evolutionary
perspective (what natural selection "wants") is not the same as the perspective of the individual – to take an obvious example, there is clearly an
evolutionary rationale for the existence of sexual desire in human beings,
but this has, at the very least, not invariably figured in the motivation of
the majority of humans who have found themselves in thrall to that desire.
Similarly, if Frank is correct about the evolutionary rationale for anger
(that the individual's long-term interest is served by the possession of a
disposition for anger which can be cultivated and communicated to others
only if that individual is likely to experience genuine anger in the relevant
circumstances), this will rarely feature in the ideation of the angry individual – if anger is to deter others, they must believe that its patient is liable
to lose sight of his or her interests in satisfying angry impulses whatever
the cost. At the same time, however, the evolutionary explanation of anger
does prescribe and specify the kinds of cognition which the individual will
exhibit, for Trivers, Frank, and others agree with Aristotle that anger is
fundamentally a response to perceived offense. It is a feature of all three
accounts of anger under consideration (the Aristotelian, the evolutionary,
and the cognitivist account of Lakoff and Kövecses) that anger is fundamentally ethicized in this way, and it is, in my view, a strength that there
is this relatively close fit between what the evolutionary account says anger
is for and what we (and Aristotle) think it is for. But while it is undeniable
that anger, both in general and (as we shall see below) in Homer, typically
rests on the notion that one has been offended, this is not invariably the
case. In considering subjective experiences of anger we also have to reckon
with the possibility that episodes of that emotion may be caused by states or
events in the subject rather than by states of affairs or events in the world;[29]
similarly, we must accommodate the tendency of individuals disposed to
anger (whether on a long- or a short-term basis) to discharge the emotion at a convenient (but not necessarily legitimate) target;[30] and we must
(I think) accommodate the intuition that some forms of anger express mere
frustration or annoyance, sometimes focusing, perhaps, on the individual's

---

[29] On acausal, objectless, pathological occurrences of anger, see Oatley and Johnson-Laird (1998) 89;
de Sousa (1987: 66) notes that in some such pathological instances (or where an emotion is produced
by direct stimulation of the brain: cf. Eibl-Eibesfeldt [1989] 385) the subject nevertheless supplies an
appropriate evaluation to rationalize its occurrence.

[30] See Berkowitz (1990).

public status, but not entailing a claim that that status has been affronted by another's offense.[31] We have seen that Lakoff and Kövecses are happy with the notion that the model of anger which they establish for modern American English should serve as a prototypical scenario around which other, less prototypical forms cluster and to which these less prototypical forms are related by (Wittgensteinian) "family resemblance."[32] It seems to me that it is also for a prototypical case that the evolutionary account establishes its rationale; it would thus be a mistake to expect that rationale to function as a rigid template for absolutely every form of the emotion. The complexity of emotions as evolved psychophysical mechanisms – in particular the role of distinct but interrelated regions of the brain in the experience of emotion – suggests that the emotions which sustain co-operation will exploit capacities which existed before they were pressed into the service of co-operation and which remain as factors in the emotional experience of individuals; this seems to me particularly likely in the case of anger. Thus the prototypical evolutionary account may need to be supplemented by evolutionary considerations of a more inclusive character, and these may in some cases account better for the empirical data on the forms that anger may take.[33]

I ask the reader to bear the above discussion in mind throughout the following examination of the terminology, ethics, and nonverbal expression of anger in the *Iliad*. In considering the Homeric evidence, we need to recognize that there exists a multiplicity of terms which we regard as anger-terms whose meaning, reference, and usage must be investigated on an individual basis; given that, as noted above, the conceptualization and labeling of emotional experience can be, to a large extent, constitutive of that experience for the individual, we need to be attentive to the possibility that the terminology of other cultures may map the emotional landscape in ways that are different to our own. The terminological study thus offers the opportunity to test whether the evolutionary rationale is too monolithic for an adequate appreciation of the specificity of such terminology, whether, indeed, there exists any substantial degree of universality behind the specificity of the terminology. At the same time, I shall focus on the

---

[31] See Durkheim (1995) 63; Elster (1999a) 48, n. 1, 62, 250. Aristotle seems almost to acknowledge this at *Rh.* 2.2.1379a11ff., but quickly reformulates frustration as focusing on perceived offense; see Cooper (1996) 250; Elster (1999a) 62; Harris (2002) 59.

[32] That is, as sharing certain but not all characteristics of the typical case; see Wittgenstein (1967) §§ 66–7; cf. Lakoff and Johnson (1980) 122–4, Lakoff and Kövecses (1987) 217–18; Kövecses (2000) 173.

[33] Several alternative (though not mutually exclusive) evolutionary explanations for a capacity such as anger suggest themselves, from its general survival value in resisting and deterring aggression to its utility in male status-rivalry promoted by sexual selection; see (e.g.) G. Miller (2000) 403–4.

degree of "fit" between the sense, reference, and application of the terms considered and the view of anger as an emotion crucial to co-operative interaction; the reference of the terms considered to perceived offense or breach of co-operation will be investigated; I shall consider the status of anger as a socially embedded ethical notion; and I shall conclude with a consideration of the nonverbal expression of anger, which will illustrate the communicative role of emotional expression in the protocols of social interaction and allow us to use emotional behavior as well as emotion-terminology as data in an attempt to establish the specificity or otherwise of Iliadic anger.

To investigate the emotion of anger in Homer through the usage of the various lexical items which appear to occur within that semantic field is to be confronted with an initially surprising combination of lack of differentiation on the one hand and specificity on the other; the former, because Homeric Greek possesses a number of terms which can be used in "anger" contexts but also cover other forms of emotional arousal or expression; the latter, because, in contrast with later classical Greek (in which the main terms for anger are *orgē* and *thumos*), Homeric Greek presents a multiplicity of terms which are routinely translated as forms or aspects of anger.

Thumos in the *Iliad* is never anger as such, always the general psychic force under whose head anger (along with other emotions) belongs;[34] on occasion, however, an application of *thumos* can amount to a reference to anger (as at 1.192, where ceasing one's *cholos* and restraining one's *thumos* are the same event).[35] *Thumos* is also important in the phenomenology of Iliadic anger as the seat of the affect described by many of the particular anger-terms (*cholos*, e.g. 9.436; *chōesthai*, e.g. 1.243–4; *nemesis*, e.g. 2.223).[36] Similarly, *achos* represents the mental distress which is part of anger and other emotions;[37] thus, on occasion, an occurrence of *achos*, in so far as it

---

34 See Schmitt (1990) 185–8, 191–206; cf. Caswell (1990) 34–44. Plato (*Resp.* 581ab) links *thumos* closely with *timē*, but not all affections of the *thumos* in Hom. are concerned with honor. Shay's definition of Homeric *thumos* ("a synonym for the English word 'character' " [2000] 33) is far too general; the most recent detailed account is now Clarke (1999) 61–126 *passim*.

35 See *LfgrE* ii.1082 s.v. *Thumos* thus appears here, in a typical (universal?) conceptual metaphor of emotion, as an opponent in a struggle: see Lakoff and Kövecses (1987) 205–6; Kövecses (2000) 37, 68–9; cf. and contrast Clarke (1999) 95–6, who does not address the metaphorical aspect. As a physical entity *thumos* is most probably to be regarded as the air in the lungs (Clarke [1999] 75); that this physical entity can also function as an emotional force is thus an example of one of the most fundamental of all emotion's conceptual metaphors, the "container" metaphor (Lakoff and Kövecses [1987] 197–8; Kövecses [2000] 37).

36 But note also *cholos* and *kradiē*, e.g. 9.636; and *ētor*, e.g. 14.367.

37 See E. M. Voigt in *LfgrE* i.1774–8 s.v.; Fernandez-Galiano (1992) on *Od.* 21.412; contrast Nagy (1979) 69–83, for whom *achos* is simply "grief."

denotes a painful, emotional response to an insult or affront to one's *timē*, can refer to the emotion of anger itself.[38] *Menos* is another similar term: in arriving to put a stop to Achilles' *menos* (1.207) or in urging Agamemnon to cease his *menos* (1.282) Athena and Nestor (respectively) are referring to anger explicitly labeled as such elsewhere in the context and adequately motivated by the insults each believes he has suffered. Similarly, the verb *meneainein* can be used in the context of anger,[39] and the individual (9.679) or his *phrenes* (1.103–4) may be "filled with *menos*" (container metaphor) in response to a perceived affront; yet *menos* may also be the force which drives a warrior to do battle, and is a force that the warrior shares with natural phenomena and with fire;[40] the verb *meneainein* may denote earnest desire or striving.[41] Thus *menos* may accompany anger, its conceptualization overlaps with that of anger, and the energy that *menos* represents may convey both something of the physiological experience of the occurrent emotion (perhaps particularly the stimulation of the autonomic nervous system) and its goal-directed, desiderative aspect (the determination to retaliate), but *menos* is not in itself a candidate for consideration as a form of anger.

This last is more of a possibility with *ochthein*. This verb, typically though not exclusively employed in the speech-introduction formula, τὴν/τὸν μεγ' ὀχθήσας προσέφη ("greatly moved, he addressed him/her"), can denote an emotional response to conduct that might be construed as an affront or lack of respect,[42] and an overlap with anger is confirmed by the use of the formula to introduce the speech of Poseidon at 15.184–99, in which he

---

[38] See esp. 1.188–92; 15.205–11; 16.48–59; for *achos* as a response when one's *timē* is impaired or under threat, see *Od.* 16.85–9; 17.468–76; 18.346–8 = 20.284–6; 21.245–55; 21.295–304. Cf. *Il.* 8.147 (Diomedes on what Hector will say); 13.417; 14.458; 14.475; 14.486 (enemy boasts over slain comrade).

[39] See especially 19.65–8: Achilles refers to the end of his anger at Agamemnon as "ceasing his *cholos*" and subduing his *thumos*, though his *achos* persists, for it is not right, he observes, to persist in *meneainein*; cf. 24.55 regarding Achilles' mutilation of Hector's body, an action motivated by his *cholos* at the death of Patroclus (17.710; 18.322 [simile]; 18.337; 19.16; 22.94 [simile]; 23.23).

[40] See Redfield (1975) 171–2; R. Führer, *LfgrE* iii.142 s.v. μένος; Clarke (1999) 111 (which seems to me slightly at odds with his p. 94, n. 85). On the warrior's *menos* cf. Hershkowitz (1998a) 142–7. Kövecses (2000: 61–86) demonstrates that the image schema of emotion as a force is basic to the concept; on the more specific metaphors here, see Lakoff and Kövecses (1987) 202–3 (anger as fire); Kövecses (2000) 38, 64, 75–7 (emotion as fire); 37, 64, 71–2 (emotion as natural force); 21, 167, 171 (anger as natural force). It should be noted that as *menos* overlaps with anger in Homer, so anger overlaps with other more general conceptions of emotion in English and other languages; many of the metaphors through which emotions are conceptualized are used either of emotion in general or of more than one emotion (Kövecses [2000] 35–50).

[41] See, for example, 4.32, Hera's eagerness to sack Troy; cf. *LfgrE* iii.126 s.v. μενεαίνω.

[42] For example, Zeus's response to Hera's own expression of anger (4.23–4, 36) at his apparent desire to resolve the quarrel between Greeks and Trojans, 4.30; or Achilles' response at 20.343 when he realizes that he has been cheated of a victory by Apollo (cf. 22.14); or Menelaus' disapproval of Euphorbus' boast at 17.18.

expresses his anger at being treated as Zeus's inferior when in fact he is (as he sees it, 186) *homotimos* ("equal in *timē*"; note the reformulation of his attitude as *nemesis* at 211). Yet there are cases in which an interpretation in terms of anger would be far-fetched. Such, for example, are those in which *ochthein* denotes the reaction of a character caught in a dilemma: Odysseus (9.403), Menelaus (17.90), Agenor (21.552), and Hector (22.98) all speak ὀχθήσας to their *thumos*, when faced with a difficult choice between behaving in the manner expected of them or ensuring their own safety (or in Agenor's case between flight and certain death and flight and possible survival); in these cases *timē* is certainly at stake (as is life itself), but there is no sense in which the individual could be construed as angry, either with himself or with others. In these and in other cases, the verb seems first of all to characterize the degree of emotional arousal with which the speech is delivered; there are elements of anxiety and frustration in their response, but it would be wrong to pin the term down to one or other of these. Rather, it seems to refer to a relatively undifferentiated (negative) affect that is elicited in situations in which the subject feels frustrated, annoyed, or constrained and that is typically expressed in exclamatory, emotional speech; it may thus take on positive characteristics of more specific emotions according to context and eliciting conditions.[43] This is a term which certainly does often focus on the individual's standing in the eyes of others, but its reference is clearly wider than that of any term which we would regard as a candidate to translate the English "anger."[44]

The verb *chalepainein* is another which is often translated "be angry"; it certainly often occurs in "anger" contexts,[45] but, crucially, it may also be used of non-reactive forms of behavior, as at 24.369, where Hermes observes that Priam and his aged attendant are ill-equipped to defend themselves against unprovoked aggression – ἄνδρ' ἀπαμύνασθαι, ὅτε τις πρότερος χαλεπήνῃ ("to keep off any man who may take the initiative in *chalepainein*"). The same line occurs (with ἀπαρέσσασθαι, "to come to terms

---

[43] It refers, for example, to Achilles' anxiety when he conjectures that the movement of the Achaean force portends bad news about Patroclus, 18.5; to the emotional manner in which he cuts his hair for Patroclus, 23.143; to his surprised irritation at seeing Lycaon once more on the battlefield, 21.53; and to the consternation of the gods when friction within the divine community seems likely (1.517) or has broken out (1.70; 15.101); cf. Zeus's annoyance at what he regards as Poseidon's misplaced concern for his own status (7.454) and Poseidon's disapproval of Hera's suggestion that he join with her in opposing Zeus (8.208).

[44] Adkins (1969: 12–13, 14–17) is basically right about the sense and reference of this verb, though I believe he is wrong to see its application in a range of different scenarios as evidence that the Homeric vocabulary of emotion reflects a society which constructs the world in ways which we must find fundamentally unfamiliar.

[45] *Il.* 14.256–7, Zeus's violent response to deception, as related by Hypnus; 16.386, Zeus's *kotos* at crooked judgments of mortals expressed in *chalepainein*; 18.108, *cholos* makes men *chalepainein*; 20.133, Poseidon describes Hera's reaction to Apollo's favoring of Aeneas.

with") at 19.183 with reference to Agamemnon's initiation of the quarrel with Achilles, in which connection the verb is also used by Agamemnon himself at 2.378. While in the two latter cases one might entertain the possibility that the relevant phrase signifies not the initiation of a conflict, but rather the initiation of anger within a conflict situation (i.e. in response to another's offense), the passage from Book 24, where this would be impossible, suggests that the verb is used of unprovoked aggression in the other passages too.[46] *Chalepainein*, then, does not refer to the experience of anger as such, but to violent or harsh behavior, in word or in deed,[47] which may form part of the *expression* of anger,[48] but may also be used in a range of other situations.

These terms do not show that Homeric terminology for anger constructs that emotion differently from modern English; rather, they indicate that, as could be predicted (given that anger is a species of the genus emotion), anger can be seen as exhibiting similarities with other forms of emotional experience; we do, indeed, need to be mindful of this in investigating the emotion of anger and its terminology, in Homer and elsewhere, but we do not need to go back to the drawing board just because some of the stock translations we learned at school turn out to be inadequate.

The fact that a number of Homeric terms cover both the experience and/or expression of anger and a wider range of emotional experiences would be a significant sociolinguistic phenomenon only if Homeric Greek possessed no terms which referred to (what we think of as) anger as such; then we should at least have to reckon with major differences in the construction and labeling of emotional experience, even if not, or not necessarily, in the experience itself. But in fact Homeric Greek possesses a number of terms which seem to me very clearly to refer to the experience of some form of anger, namely *cholos*, *chōesthai*, *kotos*, *skuzesthai*, and *nemesis*. *Cholos* is the most common of these. It is typically elicited by some form of slight or affront;[49] it is associated with the *thumos*,[50] the *ētor* (14.367), or the *kēr* (16.585; 21.136); it is a painful affect,[51] which seems to "seize," "come/fall

---

[46] Thus at 9.516 Phoenix, in claiming that he would not be advising Achilles to cast away his *mēnis* were Agamemnon still vehemently *chalepainein*, is probably not conceding that Agamemnon has, with or without just cause, been *angry* at Achilles, merely endorsing Achilles' own evaluation that Agamemnon's behavior has been excessively aggressive.

[47] Cf. χαλεποῖσιν ἐπέεσσιν, χαλεπῷ μύθῳ, χαλεποῖσιν ὀνείδεσι.

[48] Especially 16.386; 18.108; with the former, where Zeus's *kotos* is expressed in *chalepainein* in the form of high wind and torrent, cf. χαλεπαίνων of the roar of the wind at 14.399; for the "natural force" metaphor see Kövecses (2000) 37, 64, 71–2 (emotion in general); 21, 167, 171 (anger).

[49] 1.9, 78, 81, 139, 192, 217, 224, 283, 387, to cite only the examples from *Iliad* 1.

[50] 1.192, 217; 2.195–6; 9.675; 13.660; 14.50, 207, 306; 16.206; 18.113; 19.66; 23.566.

[51] 4.513; 9.260, 566; 18.112; 19.65; 23.566; 24.584.

upon," or "enter" one;[52] it craves satisfaction through retaliation (4.178) and is expected normally to lead to a vigorous response (2.195, 241–2). It can burst out in indignant speech, insults, or threats,[53] but also in violent retaliation, including killing the offender.[54] Its physical symptoms, "aura," and imagery include the swelling of the chest (or "heart," *kradiē*)[55] and "being full of *menos*";[56] it is a fire that must be extinguished (9.678),[57] a disease that must be healed by retaliation (4.36), or an appetite that must be satiated (4.35–6).[58] "Bitter *cholos*" is the response of a lion who has lost his cubs (18.318–22),[59] but it is also a passion "sweeter than honey," 18.109.[60] Quite clearly, then, the prototypical scenario of *cholos* is identical to that which Aristotle establishes for *orgē* and that which Lakoff and Kövecses establish for anger in American English; the concept of *cholos*, moreover, is constructed in terms which bear the closest comparison with English anger – its basic ontological metaphor (*cholos* is an entity) is identical;[61] the existence of this entity is conceived of as presence; it is experienced as a force or a fluid within a pressurized container; it is a fire, a beast, an opponent with whom one can struggle,[62] and a sickness or burden of which one wishes to be relieved.[63] These correspondences are systematic,

---

[52] 1.387; 6.166; 8.460; 9.436, 553; 14.207, 306; 16.30, 206; 18.322; 19.16; 22.94.

[53] 1.223–44, 387–8; 3.413–17; 4.24–9, 241–9; 8.461–8; 21.480; 24.55–63.

[54] 6.205; 23.87–8; cf. 6.166–70, plotting to have "offender" removed; 9.539–42, sending a beast to destroy "offender's" crops, etc.; cf. 24.605–6 (killing offender as expression of *chōesthai*).

[55] 9.553–4, 646; 18.110; cf. 24.584.   [56] 9.678–9; cf. 19.68; 24.54.

[57] Given the detailed correspondence between *cholos* and models of anger in other cultures (as well as the overlap between anger and other emotions in their use of the "fire" metaphor), I think it is extremely unlikely that 9.678 (Achilles is unwilling to "extinguish [*sbessai*] his *cholos*") is not a "fire" metaphor, much less that that it "is not a metaphor at all," as Clarke (1999: 94–5 and n. 85) would have it; the parallels which Clarke adduces for a less specific sense can all likewise be taken as metaphorical.

[58] Kövecses (2000: 167) notes that the "anger is hunger" metaphor, though found in English, is considerably more prominent in Zulu.

[59] That "passions are beasts inside a person" is "a very widespread metaphor in Western culture" (Lakoff and Kövecses [1987] 206); cf. "wild" or "savage" (*agrios*) *cholos* at 4.23 = 8.460; cf. also the bestial *cholos* of the snake in the simile at 22.93–5 (which has organic causes – the creature has eaten κακὰ φάρμακα). Underlying the last passage is no doubt the notion of *cholos* as a bodily humor, though this seems to become explicit only at 16.203; thus, though metaphors and metonymies which emphasize the embodiment of *cholos* are important in its conceptualization, its physical specificity as a bodily fluid is far less salient than is suggested by Clarke (1999) 90, 92–7.

[60] Cited by Arist. *Rh.* 2.2.1378b6–7 to illustrate the desiderative aspect of *orgē*.

[61] On ontological metaphors (basically reification and personification), see Lakoff and Johnson (1980) 25–34.

[62] This particular metaphor reflects the fact that the conceptualization of emotion in terms of self-division is common to both Homeric and modern English cultural models: see Kövecses (2000) 199.

[63] For all these as aspects of the cultural model of English anger, see Lakoff and Kövecses (1987); on the "disease" metaphor, see Averill (1990) 112. Harris (2002) 67–8 is too cursory to do justice to the importance of metaphor and metonymy in the study of Greek anger-concepts.

not accidental; even though the folk physiology on which it is based is in many specific details different from our own, fundamentally, Homeric *cholos* labels the same concept as English anger.

Though clearly used of an occurrent affect, *cholos* may also become dispositional,[64] in which case one can be said to be "digesting" or "concocting" one's *cholos*;[65] dispositional *cholos*, however, always has the potential to erupt into occurrence whenever the individual is reminded of its original cause.[66] *Cholos* can be deprecated as excessive, extreme, unhelpful, or inappropriate,[67] but also acknowledged as a legitimate response to an affront (9.523), and even criticized as insufficient to the circumstances (2.241–2). There is thus a rationality to *cholos*; it responds cognitively to a specific sort of scenario, and can be commended or deprecated as appropriate or otherwise to that scenario; at the same time, however, it is clearly not merely a cognitive-evaluative judgment: it is typically attended by a (paradoxically pleasant) desire for retaliation, so there is also a desiderative aspect; equally, though exhibiting rationality, it may evade the control of reason (24.584–5); it also has painful symptoms and involves specific physiological changes.

In one respect, however, the behavior of the term departs somewhat from the Aristotelian definition of *orgē*, for while *cholos* is regularly a response to some kind of offense,[68] it is not always straightforwardly the case. It appears that *cholos* can, for example, be elicited simply by failure in competition: at 4.391 the Thebans, who have been thoroughly outshone in a series of athletic contests by Tydeus, decide in their *cholos* to ambush him on his departure; the Thebans clearly feel themselves dishonored by their failure, but they could not possibly have entertained a legitimate expectation that Tydeus would refrain from trying to defeat them in the contests, and no one would have accepted this as a legitimate expectation if they had; this scenario, then, would appear not to satisfy Aristotle's condition that anger is elicited by "a perceived slight" which is "unwarranted" (μὴ προσήκοντος, *Rh.* 2.2.1378a31–2).[69] With this we might compare the response to the death

---

[64] 16.30–1, Achilles' dispositional *cholos*, cf. 9.157, 261, 299; 14.367; 16.61; 19.67; cf. Zeus 15.72.

[65] 4.513; 9.565 – not, clearly, in an effort to dissipate it, but in order to "keep it warm," like Tam O'Shanter's wife (see Clarke [1999] 93); note, however, 1.81–3, where "digesting" the *cholos* which was one's immediate response to a perceived affront transforms it into long-term *kotos*; see below. English has similar metaphors ("let him stew" etc.; Lakoff and Kövecses [1987] 198).

[66] 9.646–8; 19.16–17; see in general Darwin (1998) 234.

[67] 6.626; 10.107; 16.206; 18.107–10, 119; 20.251–5.

[68] 17.399 demonstrates that *cholos* normally disposes one to find fault, though, for rhetorical purposes, it is claimed that not even someone in the grip of *cholos* would find fault in these circumstances.

[69] Contrast the *cholos* of Antilochus and Menelaus in the funeral games of Book 23, both of whom justify their anger with reference to the legitimacy of their grievance: 23.543–54, 566–85.

of a comrade in battle, which is regularly designated as *cholos*.[70] The loss of a comrade in battle affects one's honor and requires retaliation,[71] and one's enemies in war may owe one (or one's body after death) some basic form of respect, but this cannot be felt to extend to a requirement that they refrain from killing oneself or one's colleagues out of regard for their honor. There is an apparent discrepancy between such cases and Aristotle's definition of anger in terms of the perception of unwarranted offense. This is not to be resolved by driving a wedge between Aristotelian *orgē* and Homeric *cholos*: Aristotle clearly believes that what he says about the former holds good of the latter, because he cites a statement about *cholos* to illustrate a significant point about *orgē* (2.2.1378b6–7, n. 60 above). The true resolution lies in the recognition that Aristotle's account of *orgē* establishes not an exhaustive, all-encompassing, but a prototypical definition of anger, analogous to the prototypical model established by Lakoff and Kövecses for modern English. The Homeric scenarios in which *cholos* does not straightforwardly spring from a perception of unwarranted offense are not to be dissociated from Aristotelian anger, but merely recognized as less prototypical cases which nonetheless bear a significant "family resemblance" to the prototypical scenario. There will be scenarios in which it is better to relax, rather than to retain Aristotle's insistence on unwarranted offense: just as we often feel angry when made to feel foolish, regardless of any desire on the part of anyone else to slight us,[72] so (one might say) *cholos* is likely where the individual feels that his *timē* has become vulnerable; in such circumstances individuals may feel affronted, even when not disappointed in their legitimate claim to respect, simply because of their attachment to a certain image of themselves. But we also remember that for Aristotle it is the *appearance* (*phantasia*) of unwarranted offense that is necessary for anger; such an appearance may be entirely subjective, and perhaps in warfare especially such a subjective perception that one has been illegitimately harmed is a necessary element of the warrior's motivation. As Braund and Gilbert show elsewhere in this volume in connection with Roman epic, a degree of anger, an element of personal grievance, may be a part of the martial spirit that warriors need to

---

[70] 4.494, 501; 18.337; 19.16 (this is almost certainly *cholos* at Hector elicited by the sight of the new armor, reminding Achilles of the loss of the old and whetting his appetite for retaliation; contrast Redfield [1975] 14, who takes the sight of the armor itself as the proper elicitor of Achilles' anger), 23.22–3; cf. the *cholos* of the river Xanthus at 21.146, which encompasses an element of revenge for the Trojans who have been slaughtered, but also of outrage at Achilles' lack of respect (cf. 136). On anger at the killer of a comrade-in-arms, see Lendon (2000) 5–11.

[71] Note the determination to retaliate in cases such as 4.494–7, 501–4; 18.336–7.

[72] For example, the anger of male drivers when they lose their way, often compounded by the well-intentioned intervention of female passengers.

cultivate if they are to face the enemy effectively, and it certainly seems to be a feature of soldiers' experience that the death of a comrade is the event *par excellence* that "makes it personal."[73] One might compare the commonly recognized element of anger in the grief (both spontaneous and ritualized) of those who have lost a loved one in ordinary circumstances;[74] if blame and resentment enter into the ideation of the mourner even where the loss is not attributable to human agency, it is easy to see how genuine anger might arise where a specific human being or group of human beings can be identified as killer. Such anger would not arise from an objective breach of a legitimate entitlement to respect, and to the extent that the response fails wholly to match the conditions, it is (in terms of those conditions) "irrational"; but the case of retaliatory anger for the death of a comrade, I submit, is both immediately recognizable to us as a form of anger and sufficiently close to the Aristotelian definition to count as a variant of his schema. This is certainly a case in which anger cannot objectively be characterized as identifying a failure to meet a legitimate expectation of respect between members of a co-operating group, but it can nonetheless be regarded as an extension of such a scenario *in the mind of the angry individual* to relations between members of non-co-operating groups. It is perhaps the very closeness of the bond between one comrade and another that draws the enemy who undoes that bond into a sort of notional community with his victim's avenger;[75] yet this is highly paradoxical, for the case of Achilles shows – and the evidence of real conflicts bears this out – that the minimal notion of community that turns an act of war into a perceived offense can generate an attitude in the avenger that denies the common humanity of the individual who is the target of his furious retaliation.[76] Aristotle's condition (that anger seeks revenge for a perceived and unwarranted slight) is not

---

[73] See, for example, the evidence from Vietnam and the parallels with the *Iliad* and other ancient works adduced in Shay (1994) *passim*, esp. 29, 33, 39–44, 49, 53–5, 80–1, 87–90, 95–6, 116–17; Tritle (2000) 9, n. 17, 15, 36–7, 42–3, 65–6, 70, 121–3, 131–2, 150.

[74] See Holst-Warhaft (1992) 5; Shay (1994) 40, 55; Durkheim (1995) 397.

[75] If the prototypical case of anger (both for Aristotle and for us) is highly ethicized (*qua* response to unwarranted offense), there are degrees of ethicization; though Homeric ethics does recognize impartial and generalizable standards which should apply to all equally (see below on *nemesis*), there can be no impartial or generalizable expectation that soldiers in battle should refrain from killing their enemies; yet modern soldiers would agree with Achilles and the other warriors of the *Iliad* that it is one's moral duty to avenge a comrade's death, regardless of the fact that what "they" have done to "us" is precisely what "we" were trying to do to "them."

[76] See Achilles at *Il.* 22.261–7 (he and Hector may as well be of different species), 345–54 (Hector is a dog; Achilles wishes he himself could eat his flesh; as it is, his body will feed the birds and dogs); cf. Hector at 122–8; for the simultaneous affirmation and denial of community with one's enemy, see Achilles' attitude to Lycaon, *Il.* 21.106–13. See Shay (1994) 82–4, 93–4.

to be retained at all costs;[77] yet the categories that structure his paradigm scenario may persist, albeit reconfigured, in other, non-paradigmatic cases.

Skuzesthai and *chōesthai* are very close synonyms of *cholousthai*. *Skuzesthai* and *cholos* co-occur (4.23–4; 8.459–60), and the synonymy of *skuzesthai* and *kecholōsthai* is demonstrated by Zeus's words to Thetis (reported by Thetis to Achilles at 24.134–5) at 24.113–14:

> Tell him that the gods *skuzesthai* at him, but that I above all the immortals *kecholōsthai* . . .

The logic of this passage can only be satisfied if *skuzesthai* and *kecholōsthai* signify the same response. The specific difference between the two verbs will be that the former, cognate with *skuthros* and *skuthrōpos*, refers essentially to the facial expression of anger (though often no doubt metonymously to the occurrence of the emotion itself; see below).[78]

One might be tempted to regard *cholos/cholousthai* and *chōesthai* as simple synonyms: they can be used interchangeably with reference to the same response[79] and share the same characteristics in terms of symptoms, phenomenology, and eliciting conditions. It may also be significant that, with one partial exception, no attested form of the one is metrically equivalent to any attested form of the other.[80] But there is one area in which *chōesthai* appears to depart from *cholousthai*: it is used of an agent's frustration or annoyance at his own mistake or failure. Thus Achilles predicts that Agamemnon will *chōesthai* on realizing his error in failing to honor the best of the Achaeans (1.244), and warriors frequently *chōesthai* when a weapon breaks or misses its target;[81] for Adkins (1969: 13–14, 17), these instances indicate that *chōesthai* is not an anger-term as we should understand it, but a somewhat more undifferentiated response denoting "the frame of mind of a man who has received an unpleasant stimulus from his environment" and encompassing a "positive attitude to the obstacle in his path" (17); it is "confusedly grief and anger at once." Certainly grief and anger are linked in Homeric Greek, chiefly through the usage of *achos* to cover both (and more besides); but so are they in English, in which being angry and being

---

[77] See n. 31 above, and below on *chōesthai*.

[78] On the role of metonymy in the conceptualization of emotion, see Lakoff and Kövecses (1987) 196–7; Kövecses (2000) 5, 133–4, 171–2, 176–7.

[79] 1.80–1; 3.413–14; 8.397 and 407–8; 13.660–2; cf. e.g. *cholos* at 6.205 and *chōesthai* at 24.605–6 of divine anger at human presumption; cf. *chōesthai* reformulated as *skuzesthai* at 8.477–83.

[80] The exception is ἐχώσατο = χολώσατο, which are equivalent in metrical shape, but nonetheless metrically useful alternatives by virtue of the presence/absence of the augment.

[81] 13.165; 14.406; 16.616; 22.291.

aggrieved are regularly aspects of the same emotion;[82] more generally, and perhaps more significantly, one might point to the very real sense of anger that permeates genuine human grief in both spontaneous and ritualized form (see above). But even allowing for that, Adkins' vagueness with regard to *chōesthai* is misplaced; Agamemnon's hypothetical *chōesthai* at his mistake and the others' *chōesthai* at their failure to wound an opponent in battle seem to me legitimate cases of anger, provided that we relax the prototypical requirement that the loss of face which occasions anger must be caused by another's insulting behavior; manifest misjudgment or failure in battle exposes the agent to criticism or ridicule, and the frustration of an agent in such a situation is quite clearly, it seems to me, a form of anger, directed more at the self than at others, but nonetheless like all forms of anger in having a focal reference to the *timē* of the individual (and also bearing a strong family resemblance to other, straightforward forms of anger in its expression and in the kind of conduct to which it leads);[83] again, it is the kind of anger we all experience when made to look or feel foolish (in any circumstance) – the kind we experience, for example, when attempting unsuccessfully to assemble a flat-packed item of furniture.[84]

Kotos is more easily dealt with: while it can be an occurrent affect (4.168; 14.111; 23.391) and does invariably, as *cholos* and *chōesthai* typically do, focus on the commission of some affront or offense, it can also be distinguished

---

[82] See Braund (1997) 80 and Harris (2002) 68 on Lat. *dolor*; the absence of a distinction in terminology between anger and grief is documented for several languages by Russell (1991) 430, 432, 441.

[83] Simple failure can also lead to retaliation (verbal insults at 16.617–18), but also to withdrawal (13.165; 14.408) and *katēpheiē* (22.293); for these as expressions of anger, see below.

[84] Adkins' (mis)interpretation of these cases rests less on inattentiveness to the nuances of the Greek terms than on his construction of a false dichotomy between a modern concept of anger which he never defines and ancient terms which fail to meet his undefined criteria. He is also (p. 13) opposed to the translation "be angry" for *chōesthai* at 23.385, where Diomedes sheds tears at the loss of his whip, and 21.519, where the gods, having taken part in battle on the plain of Troy (they are not mere spectators, as Adkins would have it), return to Olympus, "some χωόμενοι, others greatly exulting." But Diomedes' anger stems at least in part from his sense that the loss of his whip was *unfair*, given his performance in the race so far; in fact, its loss was more unfair than he knows, since it resulted from the direct intervention of Apollo. His tears do not disprove his anger: cf. *Od.* 2.80–1, discussed by Adkins 13, 17; Telemachus' tears parallel Diomedes' response, and similarly express a response designated *chōesthai*, but his action of throwing the sceptre to the ground in disgust at the failure of the assembly to support him parallels that of Achilles at *Il.* 1.245, following a speech which was introduced with reference to his *cholos* at 224; Adkins would presumably concede that Achilles, at any rate, is angry. As for the gods in Book 21, I cannot see why Adkins refuses to regard χωόμενοι as a reference to anger: the gods who react thus are those who have come off worst in the foregoing exchanges, exchanges which were themselves marked by mutual insults, claims, and counter-claims, and in which each side gave every impression of being convinced of the rectitude of its own position. The winners exult, the losers are angry – where's the problem? (Adkins spent some time as a lecturer in Glasgow in the 1950s, but he clearly never attended a Rangers–Celtic football match.)

from *cholos* and *chōesthai* as being a longer-term, dispositional form of anger (1.80–3: note the "container" metaphors):

A prince is stronger when he *chōesthai* with an inferior man; for even if he digest his *cholos* at the time, he retains *kotos* in his breast in the future, until he brings it to fruition.

Kotos is thus what remains when the occurrent emotion of anger becomes dispositional; like occurrent anger, it exhibits a strong desire for retaliation. This dispositional aspect of *kotos* is apparent in other passages,[85] and should probably be assumed in others;[86] thus in 5.177–8 *kotos* is presumably to be regarded as the long-term consequence of an offense which originally aroused occurrent *mēnis*, and at 16.386 *kotos* is probably the dispositional basis for the immediate expression of anger in *chalepainein*.

The last but one passage, 5.177–8, shows that *kotos* and *mēnis* can focus on the same offense (failure to honor a god in sacrifice). Indeed, in terms of its reference, there is nothing distinctive about *mēnis*: like *cholos* and *chōesthai* it responds to a perceived offense, to another individual's failure to accord *timē*. It is frequently a response of gods,[87] but may also be manifested by mortals – not just by the god-like Achilles,[88] but also by Agamemnon (at Achilles, 1.247), by Aeneas (at Priam, 13.460), and (in the *Odyssey*) by Telemachus (at the suitors, following their plot to murder him, 16.377) and even by a beggar, albeit one who is a hero in disguise (17.14). *Mēnis* and *cholos* co-occur[89] and may be used, apparently interchangeably, to designate the same response.[90] It is difficult to escape the conclusion that all *mēnis* is *cholos*, and that *mēnis*, elicited and expressed in the same sort of scenario as *cholos*, is without question a form of anger.[91]

The attempt is often made to reserve for *mēnis* the significance of "divine wrath"; this approach regards it as unproblematic that Achilles is said to

---

[85] Most clearly at 13.517; cf. 5.747; 8.391, 449; 14.191; 18.367; and 23.383, in all of which the audience is aware of long-term ill will on the part of the individual concerned – in the last case on account of an incident narrated at 5.260–73, 319–27, 433–42; see Reichl (1994) 230.

[86] 1.181; 3.345; 5.191; 10.517; 14.143; 16.449.

[87] 1.75; 5.34, 178; 5.444; 13.624; 15.122; 16.711; 21.523; cf. *mēnima*, "cause of *mēnis*" at 22.358.

[88] 1.1, 422; 2.769; 9.517; 12.10; 18.257; 19.35, 75; cf. 16.62, 202, 282 *mēnithmos*.

[89] 15.122; cf. 16.61–2, 202–3, 206, *mēnithmos* and *cholos*.

[90] For example, Apollo's *cholos* at Agamemnon's treatment of his priest, 1.9, is reformulated as *mēnis* at 1.75; the divine response to a neglected sacrifice is *mēnis* at 5.178 and *cholos* at 9.538; just so Achilles' *mēnis*/*mēnithmos* at Agamemnon is regularly designated *cholos*, 1.192, 217, 224, 283; 2.241; 4.513; 9.157, 260–1, 299, 436, 523, 646, 675, 678; 10.107; 14.50, 367; 16.30–1, 61, 203, 206; 18.108, 111; 19.67.

[91] Muellner (1996: 111) concedes that *mēnis* can be reformulated as *cholos*, but denies that *cholos* retains connotations of *mēnis* in contexts which "have not been previously defined as instances of the *mēnis* theme;" for corroboration, he refers to the dissertation of T. R. Walsh, which I have not seen; I have not been able to consult the published version, *Feuding Words and Fighting Words*, apparently published in 2002.

manifest *mēnis*, for Achilles is semi-divine, and his prodigious and terrible anger is thus assimilated to that of the gods; but it is more of a problem that Agamemnon, Aeneas, Telemachus, and the disguised Odysseus too are credited with *mēnis*. In their case, however, it is the verb, not the noun, which is used; thus the argument is advanced that the verb, being less restricted in its usage, should not be used as evidence for the semantic range of the noun.[92] This seems to me wholly implausible: not only is *mēniein* clearly denominative, it is apparent from 5.177–8 (εἰ μή τις θεός ἐστι κοτεσσά-μενος Τρώεσσιν | ἱρῶν μηνίσας· χαλεπὴ δὲ θεοῦ ἔπι μῆνις – "unless he is some god angry [*kotos*-anger] with the Trojans, having conceived *mēnis* on account of sacrifices; for in a god mēnis is difficult") that to say that one μηνίει is to say that one possesses *mēnis*. The restricted application of the noun to gods and Achilles is thus presumably accidental, and the distribution of the verb provides legitimate evidence for the concept as a whole.[93]

If *mēnis* is to be distinguished from *cholos*, then, the distinction will not reside in its reference, in the kind of scenario with which it is associated, or in the status of those who experience it, but in its connotation.[94] Precisely what that difference in connotation may be, however, is unlikely to be established satisfactorily on the basis of the Iliadic data alone – not, at any rate, without leaving oneself open to the charge of circularity in argument. Consideration of later usage of the same root sustains the impression that *mēnis* and suchlike are *largely* reserved for the gods, heroes, and the dead,[95] but even then exceptions, cases of mortal *mēnis* at the offenses of other mortals, occur.[96] The preponderance of "supernatural" applications, in Homer and after, lends some weight to the view that there is something about *mēnis* that makes it particularly *appropriate* as a term for divine anger, but a specific restriction to "divine anger" is clearly out of the question: I hazard a guess that it is the gravity and intensity of *mēnis* that makes it suitable as a term both for divine wrath and for human anger which exceeds the norm in those two respects.

---

[92] See Considine (1966) 17, (1986) 57.

[93] So W. Beck in *LfgrE* iii.189 s.v. μηνίω. The thesis of Watkins (1977a), that *mēnis* is a taboo word, rests on Achilles' use of *mēnithmos*, a supposed deformation required by a taboo on first-person uses, of his own wrath at 16.62 and 202; but as a verbal noun from *mēniein*, itself a denominative of *mēnis*, *mēnithmos* is surely an unlikely candidate to perform such a function; and if the rationale for *mēnithmos* is to permit first-person reference to the taboo concept of *mēnis*, why do we find a third-person use at 16.282? There is a (later) first-person use of the verb *mēniein* at Eur. *Hipp.* 146, and the use of the participle of *apomēniein* in the genitive absolute at *Il.* 9.426 and 19.62 is equivalent to a first-person use of the verb. Muellner's attempt to account for the difficulties in Watkins' view (1996: 189–94) fails to convince me.

[94] So Frisk (1946) 29.   [95] Frisk (1946) 31–3, 35–6, 38–9.

[96] Hdt. 7.229 (*mēnis*: Frisk [1946] 32); 5.84; 9.7 (*mēniein*: Frisk [1946] 35); other, later (incl. New Testament) examples in Frisk (1946) 33–4, 35–6.

That *mēnis* has this particular character which associates it with the prodigious and awesome wrath of gods, heroes, and the dead does not warrant Muellner's insistence that it is "a sanction meant to guarantee and maintain the integrity of the world-order" (1996: 26; cf. 32 "an irrevocable cosmic sanction"), upholding "cosmic prohibitions" (27–8) and "cosmic justice" (35), in fact "nothing less than the *nomen sacrum* for the ultimate sanction that enforces the world-defining prohibitions . . . that are basic to the establishment . . . of the world of Zeus and the society of mortals he presides over" (129). Muellner's approach has the merit of recognizing the continuity of divine and human values (34, 50–1) in Homer, but its emphasis is too "top-down" – the "cosmic" is prior in definition to the social in this approach, whereas, both logically and temporally, the opposite is the case: the mirroring of human ethical and social structures at the supernatural level is the result of the modeling of the latter on the former.[97] The effect (?goal) of Muellner's approach is to err on the side of the specific and to drive a wedge between Greek *mēnis* and anything that we might recognize as anger.

Mēnis, cholos, skuzesthai, chōesthai, and *kotos* generally designate the response of the victim/affected party or his/her partisan.[98] The same is sometimes true of *nemesis,* in which case *nemesis* bears the closest comparison with *cholos* or *mēnis.*[99] On other occasions, however, *nemesis* is the response of the bystander, even the disinterested bystander, and this marks a difference between it and most instances of the other terms, for in such cases *nemesis* is a response to an action or a state of affairs which one finds inappropriate in terms of society's general standards of the honorable, rather than to an action which directly and negatively impinges upon one's own honor.[100] The adjective, *nemessēton,* thus functions similarly to the

---

[97] See Burkert (1996) 80–102.

[98] *Mēnis* is impartial when it denotes the response of the gods to the denial of burial (22.358; cf. *Od.* 11.73); *cholos* can be a response to another's failure to fulfil his obligations (4.241; 14.49–51), though admittedly this is on the part of those who are directly affected by that failure; at 24.113–15 = 134–6 *skuzesthai* and *kecholōsthai* indicate Zeus's response to Achilles' inhumanity; cf. Apollo's *nemesis* at 24.53 (n. 100 below).

[99] 6.335–6 (with *cholos*); 8.407 (with χολοῦμαι; n.b. also χώσατ' in 397), 421 (with χολοῦται); 10.115, 129, 145; 15.103; 15.115–16, 211, 227; 16.21–2.

[100] 6.351 (where *nemesis* is envisaged as the general response to Paris' shortcomings, endorsed by Helen); cf. 5.757, 872; 13.119, 121–2; 17.91–5; 23.494; 24.53. The last passage cited shows clearly how the impartial perspective of *nemesis* may be employed by individuals who are not necessarily impartial: Apollo is Hector's partisan; but the *nemesis* he threatens here is presented as a third-party response to conduct which is futile, excessive, and inappropriate (neither *kallion* nor *ameinon,* 52, exhibiting a lack of *aidōs,* not for Apollo, but for civilized standards in general, 44). For a clear statement of *nemesis* as the potential response of the disinterested bystander, see *Od.* 1.228–9. Thus the usage of *nemesis* correlates with the dual use of *aideomai* with two categories of accusative, (a) of the direct recipients of one's actions and (b) of their witnesses; in (a), *aidōs* inhibits affronts on the honor of others, in (b) inappropriate behavior; thus both affronts and inappropriate behavior attract *nemesis.*

collection of quasi-aesthetic terms which mark breaches of the Homeric "standard of appropriateness";[101] and to reject an action as *nemessēton* is not merely to observe that it will incur the disapproval of (unspecified) others, but to endorse that (potential) evaluation and reject the action as a breach of the standards of one's society.[102]

Nemesis, in fact, bears a relation to the notion of justification which is all but analytic.[103] The locutions οὐ νεμεσίζομαι/οὐ νέμεσις/οὐ νεμεσσητόν and the like indicate that there is no justification for criticism in the particular circumstances,[104] while μὴ νεμέσα seeks to override indignation which is acknowledged as justified with reference to some more pressing need.[105] This being so, there is a case for arguing that *nemesis*, even when the response of the victim or a partisan to a personal affront, retains this notion of justification, to the extent that it characterizes the response of the offended party as the sort of response that others, in accordance with the general norms of society, would endorse. For example, the *nemesis* Poseidon feels for Zeus in Book 15 (211), and which Zeus recognizes as his response (227), is justified with reference to what Poseidon sees as an established equality of *timē* between Zeus, himself, and Hades (185–95); Poseidon thus presents his response not merely as the outrage of the victim, but as indignation at the disregard for a publicly ratified, just distribution of *timē*.[106] If *nemesis* does retain this implicit appeal to standards that others can be expected to endorse, it perhaps bears comparison with the role of "resentment," experienced by the victim but endorsed by the "impartial spectator," in Adam Smith's *Theory of Moral Sentiments*.[107]

This does leave a few problematic cases, however, which appear at first sight recalcitrant to such an interpretation: at 4.507–8 Apollo's *nemesis* appears to be motivated only by his partisan displeasure at Achaean success in battle, rather than by a sense that the Achaeans have failed in

---

[101] Long (1970); cf. Cairns (1993) 50–68, 130–5.   [102] See 3.410; 14.335–6; 24.463.

[103] At 17.91–5, where Menelaus expresses his *aidōs* at the prospective *nemesis* of any Achaean witness to his withdrawal, note that he first construes the situation in terms which would make others' disapproval justified – he is both retreating before a more powerful opponent and neglecting his duty to the dead Patroclus; then, however, in order to justify his withdrawal, he constructs an alternative scenario in which no blame could accrue, 97–101.

[104] 2.296–7; 3.156–7; 4.413–14; 9.523; 10.129; 14.80; 17.100–1; 19.182–3.

[105] 10.145; 15.115–16; 16.21–2; cf. 10.115.

[106] Similarly, at 2.222–3 the Achaeans express both *kotos* and *nemesis* at Thersites' abuse of Agamemnon; they are clearly represented as Agamemnon's partisans, and their *kotos* no doubt suggests a long-standing hostility toward Thersites; but their *nemesis* may be intended to suggest that disapproval of Thersites' behavior is a justified response – particularly as the poet is at pains not only to suggest the uniformity of the Achaeans' disapproval of Thersites and of their pleasure at his come-uppance (265–77), but also to give him a negative narrative coloring from the outset (211–21).

[107] A. Smith (1976), esp. 34–8, 68–79, 83–4, 94–7, 172, 218, 393.

aidōs and breached some accepted norm; similarly, at 8.198 Hera's *nemesis* appears to consist of nothing more than resentment of Hector's exultation and confidence in his success; 13.292–3 presents a rather different problem – Idomeneus seems to accept that he and Meriones can legitimately be criticized for "standing around conversing like children," yet expresses the concern that this may cause a witness to feel *nemesis* "excessively," ὑπερφιάλως; but can justified criticism be excessive? One could accept that these three are non-prototypical cases in which the notion of justification in the use of *nemesis*-words is attenuated, and this would not necessarily invalidate the conclusion that *nemesis* has a typical reference to justified indignation. But in each case an alternative interpretation is possible which would bring these examples into closer harmony with the mainstream. In the first two the notion of offense (breach of accepted standards) may reside in the ideation of the subject: it may be that Apollo and Hera construe what we might regard simply as a personal setback as an outrageous breach of conventional norms; perhaps, too, the element of boasting, referred to in the case of the Achaeans (4.506) and reported at length in that of Hector (8.190–7), legitimizes divine indignation at human presumption rather than annoyance. This is, in fact, very likely in the Book 8 passage, for Hector has, in the overconfidence of his self-assertion (εὐχόμενος, 198), expressed the hope that his success might even precipitate an Achaean departure that very night; for Hera, ever keen to remind Zeus that Troy must fall, this must amount not only to disregard for her own privileges and prerogatives, but also to extreme human presumption in the face of an established settlement. The third passage is also easily understood in a way which preserves the notion of *nemesis* as justified anger: Idomeneus is saying that criticism would be justified (because he and Meriones are behaving like infants), but excessive (because they are not really holding back from battle).[108]

Nemesis is not unique among anger-terms in having a reflexive aspect. (We saw how *chōesthai* could express an agent's anger that his own behavior had left his honor vulnerable.) The reflexivity of *nemesis*, however, focuses not merely on failure *per se*, but on one's failure to meet an obligation or to observe conventional standards. In a passage such as 16.544–7 it is, at first sight, an open question whether the *nemesis* that Glaucus urges on his allies (ἀλλά, φίλοι, πάρστητε, νεμεσσήθητε δὲ θυμῷ) is to be

---

[108] In 11.649, which gives us the unusual active/neutral adj. *nemesētos*, Patroclus does not necessarily endorse the *nemesis* for which he says Achilles has a propensity, but probably implies that Achilles himself typically regards his *nemesis* as justified; he is "quick to take offense," rather than merely irascible; in coupling the adj. with *aidoios*, moreover, Patroclus makes it clear that he does not wish to *offend* Achilles, the object of his respect, not merely that he wishes to avoid annoying him.

regarded as anger directed at the Myrmidons, who (themselves angered –
κεχολώμενοι – by the loss of their comrades, 546) are attempting to strip
and disfigure the body of Sarpedon, or at themselves, for allowing such
dishonor to occur, in neglect of their *aidōs* both *qua* self-respect and *qua*
respect for their dead champion. But other passages confirm that the latter
is the correct interpretation: at 17.254–5 Menelaus' exhortation urges his
hearers to consider the dishonor which would accrue to them from failure to
rescue Patroclus' body;[109] no target for reproach is envisaged other than his
Achaean audience; he is urging them to construe the situation as *nemessēton*
for themselves.[110] This reflexive use of *nemesis*-verbs arises quite naturally
out of the element of personal endorsement of social norms inherent in
those locutions in which a character rejects a certain course of conduct as
unacceptable for him/herself on the grounds that it is liable to *nemesis*,[111]
or in which an addressee is exhorted to consider the possibility of *nemesis*
as a way of suggesting a third-party evaluation of the situation which the
addressee may then endorse.[112]

Having this connection with justification, with the appeal to established
norms and customs, and with personal endorsement of society's standards,
nemesis is the Homeric anger-term which above all lends itself to universalization. The *Iliad* offers one example, in the funeral games of Book 23,
when Achilles, expressing his own disapproval (implicitly *nemesis*) at the
"unseemly" quarrel between Idomeneus and Ajax Oiliades, urges them to
apply the same standards to their own conduct as they would apply to the
conduct of others (23.492–4):

> μηκέτι νῦν χαλεποῖσιν ἀμείβεσθον ἐπέεσσιν
> Αῖαν Ἰδομενεῦ τε κακοῖς, ἐπεὶ οὐδὲ ἔοικε.
> καὶ δ' ἄλλῳ νεμεσᾶτον ὅτις τοιαῦτά γε ῥέζοι.

---

[109] ἀλλά τις αὐτὸς ἴτω, νεμεσιζέσθω δ' ἐνὶ θυμῷ | Πάτροκλον Τρῳῆσι κυσὶν μέλπηθρα γενέσθαι
("But let someone go himself, and let him feel *nemesis* in his *thumos* that Patroclus should become
a plaything for Trojan dogs").

[110] Further corroboration in *Od.* 4.158–9 (Telemachus' *nemesis*, an expression of his *saophrosunē*, clearly
focusing on his own behavior); 2.64–6 (to be understood as "reproach yourselves, and pay heed to
the reproaches of your neighbors"); see Cairns (1993) 84–5; (2001a) 208, n. 16.

[111] It is very clear, for example, from 3.410–12 that Helen is not simply refusing to meet Paris in
their *thalamos* on the grounds that this would attract others' criticism; she herself finds the notion
repugnant.

[112] Thus at 13.121–2 Poseidon/Calchas urges each of his Achaean addressees to place *aidōs* and *nemesis* in
his *thumos*: given that *aidōs* entails the thought of others' *nemesis* and the thought of others' *nemesis*
is being used to arouse the audience's *aidōs*, αἰδῶ καὶ νέμεσιν amounts to a hendiadys by which the
Achaeans are urged to see themselves as others see them and thus to recognize the inappropriateness
of their own conduct. That placing *nemesis* in one's *thumos* in this way amounts to the same thing
as putting *aidōs* there illustrates very well both the reflexivity of the pair and the reflexive potential
of *nemesis*.

Stop this exchange of harsh words, Ajax and Idomeneus; it is unseemly. The two of you would feel *nemesis* at any one else who acted like that.

The mechanism of universalization and its application as a rhetorical strategy is the same at 6.329–30, though no *nemesis*-verb is used:

σὺ δ᾽ ἂν μαχέσαιο καὶ ἄλλῳ
ὅν τινά που μεθιέντα ἴδοις στυγεροῦ πολέμοιο.

You too would fight with any else
you saw holding back from grim battle.

Paris, like the disputants in Book 23, is urged to recognize that his own behavior falls short of the standards he applies to others; μαχέσαιο probably implies the expression of *nemesis* in words of extreme disapproval (αἰσχροῖς ἐπέεσσιν, 325).[113] Similarly, in the *Odyssey*, the universalizability of *nemesis* is used in first-person locutions to reject the sort of behavior for oneself that one would criticize in others.[114]

Thus *nemesis* can be employed in the Homeric poems in ways which might appeal to the modern interpreter as exhibiting the structure of a properly "moral" argument; and it is certainly a point of some significance that *nemesis* can have this sort of application, for it demonstrates that Homeric Greek can express the important idea that an ethical (as opposed to a purely egotistical or exploitative) attitude to self–other interaction should be based on the recognition that the standards one sets for others must apply without partiality to oneself.[115] Yet while the form of some arguments which make use of the notion of *nemesis* may, in the minds of some, elevate Homeric ethical reasoning from the "prudential" to the "moral" level, the content and context of these arguments should also be considered: when Achilles invites Ajax and Idomeneus to take an impartial perspective on their own conduct he is intervening to stop a petty quarrel which arose because the former impugned the acuity of the latter's eyesight (23.473–81); and when (in the *Odyssey*) Menelaus uses a universalization argument to express his commitment to the standards by which his conduct is liable to be measured, his concern is to observe decorum in the entertainment

---

[113] For *machesthai* as equivalent to *nemesan* as response to a comrade's slacking, cf. 13.117–19.
[114] 6.286; 15.69–71; see Cairns (1990).
[115] It would be wrong to attempt to link Homeric forms of impartiality and universalization too specifically to the Kantian; impartiality, as Elster points out (1999a: 339), is not to be identified with any single conception of justice, but is "a necessary feature of any view that wants to be taken seriously as a conception of justice"; we should therefore see Homeric universalization and impartiality as rooted in an unKantian, socially embedded concept of reciprocity; see Cairns (2001a) 218–19; cf. Cairns (1999) 31.

of visitors (15.69–71). There need be nothing especially "moral" about the uses to which apparently "moral" arguments are put.

Homeric characters can appeal to universal standards, can express the difference between pique and legitimate complaint, and can recognize that generally accepted standards may be personally endorsed by individuals; but there is no absolute moral/non-moral distinction in the use of any of the terms considered above. *Nemesis* differs from the other terms in that it more regularly denotes the observer's rather than the victim's response; but the kinds of inappropriate behavior that *nemesis* identifies, even as a third-party response, cover a range of heterogeneous forms of behavior, such as brazenly returning home having made love in the open (14.336), failing to act as befits one's status (19.182; 24.462–4; cf. *Od.* 22.489), an inferior's abuse of his superior (2.223), failing to pull one's weight in battle (13.292–3), excessive and violent conduct which ignores commands to refrain from fighting (5.757, 872), and savage and inhuman denial of burial and mutilation of a corpse (24.53). As a response of the victim to another's disrespect *nemesis* is not to be sharply distinguished from *mēnis, cholos,* and *chōesthai,* all of which can share its reference to the perception of injustice (*mēnis,* in particular, normally responds to failure to satisfy a legitimate claim to honor/breach of an established distribution); thus it is important not to privilege *nemesis* as the only "moral" sentiment in Homer.[116] As a response to another's conduct by the direct recipient or patient of that conduct, too, *nemesis* and *cholos/chōesthai/skuzesthai* cover a range of eliciting conditions, from (on the one hand) conduct perceived as an affront by the patient, but unlikely so to be regarded by the impartial (e.g. the Thebans' *cholos* at Tydeus' athletic superiority, 4.391) or relatively minor forms of discourtesy/breaches of etiquette (*nemesis,* often) to (on the other) deliberately inflicted personal insult and forms of affront which disregard generally acknowledged entitlements and standards of appropriateness. Even to rank scenarios in this way is misleading, for each resembles the others in portraying an individual's emotional response to behavior on the part of another which he regards as an infringement of his own honor; there is no

---

[116] *Cholos* and *nemesis* co-occur at 6.335; 8.407 (cf. 397 *chōesthai*), 421; more importantly, a response described as *nemesis* at one point in a context may be reformulated as *cholos* at another, as when Poseidon at 15.217 threatens irremediable *cholos* if Zeus persists in the disrespect which has already aroused his *nemesis* (210); in addition, the same general type of behavior may attract *cholos* in one place and *nemesis* in another: e.g. slacking in battle (*cholos,* 4.241; *nemesis,* 13.122, 293). The behavior of Achilles which has the potential to arouse divine *nemesis,* according to Apollo at 24.53, is characterized as a potential cause of divine *mēnis* by Hector at 22.358 and elicits Zeus's *skuzesthai* and *kecholōsthai* at 24.113–15 = 134–6.

sharp distinction in these responses between saving face, status-rivalry, and defending one's legitimate entitlements.

Of the terms considered, *mēnis* responds only to violation of legitimate expectations, to offenses against established distributions of *timē*; the others can denote such a response, but may also respond to other forms of dishonor, for example that which results from simple failure in competition with others or from one's own public mistake; the reaction to perceived injustice (to the other's co-operative failure), moreover, is not sharply distinguished from the reaction to a personal challenge (to the other's competitive self-assertion); there is in general no hard and fast distinction between personal and moral offense.[117] Though anger as an emotion is central to Homeric ethical life,[118] the ethical is deeply embedded in the personal and the social, in so far as ethical attitudes are rooted in emotional involvement in concrete social practices and relationships. This being so, the "moral"/"non-moral" antithesis is not a useful tool in the discussion of Homeric ethics.

Homeric anger-terms clearly demonstrate the location of the emotion of anger in the ethics of reciprocity, whether they denote the response of the victim to a particular breach of reciprocity in a specific interaction or express the recognition that the reciprocity of honor and respect that pertains in one-to-one relationships extends generally throughout society and constitutes the basis of its ethical norms. We remember, however, that not all the above terms necessarily respond to another's failure to meet an expectation of co-operation or reciprocity; *chōesthai* and *nemesis* can focus on the self, *cholos* and *chōesthai* on the conduct of enemies; still, these cases resemble the others in that status, as a public, visible quality of the individual, is always at stake. So we must revise (or rather recognize the paradigmatic character of) Aristotle's definition of anger, but we can retain as fundamental the association he makes between anger and *timē*; Aristotle gives us the prototype, but there are numerous variants that retain enough resemblance to the prototype to qualify as forms of the same concept. The Homeric anger-terms we have considered are as one in their focus on the protection of the self-image that the individual projects and wishes to see validated in social interaction.

[117] Hence the futility of the debate, into which Frisk, Considine, Watkins, and Muellner all enter, on the "moral" or "non-moral" status of *mēnis*, a debate which depends almost entirely on the participants' different understandings of the word "moral."

[118] "Anger is to heroic what sex is to Victorian morality," Mueller (1984) 33.

Timē is fundamental to the Greek notions of selfhood and identity as social phenomena.[119] It rests both on the image of the self that the individual brings to bear and projects into social relationships and on the acknowledgment of that image by other interactants; it thus encompasses the complementary notions of "demeanor" and "deference" in Erving Goffman's description of the ritual of social interaction.[120] The focus of *timē* is thus what Goffman calls the "sacred self," the cherished image of the self which one fervently hopes will be endorsed by others; interaction ritual, in Goffman's account, largely consists of strategies of demeanor and deference designed to enhance and protect one's "sacred self" in the tricky business of interacting with others.[121] The above terminological study has shown how anger, however labeled, relates to the presentation of the "sacred self," and terminological investigation will always be required in order to ascertain how different terms belong in different scenarios or to different constructions of the same scenario; but in order to establish the precise nature of the relation between anger and honor in interaction ritual we need to go beyond the terminology of anger to the study of its characteristic signs and expressions.

In the *Iliad*, anger is expressed in a large number of different ways: in words (threats, insults, indignant complaints, etc.) and in deeds (including violence and murder);[122] all of these may be considered, on the one hand, as signals of the emotion, communicating the patient's apprehension of the

[119] Gill (1996) has performed an enormous service in alerting us to the social, "participant" character of Greek concepts of the self; but as M. W. Blundell points out (1998: 77), he could have said more about the role of *timē* in this connection.

[120] See Goffman (1967); the usefulness of Goffman's work for the interpretation of *timē* in Homer is well observed by van Wees (1992) 69–71; cf. also Macleod (1982a) 138–9, whose account of *timē* as both a "status-role" and its acknowledgment, though inspired by Beattie (1964) 35–6, is thoroughly compatible with Goffman. More generally, one might compare Elster's emphasis on esteem and self-esteem as central to the dynamics of emotion in social interaction: see especially (1999a) 417.

[121] Goffman regards interaction ritual as inevitably conditioned by the practices of a particular society, but also as exhibiting a core of universal characteristics (1967: 44–5); given that interaction ritual will typically be played out through the emotional scenarios of one's culture, I find it instructive to compare Goffman's approach with de Sousa's account of the acquisition of an emotional repertoire as a matter of activating one's adaptive phylogenetic capacities through cultural role-playing in "paradigm scenarios"; emotions are thus "the ultimate in 'method' acting," yet nonetheless rooted in phylogenetic adaptation; see de Sousa (1987) 44–5, 235–64, 332 (quotation). On the "dramaturgical" model of emotion, see Averill (1990) 114, 123–7.

[122] Achilles debates whether to kill Agamemnon, 1.188–91; Patroclus kills a playmate, 23.87–8; Artemis kills Laodameia (out of *cholos*), 6.205; 24.605–6 Apollo kills Niobe's sons, χωόμενος (and Artemis kills the daughters, 606); cf. e.g. Achilles' throwing the sceptre to the ground, 1.245; the havoc caused by Diomedes' *aristeia* leads the Trojans to conjecture that he is an angry god, 5.175–8, 191; at 14.257–8 an angry Zeus throws the gods about, ejecting Hephaestus from Olympus; threatening gestures, see 3.345; 4.167–8; even vigorous movement may express anger (Apollo, 1.43–7).

offense to the offender,[123] and, on the other, as expressions of the desire for retaliation which is one of the emotion's typical aspects. For the purposes of the present investigation of the relation between anger and honor, however, the most important expressions of anger are those which occur in the field of visual communication, for the association between honor and the visual is explicit and pronounced in the Greek context. *Aidōs*, for example, the emotion which both protects one's own and responds to others' *timē*, is very much a matter both of how one is seen by others and of how one responds to them visually; as a way of ensuring proper forms of eye contact and visual attention between oneself and others it is correlated with *anaideia*, typically expressed in forms of visual contact which manifest lack of respect for both self and other.[124] But though *aidōs* and *anaideia* are culture-specific concepts, the importance of visual communication in interaction is not a culturally specific phenomenon. Universally, recognition of others' status is correlated with visual attention: we reward those whom we respect with our visual attention; and we regulate mutual eye contact in accordance with the degree of intimacy which exists between ourselves and our interlocutors; from the earliest age, we use eye contact to initiate, maintain, and interrupt interactions;[125] in particular, from earliest infancy onwards, we develop the capacity to strike the fine balance that must be struck between too much visual attention and too little, between the unbroken stare and the shifty inability to look others in the eye.[126]

The role of ocular interaction in the Homeric expression of anger (as in the expression of anger universally) is twofold: the gaze may be used to express one's anger aggressively, in escalation of the breakdown in interaction, or it may be incorporated in less aggressive strategies which permit both escalation and resolution. In the first case, anger makes use of the communicative possibilities of that brightness of the eyes which is a concomitant of many forms of emotional arousal, but also universally characteristic of anger.[127] Agamemnon's reaction to Calchas' revelation of the cause of Apollo's anger is instructive (1.101–5): "Agamemnon, son of Atreus, wide-ruling, stood up among them, vexed; his black *phrenes* were filled with *menos* all around, and his eyes were like blazing fire; κακ' ὀσσόμενος, he

---

[123] The physiological symptoms mentioned above, though largely portrayed as subjective aspects of the experience, no doubt may often be regarded as entailing characteristic signals of emotional arousal.

[124] See Cairns (1993) Index, s.v. "*aidōs* and the eyes."

[125] See Eibl-Eibesfeldt (1989) 173–4, 195, 206, 241, 298–9, 305, 335–7, 373, 405, 488, 499, 540, 560, 567; cf. Bruce and Young (1998) 212–19, 247–54.

[126] Eibl-Eibesfeldt (1989) 170–84, 335–7.

[127] Other emotions: Darwin (1998) 205, cf. 177 (the dull eyes of grief); anger: Darwin (1998) 237.

addressed Calchas first of all."[128] *Menos*, here as elsewhere, refers to the
arousal and goal-directed determination of anger, and the blazing eyes convey to Calchas the threatening intentions which are referred to in κακ'
ὀσσόμενος.[129] The capacity of the eyes to convey aggression is confirmed
at 12.466, where Hector's eyes "blaze with fire" as he storms the Achaean
wall, and at 15.607, where his eyes shine under his brows as he rages in battle
like Ares or fire; the specific link to anger is apparent at 19.16–18, where the
terrible shining of Achilles' eyes signals the *cholos* that grows in him as he
contemplates the divine armor which is to replace that lost with Patroclus
and which thus rekindles Achilles' passion for revenge. In the context of an
interaction between two individuals, shining eyes convey an anger which
is invasive and threatening: the normal protocols of ocular interaction are
abandoned as the angered party uses his gaze to retaliate by violating the
offender's personal space.[130]

The aggressive gaze may be accentuated by a frown, a universal and
typical sign of anger.[131] The *Iliad* typically expresses this by means of the
expression ὑπόδρα ἰδών (regularly in the speech-introduction formula
τὸν/τὴν δ' ἄρ' ὑπόδρα ἰδὼν προσέφη . . . , and always in some form

---

[128] 1.103–4 = *Od.* 4.661–2 (of Antinous). The symptoms and expressions identified in these lines also
constitute, metonymously, aspects of the conceptual model of anger in Homer, just as the same
elements (the filling of the container, the comparison with fire, the aggressive visual behavior) do
in our own and other languages: see Lakoff and Kövecses (1987).

[129] This phrase refers here primarily to Agamemnon's threatening look; but because the eyes convey
intentions similar phrases come to express good or ill will (24.172, *Od.* 1.115), and the "looking" may
be figurative (as at *Od.* 10.374, where *thumos* is the subject; cf. 18.154). (For the metaphor, "the eyes
are containers for the emotions," see Lakoff and Johnson [1980] 50.) The eyes of the living (and
the immortal) are typically bright in the *Iliad* (13.3, 7, 435; 14.236; 16.645; 17.679), in contrast to
their darkening in death, but this does not mean that their brightness should not express specific
emotions in particular passages; see G. I. C. Robertson (1999) (though I remain convinced that
the bright eyes of 1.200 are those of Athena). There is a very brisk survey of the role of the eyes
in Homeric nonverbal communication in Malten (1961) 9–14; Lateiner (1995) is also suprisingly
unsystematic on this topic; but see 12, 89.

[130] See Eibl-Eibesfeldt (1989) 337. Eye contact is a significant issue in the aggressive interaction between
Achilles and Agamemnon in *Iliad* 1, especially from the perspective of Achilles, who frequently
locates Agamemnon's *anaideia* in the attitude of his eyes (149, 158–9, 225). That Agamemnon, in
attempting to resolve the conflict, should adopt the correct demeanor in visual communication
is also Achilles' demand in Book 9 (372–3). Agamemnon, in his turn, is all too conscious of the
importance of nonverbal behavior and visual communication when, in finally resolving the quarrel
in Book 19, he is careful to retain a demeanor of superiority in refusing to rise from his seat (19.76–7);
see Lateiner (1995) 54, 97.

[131] Darwin (1998) 226–8, 237, 242; cf. Eibl-Eibesfeldt (1989) 369 (with evidence from deaf-blind infants).
Since open-faced expressions, and especially that which Eibl-Eibesfeldt (1989) calls "eyebrow-flash"
(31, 117–18, 209–10, 228, 435, 457), indicate contact initiative, interest, and affection, the use of the
frown to indicate aggression may be explained on the basis of Darwin's "principle of antithesis" (see
Darwin [1998] 63–4). If it is true that the pupils contract in anger (Darwin [1998] 237), then this
phenomenon stands in direct antithesis to the well-known dilation of the pupils in contact-seeking
and attraction (Eibl-Eibesfeldt [1989] 253–4, 444).

of speech-introduction). ὑπόδρα ἰδών, that is, a fierce and piercing look from under gathered and lowered brows, expresses (metonymously) anger of several different hues: Holoka, in his study of the expression,[132] notes that the most common formula in which the locution occurs is metrically equivalent to τόν/τὴν δὲ μέγ᾽ ὀχθήσας προσέφη, but while both introduce emotionally aroused speech, the ὑπόδρα ἰδών formula seems more specifically linked to anger than is *ochthein*: it is used, for example, at 1.148 of Achilles' outrage at Agamemnon's suggestion that another of the Achaeans give up his prize to compensate him for the loss of Chryseis, and, while the formula is used to introduce a μέγ᾽ ὀχθήσας-type exclamation ("Atreides, what sort of speech has escaped the barrier of your teeth?") at 4.349–50, the narrator links the expression rather to *chōesthai* when he describes Agamemnon's smile in recognition of the anger that Odysseus has just expressed (356–7). As an anger-expression, ὑπόδρα ἰδών is used when *timē* is at stake: when an established distribution of *timē* is threatened to one's own cost (1.148), when an inferior gets above himself (2.245), when one's own *timē* is directly impugned (4.349), when a companion reacts with *nemesis* rather than *aidōs* to an affront (4.411), when a course of action is suggested that the speaker finds dishonorable (5.251; 12.230; 14.82; 18.284), when an irritating and recalcitrant individual frustrates one's plans (5.888; 15.13; cf. 24.559, where Achilles reacts angrily to Priam's initial refusal to accept his invitation to sit), when an ally fails to reciprocate (17.141), or when an ally unfairly charges one with failure to reciprocate (17.169). The element of threat in the expression is apparent at 20.428–9, the first of three occasions when Achilles "looks darkly" at Hector:

> He spoke, and ὑπόδρα ἰδών he addressed Hector:
> "Come closer, so that you may sooner reach your appointed destruction."

At 22.260 and 344, too, ὑπόδρα ἰδών prefaces speeches which express implacable hatred, desire for vengeance, and determination utterly to extinguish the prestige that Hector won in killing Patroclus. In these, as in other passages, the speech thus introduced gives off a strong flavor of contempt (cf. 14.82–103, where Odysseus' outrage at Agamemnon's suggestion that the Achaeans flee by night from Troy leads him to question the latter's fitness to command); this element is to the fore in 10.446, where ὑπόδρα ἰδών seems to convey Diomedes' contempt for Dolon as an individual and for his lack of self-respect.

---

[132] Holoka (1983).

ὑπόδρα ἰδών thus does indeed, as Holoka observes, focus on questions of status; but Holoka is wrong to suggest that it presupposes a hierarchical relationship between angry superior and offending inferior.[133] It would be better to say that the phrase requires the assumption of an aggressive, self-assertive role in interaction, and that the enforced intimacy, the invasion of the interlocutor's space that it entails, presupposes a claim to superiority only in the sense that it takes upon itself the right to rebuke, to criticize, or to protest.

But ὑπόδρα ἰδών is not the only Iliadic term for the facial expression of anger. *Skuzesthai*, cognate with *skuthros* and *skuthrōpos*, must originally have referred to the expression of anger in frowning or scowling; in the *Iliad*, however, it is also used metonymously for the experience of the emotion itself,[134] with the result that, while a few contexts make it clear that the verb's reference is to facial expression, in others we are unsure whether it means anything more than simply "be angry." It is unlikely, for example, that at 9.198 ("you two are the dearest of the Achaeans to me, σκυζομένῳ περ") Achilles is referring specifically to his facial expression.[135] But in two or three passages of the *Iliad*, the verb has particular point: at 4.22–4 = 8.459–61 the restraint of Athena is contrasted with Hera's inability to restrain her anger (*cholos*) at Zeus; while Hera gives full verbal expression to her feelings, Athena remains silent, the only sign of the savage (*agrios*) *cholos* that grips her being the fact that she *skuzesthai*.[136] Here the verb must have its proper sense; but the frown to which it refers is not quite that conveyed by ὑπόδρα ἰδών, for the latter always prefaces indignant speech, whereas Athena is silent; and where Hera pursues the course of aggressive retaliation, Athena appears to have opted to hold her anger in check. So the frown need not be entirely aggressive; it may express anger to which one is trying not to give full rein.[137]

The frown may also *betray* anger which one is actively endeavoring to conceal, as the poet makes clear in one of his acutest observations of the nuances of nonverbal behavior at 15.100–4. Hera has left Zeus on Mount Ida

---

[133] Holoka (1983) 16. He seeks to accommodate the fact that several instances of the phrase involve the anger of inferior at superior (1.148; 4.349; 17.141; 14.82) by arguing that in these the inferior inverts the pre-existing hierarchical relation for the sake of the immediate occasion.

[134] For the same metonymy in modern American English, see Lakoff and Kövecses (1987) 208.

[135] Cf. 9.372; 24.113, 134; also the only Odyssean occurrence, 23.209.

[136] Note the familiar metaphors, "anger is a wild beast" (see n. 59) and "anger is an opponent in a struggle."

[137] Zeus himself refers to Hera's response – an angry outburst of *cholos* – as *skuzesthai* at 8.483, when it was Athena who was σκυζομένη at 8.460; but Zeus is referring to Hera's anger once she has been banished to Tartarus, where presumably frowning will be the only expression left available.

and returned to the company of the gods on Olympus; Hera is disgruntled following her dressing-down from Zeus, and pays only the most basic lip-service to the etiquette of divine festivity, taking a cup from Themis, but delivering a denunciation of Zeus which causes consternation among the other Olympians (85–101); it is at this point that her demeanor is described (100–4):

> Ἡ μὲν ἄρ' ὣς εἰποῦσα καθέζετο πότνια Ἥρη,
> ὄχθησαν δ' ἀνὰ δῶμα Διὸς θεοί· ἡ δὲ γέλασσε
> χείλεσιν, οὐδὲ μέτωπον ἐπ' ὀφρύσι κυανέῃσιν
> ἰάνθη· πᾶσιν δὲ νεμεσσηθεῖσα μετηύδα·
> νήπιοι οἳ Ζηνὶ μενεαίνομεν ἀφρονέοντες [κτλ].

Having spoken thus Queen Hera sat down, and the gods were vexed throughout the house of Zeus. She laughed with her lips, but above her dark eyebrows her forehead did not relax, and in her indignation she spoke among them all: "We are fools who in our folly rage against Zeus . . ."

Nemesis (here presumably directed at Zeus, rather than at the other gods; πᾶσιν goes with μετηύδα) only rarely is manifested in any physical form,[138] but here its association with the frown indicates its status as a form of anger. Homer is clearly familiar with the phenomena of affect-masking, when one attempts to conceal one's feelings by assuming an opposite facial expression,[139] and of leakage, when the underlying affect shows itself despite the individual's attempt to mask it.[140] The acuteness of his observation is confirmed by Darwin (after Duchenne) and Ekman, who comment on the characteristic betrayal of the false smile in the attitude of the eyes.[141]

The frown, though still a sign which communicates displeasure, may thus be used in responses which inhibit or mask aggression as well as in its uninhibited communication. Thus these passages (4.22–4 = 8.459–61, 15.101–3) provide a bridge between my first main category, aggressive facial expressions, and the second, in which visual contact is broken off in a way that avoids unmediated counter-aggression.

One of the universal and instinctive responses which demonstrate the importance of visual communication in interaction is the use of visual "cut-off" to demonstrate that offense has been taken and thus to terminate

---

[138] It occurs in the *thumos* (2.223; 16.544; 17.254) or the *phrenes* (13.121–2), but otherwise is not linked with any of the physical symptoms or expressions which characterize some of the other anger-terms.

[139] This familiarity is, of course, prominent in the *Odyssey*'s representation of its hero's self-control: see (e.g.) 20.9–21, 301, where what are normally visible, external expressions of emotion are portrayed as undetectable inner experiences.

[140] See Ekman and Friesen (1969); Ekman (1992a); cf. Lateiner (1995) 83–8.

[141] Darwin (1998) 202–4, with Ekman's commentary.

the interaction. Infants throughout the world do this from the age of about two months; it is found also in non-human vertebrates.[142] This is a complex and interesting response: it demonstrates to the offender the victim's loss of face (lack of respect from the offender), and so entails adoption of the passive role of the victim; at the same time, it punishes the offender by withdrawing visual attention and abruptly ending the interaction (thus demonstrating lack of respect *for* the offender); it also, as we shall see, leaves the greatest number of options open[143] – it can have an appeasement function, and thus repair the interaction, but it also demonstrates displeasure and allows for an escalation of aggression in future retaliation;[144] at the same time, however, it carries considerable risks for the "face" of the angered party.[145]

That the averted gaze, the avoidance of eye contact is a typical sign of anger in Homer is apparent from 3.216–20, where Helen describes how from Odysseus' demeanor (looking down, eyes fixed on the ground, 217) one would conjecture that he was unintelligent, the bearer of an intense long-term resentment (220, φαίης κε ζάκοτόν τέ τιν' ἔμμεναι ἄφρονά τ' αὔτως). The response has some affinity with the downcast, dejected expression which expresses Hector's anger (*chōesthai*) at throwing his spear in vain at 22.291–3, at least in so far as the averted gaze conveys both anger and the agent's sense that his *timē* has become vulnerable. But the most characteristic application of visual cut-off as an expression of anger in the *Iliad* is in the theme of the hero's withdrawal.

This is a theme which permeates early Greek oral poetry;[146] such is the correlation between anger and withdrawal that Hector's immediate conclusion on noticing that Paris has withdrawn from the fray is that he must be in some way angry (6.325–31). But the classic case of withdrawal, and the most interesting from the point of view of its character as an interaction strategy, is that which expresses the anger of Achilles.[147] Achilles,

---

[142] See Eibl-Eibesfeldt (1989) 205–6, 373, 488, 499, 560; cf. Darwin (1998) 231; Goffman (1967) 23; Kendon (1977) 164–5; Morris (1977) 164–5; in animals, see Lorenz (1996) 183–4; Eibl-Eibesfeldt (1989) 170.

[143] Eibl-Eibesfeldt (1989) 499.

[144] Contrast the erect posture, forward inclination of head and body, and threatening expression of eyes and brows in the aggressive expression of anger (Darwin [1998] 234–49) with the element of appeasement in avoiding face-to-face, eye-to-eye confrontation and withdrawing from the interaction; the contrast is accentuated when the latter response involves veiling the head (below).

[145] See Goffman (1967) 23.

[146] See Richardson (1974) on *H. Dem.* 90–7; Sowa (1984) 95–120; Foley (1994) 91–3; Muellner (1996) 23–9, 116, 123, 136–7.

[147] Achilles' withdrawal: *Il.* 1.306–7, 327–30, 348–50, 488–92; 9.356–63, 428–9, 650–5, 682–92; 16.61–3. Muellner (1996) is especially good on the role of withdrawal in registering the breakdown of solidarity: see 23–4, 114, 136–8, 142–3, 146–8. Withdrawal thus instantiates the alienating

as noted above, first reacts aggressively (with aggressive facial expression: ὑπόδρα ἰδών, 1.148) to Agamemnon's assault on his *timē*; he even considers killing him (188–91), but is persuaded by Athena to withdraw and await compensation. Thereafter he remains apart from the other Greeks, spending most of his time secluded in his quarters.

His response thus (a) takes the place of a more violent alternative, and (b) registers with Agamemnon the latter's offense in breaching the reciprocal and co-operative relationship which should exist between the two, while at the same time leaving room for the restoration of that relationship (on Achilles' terms) in future. As a strategy to effect the restoration of one's injured honor, however, this is not without risk. Thersites, for example, is able to argue in Book 2 (239–42) that Achilles' response to Agamemnon's affront showed a reprehensible lack of anger (and thus by implication a reprehensible lack of self-respect).[148] Thus the strategy can be criticized for being insufficiently aggressive, for showing too little concern for one's "sacred self." It can also, since it depends for its success on the offender's desire to repair the relationship, be criticized for its uncertain efficacy, as it is by Phoenix in the Meleager-paradigm of Book 9. Phoenix's explicit point is that Meleager had in the end to abandon the strategy of withdrawal without attaining his objective (the visible demonstration of his status and value in the community and of the offending parties' need for his prowess), but he also presents the paradigm in such a way as to paint the strategy of withdrawal in an unattractive light. For Meleager does not merely withdraw, he withdraws to his bedroom and takes to his bed, where he lies beside his wife, shut away in the *thalamos* behind barred doors (9.556–65, 574–6, 581–3, 588). Thus does a first-division hero wilfully deprive himself of the opportunity to exercise his heroism; instead he remains in his *thalamos*, like a woman, spending his time in bed with his wife, like a Paris. Phoenix thus makes obliquely the point that Thersites made more openly – that the strategy of withdrawal, demonstrating as it does one's dishonor to the world and requiring that one assume the status of victim, has dangerous

---

effect of anger (n.b. the antithesis of anger and *philotēs* in 9.628–32; 14.207 = 306; 16.282); see Most (this volume, ch. 2) on the opposition between anger and pity (*eleos*) in the thematic structure of the poem, and note the association between *eleos* and *philotēs* established by Scott (1979) and Roisman (1984) 12–13; contrast Konstan (2001) 57–62, 73–4.

[148] The evaluation varies with the rhetorical purpose of the speaker; for Thersites, whose policy is to criticize rulers where he can, Achilles' nonviolent response is insufficiently angry (Austin [1999] 26); for Nestor, attempting to heal the breach, Achilles should not be angry with Agamemnon at all (1.277–81, 283–4); for Phoenix, expressing one's anger in refusal to fight is perfectly understandable, but open to criticism if anger persists after compensation has been offered (9.523). On notions of excess and deficiency of anger in Homeric society, see van Wees (1992) 126–38; more briefly, Harris (2002) 141–3, 149–50.

implications for the agent's status, especially (but not solely) if ultimately unsuccessful.[149]

As a strategy to demonstrate that offense has been received and taken, withdrawal has very close affinities with veiling, another cultural elaboration (in this case a ritualization) of the instinctive response of visual cut-off. No character veils in anger in Homer,[150] but Demeter combines veiling with withdrawal in expressing her anger in the Homeric Hymn,[151] and Achilles veils to express his anger at Agamemnon both in art[152] and in Aeschylus' *Myrmidons*.[153] Veiling is used in a variety of situations in which *timē* is vulnerable or in question;[154] used to express anger it signifies that the offender's conduct has impaired the victim's honor, while at the same time conveying the victim's lack of regard for the offender, but in assuming the passive role of the dishonored victim it may also perform a quasi-appeasement (self-abasement) function that increases the pressure on the offender to make reparation, if s/he wishes to save the interaction and/or the relationship.[155]

Finally, an interaction may also be terminated by verbal as well as visual cut-off; just as aggressive angry looks contrast with less aggressive tactics of gaze avoidance and withdrawal, so aggressive, insulting, and threatening verbal expressions of anger contrast with the complete refusal of verbal communication. Like gaze avoidance or veiling, too, silence may be both a way of restraining one's anger which avoids more aggressive forms of retaliation[156] and, when it involves protracted and obstinate refusal to speak, an effective form of retaliation in itself.[157]

---

[149] Phoenix's implication that withdrawal involves quasi-feminization is taken up in, for example, Sophocles' *Ajax*, where the hero spends much of the earlier part of the play in the seclusion of his tent (the place to which he consigns Tecmessa to conduct her lamentations at 578–82), lamenting his humiliation in an extravagant, emotional fashion that (Tecmessa tells us, 317–20) he had previously declared appropriate to the cowardly and the depressed; see Zeitlin (1990) 82; Wißmann (1997) 116–17. Ajax, of course, refers ironically to his own feminization at 651.

[150] *Pace* Slatkin (1986).

[151] Withdrawal: 90–4, 301–7, 318–39, 346–56; veiling 40–2, 180–3, 192–205 (n.b. downcast eyes, 194; silence, 194, 198; refusal of food and drink, 200).

[152] See *LIMC* i.2.103–6 Achilleus 440–2, 444–6, 448, 453, 464; iii.2.133 Briseis 1, 136 Briseis 14; cf. London E 69 (*ARV*[2] 185.39); cf. the veiling of Ajax at the judgment of the arms: *LIMC* i.2.243–4, Aias 1, 81, 84.

[153] *Myrmidons* fr. 132b Radt with Taplin (1972), esp. 62–76; for veiling as an expression of anger, cf. Hdt. 6.67, Eur. *Med.* 1144–55, and see Cairns (2001b).

[154] For full discussion, see Cairns (2002).

[155] Since, however, veiling is associated with humiliation and failure (see esp. Plut. *Vit. Dem.* 28–9, with discussion in Cairns [2002] 79–80), as a strategy designed to register anger at an affront it carries the same risks to the "face" of the individual as does withdrawal.

[156] See 4.22–3 = 8.459–61, where silence is accompanied by frowning; 8.444–5, 449.

[157] See *Od.* 11.563–7; cf. *H. Dem.* 194, 198, where Demeter's silence is reinforced by her averted gaze in 194, and her veiling in 197.

The scenarios of anger discussed above exhibit many universal features of the role of anger in interaction ritual, especially in areas of expression and nonverbal behavior, but also in the actual affective experience that is labeled by specific lexical items and conceptualized in terms of typical conceptual metaphors and metonymies. Homeric mechanisms of anger and their fundamental focus on the notion of *timē* demonstrate the affinity between that concept and Goffman's notion of the publicly projected "sacred self," the object of one's own demeanor and one's partner's deference in the ritual of social interaction; this in turn corroborates the emphasis placed by Aristotle and by modern theorists on the fundamental sociality of such emotions. In its eliciting conditions and typical behavior patterns, as well as in its symptoms, aura, imagery, and expression, Homeric anger regularly exhibits fundamental and universal features of this basic human emotion, though there are undoubtedly forms of expression in which a universal response has been culturally remodeled and developed (e.g. the development of the visual cut-off into the full-scale oral-poetic theme of withdrawal; cf. the ritualization of the same response in the practice of veiling). But though the concept of *timē* and the notions of reciprocity which it entails encompass universal characteristics of human sociality, *timē* is also particularized by specifically Greek notions, both in itself and in its relation to terms such as *aidōs* and *nemesis*, which, while intelligible, even in many respects familiar to us, are nonetheless in the totality of their conception specific to Greek language and culture. The Greek evidence helps to indicate how, in the social construction of human emotion, the specific encompasses the universal, how cultural practices and "mentalities" incorporate phylogenetic capacities: these are not discrete and separable components of nature and culture, but exist in a relation of mutual entailment, in which all natural capacity is actualized under environmental stimulus and expressed within a certain norm of reaction; the complex relation of familiarity and dissimilarity between "us" and "them" requires the closest attention to the specificity of Greek ethical and social notions, but this must be set in the context of a wider awareness of the commonality of human nature and the constraints on cultural elaboration that this imposes. Thus in order to fulfil its potential, the dialogue between ourselves as classicists and the societies we study must be supplemented by dialogue between classics and other disciplines – not only historical, philological, and literary, but also philosophical, sociological, and scientific.

CHAPTER 2

Anger and pity in Homer's Iliad

Glenn W. Most

"The rage (Μῆνιν) – sing it, goddess, that of Peleus' son Achilles: accursed (οὐλομένην) rage, which laid countless woes upon the Achaeans" (1.1–2): this is how the poet addresses his Muse at the opening of his *Iliad*. What precisely does he have in mind? On its own, the opening line could be taken simply to be asking in general for some poem about an anger – any anger – of Achilles. But the highly pejorative epithet οὐλομένην ("accursed"),[1] which begins the second line with a conspicuous and there-fore presumably significant enjambment, and above all the relative clause that goes on to fill out that line and specifies just which anger the poet means make every appearance of promising his listeners a poem not just in general about some anger of Achilles, but specifically about that celebrated anger of his, which was directed against Agamemnon and which cost so many Greek warriors their lives.

But it is well known that, if we measure the *Iliad* as we have it against this opening announcement of its theme, the Muse seems to have given her poet rather more than he asked for, and this in two regards.[2] First, Homer does indeed tell of Achilles' wrath – but he recounts not only, first, his wrath against Agamemnon, "which laid countless woes upon the Achaeans," but also, second, his wrath against Hector after Hector has slain Patroclus and after Achilles has formally abjured his wrath against Agamemnon; and this wrath of Achilles against Hector, so far from causing any sufferings whatsoever for the Greeks, was one which brought them considerably closer to their final victory and laid countless woes upon the Trojans. This doubling of Achilles' wrath is of a different order from the many extraneous episodes which the poet has inserted into his account of

---

[1] As pointed out in LSJ s.v. οὐλόμενος, in this word is always implied the wish, "may it be destroyed" (ὄλοιο), and a contrast with "beneficial" (ὀνήμενος); cf. *Il.* 5.876; 14.84; 19.92; *Od.* 4.92; 10.394; 11.410, 555; 15.344; 17.287, 474, 484; 18.273; 24.97.

[2] So already Grafton, Most, and Zetzel (1985) 119–21; and see, e.g., Geddes (1878) 38–9; and Bethe (1914) 311, n. 1.

Achilles' wrath against Agamemnon (episodes like the catalogue of ships, the Teichoskopia, or the Doloneia), for these expand that subject, providing it with a background and foil and thereby permitting us to understand all the more clearly the general context of Achilles' withdrawal; but Achilles' wrath against Hector might well be thought to be just one more of his angers and hence to provide only in the most superficial sense a relevant illustration of one aspect of his wrath against Agamemnon (demonstrating at most what Achilles could be like when he did not withdraw from battle), and this second wrath of his seems at any rate to have been excluded as a theme from the poem by the qualifications of μῆνιν ("rage") which fill its second line. And second, Homer tells not only of Achilles' extraordinary wrath against first Agamemnon and then Hector, but also of his no less extraordinary gentleness with regard to Priam, and thereby chooses to conclude an epic of bloody-minded warfare with a scene of compassion and mutual respect and understanding. The shift in subject can even be roughly measured statistically: 36 percent of all the occurrences of words for anger in the *Iliad* and only 9 percent of those for pity are found in its first five books; 10.5 percent of those for anger and 50 percent of those for pity are found in its last five books.[3] What does it mean that an epic that begins with the word for wrath culminates in an episode of pity?[4]

Both of these apparent anomalies have played a central role in modern Homeric philology. They were signaled, conspicuously and dramatically, as signs of incoherence and interpolation by Friedrich August Wolf in his *Prolegomena ad Homerum* of 1795, and were taken by him (together with many other pieces of evidence) as compelling proof of the lack of organic unity in the poem and hence for the impossibility of its having been composed by a single poet.[5] Throughout the nineteenth century, these apparent problems continued to provide favorite fissures for the crowbars of Analytic philologists, who used them both to pry apart the transmitted form

---

[3] Θυμός (in the meaning of anger), κότος, μῆνις, χόλος and related words for different kinds or degrees of anger are found approximately 114 times in the *Iliad*, of which 42 times are in Books 1–5 and 12 times in Books 20–4; ἔλεος, οἶκτος, and related words for different kinds or degrees of pity are found approximately 56 times in the *Iliad*, of which 5 times are in Books 1–5 and 28 times in Books 20–4. These statistics are imprecise, but surely indicative.

[4] For the importance of pity, and of Achilles' pity in particular, for the meaning of the *Iliad*, see above all Burkert (1955); also Casadio (1970–72); Scott (1979); Monsacré (1984); and now especially Kim (2000), to whom I refer the reader for the most coherent and nuanced treatment of this topic. I am grateful to Dr. Kim for her kindness in sending me the proofs of her important study in the summer of 2000 before its publication and in meeting with me in the spring of 2001 to discuss the fundamental convergences in our interpretations as well as the relatively minor differences in our emphases (above all, Dr. Kim tends to understand pity and pitilessness as alternatives, while I prefer to stress the interdependence of anger and pity).

[5] Grafton, Most, and Zetzel (1985) 132–4.

of the epic into what they took to be the earlier, more unified poems (one on Achilles' anger against Agamemnon, another on his anger against Hector) which had been patched together by a late and incompetent redactor, and to assign Book 24 as a whole, on grounds of linguistic anomaly and ethical incompatibility, to a different poet from the one who was largely responsible for putting the rest together.[6] To be sure, most of the premises and results of the older Analytic school, including these particular ones, were first roundly condemned – Lesky for one called the athetesis of *Iliad* 24 "the worst mutilation [. . .] that has been committed by Analysts upon this poetry"[7] – and have since then been largely forgotten by most contemporary Homerists. But it is too easy to simply dismiss or ignore the Analysts' complaints: in the present instance, as in many other cases, it turns out upon closer inspection of the texts in question that even though the Analysts' answers depended too much upon outmoded conceptions of oral poetry to be of much use to us today, nonetheless their questions were sensitive to real problems and issues in the epics as they are transmitted; and it emerges that, if these questions are reformulated by being detached from the issues of genesis and development that obsessed the Analysts and instead are redirected toward the ones of structure and meaning that obsess us, they can be turned to considerable interpretative advantage, at least for our own hermeneutical interests. In other words, some at least of the Analysts' questions are worth exhuming – those that have been not answered, but merely forgotten.

Perhaps it might be suggested that, to answer the Analysts' objections, it would suffice to point out that Achilles' two angers and his compassion in Book 24 are causally connected with one another within the chain of events of the plot of this epic and of the legendary history of the Trojan War. But in fact, such an explanation falls far short of dealing satisfactorily with this issue. To be sure, Achilles' first anger, against Agamemnon, leads causally to his second anger, against Hector: for it is only because Achilles' anger against Agamemnon has led him to withdraw from the battle that Hector and the Trojans can obtain such success on the battlefield that they can drive the Greeks back into their walled camp and threaten to set fire to their ships; and it is only in order to ward off the destruction of the Greek fleet and army that Achilles agrees to send Patroclus, disguised in his armor, against the Trojans; and had he not done so, Hector could not have killed Patroclus, at least not in this way and not at this stage

---

[6] A few celebrated examples: Lachmann (1847, 1865, 1874); Peppmüller (1876), especially xxxi–xl; Cauer (1895); Bethe (1914). See also the two works listed at n. 17 below; and in general Volkmann (1874).
[7] Lesky (1953) 131.

of events. And, to be sure, Achilles' compassion for Priam does indeed come after the conclusion of his anger at Hector, and his restitution to the old man of his son's corpse rescinds the violation of that body he had hitherto perpetrated, in an anger for which the mere death of Hector could not provide an adequate satisfaction. But such narrative connections are only a necessary, not a sufficient condition for the co-presence of all these elements in the same poem, and they cannot explain why the poet has chosen to conjoin them. For, as Aristotle demonstrated in chapters 7 and 8 of his *Poetics*, it is not enough for a plot to have unity for its elements to be connected causally with one another: they must be constituted in terms of a beginning, a middle, and an end, in the precise sense that he defines;[8] and he singles out Homer as having understood this point better than all other ancient epic poets.[9] Now, it is certainly conceivable that he was mistaken about Homer. But if he was not, then mere causal connection will not be enough to justify the structure of the *Iliad*, for (1) other, causally no less closely related events occurred before the beginning of Homer's story (most immediately the capture of Chryseis and Briseis, to name but two events) and after its end (most immediately, the resumption of battle after the burial of Hector and the death of Achilles, to name only these), but Homer has chosen to exclude these from his explicit direct narrative and thereby to focus attention upon those which he has included; and (2) in purely causal terms there is no reason why Homer might not have ended his epic at some earlier episode (for example, the death of Patroclus, the death of Hector, the funeral games for Patroclus), so that if he has chosen to go beyond such possible stopping-points it must be because in his eyes they did not provide an entirely satisfactory conclusion for his story. In both cases, the motivation for Homer's choice cannot have been purely causal but must have been some other consideration (e.g. formal or thematic): so too, within the plot structure of the *Iliad* as we have it, a strictly causal connection seems to be capable of explaining satisfactorily not the compositional necessity, but only the compositional possibility, of Homer's decision to link together within the compass of a single poetic design the two separate angers of Achilles with one another and with his compassion toward Priam.

Instead, it seems more plausible to presume that the poet of the *Iliad* has designed the narrative structure of his poem precisely in order to explore, and to invite his audience to explore with him, the various kinds of thematic relations that obtain between the stories that he has chosen to set thereby

[8] Arist. *Poet.* 7.1450b26–32.   [9] Arist. *Poet.* 8.1451a22–30.

into relation with one another. In other words, his point would seem to be to consider the similarities and differences between the two episodes of anger manifested by Achilles in the two stories combined into this poem; and to consider the relation between the sentiment of anger which marks those two stories and the sentiment of pity which marks the final episode of the poem. If so, the theme of the poem is not just anger, but the relation between anger and pity; and the poet has chosen precisely that particular causal concatenation of events which would permit him to explore this theme in all the dimensions he deemed appropriate.

The suggestion that it is not so much anger itself as the relation between pity and anger which is at the thematic core of the conception of Homer's *Iliad* will doubtless strike at least some of its readers as strange. After all, it is μῆνιν ("rage") which is its first word, and so manifold and memorable are the varieties of anger which the poem presents to us – think of Agamemnon's haughtily self-righteous fury, of Achilles' astonished indignation, sullen resentment, uncontrollable rage, and glacial wrath, of Thersites' obstreperous defiance, of Odysseus' irate disdain, of Helen's partly relieved contempt, of Apollo's bland vengefulness, of Zeus and Hera's marital squabble, of Aphrodite's admonitory scorn, of Ares' insane ferocity, to name but a few – that it is easy to think of the *Iliad* as being in essence the epic of anger.[10] Moreover, for a long tradition which began well before Catullus,[11] Virgil,[12] and Horace[13] and will continue no doubt long after Christa Wolf,[14] Achilles, the protagonist who most fully embodies the ethos of this poem, has been thought to be characterized supremely by implacable wrath.[15] Even looking beyond the character of Achilles himself, pity might at first glance seem in general to be rather out of place on the Homeric (or indeed on any other) battlefield. It is not accidental that most of the episodes in the *Iliad* in which pity is invoked during battle scenes are ones in which a suppliant casts away his weapons, throws himself upon an enemy soldier's mercy, and asks that his life be spared in pity – nor that in every single one of these scenes narrated within the present world of the *Iliad*, the appeal is

---

[10] On μῆνις ("rage"), especially with regard to Achilles, see Frisk (1946); Watkins (1977b); and now especially Muellner (1996). On anger in the *Iliad*, see, for example, Irmscher (1950); Adkins (1969); Shay (1994), especially chapters 3–5; and now Manakidou (1998) 242–4.

[11] Cat. 64.339ff.

[12] Virg. *Aen.* 1.483–4. Achilles is *saeuus* ("savage") at *Aen.* 1.458 and 2.29, *immitis* ("cruel") at 1.30 and 3.87.

[13] Hor. *Ars P.* 120–2.

[14] Wolf (1983) uses "das Vieh Achill" ("the beast Achilles") repeatedly as a vicious parody of Homeric formulaic epithets.

[15] Recent studies on the image of Achilles in Western literature after Homer include King (1987); Latacz (1995); and Heusch (1997).

refused and the suppliant is mercilessly slain.[16] The first of these episodes, in Book 6, seems paradigmatic, and may even have been supplied for this very reason: Adrestus has almost succeeded in persuading Menelaus to take him alive and accept a large ransom, but then Agamemnon rushes up, reproaches his brother for his kindness to the Trojans, and urges that not one Trojan should escape death, not even the male child in his mother's womb; Menelaus then thrusts Adrestus away, and Agamemnon kills him with his spear. Might some listener think that Agamemnon's attitude is inordinately cruel? Just to preclude any such potential tenderheartedness, Homer expresses explicit approval of Agamemnon's words, calling them αἴσιμα ("fated, fitting") (6.62).

Thus it might be thought that pity and anger strictly exclude one another, and that only the latter has a place on the battlefield. For such a view, the *Iliad* might seem to fall into two discrete and unconnected parts, one military and bloody-minded, set on the wind-swept plains of Troy, and the other merciful and conciliatory, staged within the tent of Achilles. Indeed, at the limit, the compassionate ending of the *Iliad* might even be supposed to have been pasted inorganically onto a sanguinary story with which it does not really fit – as though a later, more humane poet had inherited a primitive tale of brutal violence and, after first recounting it precisely as he had received it, without making any changes, had then gone on to add a civilizing epilogue more in taste with his own comparatively enlightened stage of cultural development.[17] But in fact this view is not supported by a closer inspection of all the battlefield scenes of the *Iliad*, for it turns out that pity does have a constructive contribution of its own to make within the conventional mechanism of heroic slaughter.

Consider a battle scene from Book 5. Aeneas kills two Danaan champions, the brothers Crethon and Orsilochus, whose deaths are highlighted by an extensive obituary, including detailed notices about their genealogy and their enlistment in the expedition, and by a heroic lion simile. Menelaus sees them fall and, moved by pity for them, strides forward to attack with his spear: "as they both fell, Menelaos, dear to Ares, pitied (ἐλέησεν) them, | and he went through the warriors fighting in front, helmeted in gleaming

---

[16] *Il.* 6.46–65; 10.372–457; 11.130–47; 20.463–72 (ἐλεήσας, 465); 21.36–119 (ἐλέησον, 74). See on these scenes Griffin (1980) 53–6; Pedrick (1982); Thornton (1984); Yamagata (1994) 40–5; and especially Crotty (1992). The sole exceptions are from earlier times (*Il.* 21.77, 100–2: no doubt by the tenth year tempers have become rather frayed) or from the different world of the *Odyssey* (*Od.* 14.278–84; 22.331ff., 361ff.).

[17] This bizarre view of the relationship between Book 24 and the rest of the *Iliad* has been held by a number of first-rate scholars, for example Wilamowitz-Moellendorff (1916) 70–9; Von der Mühll (1952) 369–91.

bronze, | shaking his spear" (*Il.* 5.561–3). So too, a few lines later, Hector kills two Greek warriors in a single chariot, Menesthes and Anchialus; this time it is Telamonian Ajax who feels pity for them and is thereby moved to throw a spear which kills Amphius: "as they both fell, great Telamonian Ajax pitied (ἐλέησε) them, | and coming very close he stopped, and hurled with his gleaming spear, | and struck Selagus' son Amphius" (*Il.* 5.610–12). Two victims, linked by the same father or chariot, designated by the dual, in two passages; is it by chance that the same formula recurs in another pair of passages, much later, in Book 17? Once again it is Aeneas who begins by mortally wounding Leocritus, a companion of Lycomedes; Lycomedes feels pity for him and is thereby impelled to kill Apisaon with his spear: "as he fell, Lycomedes, dear to Ares, pitied (ἐλέησεν) him, | and coming very close he stopped, and hurled with his gleaming spear, | and struck Hippasus' son Apisaon, shepherd of the people" (*Il.* 17.346–8). And only a few lines later, Asteropaeus, Apisaon's comrade from Paeonia, is said to have felt pity for the fallen Apisaon in turn and therefore to have rushed forward into the melee: "as he fell, warlike Asteropaeus pitied (ἐλέησεν) him, | and he too rushed forward, eager to fight with the Danaans" (*Il.* 17.352–3).[18]

This might well seem to us an odd way for these Greek warriors to express pity; or, to put this point better, it might well seem odd to us that Homer has chosen to focus upon pity as their central motivating reaction to the sight of their slain comrades. Might we not rather expect grief for the death of a friend, or shame at the offense to the honor of the group, or dread at what might happen to themselves, or an immediate and instinctive desire for vengeance, to be the more appropriate term for describing their reaction? After all, the warriors in question, so far from deliquescing into a pool of sentimental compassion, are moved by the emotion they feel to undertake immediate action in order to seek bloody revenge. Indeed, in other passages in the *Iliad* similar situations are said to provoke not pity but ἄχος ("grief"), χόλος ("anger"), or θυμός ("rage") and to lead to similar actions.[19] Obviously, pity is not synonymous with grief or anger; but just as obviously, if anger or grief can be said by Homer to be the reaction to the very same experience, and to lead as a result to exactly the same action, as ἔλεος ("pity") does, then we must take great care to try to understand the latter term as far as possible in Homeric terms, and as little as possible in our own.

---

[18] On these passages see Burkert (1955) 69–70; Casadio (1970–72).
[19] See, e.g., *Il.* 4.494, 501; 5.670; 13.206–7; and see Burkert (1955) 69 and nn. 1, 2.

Later Greek discussions of pity, though they derive from a highly technical philosophical and rhetorical tradition which is remote in many regards
from the world of Homer, may nonetheless, if handled with caution, provide a useful starting-point for understanding Homeric pity and its relation
to anger.[20] Aristotle defines ἔλεος ("pity") in his *Rhetoric* as "some kind of
pain as response to an apparent[21] fatal or painful evil which happens to
someone who does not deserve it, which one might expect oneself or one
of one's friends to suffer, and this when it appears to be near."[22] Aristotle's
definition picks out certain features that recur in later philosophical for-
mulations, such as Chrysippus' "pain as response to evils that happen to
someone else when that person suffers them undeservedly":[23] mental pain
or suffering on the part of the pitier, as a response to physical and/or mental
suffering on the part of the pitied person; the pitier's judgment that the
pitied person's suffering is undeserved (for otherwise it would be welcomed
as a merited punishment).

These features are certainly applicable to many passages in the Homeric
epics in which humans and gods pity, or do not pity, one another. But
in at least two important regards, these later definitions raise interesting
problems.

First, Aristotle emphasizes that we only pity people who are like us, and
that we pity them because they have experienced an evil which we too
might experience;[24] yet in Homer the gods are certainly capable of feeling,
and expressing, pity for human mortality, even though they themselves are
immortal.[25] To be sure, we may interpret this feature in part as further evidence that the Homeric gods function as an idealization of Homer's human
audience (and hence ultimately share his human characters' mortality),[26]
or see in the gods' sympathy merely their recognition of the fact that, like
humans, albeit somewhat less so, they too are under the sway of forces,
like fate, which are stronger than they are. Nonetheless, Homeric pity does

---

[20] See Herwegen (1912).

[21] There has been much discussion concerning the precise meaning of the participle φαινομένῳ
("apparent") here. Cope (1877: 10, 93–4), takes it to refer to the objective seriousness of the evil
involved, and this view has been adopted by many others; see in general Fortenbaugh (1975). I take
it, on the contrary, to mean that the person who feels this emotion does so because the situation in
which he finds himself seems *to him* to be of a certain kind, whether or not it really is and whether
or not someone standing outside that situation would judge it to really be so; so too, for example,
Cooper (1996) 255–6, n. 23.

[22] Arist. *Rh.* 2.8.1385b13–16.

[23] This is the formulation in *SVF* 3.100.43; for other versions, cf. *SVF* 3.99.38, 100.7–8, 43, 101.10, 21–2,
106.2–3, 109.43–4, 110.8–9.

[24] See Arist. *Rh.* 2.8.1385b16–19.

[25] E.g. *Il.* 8.33–4, 201–2, 464–5; 16.431; 24.23. See Burkert (1955) 147. [26] See Griffin (1978).

seem in this regard to be rather more generous and less self-regarding than its Aristotelian counterpart.

And second, Aristotle and Chrysippus agree that we only feel pity for other people's misfortunes, not for our own. This may seem to be a surprising restriction. If we define pity, for the purposes of the present argument, as "distress at someone's real or threatened undeserved suffering," then there is no evident reason why the pitier and the pitied might not be the same person. After all, if one can feel distress at the sight of someone else's real or threatened undeserved suffering, why should one not also be able to feel it at the sight of one's own?[27] And indeed, even though one particular tradition in modern British moral philosophy has defined pity in such a way (as distress at someone else's suffering) as explicitly or implicitly to deny the very possibility of self-pity,[28] there seem in general to be few passions which in our daily lives we have such ample opportunity to observe expressed so richly, so deeply, and so sincerely, both around us, and within us, as self-pity. No doubt this is due to the consolatory effect of the splitting of the unhappy self into two parts, one which has no choice but to suffer, presumably unjustly, but another which, by pitying the former, can provide at least the appearance of compassionate companionship for it and relative freedom from such suffering in its own right; and if so, then self-pity seems likely to provide forms of psychological compensation, in this vastly

---

[27] Similarly, a large number of other forms of behavior can be directed indifferently either toward oneself or toward others. Helen can direct against herself (e.g. *Il.* 3.173ff., 410–11) the same reproaches that others (would) direct at her (e.g. 3.411–12; 24.767–72). When Agamemnon sees that Menelaus has been wounded, Agamemnon shudders – and so does Menelaus (4.148–50). In Aristotle at least, such an easily understandable eventuality is suppressed because he seems to have attempted to constitute his catalogue of πάθη ("sufferings") precisely on the basis of the opposition between the subject of the emotion and the person at whom it is directed: on the one hand, pity is directed at someone else's real or threatened undeserved suffering; on the other hand, if the real or threatened undeserved suffering is one's own, then, according to Aristotle, one ought to feel not pity but either (1) anger, if the suffering is real (Arist. *Rh.* 2.2.1378a30–2: it is because Aristotle is speaking of the courtroom rather than the battlefield that he focuses here upon ὀλιγωρία ("offense"); for anger at physical injury, which of course was far rarer in the city, cf. *Rh.* 2.2.1379a32–3) or (2) fear, if the suffering is threatened (*Rh.* 2.5.1382a21–2: nowhere in this chapter does Aristotle ever even hint that one could possibly fear for anyone other than for oneself, see especially also *Rh.* 2.8.1386a27–9). Yet the systematicity of Aristotle's analysis fails manifestly in the case of anger, which, according to him, one can feel for an unjustified slight suffered not only by oneself, but also by one of one's friends. If one can feel anger both for oneself and for others, why cannot one feel pity or fear both for oneself and for others? It may be that Aristotle's peculiar emphasis upon the fact that the person we pity must be very much like us but not too much like us (*Rh.* 2.2.1378a34) is a further sign of the strain under which his categorization is laboring.

[28] E.g. Hobbes (1966) IV.44–5: ch. 9, § 10; Butler (1850) II.53–4: "Sermon 5. Upon Compassion"; Hume (1978) 368–71, 381–9: Book 2, sections 7 ("Of Compassion") and 9 ("Of the Mixture of Benevolence and Anger with Compassion and Malice"). Some modern scholars adopt the same artificially restrictive terminology, for example Wierzbicka (1999) 101.

imperfect world of ours, which can yield satisfactions intense enough to make it an extremely widespread if not universal phenomenon within the history and geography of human experience.

Yet it is a remarkable aspect of ancient Greek ethical thought that, for the most part, pity seems in fact to have been understood in such a way that it was restricted to the relation between self and other, and hence could not readily be applied to the relation between the self and itself.[29] There is no word for self-pity in Greek; what is more, while self-pity becomes a familiar motif of such later Greek genres as historiography and romance,[30] there is only a surprisingly small number of scenes of self-pity in the ancient Greek literature of the archaic and classical periods.

Three such scenes might help us to understand better why this emotion seems to have played such a marginal role for the earliest Greeks.

(a) The first one occurs when the dead Patroclus is mourned in the *Iliad*. Here the female slaves are said to respond to Briseis' lament in the following terms: "So she spoke weeping, and in response the women groaned | on account (πρόφασιν) of Patroclus, and (or "but": δέ) each one for her own woes" (*Il.* 19.301–2). Whether we are to take this to mean that the women did not really mourn Patroclus himself but only used him as a pretext in order to express sorrow for themselves or whether, as is no doubt far more likely, it means that they mourned both for Patroclus and for their own sufferings,[31] this is certainly an instance in which the public expression of self-pity is being depicted.

(b) Another, more complex passage, describes Odysseus' reaction to Demodocus' song about the Trojan horse: he weeps like a woman weeping for her dead husband, fallen in defense of their city (*Od.* 8.521–31). This extraordinary simile is rich in psychological, literary, and meta-literary complexities, which exert a fascination in their own terms and at the same time have the immediate narrative function of helping to prepare for the imminent climax of Odysseus' self-revelation.[32] But leaving aside in the present context these more subtle dimensions, one might instead simply ask for whom it is exactly that Odysseus is weeping here. The comparison made

---

[29] See especially Konstan (1999). My thinking about these issues has benefited greatly from lively discussion with David Konstan and from this and other studies of his, but I continue to disagree with him about the nature of self-pity and its incidence in Greek culture.

[30] For post-classical historiography, see, for example, Polybius 9.10.9. On scenes of self-pity in the romance, see Most (1989); and note the conventional reinterpretation in the Greek romances (Chariton 8.5.2; Ach. Tat. 2.34.7; Heliod. 1.18.1) of the Homeric phrase Πάτροκλον πρόφασιν ("on account of Patroclus": see the following note) as designating pure self-pity under the guise of lament for another person's troubles.

[31] See M. W. Edwards (1991) 271 ad 19.301–2.   [32] See Rohdich (1987).

between his tears and those of a woman mourning her fallen husband might for a moment make us think Odysseus is lamenting the dead Trojans, such as Hector, whose lamentation on the part of Andromache helps to close the *Iliad* (24.723–45). But this is surely impossible: after all, Demodocus has just now concluded this very song by recounting, as the climactic moment of Odysseus' divinely assisted victory over the Trojans, the story of how he and Menelaus went to the home of Deiphobus in order to slay him (8.517–20); for Odysseus' sympathy to be directed in the first instance toward the Trojans would imply a self-reproach on his part and a repudiation of Demodocus' apparent intent which would be out of character for the invariably courteous, generally self-confident, morally untroubled Odysseus. Instead, we should notice that, whenever he complains about sufferings in the preceding and following lines, it is always those of the Greeks, and especially his own, that he has in mind (8.490; 9.14–15). Hence it is far more likely to be the case here as well that Odysseus is weeping for the Greeks, and most especially for himself, both for the glory he once had but has since lost, and for the sufferings that once accompanied his triumphs without vitiating them but that now threaten to obscure them altogether.[33]

(c) Finally, a third passage occurs in Euripides' *Hippolytus*. This is Hippolytus' frustrated outburst when he finds that there is no way in which he can convince his father of his innocence: "Oh woe! If only it were possible for me to look upon myself, standing opposite | to myself, to see myself weep for the evils we are suffering!" (Eur. *Hipp.* 1078–9).

All three of these passages are certainly quite remarkable, but it should not be forgotten that they are in fact rare exceptions within the larger context of the general neglect of self-pity in the earlier period of ancient Greek culture. Indeed, they may even help to explain why it is that self-pity seemed less interesting to the Greeks than it does to us. For the two Homeric passages suggest that the public expression of self-pity may have been thought to be more acceptable for women than for men, and if so was likely to be marginalized in a literary and philosophical tradition that was far more concerned with the proper form of behavior to be displayed by men than with that appropriate to women; while the Euripidean passage suggests that the earlier Greeks tended to think of the pitier as standing apart from, and above, the person he pities, so that the very notion of someone pitying himself may have been hard for them to conceive of in any straightforward or simple manner.

[33] See Lloyd (1987) 88.

If we consider pity, then, as at least the Homeric Greeks seem to have, as a special case of distress at someone's real or threatened undeserved suffering – namely the case when, among other relevant circumstances, the observer and the sufferer are two different people – then we can understand in terms of the perpetrator and sufferer of that suffering the link between this distress and anger, which we noted earlier in certain battle scenes in the *Iliad*. For when we feel distress at someone else's real or threatened undeserved suffering, we can focus either upon the dimension of the person who experiences that suffering or upon that of the person who causes it: in the former case we feel Homeric pity; in the latter case, Homeric anger. Four possible cases can be imagined. (1) If the suffering is about to be inflicted by ourselves but has not yet happened, our pity can lead us to refrain from inflicting it; this is what happens when a suppliant's request for pity is granted (so, e.g., *Il.* 21.77; 24.156–8). (2) If the suffering is about to be inflicted by someone else but has not yet happened, our pity can lead us to take steps to prevent that other person from inflicting it; for example, the gods, or such mortal warriors as Achilles or Hector, can ward off suffering from other persons upon whom they take pity, by fighting in their defense, by killing those who would kill them, or by protecting them in other ways (so, e.g., *Il.* 5.677–82; 13.15–16). (3) If, on the other hand, the suffering has already been inflicted by ourselves, our sense of pity at the sufferer and anger at the perpetrator (in this case, ourselves) can combine to become a potent sense of guilt and self-torment (so, e.g., *Il.* 18.34, 98–9). (4) If, finally, the suffering has already been inflicted by someone else, then our pity at the sufferer can become mourning (in the special case that the sufferer has died) and our anger at the perpetrator can become a desire for revenge, the wish that he, who caused someone to suffer to whom we were close, might suffer himself as well (so, for example, in the four battle scenes discussed above).

I apologize for this admittedly somewhat mechanical classification, which, I trust, will provoke neither pity nor anger. It will have achieved its purpose if it succeeds in illustrating the fact that, at least in the Homeric world, pity and anger, so far from being mutually exclusive opposites, are intimately interconnected: pity for someone's undeserved suffering is certainly not the only reason why people become angry in Homer's world,[34] but it can easily become a potent component in a highly unstable psychological mixture that is capable of issuing forth explosively in wrathful

---

[34] In his exhortations to battle to various soldiers in Book 4, Agamemnon provides a whole set of different motivations for military anger: *Il.* 4.223–64, 338–48.

action. Indeed, we may go so far as to suggest that a Homeric character cannot ever feel pity, at least for suffering provoked by humans, without at the same time actually or potentially feeling some degree of anger at the agent or agents who caused this suffering; and that it is precisely the intense painfulness of the pity which such a character feels, combined with the distressing mixture of this pity with feelings of anger and resentment, that can motivate him to relieve himself cathartically by giving outlet to his violent rage in murderous action.

This is a concept of pity which is not entirely familiar to us. For a Christian view, which awards a high privilege to the qualities of meekness and humility, anger is a sin of arrogance and self-affirmation which leads to actions that injure other people, while pity is a virtue which passes on to our fellow-humans God's own love for us and expresses a sense of the solidarity of all creatures by refraining from any kind of hurtful action against them: "blessed are the pitiers (οἱ ἐλεήμονες), for they themselves will be pitied (ἐλεηθήσονται)" (Matt. 5:7); "become pitiers (οἰκτίρμονες) just as your father is a pitier (οἰκτίρμων) of you" (Luke 6:36). In Homer, on the other hand, ἔλεος ("pity") and χόλος ("anger") are two sides of the very same coin, two thoroughly interdependent ways of viewing precisely the same situation, two modes of subjective response to a highly specific kind of objective experience which in neither case remains locked into the privacy of an unexpressed sentiment but instead issues forth in all the external manifestations of socially recognized forms of behavior: sighs, tears, groans, laments, rolling in the dust and manure, tearing one's hair, gnashing one's teeth, gashing one's cheeks – and also, committing murder.

Viewed in the light of this classification, it becomes possible to understand the peculiar structure of the plot of the *Iliad* – first Achilles' anger at Agamemnon, then his anger at Hector, then his pity for Priam – as the narrative formulation of a profound meditation upon the interrelation between various kinds of compassion and various kinds of anger. From this perspective, the story of the *Iliad* as a whole can be seen as the succession of three stages: first, Achilles reacts to what he sees as his own sufferings at the hands of Agamemnon, and as the Greeks' failure to prevent them, by abandoning his previous concern for the well-being of the Greek army as a whole and instead focusing his attention primarily upon his own mistreatment, feeling above all compassion for himself and anger at Agamemnon and most of the other Greeks (Books 1–19); second, Achilles reacts to what he sees as Patroclus' sufferings at the hands of Hector and the Trojans by definitively abandoning his anger against Agamemnon and the Greeks, and instead feeling pity for Patroclus and anger at Hector and all the other

Trojans (Books 19–23); and third, Achilles reacts to what he sees as Priam's sufferings at his own hands by temporarily abandoning his anger against Hector and the other Trojans and instead feeling pity for Hector's father (Book 24).[35] Between the first and second stages the dividing line is deliberately blurred by a gradual transition whose subtlety indicates the poet's extraordinary psychological sensitivity – Achilles begins to feel concern for the Greeks as early as Book 9, and especially in Book 11, and he feels pity for Patroclus at first in Book 16 while he is still alive, but he does not formally abjure his anger against Agamemnon until Book 19 – but the underlying clarity and coherence of the structure can hardly fail to be recognized. From almost the very beginning to almost the very end, distress, compassion, pity, and anger intertwine almost inextricably as Achilles' fundamental emotions and motivations for action; their specific objects change, as do their modes of actualization in externally perceptible behavior, but the unbroken continuity of this mixture of passions provides the coherence and unity both of Achilles' character and of the plot of the *Iliad* insofar as this is his story.

Working out this interpretation in detail would require the kind of close analysis of the entire poem which could not possibly be undertaken within the limits of the present paper; nonetheless, a brief survey of some of the salient moments of the epic, as seen in this light, may help to flesh out the dry and schematic skeleton of these claims and thereby render them somewhat more plausible.

At the very opening of the *Iliad*, before the eruption of the quarrel between Agamemnon and Achilles, Achilles is characterized unambiguously by his concern for the welfare of all his fellow-Greeks: it is after all into his heart that Hera, distressed by their suffering, puts the idea of summoning an assembly (1.55–6), and at that assembly it is he who begins with an earnest attempt to rescue them from the plague. But once that quarrel breaks out, it follows a pattern already exactly prefigured in the preliminary episode involving Chryses. There (a) Agamemnon committed an offence, what Aristotle would have termed an ὀλιγωρία, against the priest of Apollo by contemptuously refusing to restore Chryseis to him; and (b) Chryses became angry at the perpetrators, Agamemnon and the Greeks, because of the undeserved suffering he experienced at their hands. But (c) obvious circumstances made it impossible for him to move directly to express this anger by violent action against those who had made him suffer, so (d) he

---

[35] This structure does not contradict, but instead complements, counterpoints, and enriches other narrative patterns that have been observed in the *Iliad*, for example the three-part movement in performance (*Il.* 1–8, 9–15, 16–24) for which B. Heiden has recently argued: (1996) with further bibliography p. 8, n. 10; (2000).

withdrew from human society and went above Agamemnon's head to the
god Apollo, to whom he was specially linked as his priest: (e) he invoked
Apollo to witness what he had suffered and implored him to become angry with and to punish the Greeks for his sake (1.34–42). At the Greeks'
assembly, precisely the same sequence of steps now takes place a second
time: (a) Agamemnon commits an offense against Achilles by contemptuously depriving him of Briseis; (b) because of the undeserved suffering he
has experienced, Achilles is angry at the perpetrators, Agamemnon and the
Greeks; but (c), though as a heroic warrior he is strongly tempted to kill
Agamemnon on the spot, he is dissuaded by Athena's intervention from
moving directly to express this anger in violent action against the man who
has made him suffer. Hence (d) he withdraws from human society and goes
above Agamemnon's head to the goddess Thetis, to whom he is specially
linked as her son, and through her to the supreme god, Zeus (1.348ff.); (e)
he asks Thetis and, by her mediation, Zeus to witness what he has suffered
and to become angry with and to punish the Greeks – the very people he
had done his best to save at the beginning – for his sake (1.365ff.). Thetis'
response, as throughout the *Iliad*, is to pity her son and to mourn him while
still alive (1.414–18) – and simultaneously to promise that she will ask Zeus
to make the Greeks suffer, as he had requested of her (1.419–20, 426–7).

Thus, almost from the very beginning, the very same emotions, anger at
others and a compassionate focus upon one's own suffering, are intertwined
as motivations both for Achilles and for other characters, though of course
in a different mixture and with varying intensity in each case. The doubling
of the narratives of Chryses' and of Achilles' reactions to their mistreatment
serves to illustrate the differences in their characters and status, to confirm
by repetition the injustice of Agamemnon's behavior (which is of course
not to suggest that Achilles is entirely faultless), and to indicate the path
that anger at others and compassion for oneself can take when their most
immediate and natural outlet, violent action, is blocked by circumstances.

Achilles' situation from Book 1 to Book 9 is one of psychological stand-
still corresponding to his physical withdrawal. Whenever he is referred to
throughout these books, he is described as still being unrelentingly angry with Agamemnon.[36] When his comrades accuse him of being νηλεής
("pitiless"), as they do twice in Book 9,[37] they are claiming thereby that he
is showing himself to be devoid of the fundamental human sentiment of
pity, altogether and for anyone to whom it could reasonably be expected

---

[36] *Il.* 2.689, 769, 771–3.
[37] *Il.* 9.497 (Phoenix), 631 (Aias). νηλεής ("pitiless"), a term usually applied by Homer to bronze and
the day of death, is used by him in reference to only two living beings: Achilles and the Cyclops.

to apply; but, given the early Greek insensibility to self-pity, they are not reproaching him with having pity for no one but himself nor asserting that he does not even pity himself. The scene between Hector and Andromache in Book 6, whatever its other functions, is also clearly designed to suggest by contrast the possibilities for rich and humane personal interchange which, at this moment, are denied to Achilles by his obsessive self-absorption but are still available to his Trojan counterpart. For Andromache begins by accusing Hector of feeling no pity (ἐλεαίρεις) for her son or herself (6.407) and urges him out of pity (ἐλέαιρε) for them to remain on the wall with her (431); Hector rejects her urgent request for pity by appeal to a countervailing claim upon him, his respect (αἰδώς) for the judgment of the Trojans (442), but he makes no secret of the pain he feels for what he fears will be her future suffering (ἄλγος) (450). It is only when the very epitome of what is pitiable, his baby son, is frightened by his helmet (the very same helmet which Hector wears, ultimately, precisely in order to protect Astyanax from the destiny which no human effort will be able to ward off) that Hector can finally find an expression for the profound pity (ἐλέησε) for his wife which earlier she had requested and he had been unable to grant (484): yet nonetheless he allows what he claims to perceive as his duty to oblige him to break off the conversation they have begun and to return to the battle he has temporarily abandoned. Part of the pathos of this extraordinary scene derives from our tragic foreknowledge not only that Hector is doomed to be slain very soon by Achilles, so that all his forebodings for Andromache are true and all his hopes for Astyanax are in vain (Achilles' son will enslave Hector's widow and kill Hector's orphan son) – but also that, at the moment when Hector speaks these words, Achilles himself is so restrictively focused upon his own suffering that he could not possibly feel the human impulse of pity that Hector, too human to be a perfect soldier, has tried in vain to suppress but has then so movingly displayed.

The embassy in Book 9 offers Achilles a parallel opportunity to display pity toward those to whom he is closest, but the opportunity is one that he – almost – completely refuses. Agamemnon's offer of gifts and the restitution of Briseis seems to count as a complete fulfillment of the ordinarily expectable obligations of the heroic code (this is certainly how Nestor, one of that code's supreme embodiments, judges it, *Il.* 9.163–4): if Achilles were moved only by questions of self-interest and his public standing, they would be enough to resolve the issue once and for all. But of course he is not: Achilles can be won over neither by Odysseus' shrewdly tactful catalogue of Agamemnon's offer and his appeal to Achilles to pity (ἐλέαιρε) at least the other Greeks (302, cf. 247–8); nor by Phoenix's more emotional and personal speech, with his plea to Achilles not to have a pitiless heart (νηλεὲς ἦτορ, 497) and his illustration of the importance of allowing oneself to be placated with the allegory of the Λιταί and the story of Meleager; nor by Ajax's gruff and soldierly reproach that Achilles has made his heart bestial and inhuman (629), that he cares nothing for the love of his comrades (630–1), and that he has become pitiless (νηλής, 632). For, as Achilles' own speeches to the various ambassadors demonstrate, his obsessively restrictive focus upon the wrongs he feels he has suffered has not changed or developed in the least during the time intervening since his laments about the way he was mistreated back in Book 1. The failure of the embassy demonstrates that Achilles is so locked into his blind self-absorption and anger that even the most powerful considerations of rational self-interest, of social prestige, and of the professed love of his friends are not capable of swaying him. But in that case, what factor possibly could? A hint of an answer that points in the direction of future developments is provided by the fact that, in the course of this book, Achilles' responses, though they remain refusals, become nonetheless progressively less categorical: although he tells Odysseus that he will leave Troy and sail home at dawn the next day (356–63, 427–9), he asks Phoenix to spend the night with him so that they can decide together at dawn the next day whether or not they should both return home (618–19), and he says to Ajax that he will actually return to battle, but only if and when Hector starts to burn the Greek ships (650–3). Evidently, the presence of those three of his comrades who are the dearest to him among all the Greeks (198) has begun to permit him to recognize that his anger is in fact directed only against Agamemnon, and that for his fellow-Greeks, on the contrary, he is not incapable of feeling some degree of solidarity. But as yet his anger and self-absorption do not permit him even to voice this recognition, let alone to act upon it.

Yet as Hector bears the war into the Greek camp in the course of Book 11, a subtle, and as yet unacknowledged, shift in attitude on Achilles' part begins to make itself manifest. No longer withdrawn within his tent in the splendidly self-consoling isolation of music and heroic legend, Achilles is now standing by the stern of his ship, observing the carnage as a suddenly interested spectator (11.598–601); and when Nestor drives back from the battlefield, bearing in his chariot a wounded man whom Achilles thinks he recognizes as Machaon, Achilles requests Patroclus to go and find out who the injured warrior is (611–15). To be sure, the justification that Achilles gives for his request is not pity for his endangered comrades but rather the self-satisfied expectation that now the Greeks are evidently in such danger that they will soon be supplicating him (609–10); but such a consideration does not really suffice to motivate his curiosity and seems instead an attempt to conceal behind a façade of apparently continuing anger the still small, but ever growing, degree of his emotional participation in the danger facing the Greek army. In any event, Achilles' request is one of the turning points of the epic as a whole, for it is the first time since the beginning of his anger that he has broken out of the confines of his angrily self-absorbed indifference to others and performed an action (albeit a purely verbal one) which demonstrates that he has begun to return to the compassionate concern for his fellow-Greeks that he manifested at the very beginning of the epic – indeed, Nestor will ask with only partly feigned astonishment why Achilles has now started to feel pity (ὀλοφύρεται, 656) for the Greeks. And it sets in motion the inexorable chain of events that will lead, step by step, to Patroclus' death, to Hector's, and to his own – as Homer puts it with reference to Patroclus, "this was the beginning of evil for him" (604).[38]

Patroclus, of course, is characterized throughout the *Iliad*, precisely in contrast to Achilles, by his universally acknowledged kindness and pity.[39] Thus it is entirely appropriate both that it is ultimately only Patroclus, who is gentle to all and whom Achilles himself loves beyond all others, who proves himself capable of wrenching Achilles out of his self-absorption and reminding him of his participation in humanity, by making him feel pity for someone other than himself – and that that someone is Patroclus himself. At the beginning of Book 16, when Patroclus finally returns from the mission on which Achilles had sent him back in Book 11, Achilles sees him bathed in tears because of the plight of the Greeks (16.2–4); and – for the very first time in the whole epic – Achilles feels pity for someone, that is, compassion for someone other than himself:

> τὸν δὲ ἰδὼν ᾤκτειρε ποδάρκης δῖος Ἀχιλλεύς,
> καί μιν φωνήσας ἔπεα πτερόεντα προσηύδα·
> τίπτε δεδάκρυσαι Πατρόκλεες, ἠΰτε κούρη
> νηπίη, ἥ θ' ἅμα μητρὶ θέουσ' ἀνελέσθαι ἀνώγει
> εἱανοῦ ἁπτομένη, καί τ' ἐσσυμένην κατερύκει,
> δακρυόεσσα δέ μιν ποτιδέρκεται, ὄφρ' ἀνέληται·
> τῇ ἴκελος Πάτροκλε τέρεν κατὰ δάκρυον εἴβεις.
>   (16.5–11)

---

[38] Taplin (1992: 176–7) analyzes well the movement that leads from Nestor's exclamation about Achilles' (lack of) pity to Patroclus' pity to Achilles' pity to Patroclus' death, and concludes, "It is the current of compassion, set in movement by Nestor, that sends Patroklos to his death. In the Iliad, pity advances suffering as well as to some extent redeeming it" (177).

[39] *Il.* 11.814; 15.390–404; 17.204, 670–2; 19.287–300; 21.96; 23.281–2. This is indicated by his epithets as well: ἐνηής ("kind"), ἤπιος ("gentle"), μείλιχος ("honeyed"). Obviously, Patroclus' *aristeia* in Book 16 is an exception that proves the rule.

Seeing him, swift-footed godly Achilles *pitied* him, and addressing him he spoke winged words to him: "Why are you weeping, Patroclus, like a silly girl, who runs beside her mother and urges her to pick her up, clinging to her robe, and hinders her as she rushes along, and looks at her as she weeps, until she picks her up? Just like her, Patroclus, you are pouring forth a rounded tear."

At line 5, Aristarchus wished, astonishingly, to replace the manuscripts' unanimously transmitted ᾤκτειρε ("pitied") with the unsupported conjecture θάμβησε ("was astonished at") on the grounds that, if Achilles had really felt pity for Patroclus, he would not have made fun of him by comparing him to a little girl.[40] But in fact the transmitted reading is crucial here, as an unmistakable sign of a fundamental shift in Achilles' attitude, and the tenderly mocking tone of his first words to Patroclus may not only testify to the warmth and intimacy of his emotional bond to his older friend but also suggest that he does not yet feel quite comfortable with the pity he is feeling and expressing verbally now for the very first time in the whole poem.[41] Hence Patroclus' passionate reproach that Achilles is νηλεές ("pitiless") and is so inhuman that his parents must be not Peleus and Thetis but the sea and the cliffs (33–5)[42] is no longer fully justified: by expressing for the first time compassion for someone other than himself in his opening address to Patroclus, Achilles has demonstrated that he is indeed open to the recognition of his full participation in the community of at least some other men, and Patroclus' words are perhaps best taken as a mixture of his own desperation at the Greeks' plight on the one hand, and of encouragement for someone who no longer is completely dependent upon such encouragement on the other. Thus, in his reply, Achilles can bring himself to acknowledge that, although nothing has changed in the grounds that provoked his anger, that anger itself was apparently not after all so implacable as he had thought (50–63), and he accepts Patroclus' suggestion that Patroclus put on his own armor and lead the Myrmidons into battle in his guise in order to rescue the Greeks (64–70). Indeed, when Achilles sees that the ships have already begun to burn, he becomes filled with anxiety for the Greeks and goes so far as to urge Patroclus to arm himself as quickly as possible (124–9). There can be little doubt that the mediation of Patroclus has permitted Achilles to begin, for the first time in the course of the *Iliad*, to feel pity not only for him but also for the rest of the Greeks. But it should be emphasized that at this point Achilles is only at the very beginning of this development – after all, his first speech

---

[40] Schol. Vet. ad *Il.* 16.5.   [41] So Burkert, rightly, (1955) 94.

[42] I have discussed this passage elsewhere in another perspective: Most (1993).

to Patroclus had concluded with the loving, sentimental, and thoroughly horrifying daydream that all the Trojans might die, and all the Greeks too except for himself and Patroclus, and that they two alone might take Troy (97–100).[43]

Of course, Achilles' decision to send Patroclus into battle in his own armor leads inadvertently to his friend's death; and Achilles' sense of his own undeniable (even if, in our eyes, only partial) responsibility for this outcome, coming as it does immediately after he has begun to break open his carapace of hostile indifference and to expose himself once again to the full emotional risk of involvement with other humans, leads to the consequence that, once he learns that Hector has killed Patroclus, all the emotions that had previously dominated his spirit continue qualitatively, but increase radically in intensity, while at the same time they are now directed at new objects. Achilles' earlier focus upon his own sufferings is now replaced by mourning and pity for Patroclus; his earlier anger at Agamemnon, and secondarily at the rest of the Greeks, now gives way to anger and a desire for revenge against Hector, and secondarily against the rest of the Trojans. The scene of lamentation when Achilles hears the news of Patroclus' death is horrific in its pathos[44] – Antilochus must hold Achilles' hands for fear he will otherwise cut his throat (18.33–4) – but it stands in sharp contrast to the calm, indeed the indifference, with which Achilles learns from his mother that his own death will follow soon after that of Hector (98–121). Indeed, for the rest of the *Iliad*, most strikingly in the terrifyingly dispassionate cruelty of his words to the rejected suppliant Lycaon (21.99–113), Achilles will continue to display a marked indifference to his own past sufferings and imminent death[45] which is quite different from the intensely passionate absorption in his own ills that had characterized him in the first part of the *Iliad*, and which thereby indicates how completely his pity for Patroclus has come to replace his earlier sorrow for himself. The degree to which the emotional preoccupation with Patroclus and Hector that has now come to

---

[43] These lines much troubled ancient scholars. According to Schol. Vet. ad *Il.* 16.97–100a, b, Zenodotus and Aristarchus athetized them as presupposing the later version of a homosexual relation between Achilles and Patroclus; the scholia add further reasons for deleting them as inappropriate. Instead, their tragic pathos marks them as genuinely Homeric: all the listeners know that, so far from Achilles and Patroclus alone surviving to take Troy, they are the only two of the major Greek warriors who will die before Troy is taken.

[44] So too later, e.g. *Il.* 18.235–38, 316–42; 19.312–37; 23.222–5, etc.

[45] So, e.g., *Il.* 19.56–73, 420–3; 22.365–6; 24.522ff. Even at 21.273–83, where Achilles refers to himself, exceptionally, as ἐλεεινόν ("pitiable," 273), what he complains about is not that he seemingly must die – this he accepts without hesitation – but that the death that seems imminent is not the heroic and glorious one that he was promised, but a miserable and vulgar one, appropriate for a swineherd boy.

occupy him currently exhausts the scope of his concerns is well indicated by
his refusal, against Odysseus' pragmatic and sociable advice, to eat anything
at all with the other Greeks, so long as Hector is still alive and Patroclus
unavenged (19.199–214).

In Book 22, Hector once again rejects his family's appeals to pity them and
stay within the walls (ἐλεεινὰ, 22.37, ἐλέησον 59, ἐλέησον 82) and instead
chooses to privilege his respect (αἰδώς) for the Trojans and to remain outside
the walls to face Achilles alone – and thereby seals his own (and also Troy's)
fate; for, since it was destined both that Achilles would slay Hector and that
Achilles would not take Troy, on the one hand Hector was only vulnerable
outside his city's walls (and hence those who love him are always urging
him to stay within them) and on the other hand Troy could not be taken
so long as Hector remained on or in the walls (and hence Hector's decision
to remain outside them has such catastrophic consequences). Now Achilles
can slay him and avenge Patroclus, thereby satisfying the demands of pity
for his slain friend. At the same time, Achilles has gradually developed
further, from an initial limitation of his compassion to Patroclus alone, to
a more encompassing sense of pity for all the other Greeks who have been
killed in the war. Already when he had refused Lycaon's supplication he had
said that all the Trojans would have to pay not only for Patroclus' death
but for all the Greeks who had died while Achilles had stayed out of the
battle (21.134–5); and now, when he refuses Hector's suggestion that they
come to an agreement, he does so by saying that Hector will have to pay
not just for what he did to Patroclus but for all the Greeks he had slain
(22.271–2) – indeed, in addressing Patroclus' murderer, he does not even
name him here, out of an extraordinary mixture of tactful reverence for the
dead, desperately maintained control over himself, and uncontrollable rage
at Hector. But there can be little doubt that, in Achilles' mind, the other
Greeks are still at this point as secondary in comparison to Patroclus as the
other Trojans are in comparison to Hector. It is only after he has satisfied
his anger at Hector and his pity for Patroclus by slaying the Trojan hero
and outraging his body, while burying Patroclus in pointed contrast with
full funeral honors (including the unheard-of sacrifice of twelve human
captives), that Achilles can gradually become reintegrated socially within
the community of the Greek army, which he has already begun to rejoin
psychologically by the gradual extension of his compassion beyond the sole
case of Patroclus to all his fellow-Greeks. This reintegration he achieves by
organizing and administering the funeral games for Patroclus in Book 23,
which reestablish his place within the social hierarchy of the Greek camp;
and it is appropriate that it is during these games that, for the first time

since Achilles' expression of pity for Patroclus at the beginning of Book 16, he expresses pity for another person, this time a different Greek warrior, Eumelos, who unfairly comes in last in the chariot race (ᾤκτειρε, 23.534; οἰκτίρεις, 548).

But it is only in the last book of the *Iliad* that the pity for others which has gradually come to replace self-absorption within Achilles' spirit is finally able to extend beyond even the Greek camp so as to include Priam, the king of Achilles' enemies, and thereby to extinguish, temporarily but almost completely, the anger which he has felt, first for one object and then for another, uninterruptedly since almost the very beginning of the epic. Book 24 represents the triumph of pity; but at the same time it is a coherent and appropriate conclusion for the epic as a whole.[46] It opens with the pity (ἐλεαίρεσκον) of the gods for Hector's mangled corpse (24.23) and with a council of the gods at which Apollo reproaches the other gods with feeling no pity for Hector and the Trojans, and accuses Achilles – the very man in whom we have been observing the gradual renewal of his sense of pity over the preceding books – of having destroyed the quality of pity itself (ἔλεος, 44, a Homeric *hapax*). Despite the continuing anger of Hera, Poseidon, and Athena, Zeus decides that Achilles must restore his son's body to Priam: for Achilles' mistreatment of Hector has made the gods exceedingly wrathful with him (113–16); and against such an anger Achilles offers no resistance. Simultaneously Zeus communicates to Priam his pity (ἐλεαίρει) for the old man (174) and encourages him to go to Achilles' camp to ransom his son. Hecuba is convinced that Achilles is so wild and faithless that he will have no pity (ἐλεήσει) on him (207), but Priam relies upon Zeus' pity (ἐλεήσῃ, 301) and prays that Achilles will pity (ἐλεεινόν) him (309). Zeus does indeed take pity (ἐλέησε) on him as he travels across the plain (332) and sends Hermes to guide him. When Priam arrives, he assumes the suppliant position in front of Achilles, kisses the hands that have killed his many sons, and reminds him of his own father Peleus (486–7, 503–6) – thereby establishing a bridge of similarity, not only between the two aged fathers,[47] but also between their two young sons, both destined to die prematurely and to bring grief upon their fathers, a bridge upon which compassion can travel. And Achilles responds by weeping, not for himself, but for his father and for Patroclus (511–12), and concludes by feeling and expressing pity for

---

[46] I have learned much from Macleod (1982b). See also Beck (1964); Deichgräber (1972).

[47] Priam's appeal and Achilles' compassion are lent further poignancy by the listeners' knowledge that upon the fall of Troy Achilles' own son Neoptolemus will notoriously violate his father's pity for the aged Priam by slaying him mercilessly at the altar of Zeus.

the aged Priam: "pitying (οἰκτείρων) his hoary head and his hoary cheek" (516).

It is only now that we can understand why all the earlier scenes of battlefield supplication ended with the refusal of pity and the slaying of the suppliant: they were designed to serve as a foil in order to increase our anxiety for Priam and as a contrasting measure of the change in Achilles' character.[48] To be sure, Achilles remains Achilles: when Priam pushes him a bit too quickly, he responds with a last spark (in this epic) of his wonted rage and threatens to do violence to the suppliant within his hut (559–70) – but then he runs out of the house, no doubt in order to prevent himself from doing anything of the kind, and goes instead to do exactly what Priam had asked of him (572ff.). The whole development in Achilles' character can be measured in the difference between the first scene of the epic, in which only the intervention of Athena had restrained him from acting upon his anger, and this final demonstration of his newly found capacity to master his own anger. The bond of intimate solidarity – between deadly enemies! – which had been initiated by Achilles' pity is confirmed by a scene of mutual astonished admiration (628–33) and is then sealed by Achilles' promise to hold the Greeks back from war until Hector (now like Patroclus) has been properly mourned and buried (669–70). We, who stand outside this poem and know what the future of the epic tradition will bring, can recognize the chilling irony in the fact that Achilles' negotiation with Priam concerning the length of the truce to mourn Hector before fighting will resume is simultaneously, and quite unbeknownst to him, a determination of the number of days he himself has left to live; for the day the fighting begins again will be the last one of his life. And the intimacy between Priam and Achilles is further sharpened by the explicit contrast drawn repeatedly with Agamemnon, who, if he came to know that Priam was sleeping in Achilles' tent, would doubtless feel none of the pity for him that has taken hold of Achilles but would instead seize him as a hostage against an enormous ransom (650–5, 686–8) – and by the implicit contrast between Chryses' embassy to Agamemnon to ransom his living daughter in Book 1, which had failed then because of Agamemnon's obdurate and uncontrollable anger, and Priam's embassy to Achilles to ransom his dead son here, which succeeds now because of Achilles' new-found capacity to control his anger. Then the epic can conclude with the laments for Hector, in which Andromache, Hecuba, and climactically Helen express their pity for him and provide a counterpart for the laments for Patroclus which

[48] See Macleod (1982b) 15–16.

had been repeatedly uttered in the closing books and which prefigure the laments for Achilles which we know will very soon have to be uttered over his own corpse.

Thus Achilles undergoes a certain degree of development in the course of the *Iliad*, which brings him from a concern for his fellows to an angrily self-absorbed focus upon his own sufferings, then to a first pity whose object is his closest friend among the Greeks and finally to a second pity which envisions the one man whom one might expect him to regard as his worst enemy, the king of the Trojans, the man whose son killed his best friend. This widening and generalization of Achilles' capacity for compassion, which is at the same time a return at the very end of the epic to something like the concern for his community which he manifested at its very beginning, is correlated with a gradual shift in the anger which is no less characteristic of him: first an anger directed above all at Agamemnon, who has treated him contemptuously, but also at all his fellow-Greeks, whose suffering he not only accepts but in fact even implores and engineers, with the purpose of making them all realize how much they need him and what a mistake it was not to support him against the king's outrage; then an anger directed first of all at Hector, who has killed his friend, but beyond him at all the rest of the Trojans, who are to be killed, partly as a way of getting at Hector, partly for their own sake. Finally, in the last book, he displays a brief spark of his accustomed anger but has learned to dominate this passion and otherwise seems to have been freed of it. At a crucial moment in his speech in the embassy of Book 9, just before the catalogue of the gifts Agamemnon has promised, Odysseus had reminded Achilles of the parting words spoken to him by his father Peleus when he departed for Troy:

> τέκνον ἐμὸν κάρτος μὲν Ἀθηναίη τε καὶ Ἥρη
> δώσουσ' αἴ κ' ἐθέλωσι, σὺ δὲ μεγαλήτορα **θυμὸν**
> ἴσχειν ἐν στήθεσσι· φιλοφροσύνη γὰρ ἀμείνων·
> ληγέμεναι δ' ἔριδος κακομηχάνου, ὄφρά σε μᾶλλον
> τίωσ' Ἀργείων ἠμὲν νέοι ἠδὲ γέροντες.
> ὣς ἐπέτελλ' ὁ γέρων, σὺ δὲ λήθεαι·   (9.254–9)

"My son, Athena and Hera will give strength, if they will, but as for you, restrain the great-hearted *rage* in your breast: for a kind disposition is better; cease from evil-working strife, so that the Argives, both young and old, will honor you all the more." So he commanded, the old man, but you have forgotten.

At the moment when Odysseus cited Peleus' admonition to restrain his rage (θυμός), Achilles' conduct did indeed seem to suggest that he had forgotten it; but the overwhelming sufferings, his own and others', for which he has himself been partly responsible, as well as the explicit reminder of Peleus that Priam gives him in his own embassy to him in his tent (Book 24), help him in the end not only to remember it, but also to put it into practice, by controlling the rage (θυμός) which Priam inadvertently arouses there (24.568). To be sure, Achilles does not become a different person, and the emotions with which we identify him remain the same from beginning to end; but by the end of the poem he has learned to manage those emotions, at least to a certain extent. It is difficult not to interpret this as an evolution in Achilles' character which results from a kind of education which he undergoes[49] – certainly not as a *Bildungsroman* in the nineteenth-century sense, but at least, to adapt the title of Alexander Kluge's novel, as a "learning process with a deadly outcome."[50]

This is not to make of Achilles a Christian saint: as indicated above, Homeric pity and Christian pity are worlds apart from one another. But it is to suggest that Homer was fascinated not so much by the phenomenon of epic rage itself as rather by the interdependence, within the traditional stories as he understood and interpreted them, of rage and pity – of what some might take to be the most male and violent passion with the most female and tender sentiment. It is precisely their thoroughgoing interdependence, within the vicissitudes of the self's dealings with itself and with others, that Homer chose to make the central theme of his monumental version of the traditional legends. To be sure, the *Iliad* remains a poem about anger – while no metrical constraint could have prevented Homer from beginning his epic, had he wished to, with the words, "The pity (Οἶκτον) – sing it, goddess, that of Peleus' son Achilles," we may surely presume that an epic that began that way would have been very different from, and no doubt vastly inferior to, the *Iliad* as we have it.[51] Audiences used to tales of martial glory would have protested against such a poem and sought out other singers in place of Homer; within a cultural context of oral performance and transmission, this would have resulted in the immediate annihilation of his epic. Presumably Homer inherited a traditional set of stories which emphasized bloody-minded rage and revenge but which also included scenes of deeply moving compassion – had he invented the latter from whole cloth, he would have been violating all the canons of epic truth

---

[49] For a different account of the development in the character of Achilles, cf. Kirk (1962) 353–4.

[50] See Kluge (1996).

[51] One curious ancient testimony to the importance that could be attributed to the choice of exactly the right beginning is Protagoras' objection to the opening of the *Iliad*, namely that μῆνις ("rage") should be masculine, not feminine (80 A 28 DK): evidently he felt, or at least could plausibly suggest, that an epic of masculine warfare needed to commence with a masculine word, especially since the concept denoted by the opening word was made responsible for the death of many male warriors.

and would have been rejected by his audience. So far from simply retelling a sanguinary version *tel quel* and then appending to it a civilized epilogue, he reinvented the tradition plausibly, retelling it from the beginning (from a beginning in which he begins with rage but prominently deprecates it as "accursed") in such a way that the interconnection between anger and pity would become unmistakable – or rather, considering how often the poem has been oversimplified and distorted by later readers into a tale of mere heroic rage, should have become so.

In conclusion, there can be no doubt that different parts of Homer's poem forcefully suggest to the attentive listener, or reader, mutually discrepant evaluations of the various modes of human conduct that it portrays; but the attempt, which goes back to Vico,[52] to resolve these inconsistencies by temporalizing them along the axis of a theory of cultural evolution which postulates many *Homers*, from more primitive ones to more enlightened ones, is only one possible hermeneutical approach, and by no means the one most consonant with our own modern sense of the nature of great poetry and of human personality. Instead, we can keep one Homer, by postulating many *Achilles* – or rather, only one, who develops continuously from the beginning of the *Iliad* to the end, along the line of an evolution in his character which is brilliantly conceived, intuitively plausible, and profoundly tragic.[53]

[52] Vico (1948).   [53] Cf. still Szabó (1956) 82–108.

CHAPTER 3

Angry bees, wasps, and jurors: the symbolic politics of ὀργή in Athens

D. S. Allen

What are we to do with the ubiquitous moments of emotional intensity in Greek oratory such as the following one from Demosthenes' prosecution of the wealthy Meidias on a charge of hubris: "All this bad behavior and his habit of adding to the troubles of people who justly defend themselves against him must be paid back with more than just my getting angry and upset while you look the other way! It's necessary for everyone to be just as angry!" (ἀλλὰ πᾶσιν ὁμοίως ὀργιστέον, 21.123).

Demosthenes is by no means the only Athenian orator to use arguments about anger, and specifically about ὀργή, to construct particular definitions of justice and of the just use of authoritative penal power.[1] Rather, ὀργή was a central argumentative term in all of the orators except Antiphon.[2] Aeschines, for instance, describes the moment when litigants must debate the penalty to be imposed on a convict as being when "the third water is poured in [to the water clock to time the speeches to be made] about

---

[1] In oratory, anger is the reason that orators most frequently give to explain why they, or someone else, or the city has tried to punish or wishes to punish. This is also true in stories about private non-institutional acts of punishment. For claims about anger, ὀργή and otherwise, see (this list is by no means exhaustive): Isoc. 13.1; 20.6–9; Andoc. 1.24; Lys. 1.15; 15.12; 19.6; 29.6; 31.11; Isaeus 1.10, 13, 18; 8.37; Dem. 19.265; 21.99; 28.63; 34.19; 35.31; 38.1; 59.51–5; Aeschin. 2.3; 3.3; Lycurg. 1.86, 91–2. For hostility or hatred toward an opponent, see Isoc. 13.1; Lys. 7.20; 13.1; 15.12; Dem. 53.1–3, 15; 54.33; 58.49, 52; 59.1, 14–15. Even a defendant could put his case by claiming that he had never been more angry (Aeschin. 2.3). For the anger of collective bodies, see Dem. 21.2, 6; 22.2; 59.80. Lysias sees before him in his jury an audience whose "wrath wishes to punish" (Lys. 29.6).

There is an emphasis on "showing" anger (φαίνομαι; ἐνσημαίνω): Isoc. 18.42; 20.3; 20.22; Lys. 12.90; Dem. 21.34, 183; 25.27; 41.3. See also Lys. 13.1; 19.6; 29.6; Aeschin. 2.3; 3.107, 198; Lycurg. 1.91–2; Demades 1.30.

[2] Antiphon is the only orator who disavows ὀργή or criticizes its constant appearance in the courts without elsewhere claiming anger as a justifiable inspiration to action. In *On the Murder of Herodes* he writes: "First deliberate well, and not with anger (ὀργῆς) or under the influence of slander. There could be no advisors worse than these. For it is not the case that the angry man has good judgment. For this state of mind destroys the faculty, judgment, with which he deliberates. The passing of time has great power to release the judgment from anger (ὀργῆς) and find the truth of events" (5.69, 71). For other (and uncharacteristic) disavowals of anger, see Lys. 25.6–7; 29.2; Dem. 18.121, 278; 19.227–8; 22.1.3; Aeschin. 3.3; Lycurg. 1.3, 5; Demades 1.3, 4.

the penalty and the magnitude of your anger (τῷ μεγέθει τῆς ὀργῆς τῆς ὑμετέρας)" (Aeschin. 3.197). The juxtaposition of the water in the water clock, which counts time, to the anger in the jurors, which metes out justice, underscores the way in which anger was thought of as being measurable, assessable, and finally dispensable. The job of law, it could even be said, was to determine how much anger ought to be applied to particular types of wrongdoing. Thus Demosthenes writes:

It is necessary to consider the laws, gentlemen of the jury . . . In particular, compare how much more anger and punishment the laws think that hubristic wrongdoers, who act of their own free will, deserve (μείζονος ὀργῆς καὶ ζημίας ἀξιοῦσι) in contrast to all other categories of wrongdoers. The laws draw this distinction fitly, for, while a victim rightly receives the law's support in all circumstances, the law [appropriately enough] does not direct equal levels of anger (οὐκ ἴσην τὴν ὀργήν) at the culpable party, regardless of whether he acted willingly or not. (Dem. 21.42, 43)

Authoritative definitions of what constituted anger, of when it was appropriate to be angry, and of what sorts of action were appropriate expressions of anger were woven into the definitions of law and justice that operated in the Athenian courts and that shaped life in the Athenian *polis*.[3]

Demosthenes uses the verbal adjective ὀργιστέον ("it is necessary to be angry") in the particular moment of his attack on Meidias as part of a larger effort to construct a statement about necessity and about the forms of moral obligation that are binding on his fellow-citizens. He is asking that the jurors transfer the energy of their political power as vote-givers into an act against the defendant that would be described not only as a condemnation, or an act of criminal justice, but also as an act of anger, specifically an act of ὀργή. Justice and anger would thus define one another, in whatever authoritative decision might have been handed down by the jury in Meidias' case. Demosthenes' exhortation reveals the idea of ὀργή

---

[3] The language of anger was by no means merely a matter of rhetorical flourish but was rather embedded in the ethical calculus of value used in the Athenian courts (Allen [2000] ch. 5). The discourse of anger and pity is littered with the vocabulary of "desert" (τὰ ἄξια). In oratory, requests like "I deserve to be pitied" (Antiph. 5.73, ἄξιος ἐλεηθῆναι) are as frequent as injunctions to hand out "deserved anger appropriately" (Dem. 21.127, ἀξίαν ὀργήν). E.g. Antiph. 1.3; 5.73; Andoc. 2.6; Isoc. 16.48; 20.14; Isae. 6.56; Lys. 6.55; 11.9; 13.1; 14.2, 8; 20.21; 27.11–13; 28.13–14; 31.11; Dem. 21.148, 186, 196; 24.152–3, 200, 218; 37.20; 44.57; 45.20; 54.138; Lycurg. 1.58; 1.138; Aeschin. 3.260; Din. 1.22. The language of anger and pity defined the contours of the competition between prosecutor and defendant. Thus Demosthenes argues: "Which of us is more deserving of pity?" (Dem. 54.43). A request by a litigant for pity for himself or for those whom he was defending was equally and simultaneously a request for anger at his (or their) opponent. Lysias makes this clear when he says: "You should pity these young ones . . . [but] this man is worthy of the anger of all the citizens" (Lys. 32.19).

to be an authoritative ethical and psychological norm, one with enough suasive power to structure political action.

But perhaps this is to make too much of Demosthenes' vituperative injunction that the jurors should grow angry. How is it really possible that the forms of obligation and authority that are involved in an orator's invocation of anger in fact have anything to do with real political authority in the city – either institutional or cultural? Perhaps they are merely the showy dressing on self-indulgent and disgraceful forms of rhetorical extravagance? In the *Apology* Plato's Socrates, at any rate, seems to think that the frequent oratorical calls to anger, as well as pleas for pity, were nothing more than this (*Ap.* 35aff.), and generations of scholars have agreed.[4] I, however, wish to argue a contrary position and it is this: anger – and more specifically ὀργή – was a central term in the ethical discourses that produced Athenian definitions of the good citizen, justice, and just behavior.[5]

Over the years students of Athenian democratic political authority have zigzagged between examinations of institutions and examinations of discourses or culture. A focus on the institutions of the assembly and the board of *nomothetai* reveals a city that sought to secure its norms and structures by means of written law and institutionalized procedure.[6] But a focus on the discourse of the courts, where mass juries decided the fates of elite politicians, shows us a city that kept its politics democratic by means of the power of communal norms and popular discourse.[7] A shift in attention, however, to the ethics and psychology of citizen behavior allows us to see how institutions and culture interacted with one another and also how they sprang from a single source of authority: namely, the community's determinations of how individual citizens should act.

What then was ὀργή thought to be? And what were the guidelines for using it legitimately?[8] ὀργή plays no role in the Homeric epics and makes its first appearances only in Hesiod's *Works and Days* (304) and

---

[4] Thus, Adkins (1972: 122) writes: "Emotional pleas for pity were notoriously sometimes made in Athenian courts but these speakers seem not to be asking for pity, but rather for admiration for qualities which we should not regard as relevant in court."

[5] It should be noted that the argument of this essay primarily concerns the role of ὀργή in Athenian political discourse but I have sometimes drawn on material pertaining to other forms of anger, for instance to θυμός, in cases where an argument can be made for the relative isomorphism of the different types of anger.

[6] See, for instance, Hansen (1975), (1980), (1983), (1987), (1989a), (1989b), (1989c), (1989d), (1991); Sealey (1982), (1987); Todd (1993, repr. 1995).

[7] See, for instance, Ober (1989a), (1989b); Humphreys (1983), (1985).

[8] In the context of ancient epic, Muellner (1996: 84ff.) identifies *mēnis* as the *source* of punishment and action, while *cholos* is the *trigger* for the action. He adds (1996: 187ff.) that *mēnis* comes from an Indo-European root that means "activate the mind." What is true of *mēnis* is true of *orgē*: it is a state of mind from which the unfolding of the punitive drama begins. Considine (1986: 53–6) shows that *mēnis* (as a noun) applies exclusively to divine wrath.

the Homeric *Hymn to Demeter* (203–4). In both texts the word seems to refer not so much to an emotion as to some general element of the human psychological apparatus in respect to which a person can be either positively or negatively disposed. Later, however, Theognis and Herodotus relate the passion of ὀργή to quarrels and injurious behavior.[9] And by Aristotle's era, the philosopher thinks it reasonable to make quarrels central to his definition of ὀργή. He writes:

Let anger be defined as a desire, commingled with pain, to see someone punished, and which is provoked by an apparent slight to the angered person, or to something or someone that belongs to him, when that slight is not justified. (*Rh.* 2.1.1378a)[10]

Emotions are understood in terms of the structure of action that follows from them. Aristotle treats ὀργή as a painful emotion that arises directly from one sort of action (a belittling) and that leads directly to another set of actions: punishments resulting from quarrels of ambition and status.

As it works out, the vast majority of orators and tragic characters do cite anger as their motivation for undertaking to punish. But if anger was to be channeled into a legitimate act of punishment, it had to be used correctly. In tragedy, we can find an ethics of anger and of anger-based punishment that required those who wished to act on their anger to do so openly and straightforwardly and not by means of guile or cool calculation. A Sophoclean chorus speaks for any number of other tragic characters when it is careful to distinguish guileful punishment or revenge from legitimate forms of reciprocation:

Fate's punishment never visits anyone who suffers the first blow and then exacts revenge (ἂν προπάθῃ τὸ τίνειν). But when deceitful dealings (ἀπάτα) are set against other deceitful deeds, the paybacks (ἀντιδίδωσιν) produce burdens, not fair reciprocity (χάριν). (Soph. *OC* 229–33)[11]

The structure of punishment is based not only on anger but on "paying back," but return payment can be extracted either legitimately

---

9 Theognis: 98, 1059, 1223, 1303; Herodotus: 1.61.2; 1.73.4; 1.114.5; 1.141.4; 1.156.2; 3.25.1; 3.35.1; 3.52.3–4; 3.131.1; 4.128.1; 6.85.2; 6.128.1; 7.105.1. Theognis, for instance, draws an opposition between ὀργή and "grace," "gratitude," or "favor" (χάρις, 1303), and links ὀργή to the θυμός, one of the physio-psychological organs of the Greek body which was itself a source of anger and other passions (1223, 1303).

10 At 1.10.1369b1–1370b1 Aristotle treats the θυμός and ὀργή as forces that bring honor. See also *De anima* 1.1.403a29ff.

11 Every tragic woman who fails to control her θυμός and who punishes is accused of using guile in her attempt to punish: Aphrodite in her punishment of Hippolytus (Eur. *Hipp.* 1312), Creusa (Eur. *Ion* 844, 985, 1481), Hecuba (Eur. *Hec.* 1269), Clytemnestra (Soph. *El.* 279; Aesch. *Ag.* 155, 1129, 1495, 1519; *Cho.* 1003), and even Electra (Eur. *El.* 9, 830). Medea, who is always extraordinarily self-conscious about the way in which she is treading on taboos, says explicitly that she will use guile to punish Jason. For that matter, she even goes so far as to call her own act of punishment a "murder" (391, 783).

or illegitimately. If it was unacceptable to turn one's anger into action by means of guile, neither was it acceptable to delay the moment of acting in anger once one's passion had been aroused. In Euripides' *Ion*, when Creusa wishes to punish her husband for seemingly disinheriting her and her children by adopting Ion priest of Apollo as his son, she is told that she will be murdering if she waits and fails to kill Ion immediately (αὐτοῦ νυν αὐτὸν κτεῖν', ἵν' ἀρνήσῃ φόνους, Eur. *Ion* 1026). Similarly, in *The Children of Herakles*, Iolaus' delay in killing Eurystheus makes his act one that no one would perform any longer and opens Alcmene to much blame (πολλὴν ἄρ' ἕξεις μέμψιν, εἰ δράσεις τόδε, Eur. *Heracl.* 970–4). Acts of anger, punishments, if they were to be legitimate, had to be carried out in hot blood, as it were. We moderns might use that phrase metaphorically, but the ancients thought it literally. According to Aristotle, ancient doctors defined anger as "a boiling of the blood or warm substance surrounding the heart" (*De an.* 1.1.403a30: ὁ δὲ ζέσιν τοῦ περὶ καρδίαν αἵματος καὶ θερμοῦ). The modern phrase "in hot blood" captures not only this materialist definition of anger but also the ethical criteria used by the Athenians to determine which types of action were legitimate vehicles for anger. Aristotle explicitly prefers hot-tempered (οἱ ὀξύθυμοι) to mild (οἱ πρᾶοι) men precisely because the former will be outspoken (παρρησιαστικοί) and let you know what they are doing, while the latter will dissemble (εἴρωνες καὶ πανοῦργοι) and it will never be clear what they will do and when they are about to act (ἄδηλοι γὰρ εἰ ἐγγύς, ὥστε οὐδέποτε φανεροὶ ὅτι πόρρω) (*Rh.* 2.5.1382b21–2). Anger itself was defined as an emotion that led, when used correctly, only to open and straightforward "hot-blooded" contests.

Oratory mirrors tragedy in valuing the ethic of hot blood and the idea that anger should lead to open confrontations where one citizen tests his strength, political rather than physical, against that of another citizen. Athenian prosecutors had to prove at least two things to show that their prosecution and the prosecutorial anger justifying it were valid: that they were personally and legitimately involved in some sort of feud with the defendant, and that they had acted in a timely fashion.[12] As frequently as an orator called upon his jurors to exercise a public anger, he would also invoke personal anger. More importantly, he would explain it. The frequency with which speakers narrate feuds and disputes reveals not only that orators *were* usually *personally involved* in the case at bar, and not only that they felt *obliged to be personally* involved in the case at bar, but also, and more importantly, that they felt obliged *to show* their audiences that

---

[12] See Allen (2000) ch. 7.

they were personally involved and to give an account of that personal involvement. Aeschines accurately expresses a consistent theme in Athenian opinion when he says:

When I saw that the city was being harmed by Timarchus, who was in fact serving as a politician and speaking in the assembly despite the law's disbarment, and when I myself was personally subject to his malicious prosecutions, I thought it would be one of the most shameful things ever were I not to come to the aid of myself, you, the laws, and the whole city. And so it turns out, men of Athens, that the usual things people say about public trials aren't false: private enmities do frequently set public matters straight (οἱ εἰωθότες λόγοι λέγεσθαι ἐπὶ τοῖς δημοσίοις ἀγῶσιν οὐκ εἰσὶ ψευδεῖς· αἱ γὰρ ἴδιαι ἔχθραι πολλὰ πάνυ τῶν κοινῶν ἐπανορθοῦσι). (Aeschin. 1.1–2)[13]

The expectation that orators should prove their hot blood, as it were, is also clear from the regularity with which orators display discomfort about delayed prosecutions. We hear repeatedly that the only appropriate time to be angry is "immediate" to the event that causes the anger (εὐθύς) (e.g. Isae. 3.48; Dem. 36.9; 37.2). And one orator criticizes another for a slow prosecution on the grounds that "Other people in their anger would immediately seek to punish (ὀργιζόμενοι παραχρῆμα τιμωρεῖσθαι ζητοῦσιν)" (Lys. 3.39). Institutions gave support to this norm. The statute of limitations was set at five years for all types of case except for homicide and the prosecution of unconstitutional laws or decrees. According to Demosthenes, delay made cases of crime and punishment "stale" (ἕωλα) and "cold" (ψύχρα) when they arrived before the jury (Dem. 21.112).

"Hot-blood" was, importantly, for those in the prime of life, and young men risked seeming presumptuous or out of order when they tried to prosecute or otherwise direct public actions.[14] The speaker of one Lysianic speech treated this communal norm as a given when he worried that: "some men, councilors, are already irritated (ἀχθομένων) with me, thanks to these affairs, on the grounds that I tried to speak before the people when I was rather young"(Lys. 16.20).[15] In a certain sense anger involved the pleasures of heroic manhood. Aristotle cites Achilles' comment that anger (*cholos*) is "sweeter than dripping honey"[16] and himself puts it thus: "A certain pleasure, which derives from the hope of punishing, necessarily accompanies every experience of anger (καὶ πάσῃ ὀργῇ ἕπεσθαί τινα ἡδονήν, τὴν ἀπὸ τῆς ἐλπίδος τοῦ τιμωρήσασθαι) (2.2.1378b2ff.) (see also *Rh.* 1.11.1370b29; 1378a1ff; 1380a34).

---

[13] For analogous statements, see Lys. 7.20; Dem. 21.8; 24.8.
[14] Dem. 28.2; 58.59–61. See Carey (1994) 28.
[15] Cf. Diomedes (*Iliad* 9.33).
[16] Arist. *Rh.* 2.2.1378b, quoting *Iliad* 18.109. See M. W. Blundell (1989) 27.

Here it is worth noting that the hot blood in ὀργή involved not only the passion of anger but also the pains and pleasures of erotic desire, as in Pindar's narration of Apollo's pursuit of Cyrene (*meilichos orga, Pyth.* 9.43).[17] In fact, the cognate verb ὀργάω connotes sexual passion and means "to swell with moisture," "growing ripe, and (of men) swell with lust, wax wanton."[18] When ὀργάω refers to *female* sexual desire, what is at stake is not only pleasure but fertility. The Hippocratic texts, for instance, discuss remedies for infertility caused by situations where women "do not desire to mingle with their husbands because of dampness, and do not feel sexual desire (ὀργᾶ̣), and grow thin" (*Diseases of Women* 1.57.5–6). In another instance, the author discusses how to treat women whose wombs are too dry and concludes by saying that they should go to their husbands when, after the application of the remedy, their menstruation is no longer heavy and they feel desire (ὀργᾶ̣) (*Diseases of Women* 1.12.8). Ripe fruit could also be described as growing soft and swelling (ὀργᾶ̣, ὀργῶν), and the word ὀργάς, a cognate of ὀργή, was the name used in fifth- and fourth-century Athenian historical texts for the fertile, uncultivated land dedicated to a divinity at Eleusis (e.g. *IG* 2².204, 5–12).[19]

The most explicit connection between ὀργή and fertility appears in a Hippocratic discussion of the effect of geography and environmental conditions on health. People who live in locales oriented to the east rather than to the west, the text argues, have clear voices and are better off in respect to both ὀργή and intelligence (ὀργήν τε καὶ ξύνεσιν βελτίους εἰσί). Moreover, the natural productions in such a region are superior (τὰ ἄλλα τὰ ἐμφυόμενα ἀμείνω) to those of other regions. For human beings, this means that diseases are fewer and less powerful in such a place and that women are very fertile and give birth easily (Αἵ τε γυναῖκες αὐτόθι ἀρικύμονές εἰσι σφόδρα, καὶ τίκτουσι ῥηϊδίως) (Hipp. *Airs and Places* 5.13). ὀργή was a passion that was central not only to political behavior (punishment and competitions over honor) but also to the constitution of the family (through procreation). Put simply, health and fertility reign where ὀργή is rightly constituted. The fact that a passion at the heart of enmity could also be central to sexual desire, and to the associated ideas of fertility and ripeness, will prove significant to understanding the Athenian system of punishment and politics – and, especially, the role of women within it.

---

[17] Cf. Pindar, *Isthm.* 2.35; Eur. *Hel.* 1339; Plut. *Vit. Pomp.* 47.

[18] LSJ, s.v. The link between ὀργή and desire/passion comes up in Winkler (1990a) 198. Pindar (*Nem.* 5.32) uses the phrase ὀργὰν κνίζων, and the context is sufficiently ambiguous that the sexual connotations of κνίζειν may be said to carry weight.

[19] On plants, see also Hdt. 4.199; Xen. *Oec.* 19.19. The word ὀργάς came to mean a "pubescent girl" in Byzantine Greek (Chantraine [1968], s.v.).

The *cultural* requirement that orators act according to the principles of anger and hot blood was strong enough to lie at the root of one especially notable feature of Athenian *institutions*: the persistence of the personally interested prosecutor in the face of the institutional opportunity, provided by Solon, for anyone who wished (ὁ βουλόμενος), even a disinterested, dispassionate party, to prosecute in a *graphē*. The extant oratorical corpus yields only four cases (leaving aside administrative suits like *dokimasiai* and *euthunai*) where the prosecutor was not personally involved in a feud with the defendant.[20] In other words, for the whole life of the democracy, extant sources reveal the personally interested and "hot-blooded" prosecutor to have been the norm, even in public cases where there was no institutional need for the prosecutor to be personally involved in the matter. Anger was valorized as a crucial judicial tool to such an extent that the ethics of anger constrained not only citizen behavior but also the ways in which institutions functioned in the city.

The Athenian political world – and even the functioning of its institutions – was thus constituted by a valorization of anger as socially useful and necessary. But why should anger be so valorized? How could ὀργή be as relevant to citizenship as this argument suggests? We can find an explanation of the Athenian valorization of ὀργή in Aristophanes' *Wasps*, a play which tells the story of what happens in one Athenian family when a son decides that his father is too addicted to jury service and must be kept at home in order to be cured of his excessively harsh disposition (παῦσόν τ᾽ αὐτοῦ τοῦτο τὸ λίαν στρυφνὸν καὶ πρίνινον ἦθος, 877) and the ill-temperedness of his anger (καὶ παυσάμενον τῆς δυσκολίας | ἀπὸ τῆς ὀργῆς | τὴν ἀκαλήφην ἀφελέσθαι, 883–4).[21] A chorus of jurors, represented as Wasps, come to the father's rescue, claiming to be on their way to court bearing three days' worth of troublesome anger (ἥκειν ἔχοντας ἡμερῶν ὀργὴν τριῶν πονηράν, 243); note the trope of measurable, dispensable emotion. They join the embattled father, Philokleon, in offering a defense of their jurors' anger in terms of its social value. Between them, they argue that their angry spirit allowed the Athenians to overcome the Persians and to achieve their city's independence (cf. 383; 1071–88), and that it allows them to equalize the city's internal power structure because it engenders

---

[20] The four cases are Hyp. 1 and Din. 1, which come from a single prosecution in the democracy's final years, and Lycurg. 1 and Lys. 22. In both of the last two, the speaker tries to justify the exceptional nature of his prosecution.

[21] I have used MacDowell (1971) for the text of the play. For secondary sources, I have referred to M. Croiset (1909); MacDowell (1971, repr. 1995); Vaio (1971); Reckford (1977); Konstan (1985); Edmunds (1987); Olson (1996).

fear in the wealthy and aristocratic (1107–11). Philokleon (548–630) claims that his anger makes him powerful as a king (549) since great and tall men supplicate him (552–5). His ability to raise and lower the pitch of his anger allows him to mock at wealth (χἠμεῖς αὐτῷ τότε τῆς ὀργῆς ὀλίγον τὸν κόλλοπ᾽ ἀνεῖμεν. | ἆρ᾽ οὐ μεγάλη τοῦτ᾽ ἔστ᾽ ἀρχὴ καὶ τοῦ πλούτου καταχήνη;, 574–5). The Wasps and Philokleon treat anger as the source of Athens' independence, greatness, and egalitarianism, and they conceive of anger as being necessary to their participation in democratic politics as free and equal citizens. It is perhaps difficult to say whether Aristophanes was mocking the Athenians or would have agreed with his characters' claims that ὀργή played such an important role in maintaining democratic equality and freedom, but the play does prove that the Athenians could indeed articulate a coherent rationalization for the ways in which ὀργή might be seen as a fundamental principle and constitutive component of democratic politics.

This said, the valorization of anger in the public sphere also introduced a peculiar sort of political difficulty to the Athenian polis. A political community is constituted with a view to its own survival. An implicit claim is therefore made by those who constitute a political community that the principles in accordance with which they constitute it will preserve the lives of and provide for the flourishing of its members.[22] In the Athenian context, this means that the principles that shaped the public sphere also had the task of ensuring the preservation of private households.[23] Men could carry out a politics based on angry punitive competition only on the condition that their activity would not bring about the ruin of the family. But the activities in which citizen men engaged in their political lives – anger and competition over honor – were by definition those activities that would destroy the family if transplanted into the context of the household.[24] Despite the Wasps' arguments in favor of anger, anger could also be problematized, as tragedy reveals. Tragedy revolves, to a noticeable degree, around the figure and problem of the angry woman. And worries about the use of anger by women are thoroughly embedded in a fear that

[22] See R. J. Littman who writes: "From anthropology, we learn that societies that depend on a lineage system for their organization need to maintain 'the interlocking web of social relationships . . . at all costs in order for the society to survive, and all parts of the social system, including the judicial system, are oriented toward that end" (1990: 16). At some level this is true even of tyrannical regimes, so long as the tyrant is at least interested in maintaining the bare existence of a community.

[23] According to Isaeus (7.30), the *archon* even had the explicit duty of preventing a family from being extinguished.

[24] See Michelini (1994) 254ff. The most dramatic statement of the problem probably comes in Euripides' *Hercules Furens* when the hero comes home but does not leave off his warring and, in a fit of "madness" and "anger" (e.g. 1206–13), kills his own children.

anger will enter the sphere of the household. (Take for example, the cases of Clytemnestra, Medea, Creusa, Deianira, Antiphon's stepmother.) Anger might be useful in the *polis*, but in the household, as tragedy portrays it, it is ultimately destructive. To the degree that anger threatened family relationships with vendettas, it invalidated the claims about its social usefulness that were made by the male citizens and made moot the arguments that it was necessary to securing democratic citizenship. The political valorization of anger thus brought with it a danger that people would act according to the norms of anger to the point of unrestrained vendetta within families where such action would be socially fatal.

The problem posed by a system of punishment and politics that is based on the valorization of reciprocal anger, the problem of vendetta, can be solved in one of two ways: either (1) anger can be delegitimized as a basis for punishment for all members of a community; or (2) punishment may be localized in a limited set of "legitimately angry punishers" who are not typically in familial relationships with one another. The Athenians could not choose the first method, the general invalidation of anger, because anger was ideologically necessary to the self-understanding of male citizens as political actors, so unlike almost all post-Platonic and also post-Christian philosophers, they chose the second method – the decision not to invalidate anger across the board but, to put it crudely, to establish one angry punisher per household – the adult male – and to regulate the contests among households.[25] In Athens anger, even anger arising from one's own punishment, remained a valid basis for punishment for those who were allowed to punish: fathers, brothers, and sons.[26] But not everyone was allowed to turn their anger into open, hot-blooded acts of punishment. The exclusion of women from politics effected their exclusion from the practice of anger, and this in turn secured the household and relationships between men and women from the threat of anger and its destructive force. The exclusion of women from political institutions also kept male–female relationships

---

[25] Consider this story, in which punishment is specifically assigned to the male child: "Thinking his wife pregnant, he enjoined her to tell the child, if a son, that Agoratus had killed his father and that he should take vengeance on behalf of his father [upon coming of age]" (Lys. 13.42). V. Hunter (1994: 115) writes: "Whatever the role of women in the kinship structure before the advent of the state, it was [after the advent] securely linked to the reproduction of that basic unit [the *oikos*] and with it the social structure." S. Blundell writes: "The development of democracy in Athens may have been a parallel phenomenon to the subordination of women, in that both were linked in some degree to the emphasis placed on the economic independence [that is, self-sufficiency] of the *oikoi*" (1995: 129). Foxhall describes the head of the household as the individual who was empowered to cross the boundary between the household and the community. He "mediated between the changing contexts of public and private life" (1989: 31).

[26] In tragedy, Theseus is an anomaly in forswearing rage (Eur. *Supp.* 555, 581). Socrates also proposed that the Athenians should employ the first method of dealing with vendettas.

outside the spheres and contexts in which anger was valorized and so kept women from becoming habituated to acting on anger. Finally, the exclusion of women from politics allowed for the stabilization of a politics based on anger's valorization and made the male practice of anger a socially viable activity.[27] The structure of Athenian political institutions can thus be seen as having evolved so as to accommodate the valorization of anger as a principle for public action.

The institutional exclusion of women from the political realm was complemented by a female morality of anger that instructed women not even to try to breach the boundary between private and public forms of behavior. One after another tragic character mouths gnomic statements like this one from Deianira: "it is not noble for a woman who has any sense to grow angry (ἀλλ' οὐ γάρ, ὥσπερ εἶπον, ὀργαίνειν καλὸν | γυναῖκα νοῦν ἔχουσαν·)" (Soph. *Trach.* 552–3).[28] According to Euripides' Jason, the woman who acts according to the terms of peace rather than according to the terms of enmity and anger is the temperate (σώφρων) woman, the model of female virtue.[29] The ideology of anger to be found in tragedy prescribes that women must restrain their anger not only if they wish to be *good* women but also if they wish to be women at all. The Aeschylean Clytemnestra, Deianira, and both the Sophoclean and the Euripidean Electra (Soph. *Trach.* 1062–3, 1075; Soph. *El.* 983, 997–8; Eur. *El.* 1204) are all described as manly when they act on anger. Hecuba and Medea become beasts and monsters.[30] Almost all of tragedy's female punishers are also designated as murderesses in situations where men, acting analogously, do not become murderers.[31] For that matter, the two features that distinguish murder from

---

[27] Humphreys (1989); V. Hunter (1994) ch. 2. Consider cases like that by Antiphon, *Against the Stepmother*, in which two half-brothers are on opposing sides of a court case.

[28] Cf. Soph. *El.* 177, 178; Aesch. *Eum.* 824–32; Eur. *Med.* 869–90, 908–13.

[29] Jason: "Wife, I praise what you've said, but I don't censure your earlier behavior; for it fits the circumstances when a female quarrels (ὀργάς ποίεισθαι) with a husband because he is smuggling in another marriage. But now your heart has revolved to a better state, since, with time, you have recognized the winning counsel. These are the acts of a prudent (σώφρονος) woman"; Eur. *Med.* 908–13.

[30] Schlesier (1993: 89–114) has shown the frequency with which the trope of the Maenad and words like μαίνομαι are applied to women in tragedy. See Schlesier (1993) for maenads as the model for tragedy. On Hecuba as a beast and monster, see Allen (2000) 116. Medea is also described as bestial by the end of her tragedy; she is like a lioness, like the Scylla (Eur. *Med.* 1342–3). See also Aesch. *Ag.* 1231ff., where the chorus compares Clytemnestra's daring and act of punishment to the nature of female monsters.

[31] Tragic characters who have punished or who have tried to punish are accused of murder only seven times in the extant plays (if we leave out cases where Orestes is called a matricide). Of those seven accusations, five are directed at women, despite the fact that women in extant tragedy "punish" or try to "punish" roughly eighteen times to men's (roughly) seventy-one (*phoneus*: Aesch. *Ag.* 1309, 1506; Soph. *El.* 778; Eur. *El.* 30; *Med.* 1267; *Ion* 1026).

punishment – guile and delay, features of "cold-blooded" violence – are especially associated with women.[32] In other words, women were defined as being incapable of guiding their anger into structures of legitimate action; actions that issued from their anger could never qualify as political, nor could women themselves be said to be constituted in respect to their ὀργή in a politically relevant fashion. The tremendous ideological apparatus that was layered on top of the institutional structures, which kept women out of situations of punishment and kept private differentiated from public and male–male relationships differentiated from male–female relationships, generated a political space in which it was conceptually coherent and practically realistic to treat ὀργή/anger as a principle of politics.

But a male morality of political ὀργή was also necessary before anger could be a useful and not a dangerous political force. This morality is perhaps best accessed through a consideration of sycophancy, that mysterious and vilified form of prosecution, whose name literally means "pointing out" or "displaying figs." As Todd has noted (1993, repr. 1995: 92–4): "It is easy enough to describe the sycophant as a perversion or perhaps inversion of the ideal of the volunteer prosecutor, but there has been considerable recent dispute as to what it is about him that is perverse." On the traditional view, the sycophant prosecuted for money and was thus base. Osborne, however, has argued that the term "sycophant" denotes a "vexatious litigant," one who was excessively eager to prosecute. More specifically, Osborne uncovered an association between sycophancy and violations of what I have been calling the norms of hot blood: that one avoid delays and prosecute only where personally involved. He writes: "The orators . . . frequently take the fact that the prosecutor was not himself wronged as a sign that the prosecution is sycophantic . . . The sycophant characteristically acts after the event and rakes up old charges . . . If men do not contest charges immediately but later, they are regarded as sycophants and *ponēroi*."[33]

Scholars have generally dismissed the etymology of the word "sycophant" – revealer of figs – as meaningless, but this may turn out after all to be where the answer lies. The fig tree with its pendant fruit (συκῆ, σῦκα) was used as a metaphor for the male reproductive organs; the single fig (σῦκον) represented the female genitalia.[34] Dried figs (ἰσχάδας)

---

[32] Detienne and Vernant have a good discussion of *dolos* as providing the weaker competitor with means to overcome the stronger (1978) 27–9.

[33] Osborne (1990) 99–100. On sycophants, see Lofberg (1917) 19–25; A. R. W. Harrison (1971) 60ff.; MacDowell (1978) 62–6; V. Hunter (1994) 126–7; Christ (1998). See Lys. 13.67; Isae. 11.13, 31; Dem. 21.102–3, 116; 36.54; 38.3, 16, 20; 39.2, 26, 34; 55; 57; 58; Aeschin. 1; Lycurg. 1.31. And Isoc. 15.314–15 on laws against sycophancy.

[34] Jeffrey Henderson (1991a).

mainly represented female genitalia (primarily outside Old Comedy) but may also have represented spent and satisfied male genitalia, especially since the related verb ἰσχναίνω was used to describe the satisfaction of passion.[35] The petals of the fig (θρία) were a euphemism for the foreskin. "Drawing back the fig-leaves" suggested preparation for sexual activity and behavior that was overly virile and violent.[36] "Figs" did not, however, represent only sexuality. They also represented anger, as they do in Aristophanes' *Wasps*, as we shall see below. A ripe fig was one that swelled and softened (τὸ ὀργῶν, Xen. *Oec.* 19.19) or that was, we might say, full of ὀργή. Notably, the Athenian scapegoat, the *pharmakos*, was driven out of the city with dried figs hanging around his neck; and scapegoats in other cities were beaten around the genitals with fig-wood. Comedy defines the *sycophant* (συκοφαντεῖν), our perversion of the volunteer prosecutor, as one who "screws/provokes erotically" (κνίζει ἐρωτικῶς);[37] and so the sycophant's name hints at an eroticization of the angry process of prosecution.

In *Wasps* Aristophanes first deploys the figure of the fig in his description of Philokleon, the old angry juror who tries to escape his son's house arrest. In one of his efforts at a jailbreak, Philokleon climbs out of the chimney, gets caught, offers the excuse that he is smoke, and is mocked by his son for being the stinging kind (δριμύτατος) that comes from fig-wood (συκίνου, 145).[38] Bdelykleon wryly notes the arrival of the chorus of Wasps at his house with another fig metaphor (and does it matter that the genitive of "wasp" (σφηκός) is so close to the word for "string of figs" (σφῆκος)?): he knows the jurors have arrived, he says, because he recognizes the sound of fig leaves crackling (ὡς ἐγὼ πολλῶν ἀκούσας οἶδα θρίων τὸν ψόφον, 436). The jurors are like men preparing for sexual intercourse; they are also men preparing to be "violently virile." The *Wasps* thus explicitly (and obscenely) draws a parallel between iretic and the erotic passions. In court the Wasps will "eat" lawsuits, they say (φάγοιμ', 511; φάγοις, 1367), "eating" being yet another metaphor frequently applied to sexual intercourse.[39] We are also reminded about Demosthenes' worry that delayed law suits become stale and cold.

---

[35] Henderson (1991a) 4, 46–7, 118, *et passim*; Buckheit (1960) 200–4. See Ar. *Peace* 1351ff.; Antiphanes 198; Pherecrates 197.

[36] Henderson (1991a) 118. See Ar. *Acharnians* 1102; *Knights* 707. Also for related terms *Lysistrata* 663; *Acharnians* 158–60.

[37] Henderson (1991a) 135, citing Plato Com. 255; Men. fr. 1071 (in Edmonds [1961] vol. IIIB). Note that κνίζων συκάμινα is to ripen figs (LXX Amos 7.14), according to LSJ. Also Pindar, *Nem.* 5.32: ὀργὰν κνίζων.

[38] Fig-wood (and other wild-woods) were commonly used for purificatory fires (Parker [1996] 221).

[39] On cooking and food as sexual euphemisms, see Henderson (1991a) 129, 142–3.

The Wasps' stings are a sign of their anger, but the word for their stings, κέντρα, is also, of course, a euphemism for *phalli* (407, 1115, 1121).[40] Reckford has argued: "The sting is a stand-in not just for anger, but for anger as a sexual surrogate" (1977: 307).[41] Philokleon himself links his anger to his sexual potency. He is afraid to acquit anybody for fear that he will wither away and/or dry up if he does (ἀποσκλῆναι, 160). Philokleon's fears are justified, it seems, since after Philokleon gives up on going to the courts, Aristophanes incorporates jokes about Philokleon's old-age incontinence and impotence (808, 1343, 1379ff.). The norms that regulated the male Athenian's use of anger were implicated in the norms that regulated his sexual self-representation. In tragedy women who punished were called manly and unwomanly. Men likewise affirmed their virility when they punished.

One scene of generational conflict in the play (in fact, generational conflict is a central theme in *Wasps*) makes this especially clear. One of the older jurors offers to give his young son a present and is dismayed when the boy asks for dried figs (ἰσχάδας, 297). The boy's father swears by Zeus and says that he would never grant his son's request, even if the boy were to hang himself out of disappointment. The elderly juror concludes his refusal by reiterating his amazement at the request for figs (σῦκα, 302).

The word for dried figs, ἰσχάδα, which could be used of female genitalia or of spent male genitalia, comes from ἰσχνός ("withered, lean, meager") and the verb ἰσχναίνω ("to make dry or withered, to dry up"). The verb could be used to denote what happened when the θυμός was tamed or satisfied or when a ripe and bursting feeling of anger had been dissolved (e.g. Aesch. *PV* 381–2, καὶ μὴ σφριγῶντα θυμὸν ἰσχναίνη βίᾳ).[42] The boy's request for dried figs (ἰσχάδας, 297) can be read in triplicate: it can be read as a request to have his own youthful anger/lust satisfied, and it can be read as a request for female genitalia, but it can also be read as a desire to see his father's anger spent and used up. The son's request for "dried figs/satisfied genitalia/spent lust" is both a request to be allowed to embark on public and sexual life and a request that his father retire from both forms of adult-male behavior. The boy seeks initiation into the world of adults, and his father responds by shifting the focus of the conversation

---

[40] On κέντρον see Henderson (1991a) 122; Padel (1992) 118, 121–2.

[41] E. Csapo, in his work on cockfights, has also found that the κέντρον is a symbol of the "cross-connection between sexual intercourse and physical violence and the intercourse and sport/combat homology" (1993: 1–28, 115–24).

[42] LSJ, s.v. According to Henderson, ἰσχάδας refers only to female genitalia and is never used in a sexual sense in Old Comedy. He therefore rejects Daele's interpretation of *Acharnians* 802 as including a reference to the phallus in the word ἰσχάδας. It seems to me that Daele is more likely to be right.

from dried figs to σῦκα, thus turning attention away from what is dried out and used up to what is fresh and ripe, from spent anger and lust to anger and lust that are still untapped. In other words, he turns attention away from the question of whether his own anger must come to an end and turns it toward the question of whether his son should be allowed to undertake the experiences of sexuality and anger. But "boys" are by definition too young to be asking for sexual or punitive satisfaction.

Anger, as the urge to punish, was a desire to rearrange human relationships, by harming or destroying them, according to the norms of reciprocity. *Eros* was also a desire to rearrange human relationships but by creating new ones. The passion of ὀργή, whether anger or *eros*, signaled the fact that a social disruption had arisen because an individual's desires were not in harmony with the structure of relationships in which he or she was situated and had inspired the individual to bring social relations into harmony with those desires. The isomorphism of anger and *eros* therefore rests on the fact that each produces a powerful desire to destabilize status-quo social relations. Like the fig, the vine (ὄρχος) was another euphemism for, and even pun on, the word for testicle (ὄρχις). And ὄρχις in turn was the name of a flower (the orchid) that was thought to have both aphrodisiac and anaphrodisiac properties. The orchid could, as an aphrodisiac, inspire people to create new social relationships or, as an anaphrodisiac, to end old ones; the same was true of ὀργή. In his father's eyes, the boy who requested figs was simply too young to be playing with the politically volatile practice of rearranging human relationships involved in both anger and *eros*. Like generational transitions, both wrongdoing and marriage had the power to destabilize the status quo and had to be regulated rigorously by the political order.

The meaning of the word "sycophant," the person who pointed out figs, thus depends on the symbolic weight of the fig as a representation of the intersection of anger and sexual lust. The sycophant somehow violated social norms that constrained the iretic and erotic behavior of citizens. Foucault argued that the Athenians (or Greeks in his terms) attempted to control those appetites considered "necessities" – such as hunger, the need for sleep, and sexual desire – by establishing an "economy of spending" them; the arousal and dispersal of desire had to be controlled. Like the other desires, anger could also be called a necessity and was likewise regulated by an "economy of spending," the rules of which are analogous to those regulating sexual desire.[43] In respect to sexual desire, a man had to be

---

[43] On anger as a form of necessity, see Allen (2000) 86–7.

temperate (σώφρων) and limit his indulgence, in order not to weaken himself.[44] The norms bounding sexuality also prescribed more specifically that the citizen indulge his desires neither for payment, nor for overly sensual purposes, nor (in the case of homosexuality) as the passive partner.[45] The norms for the prosecutor were parallel. He was expected to eschew prosecuting for payment, avoid indulging an excessive taste for provoking people and disrupting social relations, and reject serving as someone else's flunky. The man who followed these rules would be not merely a good citizen but also, on the analogy to sexual norms, a temperate man.

Norms for the "right use of *eros*" were transferable to the realm of anger. And, as it turns out, the metaphorical association between plants like the fig and the orchid and the passions works because the rules for using these fruits were themselves transferable to the use of the emotions. In the *Oeconomicus* Xenophon portrays Ischomachos as giving Socrates a lesson about the proper way to pick grapes, figs, and other fruit. The advice that Socrates receives helps to explain why "timing" was so important to the legitimacy of a prosecution. Xenophon writes:

The vine itself has many instructions for how to use it as well as possible . . . When its grapes are still unripe, it teaches you to shade anything in the sun throughout that season (περιπετανύουσα δὲ τὰ οἴναρα, ὅταν ἔτι αὐτῇ ἁπαλοὶ οἱ βότρυες ὦσι, διδάσκει σκιάζειν τὰ ἡλιούμενα ταύτην τὴν ὥραν); but when the moment (καιρός) comes for the bunches now to be sweetened by the sun, the vine, by shedding its leaves, teaches you to strip it and to ripen the fruit (καὶ πεπαίνειν τὴν ὀπώραν). Thanks to its fertility, the vine can expose ripe fruits, even while still bearing raw grapes (διὰ πολυφορίαν δὲ τοὺς μὲν πέπονας δεικνύουσα βότρυς, τοὺς δὲ ἔτι ὠμοτέρους φέρουσα). The last lesson is to harvest (τρυγᾶν) the fruit just as men pick figs: always go for the sexy (ripening/softening/fertile/angry) one (ὥσπερ τὰ σῦκα συκάζουσι, τὸ ὀργῶν ἀεί)! (*Oec.* 19.17–19)

The passage presents the rules for fruit gathering and nothing more. But the norms established for the farm are the same as the norms that syco-phants violated in the courtroom. The Athenian system of value included an ethics of proper use that applied to plants, objects, money, and passions. Xenophon's maxim, if read with an awareness of its potential for dense metaphoricity, reveals fundamental Athenian ethical principles and also the fact that cultural building blocks could be discussed under any number of guises. The use of the fig as a symbol for the sycophant is rooted in its actual use and treatment by the farmer.

---

[44] Winkler (1990b: 68) argues that there was a "system of balances since the prudent householder needs to control eros both in its arousal and in its dispersal"; see also Winkler (1991) 221.

[45] Henderson (1991a) 52, 205; also Foucault (1978).

Gathering figs is gathering what has ripened (τοὺς πέπονας) or what is full of ὀργή that needs to be assuaged. For that matter, the word for ripen (πεπαίνω) is also used as a metaphor to describe anger that needs to be softened or assuaged.[46] If one gathers too early, one gathers fruit that is raw (ὠμός) a typical feature of diseased ὀργή.[47] Ripeness and fruit gathering were also tropes used to discuss sexual readiness and intercourse.[48] Aristophanes was well acquainted with this metaphor. In the *Wealth* his character Trygaios, "the fruit gatherer," marries Opora, "the ripe fruit," in order to "produce grapes" (706–8). The activity of gathering that which is full of ὀργή is thus homologous both to dealing with anger and to sexual intercourse. The relation of fertility to both *eros* and anger allows for the metaphorical transfer of the rules of viticulture, fig gathering, heterosexuality, and homosexuality to processes of anger and punishment and makes punishment itself, which was the visible manifestation of anger, an analogue to sexual intercourse.

The Athenians had a number of fig-related words that could be used to insult those who misspent their erotic passions. In the *Peace* (1351) συκολογεῖν is used to describe excessive homosexual intercourse, and in *Wealth* (1970) συκοφάντρια is used for a woman who engages in excessive heterosexual intercourse. In another play, Kleon is essentially accused of being a homosexual rapist with a word that means "squeezing figs" (ἀποσυκάζω, *Knights* 259). He treats other people's "testicles" too aggressively and too lustily. Negative forms of sexual behavior included not only "fig squeezing" (ἀποσυκάζειν) but also a form of "fig gathering" (ψηνίζειν) that was another euphemism for homosexual contrectation.[49] Kleon violated the norms of *eros* by acting too aggressively.

But how did the sycophant, who "pointed out figs," violate the norms for standard use of the passions? According to Xenophon, the vine is supposed to point out to the farmer which fruits to pick and only those. There is therefore a right time and method for the exposure of ripe figs or of ὀργή. Likewise, there were rules about improper exposure in the sexual context. The desire to expose what should be hidden was a fundamental part of sexual aggression.[50] Calling attention to one's opponent's genitals was an act of

---

[46] Ar. *Wasps* 646; Xen. *Cyr.* 4.5.21; cf. *Iliad* 4.513; 9.565.

[47] Padel also points out that *ōmotēs*, in its biological sense, means "indigestion" (1992: 53).

[48] For ripeness and plants, see Theophr. *Hist. pl.* 3.6.9. For ripeness and disease, see Hippoc. *Acut.* 390. For ripeness and sexuality, see *Anth. Pal.* 12.185, 12.9; Anacreon 432 *PMG*. For ὀπώρα, see Pindar, *Isthm.* 2.4–5; Aesch. *Supp.* 998, 1015; Alexis fr. 165 Kock.

[49] Henderson (1991a) 47.   [50] Henderson (1991a) 2, 10.

violence and, according to Henderson (1971: 124), "references to testicles in Aristophanes almost always occur in threats (to rip out someone's testicles) or in violent erotic advances (seizing the testicles in preparation for sexual contact) (e.g. *Clouds* 713, *Birds* 442)."

Presumably the sycophant "showed his own figs" or manly vigor inappropriately and also denigrated other people by shaming them too aggressively and by pointing out facts about their lives that should have been kept out of the public eye. As Isocrates wrote (15.315), the sycophant "shows to all his rawness, his misanthropy, and his fondness for making enemies (τούτους δ' ἐν ἅπασιν ἐπιδείκνυσθαι τὴν αὐτῶν ὠμότητα καὶ μισανθρωπίαν καὶ φιλαπεχθημοσύνην)." In misspending in the economy of pleasures, the sycophant stood with the *moichos*, the male prostitute, and the citizen who violated the norms of homosexual love – an exclusive club for those *ponēroi* or base men who did not deserve to be active citizens.[51] The intersection of anger and sexuality in the trope of figs does not allow us to produce an epigrammatic definition of who or what the sycophant was but it does allow us to see the web of meaning within which the sycophant's bad reputation and dirty name were established. That web of meaning is based on an ethical system that coalesced around the problem of trying to deal with desire. The sycophant violates the economy of desire by initiating the processes of anger when the time or situation is not appropriate. Thus Demosthenes describes the statute of limitations as having been drawn up specifically in order to prevent sycophancy (36.26–7).[52]

The ban on the sycophant's acts of "exposure" limited excessive aggressiveness in the judicial system. The Athenian requirement that speakers explain their personal interest ensured that prosecutors had only an "honest" interest in sating a "ripe" anger and were not acting for some more savage and unseasonable ulterior motive. The economy of anger put limits on the number of public conflicts and disputes in which any individual could be legitimately involved, just as the economy of desire put limits on the number and kind of homosexual love affairs an Athenian citizen could have and still maintain a political role in the city. The vilification of the sycophant helped to ward off the much decried oligarchic activity of too frequent

[51] See Wallace (1994). Isocrates (15.314, 324) discusses the *graphē* against sycophants. The criticisms that orators launch at their opponents for their misuse of anger fit the analytical framework established by the idea of an "economy of spending." See Lys. 1.28; 25.5; Dem. 58.31–2; Aeschin. 3.3; Demades 1.1–4. On the general baseness of sycophants, see Lys. 12.5–6; 25.19–30; Dem. 58.64. The sycophant could misbehave outside the courtroom also; on this, see Aeschin. 2.145.
[52] See also Dem. 48.6 where he tells an audience how he knew when the time was not right for anger.

and too comprehensive punishment.[53] Indeed, the rhetoric of sycophancy established an ethics for the male use of anger that kept aggressive competition from doing damage to the public sphere, just as the ethics for the female use of anger kept the Athenian valorization of ὀργή from doing damage to the private sphere.

Greek and Athenian social critics, if I may call them that, were themselves aware of the centrality of ὀργή to social organization. Hesiod, Aristophanes, and Plato all used a single intriguing image to say so. One of the earliest two instances of the word ὀργή is in Hesiod's *Works and Days*. There Hesiod uses the word ὀργή as part of a comparison between busy and lazy men, where the former are like bees and the latter, like drones. Hesiod writes: "Both gods and men are angry with a man who lives idle, for in respect to his ὀργή he is like the stingless drones (κηφήνεσσι κοθούροις εἴκελος ὀργήν) who waste the labor of the bees, eating without working; let it be your care to order your work properly" (*Op.* 304). Social hierarchies and evaluative systems are thus represented as turning around assessments of an individual's relationship to his ὀργή.

Hesiod uses the bee/drone binary opposition again in the *Theogony* but there to bemoan the presence in society not of lazy men, but of women. Hesiod's narration of the creation of Pandora and the birth of the race of women includes the remark that women are like the lazy drones (κηφῆνες) who consume all the labor of men, who are the hard-working bees (μέλισσαι) (594).[54] As in the *Works and Days*, the bee/drone image separates the lazy from the hard-working, the bad from the good, the ethically impugnable from the morally respectable. But here the distinction turns around gender instead of around the positive and negative versions of ὀργή possessed by the good and bad worker respectively. Gender distinctions and distinctions turning on the ethics of ὀργή are parallels.

---

[53] On the importance of ἡσυχία, or peace and quiet, and the prejudice against hubristic activism, see I. Carter (1986). For a conflation of the oligarchs and sycophants, see Xen. *Hell.* 2.3.22; Lys. 12.4–5, 20; Andoc. 1.99; Theophr. *Char.* 26. For oligarchic over-prosecution, see Lys. 12.17; 13.45–54, 56, 66; 26.13; Xen. *Hell.* 2.3.17; Dem. 24.164–6; Aeschin. 3.220. For a false report of excessive use of whipping, imprisonment, and execution by the oligarchs, see Thuc. 8.74.

[54]
ὡς δ' ὁπότ' ἐν σμήνεσσι κατηρεφέεσσι μέλισσαι
κηφῆνας βόσκωσι, κακῶν ξυνήονας ἔργων—   [595]
αἳ μέν τε πρόπαν ἦμαρ ἐς ἡέλιον καταδύντα
ἡμάτιαι σπεύδουσι τιθεῖσί τε κηρία λευκά,
οἳ δ' ἔντοσθε μένοντες ἐπηρεφέας κατὰ σίμβλους
ἀλλότριον κάματον σφετέρην ἐς γαστέρ' ἀμῶνται—
ὡς δ' αὔτως ἄνδρεσσι κακὸν θνητοῖσι γυναῖκας   [600]
Ζεὺς ὑψιβρεμέτης θῆκεν, ξυνήονας ἔργων
ἀργαλέων·

The bee/drone opposition is, of course, central to the conceit founding Aristophanes' *Wasps*. The depiction of the jurors as wasps whose stings represent both their anger and their erotic desires seems to come direct from Hesiod. The juror-wasps are equivalent to bees and Aristophanes quotes Hesiod's image when he wants to set up an opposition between the jurors, who are wasp-like, and their demagogic leaders, who are drone-like. Just as Hesiod's bees resent drones who do not work, Aristophanes' wasps resent the demagogues "who sit among us as drones (κηφῆνες), don't have a sting (οὐκ ἔχοντες κέντρον), and are homebodies who devour the fruit of our tribute without lifting a finger" (1114–16).[55] The juror-wasps, like bees, have stings and stand in opposition to the demagogue-drones who do not. The jurors' stings represent both their anger and their erotic desires, and the symbolism of the sting implies that both passions are relevant to their role as jurors and citizens. Their stings are their badges of office. In contrast, the demagogues' parasitic nature is in part related to their lack of stings, their unsatisfactory constitution in respect to erotic and iretic ὀργή. Like Hesiod, Aristophanes draws on this bee/drone image as part of his analysis of how ὀργή and passion generate social categories and hierarchies that should be subject to ethical evaluation.

Plato is the third writer to use the bee/drone binary to discuss the role of passion in the life of a citizen, and he too treats ὀργή as being, on the Athenian account, a fundamentally relevant passion. Plato uses the symbol of the bees and drones in his Book 9 discussion of the disintegration of the ideal city, but before we get there we should note how central is a rejection of the Athenian concept of ὀργή to Plato's redefinition of anger in the *Republic*. Socrates' attempt to convince Glaucon that the soul is tripartite and divided into reason, anger, and desire aspires explicitly to undermine the centrality of ὀργή to Athenian thought. Glaucon initially and instinctually resists the suggestion that the soul is divided into reason, anger, and desire, and he argues instead that the soul is only bipartite and that anger might perhaps be identified as a twin to desire (Σωκ· ταῦτα μὲν τοίνυν, ἦν δ᾽ ἐγώ, δύο ἡμῖν ὡρίσθω εἴδη ἐν ψυχῇ ἐνόντα· τὸ δὲ δὴ τοῦ θυμοῦ καὶ ᾧ θυμούμεθα πότερον τρίτον, ἢ τούτων ποτέρῳ ἂν εἴη ὁμοφυές; Γλ· ἴσως, ἔφη, τῷ ἑτέρῳ, τῷ ἐπιθυμητικῷ, 439e). Glaucon's resistance to Socrates' ideas and his very Athenian association of anger to erotic desire inspire Socrates to tell the story of Leontios in his effort to

---

[55] MacDowell treats the *Wasps*' speech here as having primarily to do with financial issues, particularly their desire for an old age pension (1971, repr. 1995: 156).

prove to Glaucon that the soul is divided into three, and not two, parts. The story goes like this: Leontios was on his way up from the Peiraeus to the city when he noticed the corpses of executed wrongdoers lying beside the city walls. After struggling to keep himself from looking at the corpses, Leontios at last gave up, cursed his eyes, and ran up to the corpses to feast his eyes on them. Socrates glosses the Leontios story thus: "This story surely means that anger sometimes does battle against the desires as a thing distinct from the thing it battles (ὁ λόγος σημαίνει τὴν ὀργὴν πολεμεῖν ἐνίοτε ταῖς ἐπιθυμίαις ὡς ἄλλο ὂν ἄλλῳ)" (440a). Socrates uses the story to make a conceptual separation between anger and erotic desire and this separation is central to his rejection of the fourth-century Athenian approach to the role of anger in human life and politics. For that matter, Socrates rejects the word ὀργή itself as a term of analysis and replaces the fourth-century passional vocabulary that turned around it with his invented vocabulary of spiritedness (e.g. θυμοειδής).[56]

Much more could be said about the Platonic transition from ὀργή to spiritedness, and about its politics, but I will have to be content for now to note that the Socratic change from ὀργή to spiritedness in the *Republic* is central to the blueprint for the ideal city. After all, the city is built entirely out of citizens whose souls have been reorganized along tripartite lines and whose psychology has been reconstituted. Once this happens, women can even join in politics. When Socrates describes, at the end of Book 9, the inevitable disintegration of the ideal city, the descent – from oligarchy through democracy into tyranny – involves a reverse evolution in which the citizens' souls fall ever farther away from the paradigm offered by Platonic psychology. As their Platonic passions disintegrate, the bee/drone image reappears:[57]

[56] The substantive ὀργή is used in only three other places in the *Republic*: once to describe the desires and passions of a "beast" (493a), once to describe the "humors" or "tempers" of the masses (493d), and once to describe what happens when anger has not been entirely brought under control (572a). The adjective ὀργίλος is used once and the passion it represents is criticized and set in opposition to the high-spiritedness of the man who is θυμοειδής (411c). The word θυμοειδής is a Platonic invention but calls to mind Homeric words, both for its stress on the *thumos* and because of the suffix *-eidēs*. There are twenty-eight instances of it in the *Republic* and only three more elsewhere in the Platonic corpus. For that matter, the word θυμοειδής generally belongs to the vocabulary of philosophers and scientists, appearing only in Xenophon, Hippocrates, and Aristotle. Socrates has not only challenged the Athenian conceptualization of anger but he has erased it. The word ὀργή can no longer be used once desire and anger have been separated from one another. Socrates finalizes the erasure of ὀργή by inventing a new vocabulary of anger to replace it. He has replaced the Athenian soul with a new one and his work is complete because what was inconceivable to Glaucon has become conceivable. The Platonic vocabulary of passion – a vocabulary that uses new words for both anger and erotic desire – seals the transition from the Athenian paradigm for thinking about human cognitive and passional experience to the Socratic/Platonic paradigm.

[57] Compare this to the reference to bees and wasps in *Phaedo* 81e–82b.

Should we say about this man that, just as a drone arises in a cell [of the honeycomb] and is a disease for the hive (ὡς ἐν κηρίῳ κηφὴν ἐγγίγνεται, σμήνους νόσημα), this type of man in his own home is like the drone and is a disease to the city . . . and indeed hasn't god made all the flying drones stingless (ἀκέντρους) while some of those on foot are stingless and some have fearsome stings (δεινὰ κέντρα)? And from the stingless ones, beggars result by old age. And from the ones with stings, arise all those people called criminals (κακοῦργοι) . . . In such a city are there not many criminals who are possessed of stings and whom the rulers restrain with the stewardship of force (οὓς ἐπιμελείᾳ βίᾳ κατέχουσιν αἱ ἀρχαί) . . .? And shall we not say that such people come to be this way because of a lack of education, a bad upbringing, and the set-up of their constitution (ἆρ' οὖν οὐ δι' ἀπαιδευσίαν καὶ κακὴν τροφὴν καὶ κατάστασιν τῆς πολιτείας φήσομεν τοὺς τοιούτους αὐτόθι ἐγγίγνεσθαι). (552c–e)

Socrates redefines the category of drone to include not only stingless types but also drones with stings, a category that did not exist in Hesiod or Aristophanes and that does not exist in nature. Those drones without stings beg money from others in order to satisfy the basic physical desires that they are no longer capable of fulfilling on their own. They are like the drones who do not labor in Hesiod and Aristophanes. Those with stings attempt to fulfill their desires by acting too aggressively; they can be controlled only by the oversight of magistrates. In a certain sense, they are also Aristophanes' wasps, but criminalized by Plato. In introducing drones with stings, Plato reveals how much he vilifies the Athenian valorization of ὀργή. Much more could be said here but I will limit myself to the point that Plato uses the negative symbol of the drone precisely when he wants to stress the degree to which the success of his ideal city will depend on a rejection of Athenian paradigms for thinking about passion and ὀργή.

In all four cases of its use, the dichotomous bee/drone images establish a social hierarchy in which the lazy are distinguished from the hardworking, the bad from the good, the ethically impugnable from the morally respectable. The image also separates the male from the female. The construction of the bee/drone image, as it appears in Hesiod, Aristophanes, and Plato, is therefore predicated on a recognition that the ethics of ὀργή interacts with the construction of social categories and hierarchies. Secondly, the categories of social value with which the principles of ὀργή interact are those of the most rigorous and fundamental kind, which is to say binary systems of moral evaluation. Moreover, the gender hierarchy in Greek thought, which established the male as good and the female as bad, maps onto a hierarchy where those whose ὀργή is correctly constituted are superior to those whose ὀργή is incorrectly constituted. Social, ethical, passional, and gender concepts are overlaid on one another in the image of the bee and drone because citizenship, for both men and women, was defined in terms of a set of social and ethical criteria grounded in the idea of ὀργή, in a flexible and contradictory idea of desire. Sophocles gave an accurate description of politics as the Athenians knew it when, in the "Ode to Man" of the *Antigone*, he had a chorus praise humankind for having taught itself political skills that include not only judgment and voice but also ἀστυνόμους ὀργάς or "tempers that regulate (or are regulated by) the city" (354–5). The passion ὀργή has political weight. It worked within law and institutions, responding to and inflecting them, but it too, in turn, could be modified by Athens' political discourse.

CHAPTER 4

Aristotle on anger and the emotions: the strategies of status

David Konstan

In an undergraduate class to which I had assigned the second book of Aristotle's *Rhetoric* (in translation), I asked the students each to draw up a list of ten emotions. It was remarkable how small an overlap there was between their inventories and the passions analyzed by Aristotle. Anger was prominent in both sets, but beyond that, there was little agreement. Among the emotions suggested by the students which do not figure in Aristotle's discussion were grief, sorrow, sadness, happiness, jealousy, missing someone, and loneliness. None of the students, on the other hand, mentioned pity, envy, indignation, shame, gentleness, confidence, rivalry, or gratitude. The difference between Aristotle's catalogue and the composite set assembled from my students' lists is indicative of two very different points of view on the passions.[1] It also suggests that even in the case of anger, where both rosters dovetailed, Aristotle's conception is likely to diverge substantially from what our own intuitions might suggest.[2]

In this paper, I examine in detail Aristotle's account of anger, which in fact is quite foreign, in many ways, to modern notions.[3] This first part is necessarily the most technical. Following that, I attempt to situate Aristotle's treatment of anger in the context of his understanding of the passions in general, and I conclude by considering how Aristotle's interpretation

---

[1] The difference in the inventories is not just a function of the students' naive responses; modern lists of the so-called basic emotions typically include happiness, sadness, interest, disgust, acceptance, anticipation or expectancy, and panic – none of these Aristotelian categories – along with rage or anger and fear. See LeDoux (1996) 112–14 for a summary of the various theories; also Hillman (1992) 40–1; cf. Barbalet (1998) 82: "Confidence is conventionally not thought of as an emotion."

[2] Planalp (1999: 176) cites Schoeck (1966) for the view that "envy is particularly unmentionable in the United States because Americans do not want to admit that they are not all equals" (cf. Hochschild [1975] 292: "Envy without a social movement is a particularly private, unlegitimated feeling"). The ideology of equality in classical Athens does not appear to have had the same repressive effect on the concept of *phthonos*.

[3] See R. C. Solomon (1984) 242: "Anger is an emotion that would seem to be universal and unlearned if any emotion is." Solomon goes on to indicate how risky this assumption is. See also Rosaldo (1984) 144–5.

of anger relates to his treatment of other passions that are included in his survey. I shall not on this occasion investigate what principles might inform the array of emotions proposed by my students, although I have the impression that the sentiments they selected are more like inner states of feeling, rather than responses to the behavior of others – apart, that is, from the instance of amorous relations.

ARISTOTLE'S ACCOUNT OF ANGER

Aristotle defines anger as "a desire, accompanied by pain, for a perceived revenge, on account of a perceived slight on the part of people who are not fit to slight one or one's own" (*Rh.* 2.2.1378a31–3). Why "accompanied by pain"? Presumably this element is required by the definition of the *pathē* that Aristotle offered shortly before: "Let the emotions be all those things on account of which people change their minds and differ in regard to their judgments, and upon which attend pain and pleasure, for example anger, pity, fear, and all other such things and their opposites" (2.1.1378a20–3). Aristotle did not intend this as a rigorous or exhaustive account of the nature of the *pathē*. Clearly, it is designed to serve his present purpose, which is to instruct the orator in how to manipulate the emotions of his audience; hence the emphasis placed on the effect of the emotions on judgment (*kriseis*), in the sense of a verdict or decision. The introduction of pain and pleasure here may be a succinct way of distinguishing emotional responses from those based exclusively on reason or enthymemes, a topic which Aristotle treated with particular pride in the first book of the *Rhetoric*.[4]

Pain and pleasure themselves do not count, for Aristotle, as emotions. Rather, they are sensations or *aisthēseis*. A painful sensation may arise either as a result of direct perception, or else by way of *phantasia*, that is, through recollection or anticipation of something perceived. In Aristotle's own words: "since feeling pleasure is in the perception of some experience [*pathos*], and *phantasia* is a weak kind of perception [*aisthēsis*], some *phantasia* of what one remembers or expects always occurs in a person when he remembers or expects something . . . Thus, it is necessary that all pleasures are either present in perception or arise in remembering things that have happened or in expecting things that will happen" (1.11.1370a27–34).[5]

---

[4] The same criterion is invoked, however, at *Eth. Nic.* 2.5.1105b21–3.

[5] The relationship between *phantasia* and *aisthēsis* in Aristotle is controversial, and I shall not enter into the details of the debate on this occasion. The most relevant evidence is *De anima* 3.3 and *De insomniis* 2.459a15–19, where *phantasia* is said to be a motion that arises from (or as a result of) the activity of perception.

What is the pain that accompanies anger? It seems reasonable to suppose that it results from direct perception of something harmful or unpleasant, rather than from memory or anticipation, as is the case, for example, with fear, which Aristotle defines as "arising from the *phantasia* of a future evil that is fatal or harmful" (*ek phantasias mellontos kakou phthartikou ē lupērou*, 2.5.1382a21–2). If this is so, the pain of anger would differ from the pleasure that is also associated with this emotion, and which derives from the desire to avenge the slight that has been suffered. For this desire is accompanied by the expectation (*elpis*) of its fulfillment, which we regard as possible (if we did not, we would not be experiencing the emotion that Aristotle defines as anger). Aristotle offers a second reason for the pleasure we feel when angry, namely, that by dwelling on revenge in our minds (*dianoia*), the *phantasia* that thereby arises instills pleasure, analogous to that we feel in dreams (2.2.1378b1–9). I am not sure I understand the difference between the two reasons: the expectation of revenge is pleasurable, I would have imagined, because of the impression that comes with it. At all events, the pain connected with anger, unlike the pleasure, seems at first blush to derive not from a *phantasia* of past or future harm or unpleasantness, but from the perception of something that is present.

Nevertheless, it is important to note the parallel expressions Aristotle employs in the definition of anger: "a perceived (*phainomenēs*) revenge on account of a perceived (*phainomenēn*) slight." The verb *phainomai* is not so technical as *phantasia*, but in light of the discussion that follows, it is not unreasonable to understand *phainomenēs timōrias* as "imagined revenge."[6] Is the slight, then, also imagined, in the sense of being remembered rather than anticipated? It is possible, it seems to me, that Aristotle is thinking of anger as a durable feeling, which arises on the spot as an *aisthēsis* but is kept alive through subsequent reflection upon or recollection of the slight received. In his definition of pity, it is true, Aristotle specifies that it is a painful feeling in response to "a perceived evil that is either fatal or painful" (*epi phainomenōi kakōi phthartikōi ē lupērōi*) that has befallen another person who has not deserved it (2.8.1385b13–14). Here, the term may indicate simply that the other's harm or pain must be apparent to the onlooker. Or else, Aristotle may mean that the event that inspires pity must seem harmful, in the sense that, whatever view the sufferer holds of his condition, we pity him only if it seems a misfortune to us. On this view, Aristotle would be signaling by the word *phainomenēn* that the slight

---

[6] Nussbaum (1996: 307) suggests that *phantasia* is not so much a technical term as the abstract noun corresponding to the verb *phainomai*.

in question must be perceived as such – for one could always treat it as beneath one's notice, as Aristotle says we do when we are firmly of the opinion that we excel in the quality in respect to which another mocks us (1379b1–2).[7] But there is a third possibility in the case of pity: perhaps the phrase *phainomenōi kakōi* points to the difference between the direct experience or perception of the evil by the person pitied, and the mere *phantasia* of that evil on the part of the pitier, who after all does not suffer it himself.[8]

I have been assuming that the "perceived slight" that generates anger – whether it is immediate, recollected, or interpreted as such – is unpleasant in itself (just as the thought of revenge is pleasurable) and hence a source of pain. The problem with this interpretation, however, is that it appears to make the expression "accompanied by pain" redundant. Perhaps Aristotle means to indicate that not every offense, even if perceived as such and associated with a desire for revenge, is necessarily a source of anger. If we are wondering what other sort of reaction Aristotle might have in mind, we may look ahead to his discussion of hatred, which Aristotle distinguishes from anger, among other ways, by noting that "the one is accompanied by pain, while the other is not accompanied by pain; for one who is angry feels pain, but one who hates does not" (2.4.1382a12–13; cf. *Politics* 5.8.1312b25–34). Hatred is a response to what is harmful or vicious (*kakon*) in general, and not just to a slight, and certain forms of harm – Aristotle singles out vice itself (*kakia*), for example injustice or stupidity – are practically imperceptible (*hēkista aisthēta*, 2.4.1382a9–11), and hence not particularly painful. Since spite (*epēreasmos*), which is listed as one of the three types of slight in Aristotle's treatment of anger (2.2.1378b14), is also cited as one of the causes of hatred or enmity (2.4.1382a2), it would appear that a slight can generate not just anger but also a kind of hostility that is not necessarily accompanied by pain, and therefore incompatible with anger.

Does this mean that the slight, in this case, is not itself painful or unpleasant? I think that we can take it for granted that any slight is disagreeable. However, the primary characteristic or expression of anger (as opposed to its cause) in Aristotle's definition is the desire for revenge, and it is this, according to Aristotle, that must, in the case of anger, be accompanied by

---

[7] Whatever the precise sense of *phainomenos* in the passage, two solutions strike me as poor ones. The first is to take the word in the sense of "manifest," that is, "substantial" or "appreciable"; thus, W. Rhys Roberts, in the Barnes edition (1984) of the complete works of Aristotle in translation, renders the phrase "a conspicuous revenge for a conspicuous slight" (p. 2195; cf. Grimaldi [1988] 21 ad 1378a31.3, who takes it to mean "manifest" or "public"). The second is simply to delete *phainomenēs* before *timōrias*, with Spengel and Ross (most editors retain it).

[8] For a more detailed discussion of Aristotle's view of pity, see Konstan (2001) 128–36.

pain. I am inclined to think that this desire is both pleasant, insofar as it involves the anticipated consummation of the revenge, and painful, insofar as it is attended as well by the recollection or thought of the slight that has motivated the desire.[9] It is, then, the persistence of the pain deriving from the (originally painful) slight that accompanies and indeed inspires the desire for revenge, and constitutes it as anger.[10]

That anger should, for Aristotle, arise specifically and indeed exclusively from a slight, rather than from other kinds of deliberate harm that another person might inflict, is remarkable, and will be the focus of attention in what follows. A slight is a complex social event, and requires a considerable measure of judgment in order to be recognized or perceived as such.[11] Indeed, Aristotle makes it clear within the definition of anger itself that a slight as such – a particular remark or gesture, for example – is not the cause of the emotion; rather, it must be a slight on the part of someone who is not fit or suited (*prosēkōn*) to be the author of it. I shall return shortly to the question of just what it is that might befit an individual to render such an offense. For the moment, I may attend to the element of discrimination

---

[9] I cannot agree with Grimaldi (1998) 25 ad 1378b1–2 that "The feeling dominant in the emotion anger is *hēdonē*." Compare *Eth. Nic.* 4.5.1126a21–2, where Aristotle says that "revenge ends one's anger, instilling pleasure in place of pain"; the pleasure of revenge is dominant only after the revenge has been realized, and that puts an end to anger. D. Frede (1996) argues that the mixture of pleasure and pain in the emotions as described in the *Rhetoric* betrays the still lively influence upon Aristotle of Plato's account in the *Philebus*; by the time he wrote the *Nicomachean Ethics*, Aristotle had moved away from the Platonic notion of "process-pleasures" to his own mature view of "activity-pleasures" (p. 278). Striker (1996) draws the line rather between the brief account of the emotions in *Rhetoric* 1.10–11, where Plato's influence is still palpable, and the more detailed description of the individual emotions in *Rhetoric* 2.2–11; here, even if painful emotions may be associated with pleasures, pleasure is not a necessary ingredient in them (p. 291). Striker argues that in this part Aristotle is clearly moving toward a dichotomized classification of emotions according to pleasure versus pain (p. 292), which anticipates the later elaboration of this opposition by the Stoics (p. 294). I believe that Striker's account is basically correct: although a *phantasia* of pleasure accompanies the desire for revenge that constitutes anger (as it does all desires), the essential characteristic of this desire in particular is that it is accompanied by pain. Aspasius, in his digression on the emotions in his commentary on Aristotle's *Nicomachean Ethics* (pp. 42.27–47.2 Heylbut), affirms that the emotions are grouped generically according to *hēdonē* and *lupē*; contra Sorabji (1999), who would see desire or appetite (at least) as essential to the Aristotelian classification.

[10] A consideration of three passages in the *Topics* may offer some support for this view. At 4.5.125b28–34, Aristotle states that pain cannot be equated with anger, since pain is prior to anger and not vice versa (the priority is both temporal and causal here); I take it that the painful thing from which anger follows is just the slight. At 4.6.127b26–32, Aristotle argues that pain involved in anger and the suspicion (*hupolēpsis*) of a slight are two distinct aspects of anger (both of which may seem to fall in the category of essence); this pain, perhaps, is the one that accompanies anger, rather than the prior pain (associated with the direct experience of the slight) that is its cause. Finally, at 6.13.151a14–19, Aristotle states that being caused by pain is not the same as being accompanied by pain.

[11] See R. C. Solomon (1984) 250: "Anger . . . is essentially a *judgmental* emotion, a perception of an offense (as Aristotle argued in *Rhetoric*). It consists of a series of concepts and judgments that among other ingredients, involve the concept of blame."

or evaluation, involving at the very least the ability to distinguish between people who have or have not the right to speak or act in determinate ways, that is implicit in Aristotle's definition of anger. For it is clear that anger, for Aristotle, is anything but an automatic reflex or instinct.

EMOTIONS AND COGNITION

It is now more than two decades since scholars began paying serious attention to the cognitive aspect of Aristotle's theory of the emotions.[12] This development coincided with a shift of perspective in modern philosophical, biological, anthropological, and psychological accounts of the emotions, which in recent years have attended more and more to the role of cognition. Indeed, there have even been efforts to define the emotions entirely in terms of cognitive processes.[13] All this is in sharp contrast to the polarized opposition between reason and passion that has been characteristic of post-Cartesian philosophy and continues to prevail in popular thought.[14] The view that the emotions are irrational coincided with a tendency, beginning at the end of the nineteenth century, to explain emotions entirely in physical terms, thereby ignoring the element of judgment altogether. The article "Emotion" (part 1 of "Human Emotion and Motivation") in *The New Encyclopedia Britannica* (1986), by Endre Grastyán, Professor of Physiology at the Medical University of Pécs in Hungary, is concerned, as one might expect from the author's specialty, almost exclusively with the organic basis of the emotions. Dr. Grastyán writes (348): "Investigation into so-called emotional phenomena increasingly is being directed toward objective biological evidence." Noting that Charles Darwin's last treatise,

---

[12] A turning point was Fortenbaugh (1975).

[13] Lazarus, Kanner, and Folkman (1980: 198), for example, define emotion as "consisting of cognitive appraisals, action impulses, and patterned somatic reactions," and assert: "Emotions and cognitions are thus inseparable." R. C. Solomon (1984: 249) states (and endorses) a strong version of "a cognitive theory of the emotions" which holds that "an understanding of the conceptual and learned appetitive functions of emotion is all that there is in identifying and distinguishing them from each other and from non-emotions" (the weak version is that these are sufficient conditions). For a survey of modern studies of cognitive aspects of the emotions, together with a critique of definitions of the emotions based exclusively on cognitive properties, see Griffiths (1997) 21–43.

[14] See, for example, Damasio (1994) xi: "I had been advised early in life that sound decisions came from a cool head, that emotions and reason did not mix any more than oil and water"; cf. Hillman (1992) 188; Bailey (1983) 24: "The dichotomy between reason and emotion is part of our overt culture; that is, part of the shield of falsification by which we make life comprehensible"; Barbalet (1998) 29–61. The view has a long pedigree: Plutarch, for example, in his *Comparison of Theseus and Romulus* (3.1), speaks of the "irrational temper" (*thumos alogistos*) and "anger's unreasoning haste" (*orgē echousa tachos aboulon*) that drove Theseus to slay his son and Romulus his brother; see Alexiou (1999) 104.

The Expression of the Emotions in Man and Animals (1872, repr. 1955), "had a profound influence in systematizing emotion research," Grastyán explains that subsequent studies have focused on visible and ostensibly adaptive responses such as aggression, fright, and fawning, as well as stress responses, involuntary crying and laughing, sleep patterns, and the like – behaviors which scarcely qualify as emotions in Aristotle's understanding of the term. Researchers also began to explore the operations of the sympathetic and parasympathetic nervous systems: the pioneer here was the physiologist Walter B. Cannon, who emphasized the role of the emotions in fight or flight reactions. Symptoms such as rate of heartbeat, blood-sugar levels, production of adrenalin and serotonin, galvanic skin response, and respiration were carefully measured. Finally, the function of the emotions was associated with drives, energy levels, and efforts directed toward the successful attainment of goals: recall that the second part of the *Encyclopedia Britannica* article treats the topic of motivation. The heir to this research program has been, on the one hand, the studies of affect undertaken by Paul Ekman and his associates (e.g. Ekman 1982), and, on the other hand, the recent vogue of evolutionary psychology, represented by a slew of popular volumes, many of dubious scientific value.[15]

Aristotle too maintains that the emotions have a physical basis in the organism (see *De anima* 1.1.403a16-b2, esp. 403a25: *ta pathē logoi enuloi eisin*), but he does not reduce the emotions to material states such as the temperature of blood around the heart. In the *Rhetoric*, of course, he is interested in the passions above all for their role in persuasion rather than as stimuli to action; accordingly, he emphasizes the rational and evaluative components of the *pathē*, which may be influenced by speech. But the cognitive aspect is indispensable to an account of the passions as such, despite the confident claim of Lewis, Amini, and Lannon (2000: 42) that "most emotions require no thinking at all."

The weakness in the physiological view of anger is apparent in the following hypothetical situation. A woman is pushed violently from behind. Instinctively, her muscles tense and her heart beats faster. She may move to escape or defend herself, perhaps aggressively, by striking at her assailant. But is she angry?

Very possibly, but if so, it is because she has made a snap but complex judgment about the event which at least includes a supposition about

---

[15] Sober, if not uniformly enlightening, studies are Zahn-Waxler, Cummings, and Iannotti (1986), and Barkow, Cosmides, and Tooby (1992). In a more popular vein are Buss (1994), Buss (2000), and Lewis, Amini, and Lannon (2000). Anger has been defended from a phenomenological perspective, e.g. Milhaven (1989); for an accessible and sensible survey of views on anger, see Tavris (1989).

the motives of the person – let us say it is a man – who shoved her: for example, that his action was intended to harm her, and that she had done nothing to deserve it. Aristotle (*Rh.* 8.3.1380b16–18) points out that we do not respond with anger when we have done wrong and are suffering justly, for then the slight is not inappropriate, as his definition requires. If she subsequently finds out that he pushed her by accident, she will very likely cease to be angry.[16] As Aristotle observes in his discussion of gentleness or calming down, which he treats as the opposite of anger, a slight must be voluntary, and people therefore react mildly toward unintentional offenses, or toward people who wished to do the opposite of what they in fact did (2.3.1380a8–12).[17]

Suppose that she discovers that the man pushed her in order to save her life – say she was standing in the path of an oncoming car. In this case, she not only gives over her anger, but presumably feels grateful instead. She may respond physically to the sudden, though belated, awareness of the danger with symptoms that resemble those associated with anger – rapid breathing, increased heart rate – but what she feels is relief rather than rage. Or, if the bodily manifestations of anger are just what induces the emotion itself (as William James famously argued), then perhaps she will direct this anger at the driver of the car.[18]

Anger, then, involves a judgment of intentions. That is why we do not normally get angry at stones – this is particularly clear if, with Aristotle, we understand by anger an emotion entailing a desire for revenge that is accompanied, as I suggest, by an enduring pain deriving from a recollected insult. We do not stay furious with a stone, however much it hurts to stub our toe on it, since stubbing is not snubbing (see Ben Ze'ev [2000] 30). In

---

[16] Compare Strawson (1974) 5: "If someone treads on my hand accidentally, while trying to help me, the pain may be no less acute than if he treads on it in contemptuous disregard of my existence or with a malevolent wish to injure me. But I shall generally feel in the second case a kind and degree of resentment that I shall not feel in the first." One's feelings change as new knowledge of another's motives is acquired.

[17] There is reason to believe that stimuli that result in emotional responses are, in certain cases, communicated by two distinct pathways in the brain. In the case of a shove, for example, a message indicating danger may travel directly from the thalamus to the amygdala, triggering the relevant reaction; the thalamus may also transmit information to the sensory cortex, which processes the stimulus in a more refined manner, and sends these complex data in turn to the amygdala, permitting a second, more reflective response (the shove was of a sort likely to be accidental, etc.). Whether judgments of any kind are involved in transmissions by the shorter pathway is unclear; in any case, this process has a relatively small bearing on the example offered in the text. For discussion, see LeDoux (1996) 168–78; Elster (1999b) 31–5.

[18] LeDoux (1996: 43) sums up James' position crisply in the formula that we do not run from a bear because we are afraid, "we are afraid because we run;" cf. James (1884).

addition to the intentions of the other, moreover, anger depends also on one's own values, that is, what one regards as good or bad, desirable or the reverse. Suppose the woman in our thought experiment knew the car was approaching, and intended to commit suicide by hurling herself in front of it. The man, by shoving her, prevented her from taking her life. Is she angry at him? Again, it will depend, in part, on whether she believes that he was aware of her purpose and deliberately thwarted it. Note how the same act and intention that evoked the woman's gratitude in the previous scenario now rouse her ire. Anger depends, as Aristotle was aware, on an intricate and subtle set of judgments; it is anything but a reflex.[19]

It is conceivable, albeit unlikely in my view, that a sufficiently refined physiology of anger might be able to single out all cases of true anger – in which the subject had taken account of intentions and other psychological and ethical factors – from other emotions as well as from instinctive reactions such as the startle effect.[20] Such an account of anger would, nevertheless, be crucially deficient, and not only because it would be lacking a phenomenological description of the subject's inner state of consciousness.[21] On a purely physical analysis, the means of augmenting or diminishing anger reduce to the manipulation of its organic manifestations: raising or lowering blood pressure, heart rate, and so forth, as by chemical means. Let us grant that these means may be effective. It remains the case that they are not exhaustive; for another way of inducing or eliminating anger – Aristotle's way – is to alter the subject's view of the reasons for an offense and the context in which it was given, including the possibility that it was deserved. Even if a cognitive account only complements a physical theory which is capable of identifying and controlling all responses that we call anger, it adds an essential dimension to the pragmatics of the emotion. The case is entirely analogous to that of psychosomatic diseases which respond to both medical and psychological intervention.[22]

---

[19] See Oatley (1992) 19: "I may suddenly feel frightened if the vehicle in which I am traveling seems to be heading for an accident. I evaluate a perception in relation to my concerns for safety, though not necessarily consciously. This may be the common experience in such situations. But a person confident that an accident would not occur, perhaps the one who is driving, or the one who is unconcerned about personal safety at that moment, may not feel fear."

[20] On the difference between fear and being startled, cf. Oatley (1992) 19; Nussbaum (1996) 306.

[21] On the physiological basis of "feelings," see Damasio (1994) 160–4; Kim (1996: 69–70), following Hilary Putnam, argues that mental states cannot be reduced to states of the brain (or body generally) if a sense of pain (for example) is the same for creatures with different physiological systems (the "multiple realization" argument).

[22] There is some resemblance between this kind of explanation and what Elster (1999a: 1–47) calls "mechanisms."

ANGER AND INSULT

Be that as it may, there is one respect in which my story about a man shoving a woman is defective as an illustration of Aristotle's theory of anger. For what is extraordinary about Aristotle's analysis is not just that it comprises cognitive judgments concerning motives and the like but also that he limits the causes of anger to intentional offenses of a single kind, which are summed up by the term *oligōria* or "slight."[23] Aristotle defines a slight as "the activation of an opinion about something seeming worthless" (*energeia doxēs peri to mēdenos axion phainomenon*, 2.2.1378b10–11). He goes on to specify that we regard good and bad things as worthy of effort (*spoudē*), as well as whatever contributes significantly to these; things that do so in a small way or not at all are deemed worthless. To get an idea of how severe a restriction this is, we may consider the three classes of slight that Aristotle enumerates. The first is *kataphronēsis* or contempt, which he defines as believing something to be of no value; it follows *a fortiori* that we slight what we hold in contempt, since slighting is just the active belief (or acting on the belief) that a thing is, or appears to be, worthless. The second category of slighting is more interesting. This is *epēreasmos* or "spite," which Aristotle defines as "blocking the wishes (*boulēseis*) of another not in order to have something for oneself but rather so that the other not have it" (2.2.1378b18–19). The slight, Aristotle explains, lies precisely in that the offender seeks no personal advantage. The only explanation for such a gratuitous frustration of another's aims, according to Aristotle, is that one neither fears him nor seeks his friendship; he is thus deemed useless for good or ill, which is just Aristotle's definition of worthlessness.

In attaching this latter condition to the definition of spite, Aristotle is not simply seeking to describe accurately an obnoxious and familiar form of behavior. If one blocked another's desire out of self-interest, not only would it not constitute a case of pure spite – as we might ourselves agree: it would also fail to be a cause of anger, and this may appear rather more odd to us. Impeding the fulfillment of another's projects, or doing harm to him as such, are not reasons, according to Aristotle, why people become angry. So too with Aristotle's third category of slighting, namely *hubris* or arrogant abuse. Once again, this is defined as speaking or acting in

---

[23] Modern English speakers are inclined to identify a wider range of causes of anger (or irritation), including frustration, noise, and crowds; Tavris (1989) 164–77. Plutarch continues to see mockery and other insults as chief causes of anger, although he, like others of his time, believes that a wise person should rise above such provocations; cf. *On Controlling Anger* 454D, 460D-E, Alexiou (1999) 105.

ways that cause shame to another, not so that something may happen to you or because something has happened, but for the sheer pleasure of it (2.2.1378b23–5), which derives from a sense of superiority, not gain. If the abuse is in return for an injury, it does not count as insolence or *hubris* but rather as revenge. A little later, Aristotle explains that we tend to get angry with people who laugh at or scorn or mock us, for they are being insolent toward us, and indeed with anyone who does us injury (*blaptontes*) of the sort that indicates insolence; the affront, Aristotle repeats, must be neither in return for something nor advantageous to those who inflict it, for only then does it appear to be on account of arrogance (2.2.1379a29–32) – that is, a species of slighting, and hence a stimulus to anger.

One might suppose that Aristotle excludes revenge or retribution as a cause of anger on the grounds that the victim is aware that he has earned it, and, as Aristotle says, we do not get angry when we perceive that we are suffering justly.[24] But what of harm inflicted for the sake of personal advantage? Aristotle's line of reasoning is clearly the same in both cases: getting even with another, or doing harm for the sake of gain, do not in themselves betray a belief that the target of such behavior is of no importance, and hence do not count as slights, which are the only grounds for anger. Anger is not a response to harm as such, even when the harm is intentional. What emotion, then, if any, does arise as a result of suffering a deliberate and unmerited injury? The answer for Aristotle is, I believe, hatred or hostility (*misein*).

Aristotle observes that rejoicing at the misfortune of another is the sign either of an enemy or of one who is slighting you (2.2.1379b17–19). These are alternatives: an enemy may be expected to take delight in your ruin without it following that he or she despises you as being of no account. When an enemy behaves in this way, accordingly, one does not react with anger. In a similar vein, Aristotle points out that no one slights a person he fears (2.3.1380a22–3), because fear is a sign of one's own weakness, and this is incompatible with contempt for the other. In consequence, we cannot be angry with those who fear us, though we may certainly dislike them. Contrariwise, Aristotle says that "it is impossible to be afraid of and angry with someone at the same time" (2.3.1380a33). The reason for this, I presume, is that we acknowledge, by our fear, the greater strength of the other, who is accordingly in a fit or suitable position to deliver a slight. But we do not like people who are frightening (*phoberoi*), says Aristotle, for "no one

[24] Cf. *Eth. Nic.* 5.8.1135b25–9, where Aristotle remarks that "anger resides in a perceived injustice (*adikia*)."

likes (*philei*) a person he fears" (2.4.1381b33). We do not even return anger
for anger, according to Aristotle, since those who are angry do not appear
to act out of contempt for the other (2.3.1380a34–5; they are responding to
disdain), yet anger is listed as one of the three primary causes of enmity
(2.4.1382a1–2).

The sharp distinction that Aristotle draws between anger and hatred or
enmity may surprise us, but it is crucial to his understanding of anger as an
emotion.[25] Enmity, according to Aristotle, is the opposite of friendship or
affection. Aristotle takes a robust view of *to philein*: to love someone entails
wishing good things (or what one believes to be good things) for his sake
and his only – not one's own – and to act accordingly to the best of one's
ability (2.4.1380b35–1381a1). A friend (*philos*), Aristotle continues, is one
who both loves and is loved in return,[26] and those who regard themselves
as mutually so disposed consider themselves to be friends (2.4.1381a1–3).[27]
Aristotle draws from his definitions the conclusion that a friend shares
the other's pleasure or pain "for no other reason than the other's sake"
(2.4.1381a5–6). Thus, one who wishes the same things for another as he
does for himself appears to be a friend.

An enemy, in turn, is identified by the reverse: wishing bad or harmful
things (*kaka*) for the other. Aristotle says that enmity differs from anger
insofar as the object (*ephesis*) of anger is to cause pain to the other, while
that of hatred is to inflict harm (2.4.1382a8). It follows that, for an angry
person, it is important that the other perceive (*aisthesthai*) the response
(there is no such thing as unperceived pain), while to one who hates, it is
a matter of indifference whether an enemy is aware or not of the damage
done to him. We can see this clearly from the extreme instance of harm,
which is to say, death: when we hate someone, says Aristotle, we wish
that he or she not exist, but when we are angry, we desire that the other
feel in turn (*antipathein*) the (painful) thing that has provoked our anger
(2.4.1382a14–15). Death, however, would render him insensible to pain.

Anger in this sense is a personal matter. As Aristotle points out, one
can be angry only at an individual – at Cleon, for example – and not at
a class of people or at mankind generally (2.2.1378a34–5), whereas hatred
or dislike may be directed against a group, for example thieves in general
(2.4.1382a4–7). It makes sense, then, that hatred, so understood, need not

---

[25] Stocker (1996: 266–7) rightly distinguishes the causes of enmity from those of anger in Aristotle.

[26] Kassell (1976) marks this sentence as a later addition to the text by Aristotle himself, on no sufficient
grounds, in my opinion.

[27] Note that *philoi* or friends constitute a special subset of those who love, and that love itself is an
altruistic sentiment that does not imply or depend on reciprocity; see Konstan (1997).

be accompanied by pain in the way that anger over a specific slight must be. Although the term "hatred" in English may summon up the image of an intense loathing that is more palpable than anger, for Aristotle *to misein* signifies rather a settled and principled antagonism that is lasting and not subject, as anger is, to being healed by the passage of time (2.4.1382a7–8).

There is a conundrum here, however. If hatred does not entail pain, as Aristotle says, does it qualify as an emotion on the definition that Aristotle offers in the *Rhetoric*, which stipulates that emotions must be attended by pleasure or pain (2.1.1378a21–2)? I am inclined to think that both love and hatred posed classificatory difficulties for Aristotle's psychology.[28] In the *Nicomachean Ethics*, Aristotle states that *philia* resembles a settled state of character or *hexis*, since it is accompanied by deliberate choice (*proairesis*), and he coins the term *philēsis* – a "loving feeling," perhaps – to denote that aspect of love that corresponds to a *pathos* (8.5.1157b28–32). Pleasure and pain are not essential components of a *hexis*, and thus need not accompany *philia* or its opposite, hatred. In the *Rhetoric*, where both are plainly included among the *pathē* (as they are also at *Eth. Nic.* 2.4.1105b21–3), Aristotle perhaps supposed that the wish (*boulesthai*) that good things accrue to a friend (or bad to an enemy) is accompanied by a *phantasia* of its fulfillment, just as the *orexis* for revenge is in the case of anger. If so, both love and hatred would fall under the category of pleasurable emotions, and this would explain why the latter is not accompanied by pain.[29] It is less likely, I think, that Aristotle had in mind the pleasure we take in the good things that happen to a friend and the pain we experience at the bad, and vice versa in the case of an enemy.

It has been determined, then, that a slight is painful, and that the pain endures (in all likelihood) in recollection or in thought until such time as the affront is requited through an act of revenge, which is effective only if the other perceives in return the pain inflicted. The revenge, then, must be analogous to the slight itself in that it produces a sensible hurt, and not just objective harm (it will not do to kill the person, accordingly). When achieved, vengeance brings pleasure, and ousts the pain of the slight and hence the anger (the pleasure is anticipatory so long as the anger is active). Presumably, the revenge is of such a sort as to abolish the active belief

---

[28] Cooper (1996: 243) remarks that Aristotle's treatment of love and hatred "is anomalous in several ways."

[29] Cooper (1996: 248) notes that hatred ought not to be a pleasurable emotion, even though Aristotle makes it clear that it is not primarily associated with pain. The *phantasia* of revenge, however, might well outweigh recollected pain resulting from harm (e.g. loss of property in a wartime raid), especially if the harm was not of a decidedly painful kind.

in one's own worthlessness, by demonstrating that one is not inferior or powerless in relation to the other.[30]

THE WORLD OF ANGER

A slight, as we have seen, consists in a word or gesture that activates the belief or *doxa* – that is, manifests the belief in the form of an act or *ergon* – that one is of no account. The necessary response to such an act is to restore the opinion – one's own, another's – of one's own worth by an act of reprisal, which demonstrates one's significance in relation to the other (getting even [*antipoiein*] itself is not arrogance but requital: *Rh*. 2.2.1378b25–6). Anger is just the desire to restore the state of affairs prior to the insult (or to depreciate the offender in turn). But not every slight inspires anger. It is time to return to the proviso, included in Aristotle's definition of anger, that the author of the slight be someone who ought not to have delivered it.

The world implied by Aristotle's account of anger is hierarchical, consisting of people who are superior or inferior in regard to strength, wealth, status, and the like. The point of *hubris*, for example, is to demonstrate one's superiority to another; hence it is characteristic of the rich and also of young people (2.2.1378b28), who presumably are physically strong and at the same time need to prove themselves. This is why people who have doubts about themselves, whether in regard to looks or occupation or whatever they take seriously, are particularly prone to anger, while those who are confident that they excel (*huperechein*) are not (2.2.1379a36–1379b2). People who really do excel, however, whether in regard to family, power, wealth, or indeed a particular skill such as oratory (which is joined closely here to the ability to govern), expect deference (*poluōreisthai*) from their lessers (*hēttones*) on account of their superiority (2.2.1378b34–1379a6), and are especially likely to become angry if they suffer a slight instead. So too, we tend to be angry at those who oppose us, if they are our inferiors, or do not repay us in kind, as though we were their inferiors, and above all at a slight received from people of no account (*en mēdeni logōi*), for, as Aristotle says, "we have assumed that anger over a slight is directed to those who ought not (*mē prosēkontes*) to do so, and inferiors ought not to slight [their betters]" (2.2.1379b11–13).

We might describe the social situations in which anger is triggered or allayed in Aristotle's account as informed by an acute sense of honor, with

---

[30] In *Topics* 8.1.156a27–b3, Aristotle confronts the objection that anger toward parents does not entail a desire for revenge: in fact it does, he argues, although the pain to be inflicted is limited to remorse.

its intense regard for status, protocols of conduct, and the opinion of others – Aristotle specifies, for example, that we are more disposed to anger when a slight is delivered in the presence of those with whom we compete, those whom we admire or wish to be admired by, and those before whom we feel shame or who feel shame before us (2.2.1379b24–6). Aristotle himself says that disrespect (*atimia*) is a part of *hubris*, and that to dishonor (*atimazōn*) a person is to slight him, for what is worthless has no value (*timē*) whether for good or ill (2.2.1378b29–31).[31] He cites in illustration Achilles' words in regard to Agamemnon: "He dishonored me," and treated me as though I were "a despised (*atimētos*) vagrant" (*Iliad* 1.356, 9.648, etc.). The allusion to Homer suggests, I think, that the use of the word *timē* in the context of slights and anger may have had a poetic ring, since in prose usage the term referred primarily to political rights and offices or to economic value. But honor captures well the extreme sensitivity that Aristotle reports toward offenses against one's dignity and esteem in the eyes of one's fellow-citizens, provided that we do not assimilate the idea to the complex of honor and shame that has become popular in so-called Mediterranean anthropology in the past two or three decades, with its particular emphasis on the need to control the sexual comportment of the women in one's family. Athenian literature of the classical period offers little evidence of an obsessive preoccupation with dishonor in this narrow sense of defilement.[32]

Although the cause of anger is a slight requiring satisfaction on the part of someone who ought not to have rendered it, such as an inferior or a friend or beneficiary who might be expected to have a thought for one's dignity, Aristotle recognizes that there are certain states in which we are more or less disposed to be sensitive to such affronts, irrespective of their source.[33] When we are enjoying ourselves at a party or feeling particularly prosperous, we are not inclined to anger (2.3.1380b2–5). Contrariwise, we are more irritable when we are suffering (*lupoumenos*, 2.2.1379a11) because of something we want and lack, and are particularly prone to anger toward those who obstruct the fulfillment of our desire, as when we are thirsty, sick, poor, in love, and so on. It may be that our condition of want exposes us the more to insult, just to the extent that a person fails to respect our need,[34] but however that might be, it is important to distinguish between

[31] On slighting and *timē*, see Grimaldi (1988) 22 ad 1373b28.
[32] See Herman (1995) on *timē* in the Attic orators; contra, e.g., Cohen (1991).
[33] Aristotle notes at *De anima* 1.1.403a19–22 that when we are tense, we are more vulnerable to emotions in general.
[34] Kassell (1976) excises the words in 2.2.1379a15–18 that point to this line of reasoning.

the suffering that results from lack, as in thirst, ill health, poverty, and the like, and the pain that accompanies anger. Pain of one kind makes us more susceptible, perhaps, to feeling pain of another, but the two have different causes in this case, and are not the same pain.[35]

Anger for Aristotle, then, is anything but a reflex to pain or harm, even when the cause is intentional. Aristotle envisages a world in which self-esteem depends on social interaction: the moment someone's negative opinion of your worth is actualized publicly in the form of a slight, you have lost credit, and the only recourse is a compensatory act that restores your social position. Anger is just the desire to adjust the record in this way – the internal correlative to the outward loss of respect. In this regard, Aristotle's view of anger sits well with the set of emotions he chose to discuss in the *Rhetoric*, with which the inventory derived from my students' lists differed so notably. This is not the occasion on which to investigate in detail Aristotle's conception of emotions other than anger, but we may note briefly those aspects that bear on the competition for esteem.

ANGER AND OTHER EMOTIONS

Fear, which is a kind of pain produced by the anticipation of an evil that is harmful or painful (2.5.1382a21–2; cf. 2.5.1382a27–30), may arise as a result of the anger or enmity of those who have the power (*dunamenoi*) to inflict it (2.5.1382a32–3): I presume that enmity is specifically related to the desire to cause harm, while anger corresponds to the wish to inflict pain. Unjust individuals, arrogant people, those who fear us, or who have been wronged, or have done us wrong, or are our rivals, are all frightening, provided they are able to do harm; indeed, Aristotle says, human beings generally do wrong to others, if they can (2.5.1382b8–9). The chief factor in producing fear, accordingly, is the relative strength of the parties (2.5.1382b15–19), just as confidence, fear's opposite, derives from the knowledge that our competitors – if we have any – are either weak or well-disposed toward us, or that those who have the same interests as we do are more numerous or stronger or both (2.5.1383a22–5). So too, we feel confident when there is nothing to frighten people like ourselves or weaker, which we believe if we have beaten others or people like them or stronger than they are; also if we have more of the things which make one frightening, such as wealth, friends, land, and provisions for war (2.5.1383a32–1383b3). When an

---

[35] See Elster (1999a) 54. On analogous differences between kinds of pleasures, cf. *Eth. Nic.* 10.5.1175a19–30 and Leighton (1996) 219.

ordinary man stepped out of his house and into the streets of Athens, he must, on the basis of the picture that Aristotle draws, have been intensely conscious of grades of power in its various manifestations and his own vulnerability to insult and injury.

Aristotle defines shame as "a kind of pain or perturbation concerning that class of bad things, whether present, past, or future, that are perceived to lead to a bad opinion [*adoxia*, sc. of the person in question]" (2.6.1383b13–15), while shamelessness is indifference or insensibility in this regard. We feel shame for our vices (*kakiai*), such as cowardice, injustice, and the servility (*aneleutheria*) that is manifested in begging or flattering others for the sake of some advantage, and also for not having the fine things our equals have (2.6.1384a9–11); Aristotle specifies as "equals" those who are like us in respect to ethnicity, citizenship, age, and kin. He goes on to explain that since shame is an impression of a bad opinion (*phantasia adoxias*, 2.6.1384a23), and people only have concern for opinion (*doxa*) because of those who hold it (*hoi doxazontes*), it follows that we feel shame before those who are of some account, for example people who admire us or whom we admire, those with whom we compete, and so on: the kinds are similar to those before whom we do not wish to be slighted. Both shame and anger are a response to the poor opinion (*doxa*) that others entertain of us. The difference is that with shame we recognize that the fault is ours, whereas in the case of anger it is the slight that precipitates or energizes the opinion.[36] But both alike are symptomatic of a society in which one's standing or reputation in the eyes of others is of central concern, and above all the requirement that one not be seen to sink beneath the level of one's peers.

Aristotle defines benevolence or *charis* as "a service to one in need, not in return for something nor so that the one who does the service may get something, but rather so that the other may" (2.7.1385a17–19);[37] the emotion that is the subject of this chapter of the *Rhetoric*, however, is not

---

[36] I am suspicious of sharp distinctions between shame and guilt, as applied to ancient Greek sensibilities. Thus, Elster (1999a: 151) affirms that shame "arises when something one has done causes others to express disapproval." Whatever the value of this description, it is not Aristotelian, since for Aristotle shame arises when we are conscious that we have done something bad (and the disapproval of others is in response to such an act). This is as good as guilt, in my opinion. Elster goes on to observe (p. 160) that, for the Greeks, "A truly bad man was one who showed that he did not care about the opinions of others." This certainly cannot be true for Aristotle, who regards only the opinions of decent people to be worthy of consideration, and that because they know the difference between good and evil. If the vast majority of people are mistaken or bad, not caring about their opinions is the mark of a good person. I reserve a fuller discussion of these matters, on which Cairns (1993), B. Williams (1993), and Dover (1994: 236–42), have made important contributions, for another occasion.

[37] Partisans of reciprocity, take note!

charis as such, but rather the compound expression *charin echein*, that is, "gratitude."[38] Pity, in turn, is "a kind of pain in the case of a perceived fatal or painful harm of one not deserving to encounter it, which one might expect oneself, or one of one's own, to suffer, and this when it seems near" (2.8.1385b13–16). I have argued elsewhere (Konstan [2001] 128–36) that the pain involved in the emotion of pity derives from the fear that one is oneself vulnerable to the same kind of misfortune (it is this pain that qualifies pity as an emotion), but that fear for ourselves is not the reason why we are moved by another's misfortune and disposed to help him or her. Pity is excited by those who are worse off than ourselves, and may be regarded as the positive counterpart to contempt and arrogance, which exploit the weakness of the other for the sake of demonstrating one's own superiority (and therefore arouse anger). Kindness, on the contrary, looks to redress the inequalities that result from misfortune or (in the case of pity) unmerited misfortune.

The last three emotions to which Aristotle devotes a specific discussion in the *Rhetoric* are indignation (*nemesan*), envy, and emulation or rivalrousness (*zēlos*). Indignation is in one respect opposite to pity, in that it consists in pain at the undeserved success of another, whereas pity is motivated by unmerited suffering (2.9.1386b9–12). Both emotions, Aristotle adds, are signs of good character: people should neither prosper nor suffer unjustly. Envy, too, is in a certain sense opposed to pity, in that it is "a disturbing pain resulting from the well-being of another" (2.9.1386b18–19; cf. 2.10.1387b22–4), as opposed to pain at the other's misfortune, and to this extent might be thought to resemble indignation.[39] But, Aristotle goes on to explain, envy is not elicited by the fact that the other is undeserving, but simply by the fact that he is one's equal or similar (2.9.1386b19–20); in his extended discussion of envy, Aristotle adds that the object of envy is not that one have something oneself, but simply that the other not have it (2.10.1387b23–4). It is this last qualification that distinguishes envy from competitive emulation, which is defined as "a kind of pain at the perceived presence of good and honorable things that are possible to acquire for oneself, belonging to those who are similar in nature [to ourselves], not because the other has it but because oneself does not" (8.11.1388a30–3). Aristotle adds that this is why rivalrousness is a decent emotion, whereas envy is base; for emulation

---

[38] This interpretation runs counter to all translations of the *Rhetoric* known to me; I defend it in detail in a chapter of my forthcoming book, *The Emotions of the Ancient Greeks*.

[39] This contrast was commonplace: cf. Pindar, *Pythians* 1.85; Lysias 2.67, 24.2; Cicero, *De oratore* 1.185, 2.216; Andronicus, *Peri pathōn* 2 p. 12 Kreuttner = *SVF* 3.414, etc.

stimulates us to obtain good things, whereas envy merely aims to deprive one's neighbor of them (8.11.1388a33–6). But emulation too has a negative side: for its opposite, Aristotle says, is contempt (*kataphronēsis*), and those who are so disposed as to emulate others or be emulated by them are contemptuous of those who have the bad things that are the opposite of the good things that are vied for (*zēlōta*) (2.11.1388b23–7). We may recall, although Aristotle does not mention it in this context, that contempt was among the three causes of anger.

We may see, from this abbreviated survey of the passions according to Aristotle, that the world he evokes is deeply competitive. One is always jockeying to maintain or improve one's position or that of dear ones, whether in terms of goods in one's possession or one's status in the eyes of others. Our emotions are attuned to these demands.[40] We naturally strive to have the good things others have; such contention becomes nasty (and the mark of a poor character or *ēthos*) only when it is motivated solely by malice toward another, without advantage to oneself; then it turns into envy. Some passions motivate us to adjust the balance between success and failure in behalf of others; these include pity, indignation, and, within a more limited sphere, love, which presupposes an identity of pleasure and pain between two people. Anger is the impulse to right a wrong done to oneself, in regard to opinion or reputation, but it works to the same end: maintaining an equilibrium of goods or honor in a society where everyone is trying to climb above the rest (so too, gratitude). In the rough-and-tumble context of Aristotle's Athens, anger, like fear and shame, is a response to a threat of loss.

GOOD ANGER?

As other contributors to this volume indicate, discussions of anger in the Hellenistic age and later stress the need to control or eliminate it, sometimes, as in the case of the Stoics, along with other emotions.[41] Such advice is typically addressed to people in power, and is concerned with "the great wrath of kings nurtured by Zeus," as Aristotle puts it (2.2.1379a4–5), citing a verse of Homer's *Iliad* (2.196). For such a public of princes and noblemen,

---

[40] Striker (1996: 289) comments on the account of emotions in the *Rhetoric*: "Book 2 focuses exclusively on emotions relating to other people."

[41] Seneca's censure of anger in *De ira* is canonical for the Roman Stoic viewpoint; cf. also Plutarch, *On Controlling Anger*. W. S. Anderson (1964: 173 *et passim*) argues that even Juvenal came under its spell, and abandoned the severe indignation of his *persona* in the later satires.

it was important to advise restraint; anger, in particular, could vent itself in destructive rages against people helpless to resist.[42]

This is not the implied audience of Aristotle's treatise on rhetoric. Aristotle was writing for potential orators before the assembly and above all the courts, which were at their most active and popular in the fourth century. While defendants and prosecutors in the courts may have come mainly from the wealthier classes, the jurors were ordinary citizens, and perhaps predominantly poor, as Aristophanes' *Wasps* indicates. These were not people whose anger reflected the caprices of omnipotence; rather, they were far more likely to suffer an indignity than inflict one, and it was their emotions that the aspiring orator had to manipulate. They lived in a democracy, of course, but it was a democracy in which one had to maintain at every turn one's dignity and status. Equality resulted not just from political rights but from continual and universal vigilance to protect one's reputation and economic position. Every public interaction was a scene of potential gains, losses, and settlings of accounts; an insult was a put-down, and one was obliged to get even. Jon Elster (1999a: 75) deftly characterizes the social world implied by Aristotle's description of the emotions as "intensely confrontational, intensely competitive, and intensely public; in fact, much of it involves confrontations and competitions before a public. It is a world in which everybody knows that they are constantly being judged, nobody hides that they are acting like judges, and nobody hides that they seek to be judged positively. It is a world with very little hypocrisy, or 'emotional tact.' "[43] In this volatile environment, in which equality was an ideal but never a given, and had constantly to be asserted and defended if the image of a society of equals or similars was to be maintained, anger is obligatory, "insofar as the individual citizen who was sensitive to his honor and guarded it with anger was also guarding his personal independence, greatness, and equality" (Allen [2000] 129). This is why anger is one of the dispositions that admits of excess, deficiency, and the mean, according to Aristotle

---

[42] The condemnation of royal anger continued into the Middle Ages; see Bührer-Thierry (1998) 75: "If anger was reprehensible for all mankind, it was still more so for kings." There was also, however, an alternative tradition of just anger, which was not only the prerogative but the duty of monarchs. So Althoff (1998) 59: "Royal anger thus appears as a part of his [the king's] 'rulership practice,' that is, as part of a personally grounded system of rulership based on a range of unwritten laws"; White (1998) 139: "Public displays of anger are almost always made by kings or other males whose noble status entitles them to express anger"; Barton (1998) 154: "anger was frequently justified as necessary and righteous, especially when exercised by those with rightful authority." The model for royal anger was the just wrath of God.

[43] Elster concludes that "being ashamed of one's anger was not a typical Greek reaction." This is true, but only because anger is not a vice or the sign of a vicious character; being ashamed of spite or envy is entirely consistent with Aristotle's view of the emotions.

(*Eth. Nic.* 2.7.1108a4–6), and differs from those, like shamelessness or envy, that are bad in and of themselves (2.6.1107a8–11).[44]

This is not to deny that there were real status differences in Aristotle's Athens. Since anger is incompatible with fear, according to Aristotle, one cannot react angrily to a slight on the part of a person with vastly more power than one's own. Slaves, accordingly, are in no position to feel anger against their masters, but do have to know how to appease their masters' anger, for example by humbling themselves, confessing their fault, and not talking back (*Rh.* 2.3.1380a15–18). Aristotle assumes that the master's anger is not arbitrary but arises because of a slight on the part of the slave; slights are the only stimulus to anger that Aristotle recognizes. By humbling themselves, slaves acknowledge their lesser status, and since the weaker fear the stronger, and no one can slight a person whom he fears (2.3.1380a21–3), the slave in effect (we may conclude) withdraws the slight, or proves that it cannot have been intended. In relations between ordinary citizens and kings or the very rich and powerful, a similar code would obtain.

Aristotle's view of anger as a response to a slight, that is, an attack upon one's social standing or honor, entailing a desire to restore one's position by a compensating act of retribution, promises to offer useful insights into the role of anger in Greek literature generally in the classical period. I hesitate to affirm that Aristotle's analysis covers all cases, though perhaps it has wider application than one imagines. One must in any case take into account the specific purpose of the *Rhetoric*. For instance, Aristotle does not choose to discuss, in this treatise, the adverse consequences of acting under the influence of anger, although his own contemporaries worried about the problem. To take a single example, Xenophon, in the *Hellenica* (5.3.5–6), describes a scene in which a general leads his troops against a city in a fit of rage (*orgistheis*), with the result that he himself is slain and his men massacred. Xenophon draws the lesson (5.3.7) that masters ought not to punish even slaves in anger, and that by doing so they frequently suffer more harm than they inflict; indeed, "to attack opponents in anger and without intelligence (*gnōmē*) is a complete mistake, for anger is without forethought, but intelligence looks as much to avoiding harm to oneself as to doing harm to one's enemies." When Aristotle considers the virtues, however, he makes a similar distinction (*Eth. Nic.* 3.8.1117a.5–15): "when human beings are angry, they feel pain, and when they avenge themselves, they feel pleasure; those who fight for such reasons are warlike, yes, but they are not

---

[44] At *Eth. Nic.* 4.5.1125b26–9, Aristotle defines good temper, or *praotēs*, as a mean in respect to anger. Anger, Aristotle says, is the *pathos* (1125b30), whereas the disposition in respect to anger is a state or *hexis* (1126b8–10).

courageous: for they do so not for the sake of what is good or in the manner
dictated by reason (*logos*), but rather out of emotion (*pathos*)."[45] So too, he
includes anger among the forms of wickedness (*mochthēriai*), along with
self-indulgence (*akolasia*) and cowardice, that are responsible for unjust
actions (*adikēmata*) – in the case of anger, for example, striking another
person. I imagine that Aristotle is thinking here rather of a disposition to
excessive anger (what he calls *orgilotēs* or irascibility, 4.5.1125b29), but it is
revealing that the bare term *orgē* can carry such a negative connotation.[46]

The assumptions that entered into the ideological construction of the
emotions in ancient Greece are not the same as ours.[47] The difference between the range of passions that Aristotle treats and the lists my students
drew up suggests as much, and the divergence carries over into the consideration of anger too, as in the sharp distinction Aristotle draws between
anger and hatred. I expect that the change in perspective is associated in part
with the relative neglect of the categories of honor and insult in modern
social life, at least in the United States (I wrote these words in Salamanca,
in the heart of Castilian Spain, where there thrives an intense concern for
dignity and what others think). For my part, I would have hated living
in the Athens that Aristotle's account of the passions evokes, but I must
confess to feeling a certain nostalgia for his easy accommodation of anger
and enmity among the ordinary facts of life.

[45] Compare also *Eth. Nic.* 7.6.1149a24–32, where Aristotle compares *thumos* (analogous to anger) to a
slave who carries out an order precipitously, before having listened to all his master (i.e. reason) has
to say.

[46] Contrast *Eth. Nic.* 5.8.1135b19–29, where Aristotle explains that an unpremeditated act, such as
those due to anger, is indeed a wrong (*adikēma*), but the injury does not arise out of wickedness
(*mochthēria*): "for it is not he who acts in a passion who initiates [the conflict], but he who angered
him . . . For the anger depends on a perceived injustice." So too, Aristotle regards lack of self-control
in respect to anger (*thumos*, which is here equivalent to *orgē*) as more venial than carnal appetites,
insofar as they are more human and natural (*Eth. Nic.* 7.6.1149b27–9).

[47] Stocker (1996: 265–322), on "The Complex Evaluative World of Aristotle's Angry Man," notes that,
for Aristotle, anger is evaluative, and hence *orgē* is "a moral notion" (266), deeply connected with
honor. When Aristotle's man "is not accorded the rank and respect he thinks due . . . [he] experiences
the lack of respect as a deep wound to himself, that is, to his self" (268). Such dependency on others'
reassurance suggests a narcissistic personality (269–70); but it may be that "Aristotle's men and our
narcissists cannot have the same structure of feelings" (271), and Stocker concedes that he may be
describing what *we* would be like if we were similar to Aristotle's men (272). Stocker affirms: "The
psyche of Aristotle's man is, further, constituted by a desire . . . that he be a center, if not the center,
of attention, concern, and understanding" (277), and this conditions his need for friendship (280);
but the demand to be "understood" is itself a modern phenomenon; see Konstan (1997) 14–18, 152–3.

CHAPTER 5

The rage of women

W. V. Harris

This paper concerns feminism, slavery, bloody revenge, and centuries of oppression, but it has to start with philology. Since I shall be considering what seems to be the attempt of a male-dominated culture to delegitimize the expression of certain emotions, we had better know what those emotions were. This is all the more necessary because a good deal of the scholarly and scientific literature about the emotions still neglects semantics, with serious consequences. Even in recent years some scientific researchers into anger have set out to perform "cross-cultural" research without considering the likelihood that the concepts used by their non-anglophone subjects do not correspond neatly with those that prevail in English.[1]

Meanwhile, however, since about 1980, a number of anthropologists have made a crucial advance in research about the emotions by registering and exploring the fact that the emotional terms employed in other natural languages very commonly fail to correspond closely with the English terminology. This realization has come from investigating languages in the Philippines, in Uganda, and other places,[2] but it might have come from studying French or German, for as anyone quickly realizes who lectures to international audiences about "anger," that word is not a perfect match for *colère* (you sometimes need *rancune*, for instance) or for *Zorn* (you sometimes need *Raserei* or other words). What the speakers of a particular language mean by the word in their language which most closely corresponds to English "anger" probably means something more or less subtly different. William James was perhaps close to making this point more than

Having recently written a chapter on this subject for my book *Restraining Rage*, I have not been able to avoid using the same evidence and I have used some of the same phraseology; but in this version the reader will find additional discussion of certain points. I should like to thank members of audiences at Duke and at Oxford who heard and criticized earlier versions of this paper, and in particular my respective hosts on those occasions, Elizabeth Clark and Robin Osborne. I also owe a debt to all those who organized and took part in the symposium in Heidelberg.

[1] See, e.g., Sommers (1988) 27–9; Matsumoto (1990); Hupka et al. (1996); Fischer et al. (1999).
[2] Rosaldo (1980); Heald (1989); cf. Harris (2002), 34–5.

a century ago,[3] but its explicit formulation and evidentiary base are owed to such anthropologists as Michele Rosaldo, Catherine Lutz, and Anna Wierzbicka.[4]

What bearing does this have on antiquity? Scholars normally assume that the correspondence between, for instance, Greek *orgē* – the most important term of all in this discussion – and "anger" is unproblematic, and this is true even of historians of ancient philosophy, who might be expected to be on the semantic *qui vive*. I have noticed three recent exceptions to this general indifference to the precise translation of Greek and Latin anger-terms – an indifference which has had, as I hope to demonstrate shortly, some significant consequences. Veyne, for one, has commented on the inadequacy of *colère* as a translation of Senecan *ira/iracundia*.[5] And the sociologist Jon Elster, without knowing Greek, acutely inferred from translations of Aristotle's *Rhetoric* that something must be wrong with the equation *orgē* = "anger," and he was able in consequence to offer a suggestive analysis of one of the central anger-texts of antiquity.[6]

And now Danielle Allen suggests that *orgē* occasionally means "sexual desire" in high classical Greek, so that the term suffers, or benefits, from "fundamental ambiguity."[7] This view is, I fear, mistaken. For much of the fifth century there was indeed an ambiguity about the term *orgē*, which continued to mean something like "disposition" as well as something like "anger" – but not this ambiguity. Speculative etymologizing is irrelevant, and many *hundreds* of occurrences of the word and its cognates make its meanings reasonably clear. Occasionally of course there is a connection with *erōs*, naturally enough, since *orgē* and *erōs* were both conditions of the inner person which led easily to action, and since both of them, according to orthodox male thinking, needed to be resisted by women. And of course *erōs* led not infrequently to a whole variety of angry emotions.

Classical Greek is rich in anger-words,[8] and that remains true even when one makes allowances for the enormous length of time covered by the standard works of linguistic reference. The main words in the Homeric language were *mēnis* and its cognates together with *cholos* and its cognates, but a number of other words refer to something close to anger, such as *nemesan* and *chalepainein*. By the fifth century BC, however, some of the

---

[3] At least he offered the opinion that "each race of men" has "found names for some shade of feeling which other races have left undiscriminated," and that all sorts of groupings of emotions would be valid (1890: II.485).

[4] See especially Rosaldo (1980); Lutz (1988); Wierzbicka (1992).

[5] Veyne (1993) 105.   [6] Elster (1999a) 62.   [7] Allen (2000) 54, 118.

[8] As has quite often been noticed; see Seneca, *De ira* 1.4.2.

vocabulary had changed, and the principal words for the angry emotions were *thumos* and *orgē*. These two terms were quite often interchangeable but never synonymous, since *thumos* for most of its history meant "the seat or agency of anger and zeal within the person"[9] as well as (something like) "anger."

Aristotle offered a definition which was subsequently adapted by many others: *orgē* is "the desire, accompanied by pain, for perceived revenge for some perceived slight to oneself or one's own, the slight not having been deserved."[10] In antiquity of course a desire for appropriate revenge or for vengeful punishment was in the eyes of most people entirely respectable, even obligatory, and not a cause for embarrassment or shame; there were some dissenters on this matter both at Athens and at Rome, but they were apparently few.[11] It is not to be doubted that *orgē*, and *ira* too, very commonly included a frank desire for revenge.

Earlier in the *Rhetoric* Aristotle had explained that no one is angry with

those whom vengeance clearly cannot overtake, or those who are far more powerful than he is; against such people they are not angry, or at any rate less so.[12]

The implication of this statement is clear: while *orgē* may be a psychic state, it is only *orgē* if it also leads to action or comes close to doing so; the emotion by itself, restrained by the prudential inadvisability of showing anger against someone who is "far more powerful," scarcely counts.

It can be argued on the basis of this and a great deal of other evidence that in most periods most of what was described as *orgē* was by modern standards quite furious and intense, and the same may apply to *cholos* and *thumos*. This helps to explain the stance of those ancient critics of anger who maintained that one should eliminate all *orgē* or *ira* whatsoever (a point of view hardly to be encountered in the contemporary West): an ancient person who believed that the Wise Man should never be angry could easily do so without having to give up the prerogative of being annoyed or irritated, and – more importantly – without having to forgo the punishment of his slaves or the reprimanding of children. There were other Greek words to describe a more mild kind of anger, such as *chalepainō*: Marcus Aurelius claimed to be without *orgē*, but he admitted that he had often been annoyed (the word he uses is *chalepainō*) with his philosophical

---

[9] Simon (1988) 82.
[10] *Rh.* 2.2.1378a31 (for this translation see Cooper [1996] 255, n. 23; Harris [1997]; the passage is often mistranslated); cf. *Eth. Nic.* 5.8.1135b28.
[11] There is a substantial bibliography about this matter; see Harris (2002) 183–4, 211–12.
[12] *Rh.* 1.11.1370b13–15.

companion Rusticus.[13] It is because I think that the ancient discourse of anger-control is principally about intense anger that I have called my larger study *Restraining Rage*, for although the distinction is often blurred I take it that "rage" is generally stronger than mere "anger."

The strength of *orgē*-anger is also indicated by its close and frequent association with madness. King Cambyses – Herodotus' favorite example of irascibility – is mad as well as angry. The same applies to Sophocles' Ajax. Menander, another dramatist who certainly reflected about *orgē*,[14] insists on the resemblance between outbursts of domestic rage, even when they are quite comprehensible, and fits of insanity. Galen wrote that "you can see that rage is madness from the things men do when they are in the grip of rage."[15] Some of these texts were admittedly intended to detract from the respectability of anger itself. It remains true that modern anger reaches only infrequently the intensity which would justify pairing it with madness.

A final linguistic comment: there is a still more difficult question than the semantic one, and that is, to put it briefly, why do they talk about anger so much? For few regular readers of Greek and Latin texts would doubt that the vocabulary of anger comes very easily to Greek and Roman men of letters. It is not at all clear why. One might suggest that anger-discourse takes up space in Greek and Roman parlance partly because other concepts to which we are accustomed are largely absent. The most obvious candidate is depression, for it seems to be absent from the lexicon of Greek and Latin concepts, which is not to say that one cannot express in the classical languages the thought that someone is depressed: Bellerophon in the *Iliad* may be the original depressive.[16] (Greek *melancholia*, in my opinion, is drastically different from modern melancholy.) I have not forgotten that there is such a thing as *lupē* – a term which often refers to mental suffering. But no single word for "depression" or for "depressed" seems to have existed in either Greek or Latin. This does not mean that when ancient writers refer to *orgē* or *ira* they are "really" referring to what we would call depression, but it is possible that there existed emotional states labelled *orgē* or *ira* which we would locate somewhere between anger and depression.

---

[13] *To Himself* 1.1, 1.17.14.

[14] Among other evidence, his first play was actually entitled *Orgē*; its fragments are nos. 303–11 in the Körte-Thierfelder edition.

[15] *De propriorum animi cuiuslibet affectuum dignotione et curatione* 5.2 De Boer: "they strike and kick and tear their clothes, they shout and glare, they do everything until . . . they grow angry with doors and stones and keys . . ." Cf. Soranus 2.8 = 19 (p. 31, line 90 Burguière et al.).

[16] On the basis of *Il.* 6.200–3. See Kristeva (1989) 7; cf. Heiberg (1927) 3.

A full account of what a particular emotion amounts to in any culture requires not only semantic precision but also a careful examination of the way in which it is experienced and the ways in which it expresses itself. That is obvious enough, but scholars have a great deal more analytic work to do, as far as anger is concerned (and with respect to most other emotions too – *erōs* has of course received most attention). What, in other words, *was* the experience or behavior from which classical men – to anticipate the main argument of this paper – attempted to exclude women?

Here are two immediate responses to that question. The "strong-anger" emotions – *cholos, thumos,* and *orgē* – were domestic as well as civic phenomena: we must suppose, for instance, that Menander's lost play *Orgē* was about *orgē* within the household. So when we discuss the social rules about anger, we are not simply talking about political and civic activities from which women were mostly excluded in any case, but about their day-to-day lives and their relationships with those who were close to them and with their household slaves (the perspective of the slaves themselves is as usual very difficult to recover). Secondly, the Greeks recognized that anger can be long-lasting. They knew – something which contemporary science has often in effect denied[17] – that it can go on for months and years.[18] We are not, or not only, talking about rapidly quenched fits of ill-temper.

I now turn to the evolving behavioral codes that prevailed in various ages of classical antiquity, and to the main ideas that philosophers put forward about the reining-in of the angry emotions. Of necessity this will be a very brief sketch. What it will show is that while throughout classical antiquity many Greeks and Romans advocated the reining-in or the elimination of the "strong-anger" emotions – adopting, in some cases, positions that are quite extreme by the standards of the modern West – much of this criticism was less than absolute; in other words, it admitted the existence of legitimate *orgē, ira,* and so on – for men.

The poet who shaped our *Iliad* and *Odyssey* was not an enemy of the angry emotions – on the contrary he understood their essential role in the heroic life – but it is nonetheless hard to resist the notion that the *Iliad* was intended to show unrelenting anger, especially the *mēnis* or *cholos* of Achilles, in an unfavourable light. As it happens, however, a contextless fragment of Sappho is the earliest European text in which anger-restraint is

---

[17] E.g. Ekman (1992b) 185; Tafrate (1995) 111.

[18] See among much other ancient evidence Philodemus, *De ira* 5 (col. xxx.15–24) ("some people are not only continually in a rage [*thumountai*], but are taken over by long-lasting and hard-to-cure fits of anger [*orgai*] . . ."). See Harris (2002) 40–2.

explicitly enjoined. This theme is persistent. The verses of Solon, tragedy, Old and New Comedy all reflect elements in Athenian thinking on this subject. Herodotus, Thucydides, and Polybius all seem to have marked views about anger-restraint, and whereas the critique of the tragedians seems to be directed toward excessive anger, the historians establish a sharp dichotomy between sensible decision-making and giving way to *orgē*.

The prevailing behavioral code of the classical Athenians certainly left some scope for *orgē*-anger. The Attic orators doubtless reflect the citizens' view of the matter quite well. On the one side, they – or rather their clients – claim to be virtuous and deserving when they master their anger, and they assert that anger is inconsistent with sensible decision-making. Antiphon, in his famous speech *On the Murder of Herodes*, asks the jury to make up their minds without *orgē* or prejudice, which are, he says, the worst of advisers. "It is impossible for a man who is angry to make a good decision, for <anger> destroys the means by which he may make <sensible> decisions, his judgment (*gnōmē*)."[19] "An honourable citizen," Demosthenes virtuously claims,

should not ask a jury impanelled in the public service to take care of an anger or a hatred or anything like that for his own benefit, and he should not go to court for such purposes. As much as possible, he should not have such things in his nature, but if it is necessary, he should manage them in an even-tempered and moderate fashion.[20]

There is nothing individual about this argument – Aeschines used it too.[21] But such statements make no sense unless they reflect part of the accepted ideology. One should limit and moderate the expression of *orgē*-anger, and perhaps feeling it too. It was also recognized that *orgē* was a common source of crime,[22] and that a testator under the influence of *orgē* may have acted against his real wishes (and hence that his will should be set aside).[23]

The ill repute of *orgē* can be seen in plenty of other fourth-century sources, for instance in the moralistic instruction of a teacher who educated men for public affairs, Isocrates. His address *To Demonicus* (written in the 370s) included this advice:

---

[19] 5.71–2. No doubt Antiphon had said such things before. See also section 91.
[20] 18.278 (see Dover [1974] 192).
[21] Aeschin. 2.3 (where inflaming anger is contrasted with using "just arguments," and it is taken to be self-evidently bad that Demosthenes wanted "to call forth [the jurors'] *orgē*"); 3.4 (he speaks of his opponents as "obtaining judgments not on the basis of the laws, but with anger on the basis of *ad hoc* decrees").
[22] E.g. Dem. 54.25.   [23] Isaeus 1.13 – *orgē*, through which we all make mistakes (cf. 10, 18).

practice self-control (*enkrateia*) in all the things by which it is shameful for the soul to be controlled – gain, *orgē*, pleasure and pain. You will attain such self-control if you [among other things] . . . manage your *orgē* toward those who offend against you as you would expect others to do if you offended against them.[24]

In the social elite there was now, evidently, disgrace attached to displays of *orgē*, at least if they went beyond a certain ill-defined level.

But the practice of oratory, as was widely recognized, required one to stir the audience's anger. In the *Phaedrus* Plato gives the hostile view of such practices: Socrates is made to say about the sophist Thrasymachus that "the mighty Chalcedonian"

is the winner for tearful speeches aimed at arousing pity for old age and poverty, and he is also clever, as he said, at arousing the masses to anger, and at soothing them again by his charms when they are angry, and he is first-rate at both devising and eliminating calumnies on any grounds whatsoever.[25]

On the other hand Demosthenes, the leading practitioner, and Aristotle, the theorist and instructor, are both candid about the need to stimulate *orgē*-anger. Demosthenes often explicitly attempts to excite the *orgē* of his audiences in both political and judicial contexts,[26] and he owed much of his success to his ability to stir his hearers' emotions.[27] He takes it for granted that it was right and proper for the jury in, for instance, his prosecution of Meidias to feel *orgē*:[28]

But this habit my opponent has, men of Athens, this device of entangling in yet more trouble those who take just proceedings in their own defense, is not something which should cause me alone to be indignant and resentful while you overlook it. Far from it. All of us should be equally angry (*orgisteon*), for people should reason and observe that the likeliest of you to suffer easy maltreatment are the poorest and weakest, whereas the likeliest to act insolently (*hubrisai*), and then to avoid punishment for it and hire men to get up legal actions in retaliation, are the loathsome rich. So such conduct must not be overlooked.

---

[24] 1.21. 1.30–1 spells this out: "Be affable in your relations with those you deal with . . . You will be affable if you are not quarrelsome or hard to please and if you are not competitive with everyone, and if you do not harshly oppose the *orgai* of those you deal with even when their *orgē* is unjust; you should instead give way to them when they are in a passion, and rebuke them when they have stopped."

[25] *Phdr.* 267c–d (cf. DK 85 B 6).

[26] Political contexts: *Third Philippic* 31 and 61; *On the Crown* 18 and 138; *On the False Embassy* 7, 265, 302, etc. Judicial contexts: 21.57, 123 and *passim*; 54.42, etc.; [Dem.] 45.7, 53, 67.

[27] Cf. Dion. Hal. *Dem.* 22; and cf. Quint. *Inst.* 6.2.24.

[28] 21.34, 46, 147, 226. The propriety of judicial *orgē* taken for granted: e.g. Lys. 6.17; 31.11; Dem. 24.118 (it will be calibrated to the seriousness of the offense). The passage quoted in the text is 21.123–4.

Other contemporary orators commonly present judicial anger as proper and indeed desirable.[29]

One might be tempted to hypothesize that the only *orgē* which the behavioral code approved was *orgē* that was perceived to be on behalf of the *polis*, anger felt by juries or assemblies. More probably we should recognize that in the fourth century many Athenians shared a vernacular version of Aristotle's view of the matter, which was based on the conception of a mean between *orgilotēs* (irascibility) on the one hand and *aorgēsia* (habitual absence of *orgē*) or *analgēsia* (indifference) on the other. This mean has no precise name, and the closest Aristotle can get is *praotēs*,[30] which is best translated as "even temper"[31] (it can also mean "kindness"). What matters, in Aristotle's opinion, is not that one should avoid anger altogether (he speaks favourably of revenge), and not that one's character should somehow be half-way between irascibility and "habitual absence of *orgē*," but that one should be angry with the right people for the right reasons, in other words with people who have truly done one some injury, and also in the right manner and at the right moment and for the right length of time.[32] Achieving the mean requires one to meet these criteria; it does *not* signify experiencing a moderate amount of anger, for while moderate anger is sometimes appropriate, in other circumstances, according to Aristotle, the correct reaction to a provocation would be either vigorous and prolonged anger or mild irritation.[33]

Towards *thumos*-anger, furthermore, Aristotle shows himself more indulgent than he is toward *orgē*. He maintains that unrestrained *thumos*-anger is less disgraceful than are unrestrained appetites:

anger (*thumos*) seems to listen to reason to some extent, but to mishear it, as do hasty slaves who run out before they hear the whole of what one says, and then muddle the order, or as dogs bark if there is simply a knock on the door, before looking to see if it is a friend; so anger (*thumos*), by reason of the warmth and hastiness of its nature, though it hears, does not hear an order, and rushes to retaliate. For reason or imagination informs us that we have been insulted or

---

[29] E.g. Isoc. 18.4, 36; 20.6, 9, 22; Dinarchus, *Against Demosthenes* 2. For the willingness of fourth-century Athenians, both jurors and philosophers, to look benevolently on *orgē* as a plea in mitigation see Saunders (1991) 110. Allen (2000: 50 and 348), gives a radically over-simplified account of the acceptability of *orgē* in fourth-century Athens, minimizing or ignoring texts that deprecate it or put it in a bad light.

[30] *Eth. Nic.* 2.7.1108a4–9; *Eth. Eud.* 2.3.1220b38. Strictly speaking the mean does not have a name, but "since we call the intermediate person *praos*, let us call the mean *praotēs*." But the condition of *praotēs*, he thinks, "inclines towards the deficiency" (of *orgē*-anger) (*Eth. Nic.* 4.5.1125b28).

[31] Horder (1992) 44, n. 8.

[32] *Eth. Nic.* 4.5.1125b27–1126b10, developed somewhat from *Eth. Eud.* 2.3.1221a15–17.

[33] See Urmson (1973) 225–6 = 1980, 160–2. Cf. Horder (1992) 45.

slighted, and anger, reasoning as it were that anything like this must be fought against, heats up (*chalepainei*) of course straightaway [whereas appetites do not obey reason at all, and are therefore more disgraceful] . . . for the person who is unrestrained in respect of anger (*thumos*) is in a sense controlled by reason . . .[34]

It is from Aristotle that we hear for the first time of philosophers who apparently advocated *apatheia* or the elimination of all passions.[35] Whoever these philosophers were, and whatever exactly they meant by *apatheia*, it was of course the Stoics who became the great authors and defenders of such doctrines.

Both Epicurus and Zeno of Citium were interested in the ethics of anger, and so were many of their principal followers. A rather large literature grew up on the control of *orgē*-anger and *thumos*-anger. The first person to devote a monograph to *orgē* was Bion the Borysthenite some time in the first half of the third century, and by the time that Cicero wrote a letter of advice on the subject to his brother Quintus in 60 or 59 BC a man of education knew that "what is always said by learned men about irascibility . . . you can easily find out from many authors' writings." By this time the anger monograph of Philodemus of Gadara, rather less than half of which has proved to be legible on a Herculaneum papyrus, was probably in circulation. And there were many others to come – some lost, such as one which was probably written by Seneca's philosophy teacher Sotion, others that survive, namely Seneca's own *De ira* (probably written in AD 49 or 50), and the *Peri aorgēsias* of Plutarch (probably written about 100 AD).[36] Other works about the emotions, such as Cicero's *Tusculan Disputations* and particularly Galen's essay *On the Diagnosis and Care of the Passions of the Soul*, also gave anger plenty of space. And this kind of discourse did not remain the exclusive interest of philosophers or the philosophically minded. Far from it: learned discussions of the subject were, I think, known about by, if not known to, most members of the Hellenistic elite, and from the late Republic by most of the upper Roman elite too.

There was no single morality of anger in classical antiquity. There was, however, a strong and continuous tradition of both philosophical argument and therapy directed toward the limitation or the elimination of the stronger anger-emotions. The view that *orgē* or *iracundia* should be altogether eliminated spread beyond Stoicism to a number of non-Stoics, including Cicero and Plutarch, and it is evident that the very simplicity of

---

[34] *Eth. Eud. 6 = Eth. Nic.* 7.6.1149a25–1149b27.
[35] *Eth. Eud.* 2.4.1222a3–5; *Eth. Nic.* 2.3.1104b24–5.
[36] For a catalogue of such works see Harris (2002) 127–8.

this doctrine exercised some attraction. On the other hand the Stoics themselves, from the time of Panaetius onwards, watered down their teaching on this subject, so that Seneca, for instance, admits that even the Wise Man may feel "a certain light and tenuous commotion," and the first unavoidable impulse to anger,[37] and Marcus Aurelius, as we saw earlier, avoided condemning all angry emotions. Epictetus may have been more extreme,[38] and undoubtedly there were always some purists, but much of the philosophical culture and of the wider culture allowed that angry emotions were sometimes licit.

In the imagination of Greek and Roman men, women – like barbarians and children – are especially susceptible to anger. It is emphatically not a stereotype that is confined to the famous misogynistic or misogamic writers such as Semonides of Amorgos, Juvenal, and so on. It is virtually pandemic, from Homer onwards. Just as women were liable to give in to other passions and appetites,[39] so they easily surrendered to the angry emotions, and their anger was seldom, if ever, justified.

The stereotype appears in many genres; writers who conspicuously avoid it (Philodemus, for example) will require special consideration for that reason. It is not simply a cliché, it is (of course) a hostile stereotype, as appears from the beginning.

When Homeric Aeneas encountered Achilles on the plains of Troy, his address to the Achaean hero eventually comes round to this:

What need is there of strife and quarreling between us? As if we were women who get angry about some bitter conflict, go out into the middle of the street and quarrel with each other, saying many things that are true and many that are not, <for> anger urges them to.[40]

That was contemptible unmasculine behaviour, according to a Homeric hero. It should be observed that from the beginning the imaginary female anger which incurs hostile male comments is not merely anger directed against free men; anger between women themselves had a negative connotation.

The most crudely vengeful words spoken in the Homeric narratives are probably those attributed to Hecuba, who, when faced with Priam's diplomatic project in *Iliad* 24, expresses her desire to eat Achilles' raw flesh. The nurse Eurycleia in the *Odyssey* also emerges as particularly vindictive.[41]

---

[37] *De ira* 1.16.7; 2.4.2.   [38] See Harris (2002) 116–18.
[39] See Kurke (1997) 142.   [40] *Il.* 20.252–5.   [41] *Il.* 24.212–14; *Od.* 22.407–12.

It is also suggestive that the archaic spirits of family vengeance, the Erinyes, are female. Quite often in Homer, these spirits are those of a female personage who has been wronged, but even those of a male character, such as Phoenix's father Amyntor, are seen as female, and that of course was part of their later more developed character.[42] Their duties as avengers keep them in a constant state of outraged fury, such as more naturally belonged to the female – so the male presumes.

Certain angry mythical women were readily accessible to the mind of the classical Greek male, or at least to those who possessed a degree of education – above all Clytemnestra and Medea. Both of these figures had powerful reasons for their anger. Clytemnestra is nonetheless always a monster, and once she emerges as a specifically angry figure, in the *Oresteia*, that is what she remains. As for Medea, philosophers and orators returned to her obsessively, from Chrysippus to Synesius – not to mention poets and vase-painters. Numerous Attic tragedies contemplated women's rage (I shall be paying special attention later to *Medea* but also to *Hecuba* and to the two surviving *Electra*s), and some contemplated the anger of goddesses (*Hippolytus* includes a striking hint of criticism directed at Aphrodite[43]). The vengeful Alcmene who dominates the last scene of the *Heracleidae* is also relevant.[44]

Mingled in with the negative stereotype are the positive admonitions. When Athena, in the *Eumenides*, is instructing the Erinyes to forgo excessive anger, she claims that even she, with all her power, gives in to Zeus.[45] In the *Trachiniae* Deianeira, faced with her husband Heracles' unfaithfulness, resolves to win him back, but she professes not to be angered, for, she says, she does not know how to be angry (*thumousthai*) with him. For it is not proper, she continues a moment later, for any sensible woman to grow angry (*orgainein*).[46] This was, I take it, the correct attitude, according to conventional male opinion – which makes the outcome all the more

---

[42] *Il.* 9.454. The literature on the Erinyes can mostly be tracked down via Lloyd-Jones (1990).

[43] Eur. *Hipp.* 120.   [44] *Heracl.* 941–1052.

[45] Aesch. *Eum.* 794–891, with Allen (2000), 114.

[46] Soph. *Trach.* 543, 552–3. Somewhat similarly, an unidentified character in Euripides' *Phrixus* (fr. 819 Nauck) appears to take the restraining of *orgē* and *dusthumia* as one of a wife's principal merits. In Eur. *IT* 993 Iphigeneia virtuously tells Orestes that she is not *thumos*-angry with her late father. The admonition in the *Trachiniae* raises the old question whether women were present during the performance of Athenian tragedies. Scholars continue to disagree, but the balance of the evidence seems to show that *some* women were present (Henderson [1991b] seems on balance to make a stronger case than Goldhill [1994]): some female members of metic families were probably present, and a small number of citizen women. It does not follow that the dramatists ever had a female audience in mind, but the presence of women gives added meaning to such texts as this one.

terrible when she turns to the magic of Nessus in order to win Heracles back but unintentionally kills him instead.

An especially interesting author for the history of classical Greek thinking about anger is Herodotus. The novelty (at least for us) and consistency of his attitude are both remarkable: not only does he make *orgē* the vice of the tyrant and of the insane or semi-insane Persian king, he very seldom represents Greeks of whom he approves as feeling *orgē*, *thumos*, or *cholos* at all.[47] Therefore the language which he uses about angry women is unlikely to be careless. Consider Pheretime, the ruler of Cyrene: she was responsible for impalements, mutilations, and enslavement, which Herodotus calls "excessively severe revenge" such as "makes people the subject of the resentment of the gods."[48] Gender is not a mere incidental in this narrative, for when Pheretime is first introduced she behaves in a conspicuously "unfeminine" manner.[49] Not that Herodotus is generally hasty in attributing angry emotions to women.[50]

Rage on the part of citizen wives appears as part of their transgressiveness in the *Lysistrata*. When the Scythian Archers attack Lysistrata and her friends, they are defeated. "What did you expect?" Lysistrata asks; "did you think that you had come out against *slave* women, or didn't you realize that [free] women have *cholē* (bile, fighting spirit) in them?"[51] The climactic scene of the *Ecclesiazousai*, it will be remembered, consists of a long fierce squabble between a young woman and three old women in turn.[52]

Who is the most famous real-life woman contemporary with Lysistrata? Xanthippe perhaps, the young wife of Socrates. In later centuries she became a byword for ill temper, but her reputation, perhaps entirely undeserved, was apparently already in the making in the 380s, to judge from Xenophon.[53]

Changing genres again, we may note that the middle-aged Plato of the *Republic* was apparently willing to maintain that women were no more likely to surrender to *thumos*-anger than men are – though he does not explicitly state this:[54]

---

[47] Harris (2002) 175–6.   [48] *epiphthonoi ginontai*, 4.205.   [49] 4.162.5.

[50] When the women of Athens stoned to death the widow and children of the councillor Lycidas, who had been receptive to Mardonius' peace proposal (9.5), no emotion is mentioned. Herodotus seems to take their reaction to be a natural one.

[51] 463–5. That the women are angry is confirmed by 435–48 and 550, and by the *orgē* they provoke in their opponents (505).

[52] 877–1111. This was what women's rule led to. Earlier in the play, however, the women of Athens only seem to be angry when they are practicing being men (174–5, 255).

[53] *Mem.* 2.2.

[54] *Resp.* 5.455d–457b; the passage quoted in the text is 456a. In 3.396d he speaks of wrangling quarreling women, but then also holds up for disapproval men who behave similarly. A woman's influence in the public sphere being necessarily indirect, women might be suspected of goading their sons to give

May a woman then not be either philosophic or anti-philosophical, either
    spirited (*thumoeidēs*) or spiritless (*athumos*)?
Yes again.
Then there will be some women capable of being guardians, and others inca-
    pable. For these qualities were those for which we chose our male guardians.
Yes indeed.

In the *Laws*, however, Plato took the validity of the old stereotype of
women's irascibility for granted: one should pity those criminals who could
be cured and not punish them in anger and bitterness *like a woman*.[55]

Are there, by way of contrast, any Greek texts of pre-Hellenistic date in
which a woman's anger is represented as right or just, or is fully approved
of? I shall explore later the possibility that in Euripides' *Hecuba* the *orgē*
of the heroine was partially condoned.[56] A far clearer instance, and a most
unusual one, appears in the speech which Apollodorus, son of Pasion, gave
against Neaera (Pseudo-Demosthenes 59). Having tried to blacken Neaera's
reputation by calling her a whore and a whorehouse-keeper, the speaker
challenges the massed jurors with evident passion: if you acquit Neaera of
her crime (usurpation of citizen rights), what will you say to your wife,
daughter, or mother when you return home? Will not the most virtuous
women (*hai sōphronestatai*) immediately be angry with you (*orgisthēsontai*)
for deciding that Neaera should share in their privileges as citizen women?[57]
But the speaker is also, I suggest, making rhetorical use of what was to him
and his audience an obvious contrast: *even* well-behaved women will be
angry, so outrageous would an acquittal be, whereas such *sōphronestatai* do
not normally feel *orgē*.

Herodas 5 confirms that the stereotype was alive and popular in Alexandria
in the mid third century. In this brief sketch (eighty-five lines) entitled
Zēlotupos, "The Jealous One," the "heroine" is a woman named Bitinna,
who has been conducting a sexual relationship with her slave Gastron ("Mr.
Stomach") and now accuses him in crude terms of being unfaithful to her.
She rejects his pleas of innocence and his appeals for mercy, and orders
him to be whipped and to be tattooed on the face. In the last five lines,

---

vent to political anger, and that too was probably disapproved of: see Pl. *Resp.* 8.549d. Thus Athens
seems to have resembled another patriarchal society, that of the Icelandic sagas, where, according
to W. I. Miller (1993: 104), "women are expected to goad their menfolk to vengeful action, and
men use this goading as an opportunity to discourse disapprovingly about female vengefulness and
irrationality."

[55] *Laws* 5.731d (*mē akracholounta gunaikeiōs pikrainomenon diatelein*).

[56] The anger of Phaedra with her nurse in Eur. *Hipp.* 682–712 is at least very easily comprehensible.

[57] [Dem.] 59.110–11. For Apollodorus as the author see Trevett (1992) esp. 50–76.

however, on the intercession of a slave woman, Bitinna agrees to postpone the punishments for a few days. She is a disgraceful character according to the morals of free Greek men: first for having a slave lover, secondly, I think, for the fury, cruelty, and implacability of her anger against the slave when she thinks that he has been unfaithful. So, a double degradation, only a little bit softened at the end, and here we have yet another irate woman held up to contempt. In the succeeding mime we encounter still more female anger, disreputable again[58] – and we also encounter the line which represents a sort of official doctrine against a woman's anger: "a good woman is ready to bear anything" (*gunaikos esti krēguēs pherein panta*).[59]

There were other surviving texts similar in theme to these two sketches, such as an anonymous mime (Page, *Greek Literary Papyri*, no. 77) in which once again the protagonist is a raging woman slave-holder who has a sexual connection with at least one of her slaves.[60] The anger of the principal character is so sadistic that there should be no doubt that it is being offered for our disapproval. Herodas 3 also seems to hold a woman's anger up for derision, though the case is less explicit and straightforward. Metrotime, the principal character, desires to have her schoolboy son thrashed by his teacher, who readily collaborates. Eventually he desists, but Metrotime is unrelenting.[61]

The stereotype naturally passed over to the deeply Hellenized literary men of Rome. When Horace, for example, wrote a poem elegantly urging someone to cease being angry with him, the addressee was female.[62] One can believe, if one wishes, that a real person, unnamed, was concerned, but it is much more likely that the occasion was imaginary, and hence that Horace was acknowledging the force of the ancient stereotype. No doubt there had already been plenty of angry women in Roman literature – Ariadne in Catullus 64 stands out.[63] There had been angry males too of course, but it is clear that when women (fictional or otherwise) appear in literary works they have a much better chance than men do of being labelled

---

[58] 6.1–11, 27–36.

[59] 6.39. It is not sufficient to say that these characters "are designed simply to provoke our laughter" (Zanker [1987] 158). Another Hellenistic glimpse of our stereotype: Polyb. 15.30.1.

[60] Her anger: lines 13, 25, 28, 35, etc. This is a fragmentary text of early imperial date, originally published as *P.Oxy.* 3.413 verso, cols. 1–3. When Trimalchio tells his guest Scintilla not to be *zelotypa* toward a slave (*Sat.* 69.2), Petronius has in mind texts such as Herodas 5.

[61] See esp. lines 87–8, 94–7, though there are textual problems.

[62] *Odes* 1.16. I follow the general line of interpretation suggested by R. G. M. Nisbet and M. Hubbard; the poem is not a palinode.

[63] She curses Theseus, 64.132–201, her anger being especially plain at lines 192–201.

as irascible. Another part of this story is the Roman woman who cannot control her anger toward her slaves.[64]

A certain Theano was either the wife or the daughter of the philosopher Pythagoras, and she was reputed to have philosophized too. Long after her death (but in which century we have no means of knowing), someone or other composed some letters that purported to be hers. They represent her as an unusually self-controlled woman, probably in virtue of her relationship to Pythagoras. In one of these letters she is shown advising a female acquaintance not to punish her slaves to excess out of *thumos*.[65] But Theano is assumed to be incapable of maintaining this level: the next letter but one in the collection is simply a short angry letter[66] – such as women typically write to each other, we are led to think. The stereotype is in action once more.

To Greek intellectuals of the Roman period female irascibility was generally a commonplace: it was made use of by Lucian[67] and by Plutarch,[68] even though the latter was able to see that much marital anger came from the male side. In *On the Diagnosis and Care of the Passions of the Soul*, which is mainly about *orgē* and *thumos*, Galen wrote this:

I cannot say what kind of nature I had \<as a boy\> – to know oneself is a difficult thing even for full-grown men, much more for boys – but I did enjoy the good fortune of having the least irascible (*aorgētotaton*), the most just, the most devoted and the kindest of fathers. My mother, however, was so very prone to anger (*orgilōtatēn*) that she sometimes bit her slave-women; she constantly shrieked at my father and fought with him, more than Xanthippe did with Socrates.[69]

And he goes on to speak about his mother's "disgraceful passions." Of course we have no idea whether these charges were fair – Galen sometimes reproduces *topoi* as items of autobiography[70] and he may be doing so here. In any case he chose to proclaim his mother's supposed inability to control her rage.

---

[64] Clark (1998: 123–4) collects texts that propagate this image, including Ov. *Amores* 1.14.12–18; *Ars am.* 2.235–44, Petr. *Sat.* 69; Juv. 6.219–24, 475–95; Apul. *Met.* 3.16.

[65] Epistolographi Graeci, *Pythagorae et Pythagoreorum Ep.* 6 ed. Hercher (pp. 605–6) = 4 Thesleff (p. 198), lines 18–23.

[66] 8 Hercher (pp. 606–7) = 8 Thesleff (p. 200).

[67] *Abdicatus* 28: women have a great deal of irascibility (*orgilon*) in them and frivolity and excitability (?) (*oxukinēton*); they are more liable to various emotions including *orgē* than men are (ibid. 30).

[68] It appears from *Marius* 38 (the story of Fannia of Minturnae) that Plutarch regarded a woman who passed up an opportunity for revenge as unusual.

[69] *De propriorum animi cuiuslibet affectuum dignotione et curatione* 8.1 De Boer. Cf. Plut. *Ant.* 1.3, 49.2. Writing to his wife Marcella, Porphyry limited himself to instructing her not to punish slaves in anger (*Ad Marcellam* 35).

[70] See Harris (2002) 12.

The ideal woman wrote a Theano letter, or she was the heroine of a romance (in any case, she did not exist). In the romance written by Chariton, the heroine Callirhoe is propositioned by a eunuch on behalf of the King of Babylon: her first reaction is that she would like to tear his eyes out, but

being a woman of education and good sense (*phrenērēs*), she reasoned quickly . . . replaced her *orgē*, and responded to the barbarian artfully.[71]

It is possible, however, that most philosophers and people with strong philosophical interests generally avoided the cliché of the irascible female or at any rate treated it with some reserve.[72] Since Aristotle insisted on the subordination of women, we expect him to accuse them of excessive emotionalism. And sure enough, he does say that the rational part of women's souls "is not in command" (*akuron*),[73] which implies that they are more emotional than men. Elsewhere he declares that people are more angry with their *philoi*, their dear ones, than with other people, the reason being (he says) that people think that the former have obligations to them.[74] He *might* perhaps have added that that is why wives are irascible, but he did not do so.

Virtually the only reference to women in the admittedly incomplete *De ira* of Philodemus is a complaint about men who show undue anger to their wives.[75] Epicurean males in general – quite atypical of Greek society in their treatment of women – may have tended to reject the traditional sexism on this subject.[76] It so happens that the familiar *topos* is also absent from the philosophical works of Cicero.[77] Even Seneca, although he surrenders to the standard stereotype, may be less fond of it than might have been expected. A recent writer has maintained that Seneca believed in the moral equality of the sexes.[78] That may be exaggerated: once in *De ira* Seneca refers to anger as a woman's vice – "it is womanly to rage (*furere*) in anger," and

---

[71] Chariton 6.5.8.

[72] It may also be relevant that amid all his angry characters Menander seems to have included no women.

[73] *Pol.* 1.5.1260a13. The context is the assertion that there is a woman's form of virtue and of self-restraint, courage, and justice; he quotes Soph. *Ajax* 293, "Silence makes a woman beautiful" (words which Tecmessa says are trite, *humnoumena*, 292).

[74] *Rh.* 2.2.1379b2–4.

[75] *De ira* 5 (col. xxii.32–xxiii.2): "if they marry, they accuse their wives of corrupt behaviour and form hasty judgments <about them>" (that seems to be the meaning, but there is a gap in the text immediately after the last word translated here). In his edition, G. Indelli takes the meaning to be: "se sono sposati, agiscono sconsideratamente, accusando la moglie di oltraggio."

[76] See Nussbaum (1994) 194, n. 2. Some Stoics were not above passing on hostile stories about Xanthippe, the wife of Socrates: see Antipater of Tarsus fr. 65 (*SVF* 3.257).

[77] For a supposedly criminal woman furiously applying torture to slaves see Cic. *Clu.* 177.

[78] Mauch (1997).

the same sentiment appears elsewhere.[79] Yet given the length of *De ira* we might have expected more; not one of his numerous *exempla* of evil temper is female.

With Plutarch, however, we seem to have returned to the conventional attitude:

just as with the body a bruise results from a great blow, so with the most delicate souls the inclination to inflict pain produces a greater outburst of anger (*thumos*) in proportion to their greater weakness. That is why women are more irascible than men.[80]

And while Plutarch, like Cicero and Philodemus, is capable of seeing women as the victims of male anger,[81] he claims that women ought to be without anger, or at least without autonomous anger: a wife "should have no emotion (*pathos*) of her own, but should share her husband's seriousness or playfulness, soberness or laughter." If the husband commits "some little error" with a *hetaira* or a slave-woman, the wife should not *aganaktein* or *chalepainein*, that is, make a fuss or get cross (it follows that she should not even approach a state of *orgē*).[82] At the same time, however, Plutarch's somewhat novel view of marriage as a partnership includes both an unprecedented degree of concern about familial anger as well as awareness that husbands are responsible for a good proportion of it.

A properly organized city, from a Greek male point of view, was one in which women knew their place; and knowing their place involved among other things avoiding anger. When angry or punishing female characters appeared on the tragic stage of Athens, they were represented as masculine,[83] which was most definitely seen as an improper attribute by the great bulk of the audience. The stereotype I have been examining thus implies that there was almost no legitimate place for women's anger in the classical city, either at Athens or apparently elsewhere.

The point of the stereotyped angry woman is that she represents an attempt at the thorough denigration, indeed delegitimization, of female anger. The moralistic anti-anger tradition was only in part "absolutist": a

---

[79] *De ira* 1.20.3 ("contra mihi videtur veternosi et infelicis animi, imbecillitatis sibi conscii, saepe indolescere . . . ita ira muliebre maxime ac puerile vitium est. 'At incidit et in viros.' Nam viris quoque puerilia ac muliebria ingenia sunt"); *Clem.* 1.5.5.

[80] *De cohibenda ira* 8 (*Mor.* 457ab). See also 9 (457c).

[81] See *Coniugalia praecepta* 2, 3, 39 (*Mor.* 139e, 143e).

[82] *Coniugalia praecepta* 14, 16 (*Mor.* 140a, 140b); cf. 28 (141f–142a). It is assumed in 27 = 141f that *orgē* in a marriage came from the wife's side.

[83] Allen (2000) 115.

great deal of anger was actually approved of even by philosophers, particularly by Platonists and Peripatetics. The ordinary educated male Greek
of Hellenistic and Roman times (not to mention earlier Greeks, not to
mention Romans) was by no means opposed to all male anger whatsoever;
but about women's anger he knew what to think. The message of the texts
that we have been examining is, to borrow words from Elizabeth Spelman,
that while "members of subordinate groups are expected to be emotional,
indeed to have their emotions run their lives, their anger will not be
tolerated."[84]

It might be objected that there are other kinds of people who are stereo-
typically angry in ancient texts – the elderly, for instance. Was their anger
meant to be delegitimized too? To some extent perhaps it was, but attitudes
toward paternal anger were in fact quite complex, and an angry old father
might be thought to have a degree of justice on his side.

Thus the argument is that the *orgē* of women was held up for disapproval
or derision so often in Greek literature that we should detect a dominant
tradition of delegitimization. But this tradition does not refer to all anger
whatsoever, for the texts that I have been examining have for the most part
been concerned with *orgē* and *thumos*. So the campaign was not as severe
as it might at first seem. The rules established by the Greek male did not
go so far as to say, for instance, that a wife could not now and again express
some annoyance, *chalepotēs*, towards her husband.

But why exactly should Greek and perhaps Roman men have wished
to reserve anger for their own use? An ingenious theory has proposed that
the cognitive component in anger, emphasized both by Aristotle and by
late twentieth-century psychology, and indeed taken for granted by most
ancient thinking on the subject, means that anger is *judgmental*. To be
angry, it has been argued, is to put oneself in the position of judge, which
for a woman in a patriarchal society means to be insubordinate.[85] Greek
men were unwilling to have women pass judgment on them.

This is a not implausible if somewhat metaphysical interpretation. Anger
often no doubt seems judgmental to its targets, in all ages. But we may hesitate to equate the cognitive event which is invariably or almost invariably
involved in being angry with an act of judging. Appropriating anger for
themselves was, rather, a matter of strengthening men's social and sexual
control. Greek men simply wanted their wives (and also their concubines
and *hetairai*, and daughters too) to be docile and do their duty. An argument in favour of this view is that they wished not only to censor the anger

---

[84] Spelman (1989) 264.   [85] Spelman (1989) 265–70.

of women against the dominant male, but also their anger against slaves and against each other. It is hard to think that the free male found anything inappropriate in a free woman's *judgment* about a slave's behaviour – for it was part of a housewife's job to superintend the slaves. It was not that men needed to establish their control over the household.[86] Rather, a double purpose is served. A lesson is offered against a woman's extreme anger toward slaves, for such anger was an impediment to the smooth running of the slave system (male slave-holders explained to each other how anger could provoke slaves to appalling retaliation). And female anger against slaves could also be used, as in the mimes of Herodas, to reassert women's weakness of character.

This male instrumentalization of anger fits, as it is easy to see, into a wider set of beliefs about the excessive emotionality of women, a belief which goes back at least to epic times and the unfaithful wife Helen. The tragic theatre provides ample evidence, and Aristotle was doubtless merely one among innumerable Greek men who believed that women were more emotional than men. Anger, however, is – together with sexual desire – the emotion which most clearly requires, in the view of the Greeks, different rules for women and for men.

Women were expected to fulfil their socially assigned roles, and without too much complaining. In my view, Athenian women had unusually strong grounds for complaint, since they lived in a system which was not only patriarchal but, even by the standards of patriarchal societies, quite inconsiderate of their feelings. However, it is an extremely speculative business to reconstruct the emotional atmosphere of classical Athenian marriages, and in order not to complicate the argument unnecessarily I simply refer to my larger study.[87] It is evident in any case that the morality of anger between wife and husband was not usually symmetrical: in other words, it was a long time before philosophers suggested that husbands should exercise restraint over their anger towards their wives. Philodemus and Cicero are the earliest surviving authors to assert such as thing (though they are not likely to have been the very first).

The Epicureans may have rejected the traditional stereotype. It seems, however, that it had already been subjected to critical scrutiny long before, in Athenian tragedy.

First it should be said that although this is an attempt to interpret the inert texts of Sophocles and Euripides, we must allow for the probability that

[86] As Clark maintains in an important discussion (1998) 124.   [87] Harris (2002) ch. 12.

in the actual staging the actors did their utmost to exploit the theatrical possibilities of raging fury. That is to say, anger may have stood out in performance even more than it does in silent reading.

It would be wrong, of course, to simplify the tragedians' representations of women. One should keep in mind, for instance, that in the extant plays of Sophocles the role of prominent female characters is more often to placate angry passions of one kind or another than to express them. Tecmessa plays that role among others in the *Ajax*,[88] as does Jocasta in *Oedipus Tyrannus*.[89] Finally, much later, in *Oedipus at Colonus*, Antigone calms her father's rage, and then attempts to mollify her brother Polyneices.[90] These are all quite brief scenes, and they should be taken not as a message of any kind, but as evidence of one way in which Sophocles and some of his contemporaries imagined women as behaving.

Three Euripidean plays in particular show us the poet exploring the subject of women's anger: *Medea*, *Hecuba*, and *Electra* (to put them in chronological order). These plays seem to show a certain progression from an appalling demon of female anger, who, however, has an excellent reason to be angry (*Medea*), to a violent collective act of angry female vengeance which is paradoxically given a measure of approval (*Hecuba*), to an act of female vengeance which is horrible but fully accepted (*Electra*).

Medea is permeated with *orgē*.[91] Medea is also shown to us as having gone to great lengths in the service of another passion, *erōs*.[92] The consequences of her anger are recounted to us unsparingly, and while there is room for argument about the precise ways in which Euripides adapted the plot, there can be no doubt that he made Medea a more violent and ruthless character than was necessary: the tradition did not require him to make her the killer of her children.[93] Not only is she murderously angry, she is fully conscious of being so. Medea's revenge, especially the murder of her two small children, seems to be the maximum of horror that a woman (lacking armed force) could inflict. Her anger makes her into a bull or a lion.[94] Furthermore this anger, though perhaps it is natural, is unrelenting: what is most wrong is that she does not desist.[95] And in spite of her "masculine" resolution, Medea is depicted as a representative woman: "we were born

---

[88] *Ajax* 368, 588, 594; her husband is of course the target.
[89] *OT* 634–702. She intervenes between her husband and Creon.   [90] *OC* 1181–1203, 1420–43.
[91] See especially, in the first half of the play alone, lines 38–9, 91–4, 99, 109, 120–1, 129, 160–7, 172, 176, 271, 319–20, 446–50, 520, 590, 615, 637–8.
[92] On the linkage between Medea's *erōs* and her anger see Friedrich (1993) 225.
[93] See Knox (1977) 194 = (1979) 295–6.   [94] *Med.* 92, 187–8.
[95] She is *duskatapaustos* (109); cf. 878–9.

women," she says, "incapable of performing noble actions, but such skilled architects of every kind of harm."[96]

When Jason finally appears on stage, he begins by sententiously telling his wife that he has often seen what an untreatable evil harsh anger is, and he explains that the alternative is "to bear lightly the wishes of the stronger."[97] All very simple and true, but the play also contains a violently contrasting theme, namely that Medea has a case. This is not a subjective reaction to Medea's dramatic situation: chorus and cult both take us in the same direction. Medea is rescued by Aigeus, king of Athens, in the last scene of the play, and Attica becomes for her as for so many other tragic personages a final haven. The chorus of Corinthian women had said that Jason suffered justly (*endikōs*).[98] Revenge was not yet in 431 much questioned at Athens, and the quasi-masculine Medea almost inevitably exacted it.

We should conclude that Euripides intended to startle his audience out of its wits (and his trilogy was ranked third and last – of course we do not know why) by setting before them the disastrous anger of a barbarian woman who had good reason to be angry. No one would want to reduce this extraordinary work to a simple formula. The uniqueness and strangeness of the plot almost defies one to draw general conclusions. But what I think we see is Euripides' representation of a woman who – although she has all the determination and astuteness of Odysseus, so much so that she can see the value of carefully dissembling her emotions – is in the end ruled by unrelenting anger. At the same time, her anger was justifiable, at least while she was encompassing the death of the new bride Glauce.

In *Hecuba* (of about 424 BC) a woman's anger also has terrible effects. The second half of the play reveals how Hecuba's son Polydorus, the last Trojan prince, who had been sent for safety to the court of King Polymestor of Thrace, was after the fall of Troy murdered by Polymestor for his gold. Hecuba, though now an enslaved prisoner, manages to take revenge upon Polymestor: in combination with other enslaved Trojan women, she blinds him and kills his sons. The co-operation of a group of violent women[99] must have made the act seem all the more unpalatable to the male audience. Blinded Polymestor prophesies strikingly that Hecuba will be changed into a dog with fiery-red eyes.[100]

---

[96] 407–9. Cf. 569–75, 908–13 (it is unsurprising [*eikos*], Jason says, for a woman to be angry in Medea's situation; then, in his delusion, he praises her for having changed her mind).

[97] 446–7, 449.

[98] 1231–2; this is before Medea has killed her children. Contrast the simple black and white of Seneca's play.

[99] *Hec.* 1052, 1061–75, 1095–6, 1120, 1151–72, foreshadowed by 886. [100] 1265.

Agamemnon, however, the play's presiding figure, adjudicates in Hecuba's favour. In fact he is complicit in her actions, and we may therefore suspect that Hecuba's case is meant to receive sympathy – even though it is represented as a female mastery (*kratos*) over men.[101] Polymestor's crime made Hecuba into an angry and vengeful woman, and an even more resolute one than Medea, but her anger is not delegitimized – far from it. A modern critic speaks typically of the "degradation" which Hecuba brings upon herself,[102] but the common classical Greek reaction is also likely to have included the view that she delivered a justified act of revenge. It is interesting that although the play contains a lot of anger, actual *orgē* words, which are so common in *Medea*, are never heard. When Agamemnon catches sight of Polymestor after he has been blinded, he says "It was indeed a great *cholos* that the doer of this deed had for you and your children."[103] This choice of words is presumably to be taken as a sign that Hecuba's anger is not to be demonized. A recent reading of the play makes much of the moral ambiguity of the heroine's revenge,[104] which one might possibly be inclined to dismiss as the 1990s fashion – but in this instance it seems just right. The play is terrifying, but it is at the same time one of the most understanding depictions of female retaliation to have survived from Greek antiquity.

Euripides' *Electra* (produced about 416?) also shows us female vengeance in action. The heroine impels her sometimes hesitant brother to avenge Agamemnon's death by murdering Clytemnestra. Her hand as well as that of Orestes is on the sword as it does its work.[105] When the killing has been done, the Dioscuri appear and conveniently place the blame on Apollo; they also explain how the cycle of killing will come to an end. To that extent, Electra is justified,[106] and a violent woman can be said to have been presented to the audience with some understanding. It is to be noted, however, that Electra's anger against Clytemnestra is mentioned only indirectly; it may be that Electra's virile revenge is acceptable to poet and audience partly because it is *not* the product of violent and unreasoning passion.

Finally, I turn to Sophocles' play on the same subject, which was produced somewhat later.[107] The heroine's anger is an explicit theme, and she seems to gain credit from attempting to resist it, and ultimately blame for surrendering to it. Sophocles saw that Electra's revenge had to be built on her anger, and he allowed no palliation of that anger. The chorus tells her

---

[101] 898–904, 883.
[102] Kerrigan (1996) 194 ("she sinks to the level of her enemy"). I contradict this splendid book with reluctance.
[103] *Hec.* 1118–19.   [104] Mossman (1995) esp. 163–209, a first-rate account.   [105] *El.* 1225.
[106] See esp. 1296–7.   [107] On the chronological problem see Bremer (1991) 328–9.

early in the play to turn her *cholos* over to Zeus, and she is aware of her *orgē* and what can be said against it.[108] When Clytemnestra in her turn is angry, Electra regains a degree of calm,[109] but at the climactic moment she urges Orestes on to still greater violence in his murder of Clytemnestra.[110] This time there is no calm resolution: we are left with the terrible consequences of Electra's rage. What the poet and his audience imagined as happening when the play was over is a vexed scholarly question, but the poet conspicuously does not bring the Dioscuri or anyone else to Electra's moral rescue.

It is to be concluded that few male Greeks considered in any period that there was much room for legitimate female *orgē*. The limitations included in this statement must be attended to: the discussion is about intense anger, not about every minor form of irritation, and there are exceptional situations such as the one envisaged in *Against Neaera*. And there were those such as Euripides and presumably some members of his Great Dionysia audience who perceived the strangeness of the imbalance which arises when rage is permitted to one sex but not the other.

Thus the critique of the strong-anger emotions, which had contributed to the growth of Athenian civic institutions, helped not only to exclude women from political affairs but to take away from them, as far as possible, one of the foundations of an independent personality, that very dangerous thing, the right to rage.

[108] *El.* 176–7; 222; 331 and 369.   [109] 516–629.   [110] 1414–15; cf. 1483–4.

CHAPTER 6

Thumos *as masculine ideal and social pathology in ancient Greek magical spells*

Christopher A. Faraone

Among the Greek magical handbooks of the Roman period we find several charms labeled *thumokatocha*[1] – a rubric usually translated as "spells for restraining anger" despite the notoriously broad semantic range of the word *thumos*, which in addition to "anger" can among other things mean "breath," "soul," "spirit," "will," "courage," "heart," or "life."[2] These handbook charms seem to originate from two very different magical traditions, one connected with cursing or "black magic" and the other with amulets or "white magic." Thus those inscribed on lead and deposited in bodies of water or graves clearly evolve from a native Greek tradition of spells that aim at binding the body, the speech, or the mental faculties of a rival or an enemy. A second and equally popular type of Greek *thumos*-restraining spell probably originates in Near Eastern traditions and involves wearing amulets – either knotted cords or inscribed gold or silver tablets – designed to enhance the charisma of the wearer and to ward off the anger and hostility of others, usually their social superiors. As we shall see, both types of spells aim at much more than a man's anger. In this essay, then, I question and ultimately reject the very narrow definition of *thumokatocha* as "anger-restraining spells," first by surveying the extant examples of both types of charms and then by briefly discussing a third and closely related category of love potions that seem similarly designed to mollify or soothe irritated males. In the end I argue for a much wider category of "*passion*-restraining spells," namely charms that aim at controlling other things besides anger, for example: competitive zeal, heated verbal exchanges, and erotic attraction. I

I owe many thanks to Susanna Braund and Glenn Most, the organizers of the Heidelberg conference and the editors of this volume, for urging me to think about the control of anger in Greek magical texts. I am also grateful to all the participants of the conference for their stimulating questions and discussion of this paper. I have profited much from them and from David Jordan and Roy Kotansky, who read and commented on subsequent written versions. Any errors that remain are my own.

[1] A compound of the noun *thumos* and the adjective *katochos*, which is derived from the verb *katechein*, "to restrain." See Hopfner (1938) for a good general discussion.

[2] LSJ s.v.

suggest, moreover, that the spells borrowed from the cursing tradition can tell us much about how the ancient Greeks construct their notions of such passions as "typical" or "natural" components of an ideal masculinity. We shall also see, however, that the amuletic tradition of *thumos*-restraining spells points to an alternate, negative view of this ideal: namely that male *thumos* or *orgē* is a socially corrosive pathology that must be controlled or otherwise healed by women or other social subordinates, if they wish to protect themselves from it.

THUMOS-RESTRAINING SPELLS: ORIGINS, HISTORY, AND TAXONOMY

Although the rubric *thumokatochon* does not itself appear until the Roman-period magical handbooks, we do have evidence in much earlier binding spells for magical techniques designed to control or suppress the *thumos* of another individual. These "binding spells" survive mainly on inscribed lead tablets and are dated as early as the classical period in Sicily, Attica, and the Black Sea area.[3] By the late Hellenistic period we find them scattered throughout the Greek-speaking Mediterranean. The usual practice was quite simple: a person inscribed the victim's name on a metal tablet, rolled it, pierced it with a nail, and then deposited it in some underground place, such as a grave or a well. The focus of most pre-Roman binding spells is on the restraint, not the destruction of the victim, and they are primarily used in agonistic situations to inhibit the performances of rival politicians, orators, businessmen, or lovers.[4] Often the specific target of the binding action is related to the context; for example, curses aimed at orators bind their minds, tongues, and words so that they are unable to speak effectively, while those designed for charioteers bind their arms and eyes to prevent them from driving to victory.

Among the classical-era spells from Athens, we find four examples of the *thumos* as a target for binding. Three of these texts are quite short and seem to treat the *thumos* as part of a generalized sequence of human body parts or intellectual faculties, for example: "I bind the soul (*psuchē*), the mind (*nous*), and the *thumos*" (*DTA* 51), "I bind the tongue, the work, the hands, the *thumos*" (52), or "the *thumos*, the works, the tongue" (53). In these curses the word *thumos* should obviously be understood in one of its

---

[3] These types of incantations are called *katadesmoi* in Greek and *defixiones* in late Latin. See Faraone (1991) for an overview. The most important corpora and surveys of the Greek spells are: *DTA*, *DT*, and SGD; see p. x for abbreviations for magical texts.

[4] Kagarow (1929), Preisendanz (1972), and Faraone (1991) provide useful general discussions.

many positive connotations, as "soul," "spirit," "will," or "courage," and not in its narrow, negative sense as "anger." Indeed, this is confirmed by the author of a contemporary text (*DTA* 84a) who inserts an adjective to qualify these general terms when he writes: "I bind Androkleides and his evil tongue and his ill will (τὸν θυμὸν τὸν κακὸν) and his evil *psuchē* and I bind his workshop and his children." Here we find that in order to get the specialized sense of "anger" or "ill will" out of the word *thumos*, the author is forced to use the adjective "evil" (*kakos*) to make his meaning clear.

In the early *defixiones*, then, the *thumos* appears in its neutral or positive sense as one of a number of similar targets, such as "the mind" or "the hands," which are crucial for human success in any competitive situation. In short, *thumos* is a beneficial body part, which one desires in oneself but which one wishes to control or paralyze in a rival. By the Roman imperial period, however, the word *thumos* often appears in binding spells as the primary target (often in tandem with *orgē*), as in a series of third-century CE Cyprian texts, all apparently written by the same scribe or scribes for clients seeking to bind their opponents in an upcoming lawsuit, for example (*DT* 22.26–30): "bind up and lull to sleep the tongue, the *thumos*, and the *orgē* of Ariston, my legal opponent (*antidikos*), which [i.e. the *orgē*] Ariston has towards (*eis*) me, Soterianon, and toward Limbaros, in order that he be unable to oppose me in any action." Further along in the spell he adds (37–8): "seize the words of Ariston [which he speaks] against (*pros*) me and Limbaros." The binding of speech is also emphasized in the following formula addressed on another tablet to the dead buried in the grave where the tablets were found (*DT* 25.16–18): "Just as you are voiceless, speechless, and without tongues, so too let my legal opponents be voiceless, speechless, without tongues (*aphōnoi, alaloi, aglōssoî*)."

Another spell in the series (*DT* 33.3–6) reads: "seize the *thumos* of Soteria and Tryphon and Demetrius and Demetria, [the *thumos*] which they have towards (*pros*) me, Zoilos, and the *orgē*, and take away their power (*dunamis*) and strength (*alkē*) and make them cool (*psuchroi*) and without voice (*aphonoi*) and without breath (*apneumones*), cool towards (*eis*) me Zoilos." This tradition of binding spells aimed specifically at the victims' *orgē* or the *thumos* (and their speech as well) continues down into the fourth century, when we find an inscribed lead tablet from Egypt which reads:

Bind, bind down the *orgē*, the *thumos* of Paomis, whom Tisate bore . . . Restrain the *orgē*, the *thumos* of Paomis, whom Tisate bore, his mind (*nous*), his wits (*phrenes*), in order that he not gainsay me (ὅπως μὴ ἀντείπῃ ἐμοί), Horigenes, whom Ioullē (also called Theodora) bore, but so that he be obedient to us, now, now, quickly, quickly.[5]

Here, as in the Cyprian curses, although the spell restrains various other parts of Paomis (his *nous* and his *phrenes*) and prevents his speech in opposition or contradiction, it nonetheless gives special attention to his *orgē* and *thumos*. If Jordan is correct in supposing that this spell was also used in the context of an upcoming lawsuit, I suggest that a context of legal wrangling may explain the appearance of *thumos* and *orgē*, for recent studies have shown that at Athens, at least, public expressions of forceful anger at a trial could be crucial to a litigant's success.[6]

In the Roman period we also begin to see this special focus on the binding of *orgē* and *thumos* in other types of magical rituals – none of them overtly concerned with legal trials – that clearly derive from this tradition. An ostrakon, for example, begins with the rubric *thumokathukōn* (read: *thumokatochon*, "*thumos*-restraint spell") and ends with a *similia similibus* formula very much like the one in the Cyprian curses: "Just as this rock [i.e. the ostrakon] is voiceless (*aphōnos*) and speechless (*alalos*), so too let all who are against (*kata*) me be voiceless, speechless, and obedient to me."[7] A third- or fourth-century CE handbook, on the other hand, preserves a brief recipe for "a *thumokatochon* to be recited three times" which is comprised of magical words and the command: "Restrain the *orgē* and the *thumos* of Mr. So-and-so, toward (*pros*) me, Mr. So-and-so."[8] Another handbook recipe describes a similarly brief verbal spell accompanied by the performance of a simple ritual gesture (*PGM* 12.179–81):

If you wish to stop someone from being *orgizomenos* with you, inscribe on a myrrh-infused piece of linen this name of *orgē*: *Chneōm*. Grasping it in your left hand say: "I am restraining the *orgē* of all men, especially that of Mr. So-and-so."

Here we are directed to grasp the victim's *orgē* itself in our inauspicious left hands as we recite the performative utterance: "I am restraining . . ." Squeezing the inscribed linen is a magical action quite similar to rolling up the lead *defixio* and piercing it with a nail: both aim in different ways at immobilizing the *thumos* or the *orgē* of the victim.

---

[5] *SM* 57.34–44. I follow the text and translation of the editors. For discussion, see Collart (1930) and Bonner (1950) 104.

[6] Jordan, SGD no. 162 ad loc. See Allen (2000) 50–9 for the useful role of anger in Athenian courtrooms.

[7] *SM* 58, which was inscribed in the fourth or fifth century CE and discovered in Egyptian Thebes.

[8] It survives on two third- or fourth-century CE papyri from Egypt, *PGM* 79 and 80, and is discussed in detail by Hopfner (1930). Another handbook spell also calls itself a *thumokatochon*, and tells that we should "go before him and say" presumably whispering (*SM* 79.19–25): "Do not display *orgē* (*orgizou*) to me, but change your mind . . . You, Mr. So-and-so, put an end to your *orgē* against (*eis*) me."

There are also two examples of Roman-era magical gemstones used to inhibit *thumos*. The first, from Syria, has its underside inscribed in Greek: "Let all *thumos* towards (*pros*) me, Cassianus, be restrained (*katechesthō*)." The obverse is engraved with a figure who raises its right hand to its lips, a gesture that perhaps indicates silence.[9] Another gem of similar date, but of unknown provenance, has on its reverse a command, "Restrain the passionate outbursts (*tous thumous*) of Taso," that is presumably addressed to the lion-headed god on the obverse, who grasps a threatening cobra by the tail.[10] Although these two rings and the two verbal spells quoted above use different images, forms, and media for expressing or depicting the magical act, it is important to note that all of them use the verb "to bind down" (*kathechein*), which is traditionally used in *defixiones*.[11]

In all of these later spells, therefore, we see that the terms *thumos* and *orgē* are regularly used in tandem or interchangeably as equivalents. In contrast to the pre-Roman spells, moreover, *thumos* and *orgē* are frequently oriented against or toward (*pros*, or *eis*) a particular individual and are closely associated with hot, verbal activities that must be cooled or quieted. In these later texts, scholars usually translate both words as "anger" or "wrath," perfectly acceptable renditions for this period. This scholarly consensus, moreover, stems in part from the perception that, since *orgē* nearly always means "anger" in this period, whenever it is equated with or used in tandem with *thumos*, *thumos* must also be narrowly understood to mean "anger." As it turns out, however, a recently published cache of third-century CE lead tablets from the Athenian Agora repeatedly uses *orgē* and the related verb *orgizomai* to refer to passions other than anger.[12] Thus, in a spell designed "to chill and destroy the wrestling of Eutychian, the wrestler"[13] we read:[14] "As these names grow cold, so let Eutychian's name, and breath, impulse (*orgē*), on-rush,[15] mind, knowledge, and reckoning grow cold." In this formula,

---

[9] Mouterde (1930) 77–80, no. 11, with further comments in Bonner (1950) 105–6.

[10] Bonner (1950) no. 149, with comments on pp. 104–5: "a greenish stone streaked with black, perhaps serpentine." For my rendition of the plural *thumous*, see n. 24 below.

[11] Faraone (1989) 158, n. 151.   [12] Jordan (1985).

[13] This same wrestler also appears to be the target of texts 1 and 3. The former requests that the demons "chill and destroy the wrestling he is going to do in the . . . this coming Friday" (1.5–6). The latter binds the wrestling that E. is going to do with Hegomenos (3.2–7). Clearly we have three curses commissioned by Secundus and/or Hegomenos in anticipation of upcoming matches.

[14] Jordan (1985) no. 2.13–15. The text and translation here and below are all from Jordan, unless otherwise noted.

[15] Jordan translates the word *epipompē* as "charm" and in his note ad loc. (p. 247), he explains that he means a "*magical* charm," namely an "incantation," which he imagines that Eutychian has cast on someone else. His interpretation has been taken up in the most recent addendum to LSJ, but in the absence of any other indications that Eutychian was casting spells, *epipompē* probably refers (like all the other terms here) to some natural, physical human attribute, for example "attack" or "onrush" – certainly appropriate for a wrestler.

which is found on nine of the tablets,[16] we find the word *orgē*, which the editor rightly translates as "impulse" and not "anger," since it appears in a list of positive physical and intellectual faculties (e.g. *psuchē*, *nous*, etc.), very much like *thumos* in the classical-era texts from Athens quoted earlier. A spell from this same group binds the *orgē* of another wrestler named Attalos and then closes with the request using a participle *orgizomenos* in a similar manner (5.25–7): "Let him be deaf, dumb, mindless, *having no impulse* . . . having no strength at all" (Ἔστω κωφός, ἄλαλος, ἄνους, μὴ ὀργιζόμενος . . . μὴ ἰσχύων ὅλως μηδέν). Again the parallelism of μὴ ὀργιζόμενος with μὴ ἰσχύων or ἄλαλος suggests that the verb *orgizomai* does not refer narrowly to Attalos' anger, but rather to some general physical benefit (here: his "impulse"), which he normally enjoys and which must be restrained in order for the opposing wrestler to be victorious.

One might of course argue that *orgē* and its cognate verb should still be rendered here as "anger" or "ill will," since these emotions are generally appropriate to a combative sport like wrestling, but the same terms appear on yet another text in the same cache, this one designed to bind a runner named Alkidamos, so that he will be unable to get past the starting lines of the ephebic races held during the annual Athenaia festival in Athens (6.12–14). The three remaining spells from this collection, moreover, are all designed to separate lovers and suggest as well an amorous or erotic twist to the meaning of *orgē*. The first is aimed at separating a man named Trophimas and his girlfriend Karpodora (7.19–21): "As these [i.e. names] grow cold, so let Karpodora's name grow cold to Trophimas, and her breath, impulse (*orgē*), on-rush, mind, knowledge and reckoning." Here the same general formula that was used to chill the wrestlers and the runner Alkidamos is altered and focused simply by adding the phrase "to Trophimas" (ἐπὶ Τροφιμᾶ). The two other "separation spells" in the group also seek to chill the names, breath, and suchlike of three different men seeking the favors of a woman named Juliana, who is presumably the girlfriend of the man who commissioned the curse.[17] One of these spells runs as follows (8.1–7):

I hand over to you [i.e. demons] Leosthenes and Pius, who visit Juliana, whom Markia bore, that you may chill them and their purposes, so that they cannot speak together or walk about, that Leosthenes and Pius cannot sit in Juliana's place of business or send messages to Juliana . . . Let Leosthenes and Pius be chilled in order

---

[16] In addition to the eight other spells in Jordan's collection, this formula (with the word *orgē*) appears on a curse – published by Elderkin (1936) and improved by Jordan (1975) – which has a slightly different list that includes *prothumia*, "zeal," or "desire."

[17] Jordan (1985) suggests plausibly ad loc. that she is a prostitute with many male friends. In that case, the person who commissioned the spell may have been a rival prostitute jealous of her booming business.

that they be unable to chat with Juliana (ὅπως μὴ δύνωνται λαλῆσαι 'Ιυλιανῇ). As these names grow cold, so let Leosthenes' and Pius' names grow cold to Juliana, and [their] breath, impulse (*orgē*), knowledge, {impulse,} on-rush, mind, {knowledge,} reckoning.[18] Let them be deaf, dumb, mindless, harmless, Juliana hearing nothing about Leosthenes and Pius and they having no impulse toward or to speaking to Juliana (μὴ ὀργιζόμενοι μ[ήτ]ε λέγοντες πρὸς 'Ιυλιανήν).

Here the two men are chilled and prevented from spending time and chatting with Juliana. The participle *orgizomenoi* cannot, of course, have any negative or hostile connotation here, for it would be contrary to the goal of the spell to say "and let them *not* be angry toward" this woman. Clearly the impulse (*orgē*) toward Trophimas in the preceding spell and toward Juliana here is one of amorous or erotic intention.[19]

These Agora *defixiones* are, then, extremely important because they reveal that even in the Roman period an ambiguity surrounds the terms *orgizomenos* and *orgē*, which in these texts must mean something positive or useful to the victim, for example a "passion for" or "drive toward" wrestling, racing or (in the case of the erotic spells) a specific individual. As it turns out, the word *thumos* also appears in a similarly erotic connotation on a Greek ostrakon from Egypt dating to the "späte Kaiserzeit" (*PGM* O[strakon] 1):

O Kronos, you who restrain the *thumos* of all human beings, restrain the *thumos* of Horos whom Maria bore, do not allow him to speak with Hatros (μὴ ἐάσῃς αὐτὸν λαλήσεν Ἀτρῷ), whom Taeses bore, because I invoke you by the finger of the god in order that he [i.e. Horos] not open his mouth to him [i.e. Hatros], because he [i.e. Horos] belongs to Kronos and is subject to Kronos. Do not allow him [i.e. Horos] to speak with him [i.e. Hatros], neither night nor day, not even for an hour.

Preisendanz, translating *thumos* as "Groll," clearly believes that this spell aims at restraining the anger of Horos toward Hatros, the presumed author of the text. This interpretation – which has been universally adopted – depends on understanding the repeated datives with verbs of speaking (e.g. λαλήσεν Ἀτρῷ in line 5; λαλήσεν αὐτῷ line 8; and ἀναχάνῃ αὐτῷ

---

[18] The scribe is confused at this point; he jumbles the usual sequence and repeats two of the targets.

[19] I should note in passing that the spell against Alkidamos, the runner, ends with similar language (no. 6.31–5): "Let him be deaf, dumb, mindless, harmless, hearing nothing about Apollonian nor having any impulse toward him." Jordan (1985: 222) is agnostic about the unexpected appearance of Apollonian at the end of the curse: "Was Apollonian the competitor of Alkidamos in the race? Was the intention that Alkidamos should hear nothing of Apollonian's curse against him?" I suggest, in fact, that like the spell separating Leosthenes and Pius from Juliana, this spell was ultimately designed to separate Alkidamos and Apollonian, first by making Alkidamos slip and disgrace himself (i.e. before Apollonian) in the ephebic race (a perfect place for Alkidamos to show off his beauty and prowess before his lover) and then more directly by preventing Alkidamos from hearing anything about Apollonian or by binding Alkidamos' "impulse" toward Apollonian.

in line 10) to mean "to speak *against* someone."[20] Preisendanz adduces a parallel construction from a handbook recipe entitled "Another [sc. Victory Charm] and Subjugation Charm" that is to be inscribed on a lead tablet and placed under the left foot: "Restrain the *orgē* of Mr. So-and-so and of all men, and his *thumos* and his tongue, in order that he be unable to talk with Mr. So-and-so (ἵνα μὴ δυνηθῶσιν λαλεῖν τῷ δεῖνα)."[21] Here, too, modern editors assume that both words *thumos* and *orgē* refer to the "anger" of the victim and that the spell works like a legal "restraining order" that keeps an obnoxious person away from the victim and prevents him from saying nasty things to him. This is, of course, a plausible explanation, but it heavily strains the construction λαλεῖν τῷ δεῖνα, which normally cannot by itself imply hostility. The close parallel, moreover, from the "divorce spell" quoted above – "Let Leosthenes and Pius be chilled in order that they be unable to chat with Juliana (ὅπως μὴ δύνωνται λαλῆσαι Ἰυλιανῇ)" – suggests that a similar definition ("impulse" or "passion") is also suitable for the words *orgē* and *thumos* in the papyrus recipe and on the ostrakon, which was most probably designed by a third (presumably jealous) party to keep Horos away from Hatros.

We have seen, then, that the close affinities between "*thumos*-restraint spells" and "binding spells" suggest that the former evolve as a specialized variant of the latter, and that this evolution involves a narrowing of the definition of *thumos* from a positive, general meaning (e.g. "spirit," "will," or "courage") used in earlier *defixiones* to a more specific sense that embraces the realms of "anger" and "erotic passion." These later spells, moreover, often focus on binding the victim's *thumos* toward a specific person and cooling his hot, verbal behavior – either angry, abusive speech aimed at someone or spoken about them or the kind of hot, passionate speech used by lovers when they flirt.

THE AMULETIC TRADITION OF ANGER RESTRAINT AND LOVE SPELLS

As was mentioned earlier, there existed alongside this cursing tradition of *thumos*-restraint spells a second and equally important tradition of using amulets to mollify the *thumos* and *orgē* of another person. The differences

---

[20] The parenthetical addition to Preisendanz's *PGM* translation of the phrase at line 5 makes explicit: "reden mit (gegen) ihn." He has in mind, of course, those binding spells discussed above in which specific speech (usually assumed to be malignant gossip) is blocked, for example (*DTA* 96.8–14): "and may his tongue become leaden if he is about to utter a malicious word about Philon (ὑπὲρ Φίλωνος)." But in such cases, the victim and the negative type of speech are both usually spelled out, as here, where some apparently defamatory gossip "about Philon" is specifically mentioned.
[21] *PGM* 7.935–9.

between these two traditions can best be illustrated by a fragmentary late-Greek recipe that tries unsuccessfully to combine both types into a single spell. The lacunose papyrus (*PGM* 9) begins with instructions for inscribing a metal tablet (presumably lead) with an incantation that is very much like those on the Cyprian *defixiones* discussed above: ". . . subordinate, silence, utterly enslave the whole race of mortals, both male and female, [sc. and the whole race of] every sort of *thumoi*, which are under the authority, under the feet of Mr. So-and-so, especially [i.e. subordinate, silence, utterly enslave] this one (add the name you wish here) . . . subordinate, utterly enslave, silence the *psuchē*, the *thumos* <of Mr. So-and-so>."[22] We do not have the rubric of this spell, but it is quite similar to another recipe which calls itself a *thumokatochon* and a *hupotaktikon* ("subjection spell"), and commands: "Come to me . . . and silence, subject, and utterly enslave Mr. So-and-so to [sc. me] Mr. So-and-so and make him come under my feet."[23] The text prescribed in *PGM* 9, then, appears to be entirely consistent with the tradition of binding spells discussed above.

The same recipe, however, then directs us to recite over the inscribed tablet another short incantation that clearly is derived from another tradition. It is written in iambic trimeters and uses poetic language and ideas that we do not see in any of the binding spells discussed earlier:

> θυμοῦ σε παύσω καί σε πραϋνῶ χολῆς·
> σῖγ᾽ ἐλθὲ καὶ διακράτει σιγὴν φέρων·
> θυμοὺς φρενῶν στῆσόν τε πάντας καὶ σβέσον
> ὀργὰς ἁπάσας ὀργίλων <⏑–⏑–>.

I shall stop you from your *thumos* and soothe you from your rage (*cholos*).
Come silently and while bringing silence control it(?).
Stop all the emotional outbursts (*thumoi*) of hearts and extinguish all
    the impulses (*orgai*) of those inclined towards *orgē*.[24]

This metrical incantation, although surviving in corrupt form on a very late papyrus from Egypt, probably dates to a much earlier period, as the meter, the poetic word *cholē*, and the use of the performative future in the first line reveal.[25] Note, too, that here *thumoi* and *orgai* are linked

---

[22] *PGM* 9.5–8 and 9–10, a fourth- or fifth-century CE papyrus from Egypt.   [23] *PGM* 7.940–68.

[24] *PGM* 9.12–13 = *PGM* Hymn 30 (*PGM*, vol. II, p. 266). In this translation, I follow the suggestions of Roy Kotansky and render the plurals *thumoi* and *orgai* as repeated concrete manifestations of the abstract forces *thumos* and *orgē*.

[25] All are features of early Greek metrical charms; see Faraone (1995) and (1996). *DT* 198 (a second- or third-century CE *defixio* from Cumae) may provide another late example of a poetic spell that may also have been designed to attack anger. At line 18 we find a first-person future verb διακόψ[ω . . . τὴ]ν ὀργὴν ("I shall interrupt his/her anger") and then two lines later the words εἰ]ς μῖσο[ς] εἰς χ[ό]λος

in tandem with *cholē*, a word which always has a negative meaning, for example: "gall," "venom," or "rage."[26] I should also stress that although this text does implicitly connect *thumos* and *orgē* with verbal activity that must be silenced, it does not employ the language of the *defixiones* discussed above, but rather the vocabulary typical of protective or curative magic. The verbal construction of the first line, for instance, "I stop person X (acc.) from disease Y (gen.)" is regularly found in amulets used to cure fever.[27] Likewise the two verbs in line 3 that govern *thumoi* and *orgai* (στῆσον and σβέσον) appear in amulet texts used to "stop" pains in the feet or discharges from the eyes[28] or to "extinguish" fevers.[29] The use of iambic trimeters, moreover, is relatively rare in Greek magical incantations and seems to point to the tradition of protective or curative charms.[30]

There are, then, some clear-cut differences between the treatment of *thumos* and *orgē* in the cursing and amuletic traditions. In the binding spells surveyed in the previous section, we saw how *thumos* or *orgē* were treated as common and expected masculine traits, to be treasured in oneself but feared in a rival wrestler, orator, or lover. In the amuletic tradition, however, *thumos* and *orgē* are linked with pathological entities like *cholē* and need to be "stopped" like the discharge of a diseased eye, or "extinguished" like a fever. By borrowing the language of fever spells, moreover, this amuletic branch of magic expresses in a very different manner the same notion of a hot or febrile *thumos* that must be cooled.

This connection between amuletic magic and the stopping or soothing of the passions also appears in a very ancient Mesopotamian and Greek

---

("against anger, against rage") can easily be construed as the end of an iambic trimeter, a common metrical form of a curative incantation (see n. 30 below). As far as I am aware, the use of *cholos* here and *cholē* in the iambic charm are unique in the extant magical texts.

[26] See LSJ s.v. and Redfield (1975) 14–18 on the closely related term *cholos*.

[27] E.g. *SM* 4.6–8: παῦσον (amulet used against fever and shivering); 11 παύσατε (amulet used against fever); *P.Köln* 339 παῦσον (against pain in the feet).

[28] E.g. *SM* 4.6–8 "Stop (ἀπόστησον) from X all quotidian fever"; and 26: "Stop (στῆσον) the discharge, the pains in the eyes of X." In both cases the imperative is addressed to a third party. In *SM* 32.10–11, however, στῆ9ι is directly addressed to a discharge from the eyes. *P.Köln* 339 employs both strategies (e.g. παραστά9ι and στῆσον) against pain in the feet.

[29] See *SM* 2.14–20 for a silver amulet which contains the phrase: "If a fever seizes him, completely extinguish it (κατασβένοις = κατασβεν<νύ>οις) once and for all"; and Kotansky (1991c) for a fourth- or fifth-century CE phylactery from western Galilee, which asks that fever "be extinguished" (ἀποσβῆναι) from the person carrying the amulet. Kotansky ad loc. provides some helpful parallels from Greek medical literature.

[30] Jordan (1991: 343–6) recently pointed out that lines 3–4 of *SM* 26 (quoted above in note 28) also comprise an iambic trimeter: στῆσον τὸ ῥεῦμα, τοὺς πόνους τῶν ὀφθαλμῶν; and he brilliantly suggests that an address to a plant in a spell for gout preserved in Alexander of Tralles (ἵνα στάσῃς τὸ ῥεῦμα τῶν ποδῶν καὶ τῶν χειρῶν) hides a similar trimeter which he reconstructs as: στῆσον τὸ ῥεῦμα τῶν ποδῶν καὶ τῶν χειρῶν.

tradition of amuletic cords reflected in the famous "Deception of Zeus" episode in the *Iliad*, which begins when Hera calls Aphrodite aside and makes an urgent, but mendacious request (14.197–210):[31]

Now give me affection and desire, with which you subdue all the gods and mortal men, since I am about to go to the ends of the generous earth to see Oceanus, the source of the gods and mother Tethys . . .

I shall go visit them and I shall stop (*lusō*) their ceaseless quarrels, since now for a long time they have stayed apart from each other and from their marriage bed, since bitter anger (*cholos*) has fallen upon their hearts. If I could with words persuade their dear hearts and bring them back to their bed to be merged in love with each other, forever would I be called dear by them and compassionate.

Thus Hera, pretending to be worried about the dysfunctional marriage of her parents, asks Aphrodite for help in bringing them back together. Aphrodite agrees to help and gives her a specially charmed belt or strap (lines 214–17): "She spoke and from her breasts unbound an elaborate *kestos himas*, on which had been wrought all enchantments: love, desire, and the whispered endearment (*oaristus*) that steals away good sense, even from the thoughtful." Early commentators thought that this *kestos himas* was an amulet of sorts carried in the fold of Hera's garment,[32] but more recently scholars have argued that it was, in fact, an article of clothing, either worn about the breasts or on the waist.[33] There is also some confusion about the expected effects of the strap. We can see from Hera's story quoted above, that it could be used to heal a marital rift by "stopping" or "dissolving" (the verb is *luein*) quarrels and anger (*cholos*). Like the *cholē* mentioned in the iambic charm quoted earlier, this anger is clearly a pathological state that must be checked before a more cordial relationship can resume. Note, too, the focus in this passage on speech: it would seem that the "whispered endearment" or "love talk" (*oaristus*) which is wrought upon the strap is designed to replace the ongoing quarrels of Oceanus and Tethys.

But how was this *kestos himas* supposed to work? Gantz imagines that if Hera, the would-be-marriage-counselor, had kept her word, she would probably have given the *kestos himas* to her mother, Tethys, to wear,

---

[31] See Faraone (1990) for full discussion.

[32] See *kolpos* at lines 219 and 223 and Faraone (1990) 220, n. 1 for bibliography. Like most long and hotly contested questions, there are insufficient data here, I think, to make a secure conclusion either way. The Neo-Assyrian parallels discussed below suggest that it was a knotted cord worn as a belt or tied to the inside of a garment.

[33] LSJ s.v. and Faraone (1990) 220. The word *kestos* may, in fact, be related to Hebrew *keset* (Ezek 13:18 and 20) which seems to mean "magical band" and is apparently transliterated onto a Greek amulet (*GMA* 32.9) as *kastu*. See Kotansky *GMA* pp. 148–9.

presumably to attract her husband or calm his anger in similar fashion.[34] This procedure is, in fact, precisely what we find in a 1000 BCE Neo-Assyrian-cuneiform recipe for a specially charmed strap, which shares some startling similarities with the one described by Homer:[35]

Incantation to be recited when the husband of a woman is angry with her: The rite is accomplished [as follows]: you weave together into a single strand the tendons of a gazelle, [hemp] and red wool; you tie it into fourteen knots. Each time you tie a knot, you recite the [i.e. preceding] incantation. The woman places this cord around her waist and she will be loved.

Although here too the precise magical operation is not pellucid, it seems that the anger mentioned in the rubric was thought to be tied up as the knots in the cord are tied, an idea that is not mentioned in Homer, who does not, however, narrate the creation of the *kestos himas*. The incantation to be used with this recipe is very fragmentary, but we can make out that it invokes Ishtar, a goddess often equated with Aphrodite, the owner of the Homeric *kestos himas*. A different Neo-Assyrian recipe with the same rubric as the one quoted above preserves a prayer to Ishtar which gives us more precise insight into the kinds of angry behavior that these spells were thought to rectify: "I call on you, O Ishtar . . . because he does not tell me the words of his heart, because he is angry and does not talk to me . . ."[36] It would appear, then, that the Assyrian procedure is a remedy for a situation quite similar to that which Hera (falsely) proposes for her parents in the *Iliad*: a specially made strap or cord is worn by a woman to heal a marital rift by assuaging the anger of the husband and making him more affectionate and welcoming.

These spells used by wives to mollify husbands are, in fact, related to another, much larger class of Neo-Assyrian magical spells, the so-called *egalkura* spells, which often involve the use of knotted or beaded cords to enhance one's attractiveness in the eyes of a superior:

---

[34] Gantz (1993) 101. Redfield (1982: 196) suggests in passing that Hera herself would have worn it and beguiled both her parents.

[35] Scheil (1921) 21–7, no. 17, col. iii, lines 10′–14′. For a detailed discussion of the connection with the *Iliad* passage, see Faraone (1990). The tablet was found at Assur, an Assyrian city on the Tigris River in northern Iraq, some 350 miles from the important Greek emporium at Al Mina; see Burkert (1992) 11–12. I translate the French translation of Reiner (1966) 93, as there are no English versions available. Many thanks to my colleague Professor Erica Reiner, who kindly checked the English for me to ensure no distortions have crept in.

[36] Gurney and Finkelstein (1957) no. 257, rev. 2–9, translated by E. Reiner. In the prayer, Ishtar is addressed as she "who makes (men?) love, who brings back an *angry* man to the house of the bride's family" (my emphasis). This recipe has the same rubric as the recipe for the cord, but an entirely different ritual; the text is very fragmentary, but Professor Reiner informs me that there are references to an altar, loaves, incense, and an oil that is anointed.

You chant this spell seven times over a three-stranded cord of lapis-colored wool, you knot it (and) you bind it in your hem. And when you enter into the presence of the prince, he will welcome you [variant: "whoever looks upon you will be glad to see you"].[37]

These *egalkura* recipes have much in common with the Homeric strap and the amuletic cords apparently used by Assyrian wives against their husbands. In each case social or political inferiors armed with a magically enchanted cord face their "princes" with hopes of being made more welcome or attractive. A vaguely similar form of this kind of Assyrian "political" magic has survived intact in a short Greek recipe from Roman times, which bears the rubric *thumokatochon*: "Enter the presence of a king or magnate, and while you have your hands inside your garment say the name of the sun disk, while tying a knot in your pallium or shawl. You will marvel at the results."[38] In this case, the rubric suggests that the binding effects of the knot are focused directly on the *thumos* of the superior, but the result will be the same as the Neo-Assyrian spells: his increased goodwill and affection.

Two other forms of the Assyrian *egalkura* spells – special rings and facial ointments – also show up in the Greek tradition and seem to be used for very similar purposes. Both the ancient Greeks and Assyrians, for instance, apparently employed magical rings to increase their personal charisma, especially in the eyes of their kings and masters:

Neo-Assyrian Recipe: Over a copper ring chant the spell three times. You place it on your finger. And when you enter into the presence of the prince, he will welcome you.[39]

Greek Recipe: A little ring for success and for charm (*charis*) and for victory . . . The world has nothing better than this. For when you have it with you, you will always get whatever you ask from anybody. Besides it stops (*pauei*) the passionate outbursts (*orgai*) of kings and masters. Wearing it, whatever you may say to anyone, you will be believed, and you will be pleasing (*epicharis*) to everybody.[40]

---

[37] *KAR* 71.21–5, translated by E. Reiner. For a discussion of the ambiguous nature of these spells, which are often found in collections of spells which range from explicitly erotic purposes to purely political or economic ones, see Scurlock (1989–90).

[38] *PGM* 13.251–2, as translated and interpreted by M. Smith in *GMPT*. This spell has probably been borrowed from the Mesopotamian tradition, where Shamash (the sun god) is the patron of magic. The recipe itself, moreover, boasts that it was taken from the "Eighth Book of Moses." It is true that such hoary Eastern antecedents are usually fabricated by later magicians in order to make the spell more mysterious, and therefore more valuable to the customer – see Betz (1982) – but there are other indications of real Semitic influence *PGM* 12; see M. Smith (1984) and his comments ad loc. in *GMPT* 172–88.

[39] *KAR* 71 rev. 9–11, translated by E. Reiner.

[40] *PGM* 12.270–3 and 277–80, as translated by M. Smith in *GMPT*. There follows a long incantation to be repeated thrice daily.

The recipe for the Greek ring, which is to be set with a specially engraved gemstone, is preserved in a fourth-century CE handbook, but such gems were apparently known to the Greeks and Romans at least as early as the first century BCE.[41] Note, too, that the boast that this ring "stops (*pauei*) the passionate outbursts (*orgai*) of kings and masters" employs a verb typical of Greek healing magic.

Finally, the recipes for Neo-Assyrian *egalkura* rituals also include ointments that were applied to the faces of petitioners in anticipation of a meeting with a superior:

You chant this spell three times over good oil. You smear your face and your hands. And when you enter into the presence of the prince, he will welcome you [variant text reads: ". . . and then he who looks upon you will be glad to see you"].[42]

Here, too, we find a very similar tradition in a fourth-century CE Greek magical recipe entitled: "Prayer to Helios: A charm to restrain *thumos* and for victory and for securing charm (none is greater)."[43] The recipe directs us to say the prayer seven times to Helios and then to anoint our hands with oil and wipe it on our head and face.

These close parallels between Assyrian and Greek recipes for knotted cords, rings, and facial ointments suggest a long-standing Mediterranean tradition of such devices that is only partially visible in our extant evidence and that in all likelihood can be traced back directly or indirectly to Mesopotamia. We should not, however, overlook some important variations, for the Greek and Assyrian traditions differ somewhat in their treatment of passion or anger. Although anger figures prominently in the Assyrian recipes for knotted cords used by wives against husbands, it is not (to my knowledge, at least) mentioned explicitly in the three types of *egalkura* spells used against "princes." The Greek spells that derive from this *egalkura* tradition, however, all explicitly or implicitly target the

---

[41] *Cyranides*, a handbook which dates from two or three centuries earlier, boasts similar powers for a number of gemstones, for example: if a man wears a *dendrites*-stone "he will be loved and well heeded by all gods and mortals and he will be successful in whatever he wants" (1.4.45–51) or if a man wears a sapphire engraved with Aphrodite "he will be charming (*epicharis*), famous, and victorious in every lawsuit" (1.10.39–42). Another late Greek magical recipe (*PGM* 12.201–2) claims that when *aerizōn*, a special kind of jasper, is set in a small gold ring, it is "especially effective before kings and leaders," a belief that also seems to have been known to Pliny the Elder as well, who reports that sorcerers claim that a kind of jasper called *aerizousa* is "useful for those who harangue the assembly" (*HN* 37.118). See Riess (1896) 76 for discussion.

[42] *KAR* 237.13–17, translated by E. Reiner. The variant is *KAR* 237.18–23.

[43] *PGM* 36.211–230, tr. R. F. Hock in *GMPT*. The prayer which follows in the Greek recipe asks for a variety of abstract benefits: "I ask to obtain and receive from you life, health, reputation, wealth, influence, strength, success, sexiness (*epaphrodisian*), and charm (*charis*) with all men and all women, victory over all men and all women."

passions of the men in power: the recipes for the knot-tying spell and the facial ointment are both labeled *thumokatocha*, and the recipe for the ring boasts its ability to "stop the angry outbursts (*orgai*) of kings and masters." In the Greek tradition, moreover, we see great fluidity in the categories of amulets, *thumos*-restraining spells, and spells used to enhance one's beauty or charisma,[44] a fluidity that is perhaps most striking in this section of a prayer to Hermes preserved in a recipe for a good luck statue to be set up in a shop:

Soothe (πράϋνε) all men and give me power, beauty (add what you want) and incessantly provide me with gold and silver and every nourishment. Protect me thoroughly at all times forever from incantations [or perhaps "poisons," the word is *pharmaka*] and deceptions and every evil-eye and from malicious tongues, from every conflict, from every hatred of the gods and mortals. Provide me with charm and victory and business and abundance.[45]

Here the petitioner asks for abstract benefits like "beauty" and more concrete ones like "silver" and "nourishment." He also seeks protection from a host of evils, very much like a standard amulet. Note, too, that Hermes is asked to "soothe (πράϋνε) all men" presumably from their passions as in the first line of the iambic charm cited at the beginning of this section.[46]

This crossover between healing, charisma and *thumos*-restraint spells is made explicit in the rubric of another amulet: "A *thumokatochon* and a charm to secure favor (*charitēsion*) . . . it even works against kings!"[47] The prayer to be inscribed on the silver tablet reads: "Give to me, Mr. So-and-so, whom Ms. So-and-so bore, victory, charm, reputation, advantage over all men and women, especially over Mr. So-and-so, whom Ms. So-and-so bore, forever and all time." This is a recipe for a general charm that will bring success over *all* men and women, but the mention of kings and the place to insert the name of a single man as the primary target ("especially over Mr. So-and-so") suggest that here too, like the "princes" in the Neo-Assyrian spells or Zeus in the *Iliad*, we have a spell aimed originally at a male at the apex of some social group. Indeed, these spells are often designed for political situations, such as an appearance in a royal audience or a court of law, where the petitioner finds himself in "the presence of a king or magnate."[48] The text

---

44 Winkler (1991) 218–20. Much of the following two paragraphs is indebted to this groundbreaking study.

45 *PGM* 8.30–8. Graf (1991) 191–2 discusses this prayer in detail, noting the parallels with traditional Greek liturgy.

46 This verb is somewhat rare and generally limited to the poets and the philosophers.

47 *PGM* 36.35–68. For similar combinations of these three types of spells, see *PGM* 20.270–3 (all three); 36.161–77 (a *thumos*-binding spell and a victory spell) and 211–30 (all three).

48 *PGM* 13.251–2.

of an elaborate Greek amulet from Arabia gives us some sense of how such charms worked even in the practical world of an Roman provincial capital: "Give charm, glory, and victory to Proclus, whom Salvina bore, before Diogenianus, the military governor of Bostra in Arabia and before Pelagius the assessor, and before all men small and great . . . in order that he might win, justly or unjustly, every law suit before every judge and adjudicator."[49]

What is most striking about these amuletic spells is the uneven playing field upon which they are deployed. The *defixiones* discussed in the previous section are generally thought to have been used by social equals against each other in competitive situations, for example wrestlers against wrestlers, orators against orators, lovers against lovers. This amuletic tradition, on the other hand, seems to have been regularly deployed by social subordinates against their superiors, for example wives against husbands or petitioners against princes, kings, and provincial governors. The social context of the latter suggests two interesting insights: (i) that males, especially those monarchs like Zeus at the apex of their social structures, were regularly thought or even expected to have an excessive amount of *thumos* or *orgē*; and (ii) the fact that most of these devices are amulets and that the incantations written on them or recited over them regularly employ the language found on phylacteries, suggests that the male *thumos* or *orgē* they attacked was like a fever in some way pathological and in need of healing.

We have seen, then, how in ancient Greek culture, women and other culturally defined subordinates seem to employ cords, amulets, rings, and facial ointments for very similar goals: to lessen the *thumos* or *orgē* of a husband or a male superior and (in some cases) to increase his affection. There is also another parallel tradition in the Greek world, which I have discussed at length elsewhere: women such as Deianeira or the unidentified wives in Antiphon 1 and the Aristotelian *Magna Moralia* 16 – and in one case a male subordinate (Callisthenes, the freedman of the Roman general Lucullus) – who use drugs or love potions to calm or enervate the passions of their husbands or superiors and win back their affections.[50] All these techniques appear to be rooted in traditional female spheres of activity: belts, rings, and facial ointments are obvious parts in a women's *kosmēsis* (i.e. the process by which she makes herself attractive), and potions given to men to drink are part of the "natural" (in ancient Greek culture at least)

[49] *GMA* 58.12–19; see Kotansky (1991b) for an excellent discussion.
[50] Faraone (1999: 110–31) discusses Sophocles' *Trachiniae*, Antiphon 1.14–19, *Magna Moralia* 16 and (for Callisthenes) Cornelius Nepos frag. 52 (Marshall). I also focus on two important passages from Plutarch: *Moralia* 139a (a warning to wives not to use love potions on their husbands) and 256c (the tale of Aretaphila of Cyrene).

role of women as preparers of food and medicine.[51] Both technologies also show up in popular protective or healing rites, which were traditionally mastered and passed on by the female members of the family.[52] But despite the curative stance of these types of magical spells much of the male Greek discourse about them has a distinctly sinister ring. Indeed, it is notable that this kind of magic frequently appears in situations which involve what Greek males, at least, would call a worrisome and "unnatural" usurpation of male power, for example Hera's intervention in the *Iliad*, where for a time at least she subverts Zeus's control over the war at Troy. Shocking, too, were the reports (probably circulated by Octavian and his supporters) that Cleopatra controlled both Julius Caesar and Mark Antony with *pharmaka* and sorcery (*goēteia*),[53] and had tried to do so with Octavian, but failed.[54] Thus despite their apparent origins in curative or prophylactic techniques, the use of amulets and potions to calm and control passionate and powerful men was a source of anxiety for Greek males because it was deployed by social inferiors against their unknowing superiors, most notably by women against their husbands.[55]

SOME TENTATIVE CONCLUSIONS

I begin with an obvious paradox: why would sensible wives who wished to strengthen their marriages use magic that might *calm* or *bind* their husband's vigor, sexual and otherwise? Or why would political underlings, try to weaken their masters – upon whom their own power depended? Clearly these are selfish decisions of a sort: the individual attempts to shore up their own position within a hierarchy, even if it means weakening the central authority. They are, of course, caught in a bind, since the *thumos* that they seek to control was closely linked in ancient Greek and Roman belief, at least, to the cultural construction of masculinity and masculine authority. As we have seen, this conundrum is best illustrated in the wide range of meanings – from "courage" and "will" to "anger" – associated

---

[51] For instance, a North African form of magic which involves a prayer addressed to the popular eye shadow *kohl*, and the widespread belief that women put their menstrual blood and other materials in the food and drink of their husbands. See Janson (1987) 108 (*kohl*) and 111–12 (for tampering with food).

[52] See Hanson (1990) 309–11 for a female oral tradition concerned with "women's diseases." Bremmer (1987: 204–6) discusses the traditional belief that old women were knowledgeable about magic.

[53] Plutarch, *Antony* 37: "He was not the master of his own faculties, but under the influence of certain drugs (*pharmaka*) or sorcery (*goēteia*)." Compare *Vit. Ant.* 25.4 and 60.1.

[54] Aelian, frag. 57 and the *Suda* s.v. "*iunx*" report that she tried magic on all three Roman leaders but failed in the final attempt; see Johnston (1995) 187, n. 21.

[55] Faraone (1999) 119–31.

with the noun *thumos*. This noun is, in fact, derived from the verb *thuein*, "to rage" or "to swell," a verb used to describe swollen river torrents and storm-tossed seas, as well as angry men like Achilles who storm across a battlefield. It can mean "sexual passion" too, and Hipponax even uses the word *thumos* to refer to an erect phallus![56] Therefore in the Greek tradition at least, using magic to bind or soothe a man's *thumos* not only controls his anger; it also involves a much more diffuse attack on a man's will, courage, and sexual desire – character traits and emotions which are very closely tied to his masculinity.[57] We have also noted that the noun *orgē* can in a similar manner mean "natural impulse" or "propensity" as well as "anger." Here, too, the sexual element is not too far off: the noun *orgē* is closely related to the verb *organ*, which describes the state of a man "swelling with lust."[58] At the base of both word-groups, then, we see an intrinsic connection between a man swollen with anger and one swollen with sexual desire. We have also seen, moreover, that these more general meanings are preserved in the tradition of Greek binding spells, where *thumos* and *orgē* appear as neutral or positive attributes (like *psuchē* and *nous*) which wrestlers and orators seek to bind in their rivals. But even in the later tradition, when *thumos* and *orgē* are singled out for special treatment, it is often difficult to translate these terms narrowly as "anger" and to disallow any reference to a more generalized notion of hot or aggressive passion.

This close connection between masculine anger and passion is, of course, implicit in the apparently continuous popular Greek discourse – glimpsed only intermittently in our sources – about the close link between "righteous anger" and proper male behavior. We find, for instance, that speakers in the law courts of classical Athens repeatedly describe, display, and boast about their own sometimes violent anger, as a way of establishing their credentials as "real men" in their community.[59] Indeed in his *Wasps*, Aristophanes uses this perpetually angry insect as an icon for the old-fashioned courage, virility, and rugged individualism of those Athenians who defeated the Persians.[60] Stoic arguments against the passions also connect anger and sexual desire (*erōs*) in a way that suggests they are addressing a similar widespread popular understanding – at least from the Hellenistic

---

[56] Padel (1992) 30–2 and Allen (2000) 56–8.

[57] For some further connections between *thumos* and sexual passion, note that the words *epithumia*, "desire," and *epithumein*, "to desire," are often treated as synonyms of *erōs* and *eran*. See Dover (1978) 43–4.

[58] See LSJ s.v. and Allen (2000) 50–5. English "orgasm" is derived from this word-group.

[59] Allen (2000) 50–72.

[60] Taillardat (1962) 159–60; Reckford (1977) 305–7 – on their sexual aggressiveness; and Konstan (1985) 32–4.

period onwards – of the common sources of these two passions and their importance to proper male behavior.[61] In sum, when wives or political subordinates use amulets or potions to mollify a man's *orgē* or *thumos*, they are aiming at something more than his anger – something vitally connected with his individuality, his aggressiveness, and his autonomy, something that in a Mediterranean context such as this we might aptly call his *machismo*.

There is, however, implicit in much of the evidence for amulets surveyed above, the somewhat contrary notion that this idealized masculine *thumos* is, in fact, a dangerous force that in some cases must be "extinguished" like a raging fever or "stopped" like the pain of a gouty foot. This alternate tradition also seems to lie behind the powerful potions that women sometimes used to sedate their passionate husbands, even at the risk of unmanning or destroying them.[62] This second branch of *thumokatocha* is clearly related, as I have tried to show, to the tradition of healing or protective spells, since it clearly treats *thumos* and *orgē* as illnesses that must be cured. Which attitude, then, was more prevalent or important in the ancient world: *thumos* as a masculine ideal or *thumos* as a social pathology? Clearly *thumos* or *orgē* is an important element in the construction of masculinity and crucial to male self-representation in the ancient Mediterranean – as we would expect from such a collection of rabidly patriarchal cultures. What is unexpected, and therefore more interesting, is the abundant evidence for the tradition of *thumos* as a pathology. I have suggested above that this negative formulation of *thumos* as a disease may have been developed and passed from generation to generation by women, who in traditional societies were often the purveyors of amulets and curative potions, and who, in the context of the home at least, had the most to lose if they were unlucky enough to marry a man of violent passions. There is another Greek tradition that saw anger as a pathology: the philosophers, many of whom like Aristotle and Theophrastus were interested in medical lore and the power of herbs. The relation between these two traditions, however, is well beyond the purview of this essay. Suffice it to say that as far as I have been able to see, the folk tradition, already visible in the Neo-Assyrian charms and in the Homeric *kestos himas*, seems to predate the philosophical one by a wide margin!

---

[61] Nussbaum (1994) 402–83 *passim*, especially 409, where she describes the interlocutor in Seneca's *De ira* as a representative of the typical Roman view that anger is a necessary and important part of a soldier's personality and indeed essential to masculine behavior generally.

[62] Faraone (1999) 124–30.

CHAPTER 7

Anger and gender in Chariton's Chaereas and Callirhoe

J. H. D. Scourfield

A genre concerned with love and separation, attachment and loss (however temporary), is likely to have a high emotional content, and the earliest[1] of the five extant Greek novels, Chariton's *Chaereas and Callirhoe*,[2] is nothing if not emotional.[3] A central part of the author's aim is to give us an imaginative apprehension of what his characters feel, and to make us feel it ourselves;[4] the depiction of emotion is thus largely descriptive, the goal being the creation of mood, individual or collective. One emotion, however – anger – plays a critical role in the narrative. This fact has perhaps not been fully appreciated; certainly it has not received much prominence in scholarly writing on this novel, and wider implications have not been explored. In this chapter I want to look closely at the presence (and absence) of anger in the text, examining it particularly through the lens of gender and its ancient constructions.

A version of this paper was given at the Dublin Classics Seminar in October 1999. I should like to thank those who contributed to the discussion on that occasion, also those who participated in the Heidelberg Colloquium, particularly Susanna Braund and Christopher Gill; also Catherine Connors, John Dillon, Monica Gale, Richard Hunter, Brian McGing, and Christopher Pelling, all of whom either read and commented on earlier drafts or responded helpfully to questions on specific points.

[1] This is the accepted view (see Papanikolaou [1973] 9–10 with n. 7, 153–9, and most subsequent scholarship); O'Sullivan (1995: 145–70) argues for the priority of Xenophon of Ephesus, whose *Ephesiaca* is generally regarded as an imitation of *Chaereas and Callirhoe* (*C&C*). No firm dates can be established for either author. Chariton is now normally placed somewhere between the middle of the first and the middle of the second century AD (which papyri fix as a *terminus ante quem*); for a summary of scholarly positions and arguments see Cueva (2000), and for a fresh discussion of the dating of Chariton and the other early Greek novels, Bowie (forthcoming), who argues for a date of *c.* AD 50–75 for the whole group.

[2] I give the traditional title, as given in the only manuscript to survive complete; but there are grounds for thinking that the original title may have been simply *Callirhoe* (see Reardon [1996] 315–16).

[3] As Reardon (1982: 22) puts it, in discussing a passage (8.1.4) suggestive of a conscious association with Aristotle on tragedy, "But this whipping-up of emotions for the sake of emotions is not what Sophocles is *about*, in the *Oedipus*, or Euripides in the *Medea*; it *is* what Chariton is about"; one does not have to go all the way with Reardon to appreciate the contrast being drawn. On the many instances in *C&C* and the other extant erotic novels where confused or multiple emotion is expressed see Fusillo (1990).

[4] For helpful discussion see Kaimio (1996).

The essential events need first to be described; and I begin with the opening chapter of the novel. On the occasion of a feast of Aphrodite in Syracuse, the god Eros contrives a meeting between the divinely beautiful Callirhoe and the handsome Chaereas, who belong to the two leading families in the city. They fall instantly in love, and popular demand ensures their marriage despite family rivalries. But following the wedding Callirhoe's many disappointed suitors plot revenge against Chaereas, "a hopeless pauper, nobody's superior, competing with kings," as one of them calls him (1.2.3).[5] What drives them is a sense of insult, ὕβρις (1.2.2; cf. 1.2.1 ὑβρίσθαι), joined with malicious envy, φθόνος (1.2.1); the resentment or pique which they feel is described by Chariton as anger, ὀργή (1.2.1; cf. 1.2.2 ὠργίσθην).[6]

The plan which the suitors adopt aims to do harm by arousing Chaereas' jealousy, ζηλοτυπία (1.2.5; 1.2.6).[7] In a first attempt they fabricate evidence of a revel at Chaereas' house while he himself is absent in the country. When he returns, the indications of reveling put him in a rage, and he bursts in on Callirhoe, who knows nothing of what has been going on; but quickly, says the narrator, "his anger turned to grief" (τὴν ὀργὴν μετέβαλεν εἰς λύπην, 1.3.4), and following his unjust reproaches, which Callirhoe fiercely rebuts, the lovers are easily reconciled. Having failed on this occasion, the suitors devise a second scheme. A plausible stranger tells Chaereas that Callirhoe is unfaithful to him, and undertakes to prove it. In the evening Chaereas, who has purported to be leaving for the country again, watches a man, dressed in a lover's finery, gain admission to his house. This man has in fact, as part of the plot, seduced Callirhoe's maid, and it is this woman who lets him in; but the suspicions planted in Chaereas' mind seem to have been confirmed, and "Chaereas could no longer restrain himself but rushed in to kill the adulterer in the act"[8] (1.4.10). The man, however, leaves the house at once, and when Chaereas charges into the bedroom, which is in darkness, and Callirhoe (who again knows nothing of the scheme) runs forward joyfully to greet him, he is "overcome by anger," κρατούμενος . . . ὑπὸ τῆς ὀργῆς (1.4.12), and kicks her in the stomach.[9] She collapses and appears to be dead. On learning the truth, Chaereas longs to die himself,

---

[5] ἄπορος καὶ πένης καὶ μηδενὸς κρείττων βασιλέων ἀγωνισαμένων. The text used throughout this chapter is that of Goold (1995); translations are my own, though some debts to those of Goold and B. P. Reardon, in Reardon (1989) 17–124, both of which I have consulted in every case, will be evident.

[6] For the causal connection between insult and anger (for which see too below, p. 166) cf. Arist. *Pol.* 5.8.9 (1311a33–4).

[7] On the personification of ζηλοτυπία in the first of these passages see Roncali (1991) (whose overall argument, however, fails to convince).

[8] Χαιρέας οὐκέτι κατέσχεν ἀλλὰ εἰσέδραμεν ἐπ᾽ αὐτοφώρῳ τὸν μοιχὸν ἀναιρήσων.

[9] The text does not make explicit whether Chaereas takes the figure running toward him in the dark to be Callirhoe or her alleged lover; but as he continues to seethe after the event and shows no hint

but is prevented from suicide, and acquitted of murder in court of law; Callirhoe is buried in a splendid tomb.

It is from this sequence of events that the action of the remainder of the novel stems. Callirhoe's death turns out – in the way of Greek novels[10] – to be no more than a coma, from which she awakes just in time to be rescued by pirate tomb-robbers, who sail off to Miletus and sell her there; and the adventures, which for the reader revolve around the question whether the couple will be reunited, begin. There are other events, of course, which play an important part in pushing the action forward;[11] but – on the human level – it all starts with a series of acts promoted by feelings of anger. The anger of the suitors and that of Chaereas are different in quality – the suitors are piqued and calculate the steps they are to take, Chaereas is in a rage, unable to control himself – but ὀργή describes both.[12]

The causal sequence is psychologically convincing, but it has been re-garded by at least one scholar as determined by Chariton's choice of *narrative* sequences.[13] According to this view, Chariton makes an initial decision to include in his novel the episode of Callirhoe waking in the tomb and the robbers breaking in, and then (as he must) sets up the causes in a way which leads smoothly to that episode. But while it is true that in the functioning of the narrative the "realistic" causes are "as arbitrary as the contingent" (i.e. the external forces which Chariton has interfere in the action),[14] we should not suppose that the chosen causal connectors themselves are arbitrary. As I shall attempt to show, much that is of interest and significance can be seen in the choice of anger as the novel's key narrative impulse.

The kick delivered by Chaereas to his wife does not, however, mark the end of the process of anger-driven behavior which stimulates the subsequent action. There is a further stage in this process; or, to be more precise, the action is presented by the narrator as being interpretable in a way which

---

of regret until the truth is revealed (by Callirhoe's maidservants, under torture), it is reasonable to suppose that he knew (however momentarily) what he was doing – in that sense the act was intentional, even if in another sense it was not (see below, p. 171). The reference to darkness is best explained as removing any opportunity for Callirhoe to utter a defense: she is upon Chaereas before he can see and assess the situation, and he lashes out.

10 The *Scheintod* motif also appears in Xenophon of Ephesus (3.5–8) and (very prominently) in Achilles Tatius' *Leucippe and Cleitophon* (3.15–22; 5.7–19 and 8.15–16; 7.3–16); see too *C&C* 3.1.3–4.

11 For example, the chance (or providential) discovery of the pirate ship drifting aimlessly in the Mediterranean after its departure from Miletus gives direction to the search for Callirhoe (3.3–5); Callirhoe's decision in Miletus to marry the Ionian aristocrat Dionysius for the sake of her unborn child (2.11) is essential for the development of the action which leads to the trial in Babylon, the scene where Chaereas and Callirhoe first set eyes on each other after their separation, and the novel's emotional highpoint (5.4–8).

12 Chaereas' anger at Callirhoe over the supposed revel at his house is also described as χόλος (1.3.5).

13 Philippides (1988) 182–4.   14 Philippides (1988) 184.

provides a further stage. At the beginning of the final book (Book 8) the narrator discloses in advance the happy outcome, the lovers' rediscovery of each other and the end of their separation. At this point Chaereas, who has taken the side of Egyptian rebels against the king of Persia, Artaxerxes, and risen to the command of the fleet, has Callirhoe, along with the Persian queen and others left by the king on the Phoenician island of Aradus, in his possession, but does not know it. Fortune, *Tyche*, one of the external forces at work in the narrative,[15] intends that Chaereas should remain ignorant of the facts and leave Callirhoe behind, alone.

ἀλλὰ ἔδοξε τό<δε> δεινὸν Ἀφροδίτῃ· ἤδη γὰρ αὐτῷ διηλλάττετο, πρότερον ὀργισθεῖσα χαλεπῶς διὰ τὴν ἄκαιρον ζηλοτυπίαν, ὅτι δῶρον παρ' αὐτῆς λαβὼν τὸ κάλλιστον, οἷον οὐδὲ Ἀλέξανδρος ὁ Πάρις, ὕβρισεν εἰς τὴν χάριν. ἐπεὶ δὲ καλῶς ἀπελογήσατο τῷ Ἔρωτι Χαιρέας ἀπὸ δύσεως εἰς ἀνατολὰς διὰ μυρίων παθῶν πλανηθείς, ἠλέησεν αὐτὸν Ἀφροδίτη καὶ ὅπερ ἐξ ἀρχῆς δύο τῶν καλλίστων ἥρμοσε ζεῦγος, γυμνάσασα διὰ γῆς καὶ θαλάσσης, πάλιν ἠθέλησεν ἀποδοῦναι. (8.1.3)

But this seemed too cruel to Aphrodite; by this time she was becoming reconciled to Chaereas, though earlier she had been made intensely angry by his inappropriate jealousy, because after receiving from her the fairest of gifts, superior even to the gift Alexander Paris had received, he had repaid her kindness with insult. But since Chaereas had now made honourable amends to Love by wandering the world from west to east amid innumerable sufferings, Aphrodite took pity on him, and, having harassed by land and sea the beautiful couple she had originally brought together, she now decided to reunite them.

Aphrodite has featured in a variety of ways throughout the novel, most often as the recipient of prayers from Callirhoe[16] (who is also several times compared to her[17]), but hitherto there has been little explicit indication of her involvement in the action.[18] Here, however, Chaereas' journey and its sufferings are laid at her door. The reason behind this is her anger (she is ὀργισθεῖσα), engendered by Chaereas' jealousy (ζηλοτυπία); in kicking Callirhoe Chaereas has insulted (ὕβρισεν) the goddess, who gave him the most beautiful of women, frequently mistaken for Aphrodite herself.[19]

At this late stage, then, Chariton presents the whole of the main action of his work in terms of anger. The pique of the suitors sets up Chaereas'

---

[15] For *Tyche* in *C&C* see especially Robiano (1984); Van Steen (1998); also Ruiz Montero (1989) 127–30.
[16] See 1.1.7; 2.2.7–8; 3.2.12–13, 8.7–9; 7.5.2–5; 8.4.10, 8.15–16.
[17] See 1.1.2; 2.2.6, 5.7; 3.2.14, 2.17; 4.7.5.
[18] The one clear instance is at 2.2.8, where Aphrodite rejects Callirhoe's prayer that she attract no man after Chaereas, and is said by the narrator to have been planning another marriage for Callirhoe (with Dionysius), which she did not intend to preserve either.
[19] See 1.14.1; 2.3.5–6; 5.9.1.

rage, and the act to which this gives rise produces an angry response from Aphrodite. Finally, after seeing Chaereas endure a host of troubles, the goddess releases the pressure; only when her anger is removed can events move to a happy conclusion. Anger – human and divine – thus frames almost the whole of the narrative. In a text full of Homeric quotations and echoes[20] we should be reminded here of the *Iliad*;[21] but – as far as this aspect of the text is concerned – the closer connection is with the *Aeneid*, where divine anger (Juno's) is mentioned expressly at the beginning (with its removal described late in Book 12), human anger (Aeneas') at the end.[22] This pattern may serve to foreground the *Aeneid* as a more significant intertext for Chariton than is normally suggested. In the discussion of Greek novels generally it is, among epic models, the *Odyssey* that is particularly emphasized, and for very good reasons; but we ought not to forget, in considering Chariton, that the novel has a distinctly Iliadic part[23] as well as an Odyssean, and that the phrases *terris iactatus et alto* ("buffeted by land and sea") and *multa quoque et bello passus* ("and having endured much also in war") (Virgil, *Aen.* 1.3, 5) could be applied to Chaereas no less than to Aeneas.[24] The similarity with the *Iliad* alone, however, is sufficient for the framing function of anger in *Chaereas and Callirhoe* to be regarded as

---

[20] A convenient list is provided by Papanikolaou (1973) 14–16. Useful brief comments on intertextual relations between *C&C* and the *Iliad* may be found in Fusillo (1989) 27–8 and Egger (1994a) 42; both Homeric epics are included in the discussions of Biraud (1985) and C. W. Müller (1976) 126–36 (who sees Chariton as a writer of epic in prose).

[21] Achilles' anger at Agamemnon opens the poem, from the first word; his anger at Hector, still present at the beginning of Book 24, is finally removed at the demand of Zeus and Priam's supplication with gifts. We might also recall Poseidon's wrath in the *Odyssey*, which is instrumental in keeping Odysseus from his home in Ithaca (see *Od.* 1.74–5, etc.), as is Aphrodite's in separating Chaereas and Callirhoe; but there is no framing function here (Odysseus reaches Ithaca at *Od.* 13.113–19, and Poseidon's anger is discharged with his punishment of the Phaeacians who conveyed Odysseus there [*Od.* 13.125–64]), and it is to the *Iliad* that our minds should first turn when thinking of anger in Homer.

[22] Virg. *Aen.* 1.4, 11, etc.; 12.791–842; 12.946.   [23] In the war in Egypt in Book 7.

[24] Considering Homeric quotations in *C&C*, Reardon (1996: 333) refers to Chariton's awareness of the parallels between Chaereas the warrior and the heroes of the *Iliad*, and Chaereas the wanderer and the hero of the *Odyssey*, but says nothing, as he might in this context, of the *Aeneid*. Virgilian influence on Chariton in matters of detail is claimed – with reference especially to *Aeneid* 4 – by Cataudella (1927). The passage at 8.1.3 set out above suggests further connections: the phrase ὀργισθεῖσα χαλεπῶς ("having been made intensely angry") might be thought to echo Virgil, *Aen.* 1.4 *saeuae memorem Iunonis ob iram* ("on account of cruel Juno's unforgetting anger"), and the whole passage as it were to *combine* Virgil's reference to Juno's anger at this point with his account of its removal in Book 12; similarly, in ἀπὸ δύσεως εἰς ἀνατολάς ("from west to east") Chariton could be said to reverse the east–west movement of the *Aeneid*, referred to in the first lines of the poem (*Aen.* 1.1–3) and emphasized by the frequent references to Italy as Hesperia (*Aen.* 1.530, etc.). More generally, Laplace (1980: 120, 124–5) has argued for an allegorical level of meaning in *C&C* in which Callirhoe's child (for which see nn. 73, 88 below) parallels Aeneas, Aphrodite's child, destined to travel west and found an empire. This idea is picked up by D. R. Edwards (1991) 195–6 and (1996) 35, 131, and developed further by Connors (2002), a paper which focuses on the Roman imperial context of the novel. The

one of the ways in which Chariton associates his text with epic. Of course, the presence of anger is not felt throughout the text in the way it is felt throughout the *Iliad* or the *Aeneid*; but recognition of the frame can evoke or reinforce the association in a reader, just as a knowledge of the epics can help to reveal the frame. How a reader interprets the association is another matter; for some it might tend to emphasize the gap between epic and novel, just as the explicit and implied connections Chariton makes at various points between Chaereas on the one hand and Homeric heroes on the other[25] might for some underline the fact that Chaereas is in many respects distinctly *not* an epic hero.[26] But it is the connection, not the disjunction, that I wish to stress here, for reasons that will become apparent later.

First, however, I want to examine Chaereas' act of anger against Callirhoe more closely. It has been suggested[27] that the scene of the assault owes a debt to the *Perikeiromene* of Menander, an author with whom Chariton was certainly familiar.[28] While not wishing to dispute this – all kinds of generic influence can be seen in *Chaereas and Callirhoe*, and an ideal reading is a highly complex matter[29] – I would point out that the potential consequences in Chariton are far more serious than in this comic model, where the assault is directed merely at the heroine's hair. Though, as it turns out,[30] Callirhoe's death is only apparent, at the time, to Chaereas and all the people of Syracuse, it is real enough; in essence his act of rage is catastrophic. This, together with the fact of his punishment, clearly implies a negative evaluation of uncontrolled anger, and the language that

---

close connections between Rome and Chariton's home city of Aphrodisias (for which see Reynolds [1982] and Erim [1986], esp. 28–32, 80–3, 106–30, 136–8) are highly relevant to this whole area of enquiry.

[25] See, e.g., 1.1.3, 5.2 (Achilles); 3.5.6; 7.2.4 (Hector); 7.3.5, 4.6 (Diomedes).

[26] So Konstan (1994) 17 (with particular reference to 3.5.4–6); see also G. Anderson (1984) 47.

[27] By Borgogno (1971) 257–8; cf. Laplace (1980) 111.

[28] For evidence and argument see especially Borgogno (1971), noting also the quotation of *Misoumenos* 9 at 4.7.7; in the case of certain of the possible echoes enumerated by Borgogno and Papanikolaou (1973) 23–4 we may have to do with clichés or commonplaces. The links between Chariton (and the other Greek novelists) and New Comedy, however, are mainly situational; see further the excellent discussion of Fusillo (1989) 43–55, and, arguing for a particularly close organic connection between the two genres, Corbato (1968) (which has less specifically on Chariton than its title might suggest).

[29] For the generic complexity of the Greek novel see especially Fusillo (1989) 17–109. R. Hunter (1994: 1079–82), discussing this scene and that of Chaereas' trial which follows (1.5.2–6.1), argues that Chariton has deliberately made problematic what "code" we should use when reading them.

[30] And as the reader is likely to surmise, particularly if s/he observes carefully the reference to Callirhoe νεκρᾶς εἰκόνα πᾶσι παρέχουσα, "presenting to all the appearance of a corpse" (1.5.1) – though this is not to say that imaginative identification with the feelings of Chaereas and the Syracusans is impossible.

Chariton uses substantiates the point: Chaereas is κρατούμενος . . . ὑπό τῆς ὀργῆς (1.4.12), "overcome by anger," "conquered," "mastered." We are offered here an initial route to understanding the set of attitudes to anger contained in the text, which need to be viewed partly in the context of attitudes to emotion more generally.

One of the most obvious features of this novel is that Callirhoe is the object of every man's desire – every socially appropriate man, at least. When in his turn the king of Persia falls in love with her, he asks his adviser, the eunuch Artaxates, to find a remedy for his pain. The suggestion implicit in the eunuch's reply that the only remedy is the desired object itself horrifies the king, who rejects absolutely the idea of seducing another man's wife, and adds:

μηδεμίαν μου καταγνῷς ἀκρασίαν. οὐχ οὕτως ἑαλώκαμεν. (6.3.8)

Don't accuse me of a lack of self-control. I am not overcome to that extent.

For the king, the ability to control his emotions, not to be conquered by them, is a matter of great importance. Similarly, at an earlier stage in the novel, the Ionian nobleman Dionysius attempts to suppress his love for Callirhoe, and his efforts are presented in metaphors of an analogous kind:

Τότ᾽ ἦν ἰδεῖν ἀγῶνα λογισμοῦ καὶ πάθους. καίτοι γὰρ βαπτιζόμενος ὑπὸ τῆς ἐπιθυμίας γενναῖος ἀνὴρ ἐπειρᾶτο ἀντέχεσθαι. καθάπερ δὲ ἐκ κύματος ἀνέκυπτε λέγων πρὸς ἑαυτὸν "οὐκ αἰσχύνῃ, Διονύσιε, ἀνὴρ ὁ πρῶτος τῆς Ἰωνίας ἕνεκεν ἀρετῆς τε καὶ δόξης, ὃν θαυμάζουσι σατράπαι καὶ βασιλεῖς καὶ πόλεις, παιδαρίου πρᾶγμα πάσχων; . . ." ἐφιλονείκει δὲ ὁ Ἔρως βουλευομένῳ καλῶς καὶ ὕβριν ἐδόκει τὴν σωφροσύνην τὴν ἐκείνου· διὰ τοῦτο ἐπυρπόλει σφοδρότερον ψυχὴν ἐν ἔρωτι φιλοσοφοῦσαν. (2.4.4–5)[31]

Then a struggle between reason and passion was plain to see. Though overwhelmed by desire, as a man of breeding he tried to resist and, as it were, kept rising above the waves, saying to himself, "Are you not ashamed, Dionysius – you, the leading man in Ionia in virtue and reputation, admired by satraps, kings, and cities – to be suffering like a boy? . . ." But Love was eager to defeat these sound counsels, considering Dionysius' self-restraint an insult, and for that reason burned all the more fiercely a heart that was trying to be philosophical in love.

---

[31] On this passage and Dionysius' struggle with Eros generally see also Konstan (1994) 32–3, who views it in the light of Foucauldian ideas on mastery and self-control; as will be clear from my discussion, however, I disagree with Konstan's claim that "the secondary characters [in *C&C*] [are not] constructed to exhibit the virtues of self-mastery." A Foucauldian perspective on the threat which Eros poses to Dionysius and the king is also presented, and developed more fully and in interesting ways, by Balot (1998) 145–54.

Notable here is the narrator's positive view of Dionysius' efforts to control his feelings: his resistance is connected with his being γενναῖος, noble, and his reasoning is regarded as sound sense (βουλευομένῳ καλῶς). His concealment of his love is similarly praised at the beginning of the chapter, as being appropriate for a well-brought-up man – a πεπαιδευμένος – who lays special claim to virtue.[32] There is plainly a social dimension here, but the language employed in describing Dionysius' resistance to his emotions,[33] like that used in the passage concerning the king, points to a philosophical underlay, albeit of a non-specific kind. Dionysius, then, wins praise for fighting down his love for Callirhoe from a narrator who takes a broadly philosophical position; conversely, the text has Chaereas, who is overcome by another *pathos*, anger, endure suffering in consequence. But at the same time the passage suggests that we might look in a different direction for the essentials of the attitude to emotion implied in the novel. Dionysius' attempts to rise above his feelings for Callirhoe are countered by Love, conceived of in its divine form, who responds by "burn[ing] all the more fiercely a heart that was trying to be philosophical in love." Resistance to powerful emotion, the text seems to be saying, is useless. And this of course is the nub of the thought in the novel: love, when it comes, cannot be denied – it is overwhelming, and Chaereas, Dionysius, the satraps Mithridates and Pharnaces, the king, all yield to it. This is not necessarily out of keeping with the philosophical perspective; the philosophers recognized that, while a moderate or rational response to passion was the ideal, the force of passion could be overpowering.[34] And yet the strong contrast between Eros, personified and even personalized, and the philosophically striving Dionysius tends to evoke the thought of a much earlier time – a different, essentially non-philosophical world – which straightforwardly acknowledged the irresistible power of the divinities of love.[35] The narrator

[32] οἷα δὴ πεπαιδευμένος ἀνὴρ καὶ ἐξαιρέτως ἀρετῆς ἀντιποιούμενος (2.4.1). Note too how at 2.6.3 Dionysius, rejecting the suggestion that he should force his desires on Callirhoe, refers to himself as famed for his self-control (*sōphrosunē*).

[33] The image of being swamped or drowned is also applied to Dionysius in a slightly different context at 3.2.6, with a further reference (cf. n. 73) to his being πεπαιδευμένος.

[34] As far as sexual love is concerned see especially (and classically) the *Symposium* and *Phaedrus* of Plato.

[35] In a text which has a fifth- or early fourth-century dramatic date (for the chronological setting see, e.g., R. Hunter [1994] 1056–8, with further bibliography at n. 4), one thinks perhaps of tragedy, and such passages as the choral odes at Soph. *Ant.* 781–800; Eur. *Hipp.* 525–64, 1268–82; but of course one can equally look much further back (see, e.g., Hom. *Il.* 3.383–447, where Aphrodite induces a reluctant Helen to sleep with Paris; Hom. *Hymn Aph.* 1–5, 34–5; Sappho 1, esp. 23–4; and further archaic material cited by Toohey [1999] 259–69). In *C&C* note especially 6.3.2, where the king says that he had heard that Love rules (κρατεῖ) all the gods, even Zeus, but did not believe that anyone could be more powerful than he himself at his own court; but Love "has settled in (ἐνδεδήμηκεν) my heart," and "I am truly his captive (ἀληθῶς . . . ἑάλωκα)" (I am unconvinced by the argument of Toohey [1999] 269–72 that the king could have avoided this situation by a change in his behavior).

expresses approval of Dionysius' struggle to master his desire, only to add immediately that it is, in fact, pointless.

The presentation of Chaereas' act of anger possesses a similar kind of duality. Though at his trial Chaereas bitterly condemns himself for what he has done, he is not regarded by others as accountable: his father-in-law, Hermocrates, who might well be thought to have good reasons for acting otherwise, defends him on the basis that his action was (in some sense) unintended, ἀκούσιον,[36] and that he was the victim of conspiracy; the jury acquits him, and the narrator himself supplies defenses that he might have used, which include the suitors' slander against Callirhoe, and Chaereas' jealousy (1.5.4–6.1). While the jealousy is instrumental in producing Aphrodite's anger, on the human level it is represented by the narrator as a mitigating factor: far from stating or implying that Chaereas should have controlled his emotions, he suggests that he could not help himself.[37] It is, no doubt, appropriate for Chaereas to feel remorse, just as it is appropriate for Dionysius to try to subdue his love, but neither is responsible, ultimately, for being overwhelmed by passion.

Nonetheless, Chaereas is punished; but the question why needs to be answered with some care. Strictly, he is not punished for his act of jealous rage *per se*, but for its implications: what arouses Aphrodite's anger is the fact that "after receiving from her the fairest of gifts, superior even to the gift Alexander Paris had received, he had repaid her kindness with insult." In essence, what Chaereas is guilty of is ingratitude towards the goddess of love, and it is amends to love (Ἔρως) that he is required to make (8.1.3). It is not anger in itself, then, that Chariton implicitly criticizes here, but anger displayed in a particular situation, or directed toward a particular object.[38] The negative character of the specific act that Chaereas performs is underscored by an association which we are invited by the author to make: in having his hero kick his (as it turns out) pregnant wife, Chariton casts him in the role of cruel tyrant, evoking figures such as Periander of Corinth, about whom similar stories were told.[39] This suggests a further way of understanding Aphrodite's reaction to what Chaereas does: while on

---

[36] Cf. 1.5.4 (narrator's comment); 8.7.7.

[37] The same notion may be detectable at 1.4.10, if the words Χαιρέας οὐκέτι κατέσχεν are rightly understood to mean "Chaereas *could* no longer restrain himself" – which the context strongly suggests.

[38] The same position with regard to anger – namely that its moral evaluation depends on its context – is evident in Virgil's *Aeneid*: see Thornton (1976) 159–63.

[39] See R. Hunter (1994) 1080. In ancient political thought tyrants were commonly seen as not being in control of themselves, but swept beyond proper bounds by passions; see, e.g., Hdt. 3.80.2–5; Thuc. 3.62.3; Pl. *Resp.* 9.571a–576b; Arist. *Pol.* 5.9.11–20 (1314b–1315b), esp. 5.9.17 (1315a14–16) on physical violence.

one level she responds by taking a divinity's typical stance toward human insolence – focusing, that is, on her own sense of slight – on another, where her embodiment of human love rather than her own divine nature is her dominant aspect, her attitude amounts to condemnation of marital violence.[40]

The notions that there is an appropriate context for anger and that it should be subject to control come together in Book 7, in the episode of the Egyptian revolt. The decision made by Chaereas and his inseparable companion Polycharmus to join the rebels derives from a lie told (via a third party) to Chaereas by Dionysius, according to which King Artaxerxes, who had still to adjudicate the question to which of her husbands[41] Callirhoe was to belong, had determined in Dionysius' favour (7.1.3–11). Revenge, ἄμυνα, is the aim of Chaereas and Polycharmus,[42] and anger the underlying emotion.[43] This, however, is of a different order from the rage demonstrated by Chaereas in the first book; the action to which it gives rise is taken with deliberation and thought for the consequences – indeed, the scenario which Polycharmus paints for Chaereas, and which the latter accepts, envisages a glorious death, as they take vengeance on Artaxerxes for the injustice they believe he has done them (7.1.8).

Chaereas' anger thus comes to be enacted on the battlefield. Joining the forces of the Egyptian king, he rises rapidly to prominence through his good sense and courage; and in a bold attack on the city of Tyre, which he urges on a reluctant monarch and leads in person, he performs an *aristeia*, described with direct allusion to the military exploits of Diomedes in the *Iliad*.[44] After the city falls, he takes command of the fleet and wins

---

[40] In his essay *Advice to Bride and Groom* Plutarch, who may well be a contemporary of Chariton, warns both partners in a marriage against clashes (*Coniug. praec.* 3 [138E], 39 [143D-E]) – though the notion that the man should be dominant in the relationship is accepted without question (see esp. *Coniug. praec.* 33 [142D-E]). For criticism of anger shown by men toward their wives see also Harris, ch. 5, p. 136 with n. 75. I am grateful to Professor Harris additionally for drawing to my attention Cic. *Tusc.* 4.54, which, as will be seen, is especially relevant in the present context; attacking the Peripatetics who, he says, describe *iracundia* as *cos fortitudinis*, "the whetstone of bravery," advantageous in battle (*Tusc.* 4.43), Cicero writes: *quid? ista bellatrix iracundia, cum domum rediit, qualis est cum uxore, cum liberis, cum familia? an tum quoque est utilis?*, "That warring tendency to anger – when it has returned home, what is it like with wife, children, household? Is it of use in these circumstances as well?"

[41] For Callirhoe's marriage in Miletus to Dionysius see above, p. 165 n. 11.

[42] See 7.1.8, 1.11, 2.4; and cf. 7.4.5 ἀμύνεσθαι; 8.1.1, 8.8 ἀμύνασθαι.

[43] For explicit reference to ὀργή see 8.1.16; (with the story rewritten by Callirhoe) 8.3.7; for the connection between anger and revenge see n. 59 below, and also, for example, Arist. *Pol.* 5.8.9 (1311a34–6); Cic. *Tusc.* 3.11; 4.21, 44; Sen. *De ira* 1.12.5 (*Dial.* 3.12.5); Sen. *ap.* Lactant. *De ira dei* 17.13. Bowie (1985: 689), reflecting the *communis opinio*, sees Chaereas' valorous activity in the war as motivated by "despair and not any more positive quality"; this blanks out precisely what seems to me important in the picture.

[44] See 7.4.6 (where the line quoted – Hom. *Il.* 10.483, with minor variations from our text – is applied also, again in slightly different forms, to Odysseus slaughtering the suitors at Hom. *Od.* 22.308;

a further victory (7.6.1), proceeding to seize the island of Aradus, where he subsequently finds and is reunited with Callirhoe.

Although Chaereas' recovery of his wife is, as we have seen, dependent – on the divine level – on the intervention of Aphrodite, it is his own decision to fight against the king of Persia, his courageous spirit, his qualities of leadership, and his personal military prowess that lead to his being in a position from which Callirhoe is recoverable.[45] On this occasion, then, his anger obtains a desired result; and a strong contrast emerges with his earlier rage. Not only is his action in joining the rebel forces taken with forethought, he keeps his head even in the thick of battle. In the attack on Tyre, with some of the enemy trying to force their way out of the city, and others struggling to get back inside, we are told:

Ἐν δὲ τῷ ἀδιηγήτῳ τούτῳ ταράχῳ μόνος ἐσωφρόνησε Χαιρέας. (7.4.9)

In this indescribable confusion Chaereas was the only one who kept calm.

Far from being overcome by emotion, as in his assault on Callirhoe, Chaereas maintains absolute control, and is instrumental in the city's capture; he has acquired *sōphrosunē*, the very quality to which, in a different kind of situation, both Dionysius and the Persian king have laid claim.[46] He is still acting in accordance with his anger, but he is now its master, and he expresses it not in a domestic context, but in one appropriate to an epic hero.[47] For Chaereas' participation in the Egyptian war amounts to much more than "a grand suicidal gesture."[48] Deprived forever (as he thinks) of Callirhoe, he first proposes to cut his own throat at the gates of the king's palace (7.1.6); but Polycharmus persuades him that death attained through seeking vengeance is preferable (7.1.7–8), in words that embody the epic hero's view of the world:

24.184; the first *Odyssey* passage is indeed the closest textually, but the simile which follows in Chariton makes the Iliadic reference the stronger), and cf. 7.3.5 (Hom. *Il.* 9.48–9, adapted). Note too that Dionysius, fighting on the Persian side, also performs an *aristeia*, with the word actually used of his achievement (7.5.12–15); as in epic, there are heroes on both sides.

[45] With great irony, Chariton has for the second time in the novel made Chaereas take a critical step on the basis of false information: as his separation from Callirhoe arises from the slander of the suitors, so his recovery of her results from the lie of Dionysius (in whose corresponding loss of Callirhoe there is thus a degree of poetic justice). The Persian king is the undeserving victim on this occasion, but suffers little in the end, regaining both Egypt and his queen.

[46] See above, pp. 169–70; cf. also Couraud-Lalanne (1998) 538–9. For the complexity of meaning of the term *sōphrosunē* see North (1966); a few remarks are made at n. 92 below.

[47] The portrayal of Chaereas as feeling anger but keeping its enactment within due limits parallels portrayals of epic anger with positive connotations; on this see Braund and Gilbert, ch. 11.

[48] So Konstan (1994) 16; cf. G. Anderson (1984) 47, 89.

καλὸν γὰρ λυπήσαντας αὐτὸν ἔργῳ ποιῆσαι μετανοεῖν, ἔνδοξον καὶ τοῖς
ὕστερον ἐσομένοις διήγημα καταλείποντας ὅτι δύο Ἕλληνες ἀδικηθέντες
ἀντελύπησαν τὸν μέγαν βασιλέα καὶ ἀπέθανον ὡς ἄνδρες. (7.1.8)

It would be a fine thing to hurt him so much that he really repents, and to leave
to posterity a glorious story of how two Greeks who were unjustly treated by the
Great King made him suffer in his turn and died like men.

Combined here are the notions of harming one's enemies, leaving a reputation for posterity, and dying a noble death, all key elements of the heroic
code;[49] and Chaereas' being urged to action in this way by his companion
can also of course be paralleled in Homeric epic.[50]

In the first chapter of the novel, Chaereas is compared to Achilles (1.1.3).[51]
The precise point of comparison is their physical beauty, but comparisons
with the hero of the most famous poem of antiquity inevitably carry reso-
nances, especially at a point in a text where one might expect to find hints
of a literary program.[52] No ancient reader could have read Achilles' name
without his thoughts being turned, at some level, to anger; no attentive one
would have been surprised to find Chaereas behaving in an Achillean manner. But, for all the similarities in the anger and the prowess in war, there
are important differences too. Above all, Achilles is not remotely *sōphrōn*;
of course, the world of the novel, whether one regards this as belonging
to its fifth-/fourth-century setting or to its Hellenistic/imperial context of
production, is quite different from that of the *Iliad* – competence at generalship in military or naval conflict, for one thing, is not a characteristic
required of the heroes at Troy – but in this world *sōphrosunē* is, as we
have seen, an admired quality. By the standards of this world Chaereas,
in achieving both glory in battle and *sōphrosunē*, outdoes his chief epic
model.[53]

---

[49] For harming one's enemies see, e.g., Hom. *Il.* 11.122–42; leaving a reputation for posterity, notably
Il. 7.81–91 (Hector's speech before the duel with Ajax); dying a noble death, e.g., *Od.* 5.306–12. On
the heroic code generally see, e.g., M. W. Edwards (1987) 149–58.

[50] See esp. Hom. *Il.* 12.310–28 (Sarpedon to Glaucus).

[51] Strictly, he is compared to a statue or painting of Achilles; but this distancing of the comparison is
of no significance for the point I am making here.

[52] In the same passage Chaereas is also compared to Nireus, Hippolytus, and Alcibiades. That the references to Achilles, Nireus, and Alcibiades point programmatically to the epic and historiographical
character of the work has been hinted at by R. Hunter (1994) 1083–4; the inclusion of Hippolytus
similarly points to a connection with tragedy, for which I intend to argue elsewhere.

[53] For similar "outdoing" within the epic tradition see Hershkowitz (1998b) 105–89, esp. 105–28 (on
Jason in Apollonius of Rhodes and Valerius Flaccus). Egger (1994a: 45, n. 27) draws attention also to
Chariton's "improvement" on Homer in the complexity of Dionysius' role, which contains reflections
of both Paris and Menelaus.

Chaereas' transition from youth given to outbursts of weeping and thoughts of (and attempts at) suicide[54] to decisive man of action may seem uncomfortably sudden, but, that apart, the shift is highly appropriate – one might even call it crucial. The sufferings he experiences in consequence of his initial act of rage are the payment due to Aphrodite; but they must also involve personal growth.[55] Chaereas has to prove his worthiness to be the husband of a woman for whom his rival Dionysius might be thought a more suitable match;[56] and this involves becoming a man. The first mention of Chaereas (1.1.3) describes him as a μειράκιον, a youth, who marries young enough for his wife, when angered, to suggest that he still has male lovers, *erastai* (1.3.6). By the end of the novel, when he sails into the harbour of Syracuse wearing a general's uniform (8.6.8), this identity has been eradicated.[57] The urging of Polycharmus that they should die ὡς ἄνδρες, as men, as heroes (7.1.8, quoted above), is doubly significant in this context; though Chaereas does not die, the action he takes in pursuit of this goal establishes him firmly as an ἀνήρ, a man of anger, and its master.[58]

---

[54] Weeping: 1.3.4; 3.3.14, 4.4, 6.6; 4.4.6; 5.2.4 (it should be observed, however, that Dionysius and the Persian king also weep in sorrow: see 2.5.7, 5.12; 5.10.2; 8.5.12–13 [Dionysius]; 6.3.3 [king]; for the frequent mention of tears as a marker of the pathetic/sentimental quality of the novel see Ruiz Montero [1989] 144); suicide: 1.4.7, 5.2, 6.1; 3.3.1, 3.6, 5.6; 5.10.6–10; 6.2.8–11; 7.1.6.

[55] For the novel as *Bildungsroman*, or as describing a rite of passage, see also Schmeling (1974) 134–5, 137–8 (the whole section, 130–41, is worth reading, though it is not all equally persuasive); Couraud-Lalanne (1998), who argues that both Chaereas and Callirhoe can be regarded as undergoing a rite of passage into adult status; a more complex view is presented by Balot (1998).

[56] Chaereas' need to demonstrate his worthiness is stressed too by Heiserman (1977) 84, 85; for Dionysius' suitability to be Callirhoe's husband see below, p. 180, with n. 73; and also Bowie (1985) 689; Liviabella Furiani (1989) 51; Egger (1990) 193–4, (1994a) 42; Goold (1995) 14; Balot (1998) 158.

[57] Chariton uses the term μειράκιον only of Chaereas, three times in the first book (1.1.3, 1.10, 4.4), and thereafter only at 3.10.7, where the word is Callirhoe's. Chaereas is referred to as νεανίσκος ("youth," "young man") at 3.9.1, 9.5; 4.3.1, 3.12 (in three of these cases in company with Polycharmus), but never subsequently. He is described as νεανίας ("young man") twice, once at 1.1.8, and once by the Egyptian king (7.2.5), immediately prior to his feats of military prowess (cf. n. 83 below on the location in the text of his last thoughts of suicide). The use of these terms plainly underlines Chaereas' growth to maturity. For similar observations see Couraud-Lalanne (1998) 533–4. On Chaereas' generalship, which links him with Hermocrates (thus giving a clear indication of his suitability to be Callirhoe's husband), see Elsom (1992) 226; Couraud-Lalanne (1998) 538–9.

[58] Cf. Balot (1998) 157: "By understanding the importance of 'dying like a man' . . . Chaereas equally learns to live like a man . . . Chaereas' realization of his potential for manhood allows him to recover Callirhoe and to assume his rightful place in society when he returns to Syracuse." It is true, of course, as Balot (159–61) stresses, that traces of the earlier Chaereas remain in the final book, in two references to his "innate jealousy" (ἔμφυτος ζηλοτυπία, 8.1.15, 4.4); but in the first case he does not react with passion when the jealousy is aroused, but deflects it, while in the second it is offered as the reason for Callirhoe's non-disclosure to him of the letter she writes to Dionysius (on which see n. 88 below) – what we see, then, is her fear, not evidence of inability on Chaereas' part to restrain jealous feelings. Potential for another violent outburst may remain, but the much stronger suggestion is that Chaereas is now in control of his emotions.

If Chaereas' identity as a man is tied up with his ability to express anger in the appropriate context and to an appropriate degree,[59] it might be thought that Callirhoe's absence of anger following a near-fatal assault which she had done nothing to provoke reflects the female passivity that is typical of much ancient literature and is idealized in ancient male views of the socially acceptable female.[60] In the rest of this chapter I want to examine this lack of anger in the heroine, and to consider whether this easy presumption offers an adequate interpretation of the facts of the case.[61]

In the context of a work so dominated by emotion, and in which anger plays so significant a role, the attitude displayed by the character who, to our minds at least, has the most justification to be angry, may strike us as surprising. Callirhoe shows little more than mild irritation toward Chaereas. When she awakes in the tomb after her apparent death and the funeral, she rails at her lover, but in a muted way:

ἄδικε Χαιρέα, μέμφομαί σε οὐχ ὅτι με ἀπέκτεινας, ἀλλ᾽ ὅτι με ἔσπευσας ἐκβαλεῖν τῆς οἰκίας. οὐκ ἔδει σε ταχέως θάψαι Καλλιρόην οὐδ᾽ ἀληθῶς ἀποθανοῦσαν. (1.8.4)

Unjust Chaereas, I blame you, not for killing me, but for being so quick to cast me from the house. You should not have buried Callirhoe with such haste, not even if she had really been dead.

Later, alone on Dionysius' country estate near Miletus, after her purchase from the pirates, she puts the blame for her misfortunes squarely on *Tyche*, which "made my lover my murderer" (1.14.7; cf. 5.5.2). At 2.2.6 she refers to Aphrodite as "the cause of all my troubles," and at 2.2.7 criticizes her for

---

[59] Here we may detect a reflection of the Aristotelian view of virtuous anger set out at *Eth. Nic.* 4.5.3 (1125b31–2): "the man who is angry in the right circumstances (ἐφ᾽ οἷς δεῖ) and with the right objects (οἷς δεῖ) and in a fitting manner (ὡς δεῖ) and at the right time and for the right length of time wins praise." In this connection it might also be observed that Aristotle's definition of ὀργή at *Rh.* 2.2 (1378a30–2) as "a desire accompanied by pain for a perceived revenge for a perceived slight at the hands of men who have no call to slight oneself or one's friends" (I follow the translation of Barnes [1984], but have preferred D. Konstan's "perceived" to Barnes' "conspicuous": see Konstan, ch. 4, pp. 100–2) fits quite well the anger of the suitors and of Aphrodite against Chaereas, and of Chaereas against Callirhoe and her alleged lover, and against the king of Persia. In saying these things I do not mean to suggest that a specific philosophical line on anger or the emotions underpins, or even underlies, Chariton's novel; cf. my observations at p. 170 above.

[60] Plutarch's essay on marriage (see above, n. 40) remarks that wives who are sensible (νοῦν ἔχουσαι) keep quiet when their husbands are ranting in anger (*Coniug. praec.* 37 [143C]), and that wives should have no feelings of their own, but share their husbands' (*Coniug. praec.* 14 [140A]). Good wives – though of course they have a right to expect courtesy, not abuse, from their husbands – are kind and compliant; see generally Treggiari (1991) 229–61, esp. 238–43.

[61] The position taken in the following pages has certain affinities with that staked out by Kaimio (1995) 127–9. Kaimio is not, however, concerned with anger specifically, and it is by quite different paths that our papers reach this point of intersection.

not preserving the happy union in which she had originally joined her to Chaereas; in another prayer to the goddess, at 3.8.7, she describes Chaereas as "my beloved husband [ἀνδρὸς φιλτάτου]," and no angry word is uttered against him here either. Indeed, Callirhoe's love for Chaereas seems never to weaken: at the beginning of the "debate" she holds with her unborn child and the absent Chaereas over whether to marry Dionysius (2.11.1–3), she expresses a wish to have no other husband than Chaereas, and in the strongest terms:

θέλω γὰρ ἀποθανεῖν Χαιρέου μόνου γυνή. τοῦτό μοι καὶ γονέων ἥδιον καὶ πατρίδος καὶ τέκνου, πεῖραν ἀνδρὸς ἑτέρου μὴ λαβεῖν. (2.11.1)

I want to die the wife of Chaereas alone. This is dearer to me than parents, homeland, and child – to have no knowledge of another husband.

Though the result of the "debate" is the decision to marry Dionysius, and though there are difficulties in interpreting this decision purely in terms of social necessity and the wish to save her child,[62] in her own conscious mind at least Callirhoe remains committed to Chaereas. At 3.10.5, after receiving the (inaccurate) news that Chaereas is now dead, she says:

δυστυχοῦσα μέχρι νῦν ἐλογιζόμην "ὄψομαί ποτε Χαιρέαν καὶ διηγήσομαι αὐτῷ πόσα πέπονθα δι᾽ ἐκεῖνον· ταῦτά με ποιήσει τιμιωτέραν αὐτῷ . . ." ἀνόνητά μοι πάντα γέγονε. (3.10.5)

Until now I reasoned in my misfortune, "One day I shall see Chaereas and tell him everything that I have suffered on his account, and this will make me dearer to him . . ." All has been in vain.

It is almost as if, in the incident of the kick, the boot was on the other person's foot. Aphrodite, she goes on to assert, has robbed her of "my companion, my countryman, my lover, my beloved, my bridegroom" (3.10.7).

I have suggested above that the expression of anger, in the right place and properly controlled, is closely related to the achievement by Chaereas of full adult-male status. This link between anger and masculinity, which we perhaps take for granted when we think of Homer, seems to have been characteristic of ancient culture generally; the sexual aspects of the

---

[62] See Liviabella Furiani (1989) 51–2; Egger (1994a) 41. The passage at 2.11.1 just quoted also lends itself to a subversive interpretation: τοῦτό μοι καὶ γονέων ἥδιον καὶ πατρίδος καὶ τέκνου evokes Odysseus' words at Hom. *Od.* 9.34–5, where he tells the Phaeacians that, though both Calypso and Circe desired him for their husband, "nothing is sweeter than homeland and parents," which is why he is seeking to return to Ithaca. The echo both reinforces Callirhoe's express commitment to Chaereas and, via Calypso and Circe, with both of whom Odysseus had sexual liaisons, hints at sexual infidelity to come. The repetition of the echo at 3.8.4, in a context where Dionysius is thanking Aphrodite for the son Callirhoe has apparently borne him, underscores the point.

words ὀργή and θυμός, with their connotations of swelling, are discussed by Christopher Faraone elsewhere in this volume,[63] and Danielle Allen has argued persuasively for the importance of ὀργή in the self-definition of the male citizen in classical Athens.[64] Correspondingly, it can be said that legitimate access to anger was denied to women.[65] Figures such as Clytemnestra – depicted significantly by Aeschylus, as everyone knows, as a woman with the character of a man – and Medea – likened by Euripides to a beast and a monster – shatter the social norm.[66] Against this background Callirhoe's absence of anger can be regarded, from the conventional ancient male perspective, as something positive; despite Chaereas' brutal treatment of her, she is quick to forgive and remains the loyal wife, even through her marriage to Dionysius – a reassuring fact for those male readers who, despite the justifications offered in the text for the second marriage and the lack of condemnation by the narratorial voice, may have felt uncomfortable with this solution to the pregnant Callirhoe's problem.[67] It should be noted too that at 2.9.3–4, when contemplating abortion as the way out of her difficulty, Callirhoe specifically rejects the notion by reference to the Medea model:

βουλεύῃ τεκνοκτονῆσαι; πασῶν ἀσεβ<εστάτη, μ>αίνῃ καὶ Μηδείας λαμ-
βάνεις λογισμούς. ἀλλὰ καὶ τῆς Σκυθίδος ἀγριωτέρα δόξεις· ἐκείνη μὲν γὰρ
ἐχθρὸν εἶχε τὸν ἄνδρα, σὺ δὲ τὸ Χαιρέου τέκνον θέλεις ἀποκτεῖναι καὶ μηδὲ
ὑπόμνημα τοῦ περιβοήτου γάμου καταλιπεῖν. (2.9.3–4)

Are you planning to kill your child? Most impious of women, you are mad and reasoning like Medea! And you will seem more savage than that Scythian woman, for she hated her husband, while you want to kill Chaereas' child and not even leave behind a memorial of that celebrated marriage.

Though there is no mention here of anger, the references to madness and savagery or wildness (ἀγριωτέρα) are revealing.[68]

---

[63] Ch. 6; see also Allen, ch. 3, pp. 81–2 and 87–96, and (2000) 52–9, 160–5.

[64] Allen, ch. 3 and (2000) *passim*.

[65] See especially Harris, ch. 5, (2002) 264–82; also Allen, ch. 3, pp. 84–7, (2000) 111–18, 134–6.

[66] For Clytemnestra in Aeschylus' *Agamemnon* see especially *Ag.* 11, and the seminal article of Winnington-Ingram (1948); for Medea, Eur. *Med.* 92, 187–8, and esp. 1342–3 (picked up at 1358). I do not mean to suggest that the moral interpretation of these plays is straightforward; the role of Athens in Medea's escape seems to me particularly complicating. For further discussion see Harris, ch. 5, pp. 131, 140–1, (2002) 266, 276–8; Allen, ch. 3, pp. 84–5, 86, (2000) 113–16.

[67] Certainly there is here a moral gray area; Callirhoe's act, as Wiersma (1990: 118) observes, is undoubtedly bigamous. But this is not the place for a close examination of this matter.

[68] Chariton may be directly echoing Eur. *Med.* 1342–3, where Medea is described as τῆς Τυρσηνίδος | Σκύλλης ἔχουσαν ἀγριωτέραν φύσιν, "having a nature wilder than Tyrrhenian Scylla's"; cf. *Med.*

Callirhoe's reaction, or non-reaction, to the assault she suffers, then, may be seen in terms of female behavior conforming to the stereotype, the male ideal of how women should behave. Yet, passive as she is in this specific regard, she is entirely capable of anger, as her attacks on Aphrodite and on Fortune suggest. When Chaereas accuses her after the alleged revel, she is provoked (παρωξύνθη), and responds with spirit (1.3.6); the verb ἀγανακτέω ("be annoyed," "be indignant") is used of her four times, twice by the narrator directly (2.5.8; 6.7.9), once in a potential sense (Dionysius imagines her response to his concealment of the reason for their journey to Babylon, 5.4.13), and once in a minor character's description of her reaction to a particular incident (7.6.11). Of special interest here, however, is that she is capable of controlling her emotion.[69] When the pirates sail off from Syracuse with Callirhoe on board, she sees through their captain's attempts at explanation, but pretends to believe him,

δεδοικυῖα μὴ ἄρα καὶ ἀνέλωσιν αὐτὴν ὡς ὀργιζομένην. (1.11.2)

afraid that they might even do away with her if she showed that she was angry.[70]

Anger is here envisaged but suppressed, as more clearly still when the eunuch Artaxates presses her to submit to the Persian king. Her first impulse is to dig out his eyes,

οἷα δὲ γυνὴ πεπαιδευμένη καὶ φρενήρης, ταχέως λογισαμένη καὶ τὸν τόπον καὶ τίς ἐστιν αὐτὴ καὶ τίς ὁ λέγων, τὴν ὀργὴν μετέβαλε καὶ κατειρωνεύσατο λοιπὸν τοῦ βαρβάρου. (6.5.8)[71]

but as a cultivated and intelligent woman, she quickly sized up where she was, who she was, and who was talking to her, covered up her anger and from that point dissembled before the barbarian.

---

103 ἄγριον ἦθος ("wild character"). It is an ironic touch that Callirhoe cites the case of Medea in justification for not killing her child in a monologue in which she changes her mind over the action to take – just like Medea herself in Euripides' play (*Med.* 1021–80), where of course the opposite conclusion is reached.

[69] In this connection note also that in two of the passages just cited (2.5.8; 7.6.11) Callirhoe's annoyance impresses (in the one instance) Dionysius and (in the other) Chaereas: they admire her φρόνημα, spiritedness (2.5.9; 7.6.12; cf. 1.3.6), which Chaereas describes as οὐκ ἀγεννές ("not ignoble") – her level of response is just right.

[70] Goold (1995) translates "if she became petulant," putting a highly gendered gloss on ὀργιζομένην – we should not think in terms of Callirhoe stamping her little foot in rage. I owe this observation to Gráinne McLaughlin.

[71] Callirhoe's control of her anger here does not prevent Artaxates, whose overtures and threats she consistently resists, from regarding her a little later in terms of a wild beast (ἄγριον θηρίον) of which he would gladly be rid (6.9.4): beneath the restraint she remains feisty. The image picks up 2.9.4 ἀγριωτέρα, for which see above, p. 178 with n. 68.

Language and content here put Callirhoe on the same level as Dionysius (see p. 170 above, with n. 32);[72] and especially striking are the references to her *paideia*,[73] intelligence,[74] and quick thinking. Her intelligence and ability to reason are in fact prominent among her characteristics, most obviously perhaps in her consideration of what action to take about her pregnancy (2.9–11).[75] In representing her as highly rational, Chariton shuns the standard view of women as weak and emotional creatures; and in depicting her as being in control of her anger, he removes himself far from the stereotype which declares anger to be characteristically womanish, a position found, for example, in the younger Seneca:[76]

iracundia nihil amplum decorumque molitur; contra mihi uidetur ueternosi et infelicis animi, inbecillitatis sibi conscii, saepe indolescere, ut exulcerata et aegra corpora quae ad tactus leuissimos gemunt. ita ira muliebre maxime ac puerile uitium est. (Sen. *De ira* 1.20.3 [*Dial.* 3.20.3])

An angry disposition effects nothing great and beautiful; on the contrary, it seems to me the mark of a languid and unhappy spirit, conscious of its own weakness, to be often aggrieved, like sick and sore-ridden bodies which wince at the lightest touch. Thus anger is a particularly womanish and childish vice.

Similar notions occur in Seneca's *De clementia*, where female anger is associated not with children but with wild beasts:

magni autem animi proprium est placidum esse tranquillumque et iniurias atque offensiones superne despicere. muliebre est furere in ira, ferarum uero nec

---

[72] In comparing these descriptions, and noting particularly Dionysius' γενναιότης ("nobility"), it is interesting to reflect on an observation made by Galen, in his *Commentary on the Hippocratic Epidemics 1*, 17a.188: < . . . τὰς γυναῖκας εὑρίσκομεν ὀξυθύμους,> διότι τὸ γενναῖον τῆς τῶν ἀνδρῶν ψυχῆς οὐκ ἔχουσιν, "we find women quick to anger because they do not have the quality of nobility that men have in their souls." I owe this reference to Heinrich von Staden.

[73] The word πεπαιδευμένος/-η is applied *only* to Callirhoe (6.5.8; 7.6.5) and Dionysius (2.4.1; 3.2.6; 4.7.6; 5.5.1); other forms of the verb occur at 1.12.9 (again of Callirhoe) and strikingly, given this pattern, at 8.4.5, where the heroine, about to return to Syracuse with Chaereas, writes to Dionysius entrusting to him the son he believes to be his to "rear and educate (παιδεύειν) in a way worthy of us." Dionysius is also characterized by his παιδεία at 1.12.6; 2.1.5, 5.11; 5.9.8; and 8.5.10; the term is used of Chaereas only at 7.2.5, significantly in a passage which marks the beginning of his shift from immature youth to mature man (cf. nn. 55, 83). In this sharing of *paideia* the suitability of Dionysius and Callirhoe to be each other's spouse (see p. 175 above) is particularly evident. For brief discussion, with cultural contextualization, of *paideia* in *C&C* see Ruiz Montero (1989) 137–9.

[74] φρενήρης here clearly denotes something more than "sound of mind," opposite to ἐμμανής (so Liddell and Scott [1940] s.v.).

[75] Rhetorical influences are clearly evident here; see, for example, Reardon (1991) 87, 156–7. Among other passages where Callirhoe's intellectual abilities are apparent see especially 8.2.4–5, where she out-thinks Chaereas and holds him back from potentially disastrous action; in the judgment of Kaimio (1995: 129) she is "clearly more intelligent" than the novel's hero.

[76] For further instances, across a range of ancient literature, see Harris, ch. 5, (2002) 264–73, 280–1.

generosarum quidem praemordere et urguere proiectos . . . non decet regem saeua
nec inexorabilis ira . . . (Sen. *Clem.* 1.5.5–6)

Moreover, the qualities that belong to a great spirit are calmness and composure,
and the lofty disregard of injustices and vexations. It is a characteristic of women
to rage in anger, of wild beasts indeed (though not even the superior types of these)
to bite and bear down on those they have laid low . . . Savage and inexorable anger
is not becoming for a king . . .

What beasts and children share is the absence of the ability to reason,[77] and
we may see in these passages an implication that women are particularly
prone to anger because they similarly lack the faculty which enables it to
be controlled.[78] Such a belief may help to explain the denial to women of
legitimate access to anger referred to above (p. 178); conversely, it may have
been used partly to justify this denial and its accompanying exclusions –
if women's anger was not susceptible to internal control, it will have appeared necessary to impose such control externally. At all events, Callirhoe
challenges the stereotype; her lack of anger can be regarded as the result
not of the feeble and accepting passivity of a doormat but of reasonable
self-restraint. To be sure, this quality is not explicitly evoked in relation to
her lack of anger toward Chaereas, and, where it is evoked, the situation is
one of potential danger, and the anger which she suppresses is felt toward
a social inferior; but in drawing attention to her ability to resist acting on
emotional impulse in a text where Chaereas' failure to resist acting on the
same impulse is instrumental in the plot, and incurs disapproval, Chariton
invites the reader to interpret her behavior in an analogous way – Callirhoe
has surpassing love for her husband, yes, but she also demonstrates superiority to an emotion to which women were thought to be especially
disposed and by which they were negatively characterized. In doing so she
shows herself superior too to Chaereas, until he learns how to use anger
appropriately.[79]

---

[77] See, e.g., Arist. *Eth. Nic.* 3.2.2 (1111b8–9) and 3.2.17 (1112a15–16); Galen, *On the Doctrines of Hippocrates and Plato*, 5.7.19; and, for the intellectual incapacity and susceptibility to passion of children, Golden (1990) 6–7, 9 (with references to associations in Greek philosophical thought between children and women).

[78] In women (unlike beasts), however, the lack is not absolute; indeed, *cum sit inimica rationi* [sc. *ira*], *nusquam tamen nascitur nisi ubi rationi locus est*, "Though anger is the enemy of reason, it is generated only where reason has a place" (Sen. *De ira* 1.3.4 [*Dial.* 3.3.4]), and for the potential of women to acquire control cf. Sen. *Dial.* 2.14.1 *inprudens animal est et, nisi scientia accessit ac multa eruditio, ferum, cupiditatium incontinens,* "[A woman] is a creature lacking in forethought, and unless she has accumulated knowledge and acquired a thorough education, wild and incapable of restraining the passions."

[79] Cf. Kaimio (1995) 127: "Callirhoe is certainly more able to control herself than the hero and other male characters."

Gender analysis has been prominent in critical work on *Chaereas and Callirhoe* and the other Greek novels for the last ten or fifteen years.[80] David Konstan has stressed the unusual symmetry between the lovers in this genre – they are essentially of the same age and class, possess similarly remarkable beauty, fall in love with each other equally hard and at first meeting, and display other parallels – though his extension of this pattern into the heart of the action seems to me to overstate the case. "The novels eschew episodes in which the hero intervenes actively to save the heroine. There are no scenes in which the valiant lover comes to the rescue of his lady":[81] but Chaereas sets sail in search of the kidnapped Callirhoe, while we do not find her scheming to get back to Syracuse.[82] On the other hand, Chaereas' weaknesses as hero are obvious: his repeated attempts at suicide, for example, show him to be no Ajax, either in the reasons for his actions or in his ability to accomplish his will.[83] Equally, Callirhoe's role cannot be reduced to that of damsel in distress, sitting disconsolately awaiting rescue. Her presentation is, indeed, extremely complex, as some of the most interesting gender-focused work on the text has indicated.[84] She can certainly be seen as objectified, a point most obvious in scenes such as that of the trial at Babylon, where Chaereas and Dionysius engage in verbal swordplay[85] over who is her true husband, while Callirhoe stands by, looking down and weeping, saying nothing (5.8.5–6), or that at 2.2, where Callirhoe is bathed by servant women who gaze at her naked beauty with admiration and astonishment. But the commodification of the heroine in the first of these scenes and the voyeuristic character of the second possess ambivalences. The (male or female) reader's gaze on Callirhoe in

---

[80] For *C&C* see esp. Elsom (1992); Egger (1994a); Kaimio (1995); Balot (1998); more generally see esp. Egger (1988), (1990), (1994b); Liviabella Furiani (1989) (46–56 on *C&C*); Wiersma (1990); Konstan (1994); Goldhill (1995); and now Haynes (2003), which appeared while this book was in press.

[81] Konstan (1994) 34.

[82] It is true that, on the point of departure for Miletus, Chaereas attempts (absurdly) to drown himself in order to avoid having to decide between giving up his rescue mission and hurting his parents, who beseech him not to leave them (3.5.4–6); but this is best seen as an episode in Chaereas' progress from adolescence to maturity – before his parents urge him to stay he is eager to start (ἔσπευδεν, 3.5.1), and in the event he does leave, praying to Poseidon that either Callirhoe should return to Syracuse with him or he should not return at all (3.5.9) (Konstan [1994] 15–18 ignores these elements in the account). I am quite unconvinced by the attempt of Perkins (1995: 99–102) to read this episode in the context of Epictetan Stoicism and to present Chaereas' action positively, as a way of avoiding an inevitable failure of duty either as husband or as son.

[83] For suicide attempts see above, p. 175, n. 54. It is significant that his last thoughts of suicide (7.1.6) occur at the point of transition from youth to manhood (see above, p. 175).

[84] See also Biraud (1985) 23–7.

[85] They are at war: Συνήθης μὲν οὖν καὶ πρόχειρος πᾶσι τοῖς ἀντερασταῖς πόλεμος, "To all rivals in love war is normal and comes easily," says the narrator at 5.8.4, adding, with focalization through both characters, that Callirhoe is τὸ ἆθλον, "the prize."

the bath is mediated through female eyes, and her divine beauty, which causes men to fall in love with her, sometimes with devastating effect,[86] wherever she goes, empowers her;[87] her supreme status as a commodity, a role which in various ways she endorses, gives her a degree of subjectivity and possibilities within the framework of the patriarchal culture in which she lives: as the most desirable of women she will go on being desired.[88] Less ambiguously, Callirhoe displays positive moral qualities which Chaereas lacks. Her generosity of spirit, for example, is evident in her attitude to the Persian queen, Statira, after Chaereas' capture of Aradus: she is shocked at Chaereas' notion that Statira should be enslaved as a maidservant for her, not only because she is the queen of Asia but particularly because of the hospitality and protection which Statira afforded her during the war.[89]

Though the social construction of the world of *Chaereas and Callirhoe* is ineluctably male-dominant,[90] the text offers more than one perspective on the female. It has been suggested[91] that Chariton's novel has not one but two implied readers, in essence distinguished by gender. The representations of

[86] At the first sight of Callirhoe Chaereas can hardly stand (1.1.7); Mithridates actually falls in a faint (4.1.9).

[87] "Her irresistibility amounts to erotic omnipotence" (Egger [1994a] 39; the whole article is highly relevant).

[88] "Chaireas the general may be in a better position to hold on to Callirhoe than Chaireas the wimp who married her at the start of the narrative; but as long as she is desirable, he faces competition": Elsom (1992) 227. There is much of interest and relevance in this article, which considers Callirhoe as "phallus," the sign of male sexuality and power, within the political economy of the culture. Callirhoe's awareness of her erotic power and the possibilities it offers is strikingly indicated at 8.4.4–6 (on which see also Liviabella Furiani [1989] 52), where she conceals from Chaereas the letter she writes to Dionysius concerning "their" son, urging him to bring up the boy without remarrying: this can be seen not only as a way of sparing the child the domination of a (traditionally negatively characterized) stepmother but as a way of leaving a door to an alternative life open for herself, and (through the secrecy) keeping a part of her present life – and one with erotic content – free from her husband's control.

[89] For this contrast between Chaereas and Callirhoe (8.3, esp. 1–2) see Wiersma (1990: 119), who also (119–20) points, less persuasively, to differences in tone between the letter written by Chaereas to the Persian king and that written by Callirhoe to Dionysius (8.4.2–3, 5–6). As regards Statira, though there are practical advantages in returning her to the king (see 8.8.10, where Chaereas tells the Syracusans that he has won the king's friendship for them by doing this), the text at 8.3 stresses Callirhoe's magnanimity; and even on a subversive reading Callirhoe would outdo Chaereas, this time in a political sense. The dismissive judgment of G. Anderson (1984: 64) that "Callirhoe has few positive qualities" must surely be rejected.

[90] Indeed, in the genre of the Greek novel as a whole female life is in certain respects even more subject to male control than in contemporary historical reality; on this archaizing feature of the texts see Egger (1988) 55–61; (1994b) 266–74.

[91] By Konstan (1994) 78, with the idea more fully developed by Kaimio (1995); cf. Elsom (1992) 229 ("Callirhoe and the other heroines of romance offer themselves willingly to confirm the phallus, the male subjectivity, of men who feel insecure. For women readers, they offer themselves as models of strength and subjectivity who nevertheless willingly take their place in the patriarchal order"; modern scholarly readers are said to have another perspective again); and, with particular reference to Longus' *Daphnis and Chloe* and Richardson's *Pamela*, Montague (1992) 234–5.

anger in the text fit and support this kind of view. Interpreting Callirhoe's relation to anger is very much a matter for the individual reader. On the one hand, she may be regarded as a woman whose love for her husband overrides an unjustified and near-fatal physical assault; this perspective would seem to appeal to the standard male view of appropriate or desirable female behavior, and to women who wish to buy into it. On the other hand, her absence of anger can be seen as something positive in a very different way: her ability to resist acting on the impulse endows her with a strength that marks her (in ancient terms) as an unusual and admirable woman, and raises her above the level of her male counterpart. In this manner she both provides a yardstick by which Chaereas can be measured and offers a model to which female readers can aspire in an empowering way – even though this might be said to be an empowerment deriving from the appropriation of a quality culturally constructed as male.[92] The coexistence of these different options for reading the heroine's (lack of) anger helps to demonstrate how it is not only in its receptivity to a wide range of generic influences[93] that *Chaereas and Callirhoe* should be seen as an 'open' text.[94]

---

[92] Observe the fine irony in the reflection of the standard view of male and female emotional control at 6.6.5, where Callirhoe, imagining the Persian queen's jealousy at the king's desire for her, says to herself: ἦν οὐκ ἤνεγκε Χαιρέας, ἀνὴρ Ἕλλην, τί ποιήσει γυναῖκα καὶ δέσποιναν βάρβαρον; "Chaereas – a man and a Greek – could not endure jealousy; what will it do to a woman, and a barbarian queen at that?" For self-restraint as an essentially male virtue see generally North (1966); in contradistinction to the developing and shifting semantics of masculine *sōphrosunē* through Greek history, North remarks (p. 1, n. 2) that feminine *sōphrosunē* remains constant, and sums it up as "chastity, modesty, obedience, inconspicuous behavior." Helpful too are the comments of Carson (1990) 142–3. An exception to the rule is afforded by the Stoic Musonius Rufus, for whom a *sōphrōn* woman should, among other things, control anger and other passions – a view in keeping with the Stoic position that there is no sex-differentiation in virtue (see North [1966] 230).

[93] See above, p. 168, n. 29.

[94] This view challenges the notion of Fusillo (1996: 288–9) that the relationship between the author and implied reader of the novel is simple and straightforward, and that this has to do with the novel's "popular," pre-sophistic, character ("pure entertainment," Fusillo calls *C&C* at 290): the "implied reader" is not so easily identified.

CHAPTER 8

"Your mother nursed you with bile": anger in babies and small children

Ann Ellis Hanson

Achilles was convinced that one of his Myrmidons, chafing at absence from the battlefield, muttered behind his back, "Your mother used to nurse you with bile" (χόλῳ ἄρα σ' ἔτρεφε μήτηρ, 16.203).[1] The anger displayed by Achilles over Agamemnon's behavior in *Iliad* 1 and the failure of the embassy in Book 9 to persuade Achilles to rejoin his fellow Achaeans in the fighting against Trojans occasioned the Myrmidon's remark. Yet the action of the story was already taking a new turn, for Achilles heeded Patroclus' plea that he go out in Achilles' stead, dressed in Achilles' armor, and Achilles was ranging his men in battle order to accompany Patroclus at the very moment when he recalled the blame that he supposed some Myrmidon earlier heaped upon him. Late-antique commentators to the line suggested that the remark might be taken literally: scholia glossed it with "in exaggeration, not with milk, but with bile," and "[it was] because of the excessiveness of his wrath,"[2] while Eustathius in his *Commentary* paraphrased, "You used to suckle bile in place of milk and due to this your body has been compacted from bile."[3] Such explications no doubt gained conviction from the *Iliad* simile of the snake, said to draw *cholos* from the evil plants on which it fed, for this too was a nutritional explanation for the venomous malevolence of snakes.[4] Nonetheless, such an explanation

---

I am grateful to Glenn Most and Heinrich von Staden for helpful comments on the oral version of this paper, for these led me to substantial revisions.

[1] References to passages in the *Iliad* are cited throughout only by book and line number, without repetition of "*Iliad*."

[2] Ad 16.203, 4.214.52–5 Erbse: A – ὑπερβολικῶς, οὐ γάλακτι ἀλλὰ χολῇ. Τ – διὰ τὸ ἄμετρον τῆς ὀργῆς.

[3] Ad 16.203, 3.334.15–16 van der Valk: χολὴν ἐθήλαζες ἀντὶ γάλακτος καὶ διὰ τοῦτό σοι ἐκ χόλου οἷον τὸ σῶμα συμπέπηκται. The χόλος of 16.203 is often said to be the only Homeric occurrence with the later sense of χολή, "bile": e.g. Chantraine (1999) 2.1267; Janko (1992) 345 (ad 16.203–6). There is useful discussion with earlier bibliography in W. D. Smith (1966) 547–56.

[4] 22.93–5: ὡς δὲ δράκων ἐπὶ χειῇ ὀρέστερος ἄνδρα μένῃσι | βεβρωκὼς κακὰ φάρμακ', ἔδυ δέ τέ μιν χόλος αἰνός, | σμερδαλέον δὲ δέδορκεν ἐλισσόμενος περὶ χειῇ. See Richardson (1993) 116 (ad 22.94) for statements from Aelian and Pliny that endorse nutritional explanations for the snake's venom.

for excessive accumulation of *cholos* within the human body was already countered during the first assembly of the Achaean forces in Book 1, when the prophet Calchas explained that *cholos* was likely to sojourn longer in a more powerful man's body, and, if not cooked down, softened, and digested, resentment remained in him thereafter (1.80–3). Although Calchas' remarks were aimed at Agamemnon, the more powerful man on the scene likely to retain and savor his anger in the immediate future, in the end it was Achilles' anger that proved difficult to dissolve. Authors of the Roman period returned to nutritional explanations for Achilles' wrath, offering witticisms on the food the lad received from Cheiron, in addition to other lessons, but to the poet of the *Iliad* Cheiron was the "most righteous of centaurs" and a teacher of medicinal herbs (11.830–2).[5]

After the death of Patroclus, Achilles' anger, now mixed with grief, solidified into a fixed desire for vengeance upon Patroclus' killer, and this led not only to the despoiling of Hector's corpse, but to a reluctance to consign Patroclus' body to the pyre. In this same period, however, Achilles twice assured his mother that he had mastered the wrath in his breast against Agamemnon, a process painful for him, he claimed, for he had come to hold it dear.[6] Achilles' ability to check the anger he had transferred to Hector and the Trojans came only later, being sparked in Book 23 not only by pleas for burial from Patroclus' ghost, but also through his burgeoning ability to perceive wrath as it rose up in fellow Greeks at the funeral games and through his successful interventions when tempers flared.[7] He honed that ability in Book 24, in which he not only complied with Zeus's command to accept ransom for Hector's body, relayed to him by his mother, but he also took the precaution of having his servants bathe and anoint the dead Hector, lest Priam, enraged by the sight of his son, also rouse Achilles' own wrath, such that he kill Priam while a suppliant in his tent (24.582–6).

Centuries later the Greek physician Galen, living and practicing at Rome in the second half of the second century AD and into the first decades of the third century, found the choleric motions within the *Iliad* familiar, as

---

[5] For the tradition that Cheiron fed Achilles on the guts and marrow of wild beasts, see, for example, Apollodoros, *Bibl.* 3.13.6, and his etymologizing of Achilles' name from Ἀ-χείλη, because his lips never touched the breast, and Libanius, *Progym.* 9.1.3. For the suppression of Cheiron in the *Iliad* in favor of Peleus and Phoenix, see Janko (1992) 335–6 (ad 16.141–4).

[6] 19.65–8: ἀλλὰ τὰ μὲν προτετύχθαι ἐάσομεν ἀχνύμενοί περ | θυμὸν ἐνὶ στήθεσσι φίλον δαμάσαντες ἀνάγκῃ· | νῦν δ' ἤτοι μὲν ἐγὼ παύω χόλον, οὐδέ τί με χρὴ | ἀσκελέως αἰεὶ μενεαινέμεν. Achilles speaks lines 65–6 to Thetis also at 18.112–13, but there they are preceded by ὡς ἐμὲ νῦν ἐχόλωσεν ἄναξ ἀνδρῶν Ἀγαμέμνων.

[7] For example, the quarrel between the lesser Ajax and Idomeneus, over which Greek was leading in the chariot race (23.450–98) and the squabble over prizes between Antilochus and Menelaus (23.539–623).

these rose to overpower reason and then receded, and he easily paraphrased Homeric passages in his own terms.[8] In his *Opinions of Hippocrates and Plato* (*De placitis Hippocratis et Platonis*), Galen explained anger as a passion he expected to be stronger than reason in barbaric peoples, as well as in the young, the untrained, and the uneducated. Anger was no different in children and adults, he argued, but the mature person had made reason the guide of life and accordingly checked wrath in most circumstances.[9] Thus Galen thought the poet portrayed both Hector and Achilles as "young men enslaved to anger," but "Odysseus and Polydamas and Nestor as men who overcame anger with reason."[10] Through this latter grouping Galen implied that the ability to restrain anger and the other passions was not a matter of chronological age, so much as one of intellectual maturity, for the prudent Polydamas was born on the same night as Hector (18.251). In particular, Galen warmly commended Odysseus' exhortation to his heart, when pondering the question of how he, a man alone, might wreak vengeance on the suitors. Odysseus' words at *Odyssey* 20.18, "Endure it, my heart, for you have already endured a more shameful thing," provided Galen with the perfect example of how reason overcomes anger:

These are the words Homer made Odysseus say to himself when the heat in his heart boiled up at the sight of what was being done in his house by the servant women. Had anger conquered his reason, it would lead him to a premature punishment of the women. For as the rider is to his horse or the hunter to his dog, so reason is to anger. It is all the more just for that which is naturally superior to rule and dominate in everything: rider over horse, hunter over dog, reason over anger, although it does not always happen that the pair observes this law of nature. Sometimes a disobedient horse, running helter-skelter, has carried off his rider, conquered by his own bodily weakness or his ignorance of horsemanship.[11]

The Myrmidon's taunt, "Your mother nursed you on bile," may, in fact, represent no more than a pun on the sound-similarity between *cholos* and *gala* ("milk"). Yet Patroclus too suggested that *cholos* held Achilles in its grip, since he remained adamant in his refusal to rejoin his friends against

---

[8] For Galen's dates, see Nutton (1995) 25–39.
[9] Galen, *De plac. Hipp. et Plat.* 5.7.74–82, 1.354–6 De Lacy = 5.499–502 Kühn, where Galen quoted from and expanded upon Plato, *Resp.* 441a7–c2, in order to refute Chrysippus.
[10] Galen, *De plac. Hipp. et Plat.* 3.3.7, 1.184–6 De Lacy = 5.303–4 Kühn.
[11] Galen, *De plac. Hipp. et Plat.* 3.3.2–5, 1.184 De Lacy = 5.302–3 Kühn. Similar comments on reason overcoming the emotions in, for example, Galen, *De moribus*, are now preserved only in Arabic; see Mattock (1972) 235–60. The material from the *De moribus* considered here derives principally from 239–41 Mattock.
  As the *Odyssey* repeatedly made clear, not only was Odysseus skilled at restraining his own anger (e.g. *Od.* 8.204–5; 18.20–1; 24.544), but he frequently benefited from arousing others to wrath (e.g. *Od.* 9.480–1; 14.281–2; 17.458; 18.25; 22.26).

the Trojans, and his henchman went so far as to suggest that Achilles' engendering did not result from the coupling of Peleus and Thetis. No, he must have been born from the gray sea and the towering rocks to be so hard (16.30–5). The angers Achilles exhibited at Troy, especially as they magnified to excess, were inextricably linked with his preeminence on the field of battle. The mere sight of the weapons that Hephaestus made for him caused *cholos* to insinuate itself through Achilles' body, and his eyes flashed sparks.[12] Arousal of *cholos* frequently did prove useful to heroes in the midst of battle strife.[13] Still, anger was not always the more appropriate response, and the effects of *cholos* at times required tempering. Nestor reminded Patroclus of this when he rehearsed the farewell scene between the fathers and sons when the lads left Peleus' palace for Troy. Peleus told Achilles to be best in battle always and conspicuous above others, while Menoetius charged Patroclus, as the elder, to give Achilles good advice (12.782–9). Although Nestor was pursuing a personal agenda at the time when he recalled the farewell scene, his remarks, like those from the Myrmidon and Patroclus, raise questions about Achilles' nurturing in his earliest days: did the poem intend to imply that Achilles was early schooled in restraint over infant angers, or was he allowed to practice wrath unchecked from babyhood? And, more generally, what child-rearing practices does the *Iliad* present as normative, insofar as childhood angers are concerned? In what follows, I probe what the *Iliad* tells about the early life of Achilles and other young children of epic, juxtaposing the child-rearing practices of epic to the theory and advice given by Galen to the parents of noble Roman youngsters, for I believe such a comparison not only highlights some repetitive themes in the conservative atmosphere of raising Greek children over the *longue durée*, but also reveals that the *Iliad* presupposes the young Achilles to have enjoyed a normative upbringing.

TERMINOLOGY FOR BABIES

A discrete section of Galen's *Hygiene* (*De sanitate tuenda*) was devoted to the inculcation of healthy habits in infants and children up to age fourteen years. Galen labeled the infant *brephos* or *smikron paidion*, and observed a strict age-distinction between the *paidion* (the child in its first hebdomad,

---

[12] 19.15–17: αὐτὰρ Ἀχιλλεύς | ὡς εἶδ᾽, ὡς μιν μᾶλλον ἔδυ χόλος, ἐν δέ οἱ ὄσσε | δεινὸν ὑπὸ βλεφάρων ὡς εἰ σέλας ἐξεφάανθεν. For ἔδυ χόλος in the simile of the snake (22.93–5), see above, n. 4; Phoenix also applied the phrase to Meleager's anger at 9.553.

[13] *Cholos* stimulated him to avenge the death of a fallen comrade (e.g. 4.494, 501; 13.203, 660; 16.320, 546, 585; 17.399), and it motivated the lion to search for its stolen cubs, 18.318–22.

or seven-year period of life, usually between two or three years and seven) and the older *pais* (the child in its second hebdomad, from seven to fourteen years).[14] Soranus employed this same terminology a generation or so prior to Galen, although his pediatric discussions focused on the *brephos* and *paidion*, and he terminated his account well before the small child became a *pais*. In Soranus' view a child's upbringing at the hands of a *paedagogus* belonged more to the realm of philosophy than to that of medicine.[15]

Earlier practice lacked this precision. Solon's poem on the ten ages of man identified a prime characteristic of each age, from the child in his first seven years, who grew his first set of teeth and then lost them, to the old man in his tenth period of seven years, "for whom death comes not prematurely."[16] His elegy was much admired in subsequent literature, and Philo Judaeus, Clement of Alexandria, and Anatolius repeated it in full.[17] In both Philo and Anatolius Solon's poem was juxtaposed to chapter 5 of the *De septimanis*, a treatise in the *Hippocratic Corpus* with numerological and medical sections, preserved in Latin and partially in Greek.[18] Solon's terminology was vague, employing *pais* plus descriptive adjectives to specify the child in his first seven years, but eschewing any identifier for the lad in his second hebdomad and noting only that at its close signs of puberty were apparent. By contrast, *The Sevens* 5 listed a full complement of nouns, from *paidion/puerulus* and *pais/puer* for the first two hebdomads all the way to *presbytēs/senior* and *gerōn/senex* for those in their ninth and tenth hebdomads. The detailed study by Jaap Mansfeld demonstrated that *The Sevens* was a late addition to the *Hippocratic Corpus*, influenced by the Stoics and Posidonius, and should be dated after 100 BC. The terminological precision *The Sevens* exhibited for distinguishing children in their first and second hebdomads complements Mansfeld's arguments on the treatise's late date. Such terminology for children was not operative among those Hippocratic treatises generally agreed to have been written in the last decades of the fifth century BC and the earlier decades of the fourth. The Hippocratic *Epidemics*, for example, tended to note the effect of diseases on discrete

---

[14] Galen, *De san. tuenda* 1.12, 28 Koch = 6.59–60 Kühn.

[15] Soranus, *Gyn.* 2.57, 2.65 Burguière. For Soranus, see Hanson and Green (1994) 1025–9.

[16] Solon frag. 27 West; see especially lines 1–4: παῖς μὲν ἄνηβος ἐὼν ἔτι νήπιος ἕρκος ὀδόντων | φύσας ἐκβάλλει πρῶτον ἐν ἕπτ' ἔτεσιν. | τοὺς δ' ἑτέρους ὅτε δὴ τελέσηι θεὸς ἕπτ' ἐνιαυτούς, | ἥβης † δὲ φάνει † σήματα γεινομένης.

[17] Philo, *De opificio mundi* 104; Clement, *Stomata* 6.144.3; Anatolius, Περὶ δεκάδος; see West (1972) 135–7, for other quotations and textual variants; and Mansfeld (1971) 161–4, for other authors, both Latin and Greek, who paraphrased the elegy.

[18] The Latin version of *De septimanis* 5 is supplemented with Greek from Philo, 8.636 Littré; cf. also 9.436 Littré with n. 1 (9.433–4).

groups within a community during a particular year, including women and children; they labeled the latter *paidia*, or occasionally *nēpia*. At the same time, they sometimes referred to the fetus *in utero* as *paidion*, along with the more precise *embryon*; conditions of *paidia* and *nēpia* were also explicitly said to extend until puberty – thus implying that both *nēpion* and *paidion* were terms appropriate even for a lad approaching fourteen years.[19]

The lack of age-specific terminology for the young was as common a characteristic of earlier medical writers as it was of Attic tragedy and Homeric epic. Terminological precision seems not to have entered the discourse about children until the second century BC.[20] When Patroclus' ghost remembered his slaying of a playfellow at the beginning of *Iliad* 23, he stressed that he was *nēpios*, "childish," or "small," or "foolish" – or all of these at once. To be *nēpios* was a matter of chronological age only in part, since the word was likewise used for adults whose conduct was imprudent and unwise. It was the prerogative of the Homeric poet to label adults "childish"/"foolish" for unthinking behavior, although Iliadic characters freely applied the vocative *nēpie* to opponents in direct speech as a taunt or rebuke.[21] Nonetheless, only Patroclus in the *Iliad* applied the term to himself. By contrast, Telemachus did so not infrequently in the *Odyssey*, manipulating the admission to considerable effect when concealing his growing maturity from those in the palace.[22] Phoenix also claimed that Peleus sent him to Troy, because Achilles was even then *nēpios*, knowing neither the craft of war nor persuasion in the council and the assembly – marks of the consummate hero (9.439–41). Such remarks provoked subsequent speculation about Achilles' chronological age at the time of his departure from Phthia. The Apollodoran *Bibliotheca*, for example, suggested that Achilles was a nine-year-old at the time (3.13.6), despite the latter's brief allusion in the *Iliad* to his son Neoptolemus, whom he had left behind on Skyros (19.326–7).

Ages were not supplied for Iliadic children, and one can only guess from their capabilities and activities whether they should be grouped with Galen's

---

[19] For the fetus as *nēpion* or *paidion*, see, e.g., Hippocrates, *Epid.* 3 case 10, 3.60 Littré, and *De generatione/De natura pueri* 10 and 18, 7.484 and 498 Littré; for *nēpion* or *paidion* referring to a child until puberty, see, e.g., *Epid.* 6.1.4, 5.268 Littré, and *Epid.* 3.8, 3.84 Littré.

For the difficulty of separating slaves from children in the case histories of the *Epidemics*, see Demand (1994) 143.

[20] The empiric physician Zeuxis noted the imprecision with regard to *nēpia* in both Hippocrates and the mid third-century BC Herophilus, and his remarks were quoted by Galen in his commentary to *Epid.* 6.1.4 (*CMG* 5.10.2.2, 20–1 Wenkebach); for the passage, see also von Staden (1989) 436–7 (T267a) and 430.

[21] *Nēpie* remained a "high-register insult" in classical and Hellenistic authors – see Dickey (1996) 168 and 290.

[22] E.g. *Od.* 18.229–30; 19.9–20; 20.309–10. Athene had early told him he was too old for childishness (*Od.* 1.296–7), for which see Heubeck et al. (1988) 113 (ad 1.297).

brephos, or with his *paidion* or *pais.*[23] Nonetheless, epic's children exhibit similarities with Galen's infants and children, as the latter marked out with considerable precision the stages of childhood development.

CRYING BABIES

From the late classical period onward, theorizing about what constituted the good life, lived with a healthy body and sound mind, occupied philosophers and medical writers with increasing intensity. Infancy and childhood attracted serious attention from both theoretical and practical perspectives, and rules proliferated as to how responsible adults could best prepare children for the later life that hopefully awaited them. Galen supplied fulsome information on the pediatric theory and practices that well-educated and sophisticated Greek doctors were purveying at Rome, although he never specialized in pediatrics. If Galen drew information from Soranus, especially from the latter's *Gynecology* 2 (*Gynaikeia*), that section of Soranus' practical handbook which considered neonates and small children, he neglected to say so. There is, however, considerable overlap between the two authors, especially in the pediatric topics they chose to discuss and the advice they proffered. Details the physicians provided about infant crying and swaddling, or young children's early attempts to walk and stand, also recalled opinions from Plato and Aristotle; nonetheless, in their discussions of pediatric practices both physicians emphasized instead knowledge they acquired from midwives and nurses, rather than from philosophers. Galen, in particular, cited his own interventions in the cases of specific infants and prepubertal children, including those resident in the imperial palace on the Palatine.[24] Wet-nursing contracts from the Roman province of Egypt exhibited some of the same concerns about care of infants and young children, thus tempering, to some extent, the notion that Galen and his medical fellows wrote about babies and small children only from books, cloistered away with their writing tablets in the study.[25]

---

[23] Cf. modern discussion over the drawings of babies and small children on *choes* and the relation to 'crowning of three year olds' in Philostratus, *Heroicus* 12.2, for a summary of which, see Hamilton (1992) 63–81, and Demand (1994) 188–9 and n. 29.

[24] E.g. Galen, *De praecognitione* 7 and 12, 104–10 and 130–4 Nutton = 14.635–41 and 14.661–5 Kühn; see further, below in this section. For Soranus' apparent unacknowledged debts to Platonic pronouncements, see Hanson and Green (1994) 988.

[25] The contracts are collected in Masciadri and Montevecchi (1984); many, for example, forbade the wet-nurse to engage in sexual intercourse, a hardship for the married woman nursing for hire, yet both Soranus (*Gyn.* 2.19, 2.30 Burguière, and n. 152 ad loc., 2.96 Burguière) and Galen (*De san. tuenda* 1.9, 22 Koch = 6.46 Kühn) said the same, explaining that semen spoiled the milk. See also Bradley (1980) 321–5.

As one trained in both philosophy and medicine, Galen accepted as a given the notion that mastery of anger, together with that of the other passions, was a matter of habit and practice.[26] From observations of the angry infant whose face reddened and became hot and swollen, Galen concluded in his *Habits (De moribus)* that anger came naturally to human beings and that infants at birth possessed the same passions present in irrational animals: "they feel the things that happen to their bodies and conceive that some of these suit them and some do not; they desire that which suits them and avoid that which does not suit them."[27] No action, accident, or trait of character existed in the grown man, unless it was likewise present in him from earliest childhood. The infant, although it experienced pleasure and pain, was only just acquiring habits of response to these feelings, and Galen exhorted the responsible adults to avoid, at all costs, inculcation of unhealthy behaviors in feeding and exercises that would, in turn, exacerbate the infant's feelings of annoyance and hatred. The young child was, of course, easier to bend toward obedience, for like an immature tree, its will was still pliable, and acquiring good habits through the discipline imposed by parents and other caregivers was of considerable importance. In his *Opinions of Hippocrates and Plato* Galen quoted Plato's remark from the *Republic* that "right from birth children are full of anger" (441a7); yet in the pediatric sections of *Hygiene* he merely alluded to Plato's portrayal of Socrates in the *Lysis*, in which Socrates noted that even the newborn, while yet incapable of love for its parents, nonetheless hated them, whenever they turned to discipline it.[28]

Galen counseled immediate application of the breast to relieve infant crying, coupled with moderate rocking and soothing noises to calm the child, and advocated continuous tending up to the third year from birth, for this prevented immoderate motions from stirring up the child's mind. Anger, weeping, and rage caused a wakefulness that kindled fevers and were the precursors of severe diseases; it was the duty of all who cared for babies to provide for their wants before their distress increased to the point of throwing their minds into excessive and disordered activity together with their bodies:[29]

Often they cry and roll back and forth because they are teething; sometimes the disturbance comes from external circumstances [such as being too cold or too warm], or because they want to evacuate their bowels or urinate, or eat and drink.

[26] Cf. e.g. Aristotle, *Nicomachean Ethics* 2.1, 1103a31–b6.   [27] Galen, *De moribus* 239 Mattock.
[28] Galen, *De plac. Hipp. et Plat.* 5.74–5, 1.354 De Lacy = 5.500 Kühn, and Plato, *Lysis* 211e6–213a4.
[29] The material considered here is derived largely from Galen, *De san. tuenda* 1.7–12, 16–28 Koch = 6.31–60 Kühn; the following quotation is from 1.8.25, 21 Koch.

Galen boasted of having diagnosed what ailed a crying baby, when its nurse was at a loss after day-long efforts had failed to quiet her charge. His inspection of the baby's bed revealed that its coverings and clothes were dirty and unwashed! After the nurse followed his orders to replace the linens with freshly laundered ones, the baby quietened down.[30] Galen's recommendations on coddling to prevent infant crying echoed those of the Athenian in Plato's *Laws*, where a continuous regimen of nursing, cradling, and rocking, accompanied by gentle crooning day and night, was considered salubrious for all infants, especially the youngest ones. The gentle movements of the caregiver exercised the tiny body and prevented inner fears and frights from rising up in the young soul and overpowering it (790c-791a). The Athenian exhorted nurses and baby-tenders to judge what the little one wanted by the fact that it became silent when the desired object was offered, but wailed and cried all the more should the wrong thing be proffered (792a). The Athenian's goal was to make the little child calm and cheerful during its first three years, avoiding, on the one hand, the timidity born of constant terrors, and, on the other, pampering and overindulging it with infant pleasures.

A less permissive school of thought regarding infant crying can be traced through Aristotle and Soranus, for in the *Politics* Aristotle took specific issue with Plato's Athenian lawgiver, claiming instead that violent spasms of wailing exercised the baby and small child and gave them practice in holding their breath. The latter, in particular, was useful training for the hard labors of adulthood.[31] Soranus warned wet-nurses against giving children the breast as soon as they cried, because crying provided a natural form of exercise; still, he cautioned that the crying should not be allowed to continue for too long, lest it force the intestines downward and cause herniation. There were, he went on, many reasons why infants wailed, and all possibilities must be examined prior to overstuffing them with food, or attempting to wear them out through repeated baths. Omnipresent in those who gave advice on the care of infants was the fear of inculcating bad habits, and this appeared repeatedly in the details. Thus, for example, Soranus ordered the wet-nurse to cover the infant's eyes when it suckled, in part to prevent an object falling into them and doing damage, but also to prevent the baby from acquiring the habit of squinting at the light.

When children reached their second year, Galen saw them showing themselves aware of what it was that caused them pleasure and pain. Thus, they

[30] Galen, *De san. tuenda* 1.8.30–32, 21 Koch = 6.44–45 Kühn.
[31] Aristotle, *Pol.* 7.15, 1336a34–9; Soranus, *Gyn.* 2.30 and 38–40, 2.42 and 2.48–51 Burguière.

smiled and laughed at their nurses, but tried to take vengeance on those who brought them pain by biting and striking out at them, a more sophisticated exhibition of their desire to avoid pain and pursue what was pleasing.[32] In his *Hygiene* Galen advocated a kind of early obedience training that habituated babies to having their bath and massage after awaking, but prior to being fed, on the grounds that such a regimen was the more healthful one. Whenever bathing and rubbing took place after eating, however, the undigested food moved on to fill the body and congest the head. Galen found the majority of infants amenable to the regimen of bath before food in the morning, once spanks, threats, and other forms of discipline were applied.[33] If the child-minder were unable to follow this routine on a specific day, the baby should be given a bit of bread, allowed to play until it again felt hunger, and then the regimen of bath and massage before eating was to be imposed once more.

While no newborns appeared in the *Iliad*, concerned parents stroked and caressed their grieving adult children and asked them what was wrong, replicating the soothing gestures and words that originated in the anxieties of babyhood, as parents reached out to calm their wailing infants. This parental consolation appeared repeatedly – in the Greek camp, inside the walls of Troy, and among the gods of Olympus – suggesting that in Homer's imagined world parents readily responded to the distress of their children from infancy onward, far away from the thought that crying was salubrious for infants and useful training for holding their breath. At the first report of Patroclus' death Achilles' groans reached his mother and her Nereid sisters in the depths of the sea, and she came to comfort her son, cradling his head in her arms and sorrowing with him. She asked, even though she already knew, "Child, why are you crying? What grief has come to you?"[34] In the exchange that followed, Achilles not only determined to kill Hector, even though his mother assured him his own death would follow thereafter, but wished the impossible – that *cholos*, together with strife, perish from among gods and men, since *cholos* impelled to wrath even the man who was prudent, seeming to him sweeter than drips of honey. In Book 24 Thetis again rehearsed the comfort she brought to her son from his earliest days, accompanied by the mother's soothing gestures – caressing and calling him child, asking him about his grief.[35] She need only mention the threat of Zeus's anger, and

---

[32] Galen, *De moribus* 239 Mattock.

[33] Galen, *De san. tuenda* 1.10.9–14, 23–4 Koch = 6.49–50 Kühn.

[34] 18.71–3: ὀξὺ δὲ κωκύσασα κάρη λάβε παιδὸς ἑοῖο, | καί ῥ' ὀλοφυρομένη ἔπεα πτερόεντα προσηύδα· | τέκνον τί κλαίεις; τί δέ σε φρένας ἵκετο πένθος; . . . For τέκνον employed especially by parents as a form of address in later Greek literature, see Dickey (1996) 65–74.

[35] 24.127–8, χειρί τέ μιν κατέρεξεν ἔπος τ' ἔφατ' ἔκ τ' ὀνόμαζε· | τέκνον ἐμόν, τέο μέχρις ὀδυρόμενος καὶ ἀχεύων | σὴν ἔδεαι κραδίην . . .; Cf. Thetis at 1.361–2, χειρί τέ μιν κατέρεξεν ἔπος τ' ἔφατ' ἔκ τ'

Achilles was persuaded by his mother to relinquish his anger and accept ransom for Hector's body (24.134–6). Other parents in the *Iliad* continued to employ these soothing gestures to their grown-up children when sorrows came to them,[36] and there is no sign that the mothers, whether goddess Dione or queen Hecuba,[37] or the adult daughter Aphrodite, or the adult son Hector, found this behavior inappropriate. While the gestures more often came from a mother, questioning the cause of a child's sorrows was also appropriate for a father. Zeus embraced Artemis and laughing gently asked her about the distress Hera caused her by grabbing her wrists, boxing her ears, wrenching away her bow and arrows, and sending her scurrying from the battlefield.[38] The *Iliad* repeatedly suggested that parents had the habit of turning speedy attention to mewling infants, crying toddlers, wailing children, and even to offspring who were grown.

The gesture's emotive warmth also deepened the portrayal of the relationship between Hector and Andromache in Book 6, as she stroked Hector with her hand, despite her tears, and called to him. She had already told him that he was mother, father, and brother to her, as well as young husband, for Achilles had killed her kin. By her caress and soothing word, addressed to him alone, Andromache implied that she saw herself as protective mother to him as well. Hector reciprocated before sending Andromache back to their home and to her weaving among the handmaidens.[39] In using the gesture to his orphaned wife, Hector acknowledged his role as her nurturer, although his final words effectively excluded her from the concerns that occupied the prince of Troy, for war was the work of the men.

The first appearance of the gesture and its accompanying questions of concern to appear in the *Odyssey* underscored the emotional potential, for this time the adult child rejected it. Telemachus called an assembly of Ithacans at the outset of *Odyssey* 2, but Antinous, Eurymachus, and Leocritus made fun of his claims that the suitors were devouring his household. When

ὀνόμαζε· | τέκνον τί κλαίεις; τί δέ σε φρένας ἵκετο πένθος; and 19.7–8, ἔν τ᾽ ἄρα οἱ φῦ χειρὶ ἔπος τ᾽ ἔφατ᾽ ἔκ τ᾽ ὀνόμαζε· | τέκνον ἐμὸν . . .

[36] d'Avino (1969: 7–33) has demonstrated that the phrase ἔκ τ᾽ ὀνόμαζε often meant no more than "speak aloud." Nonetheless, the parents surveyed here were addressing their children directly, beginning with τέκνον/τέκος.

[37] Dione to Aphrodite, 5.372–3, χειρί τέ μιν κατέρεξεν ἔπος τ᾽ ἔφατ᾽ ἔκ τ᾽ ὀνόμαζε· | τίς νύ σε τοιάδ᾽ ἔρεξε, φίλον τέκος, Οὐρανιώνων . . . ; Hecuba to Hector, 6.253–4, ἔν τ᾽ ἄρα οἱ φῦ χειρὶ ἔπος τ᾽ ἔφατ᾽ ἔκ τ᾽ ὀνόμαζε· | τέκνον, τίπτε λιπὼν πόλεμον θρασὺν εἰλήλουθας;

[38] τὴν δὲ προτὶ οἷ | εἷλε πατὴρ Κρονίδης, καὶ ἀνείρετο ἡδὺ γελάσσας· | τίς νύ σε τοιάδ᾽ ἔρεξε, φίλον τέκος, Οὐρανιώνων | μαψιδίως ὡς εἴ τι κακὸν ῥέζουσαν ἐνωπῇ; (21.507–10). Cf. also Aphrodite's epiphany to Sappho, frag. 1.15–20 Lobel–Page, in which she called Sappho by name, asked what she suffered, and why she cried.

[39] 6.406–7 ἔν τ᾽ ἄρα οἱ φῦ χειρὶ ἔπος τ᾽ ἔφατ᾽ ἔκ τ᾽ ὀνόμαζε· | δαιμόνιε, φθίσει σε τὸ σὸν μένος . . . , and 6.485–6: χειρί τέ μιν κατέρεξεν ἔπος τ᾽ ἔφατ᾽ ἔκ τ᾽ ὀνόμαζε· | δαιμονίη, μή μοί τι λίην ἀκαχίζεο θυμῷ . . .

the assembly broke up, the suitors returned to Odysseus' house to feast as before, but Telemachus headed for the seashore and prayed to Athene, and, in the guise of the old man Mentor, she revived the lad's courage. Upon his return home, Telemachus encountered Antinous, who mockingly stroked Telemachus and called him by name, first chastening him for his outspoken words before the assembly of Ithacans and then inviting him to return to the banquet as before.[40] Antinous capped his remarks with an assurance that the Achaeans would accomplish Telemachus' desires to sail to Pylos and inquire about his father. In response Telemachus claimed that he knew nothing about the wrongs committed against him and his inheritance, so long as he was a *nēpios*, but now that he was grown, he was learning about them from the stories that were being told (*Od.* 2.312–15). Neither Antinous' invitation nor his promise soothed or reassured Telemachus, and he decisively rebuffed the gesture, thrusting his hand away from Antinous' grasp.[41] The rejection effectively denied Antinous any role as prospective father for this maturing young man, however much Telemachus felt the absence of Odysseus.

SWADDLING

Galen called for swaddling the neonate as soon after birth as its body had been cleansed and massaged, its umbilical cord examined and severed – and prior to its taking first nourishment.[42] Swaddling, in his view, shaped the tiny, pliable limbs. Elaborate directions on how to swaddle derive largely from Soranus, as he instructed the midwife on the need to wrap "to the very tips of the toes." Females were to be bound more tightly in the breast, but loosely in the hips, since this promoted the shape attractive in women; but should the male infant appear to have no foreskin, the midwife was to draw its tip forward and tie it with a strand of wool to correct the shortcoming.[43] The nurse removed swaddling clothes for the daily bath and massage, molding the infant to make its spine straight, its head round, its limbs flexible. Neither physician referred to the recommendation of

---

[40] *Od.* 2.302–3: ἕν τ᾿ ἄρα οἱ φῦ χειρὶ ἔπος τ᾿ ἔφατ᾿ ἔκ τ᾿ ὀνόμαζε· | Τηλέμαχ᾿ ὑψαγόρη . . .

[41] *Od.* 2.321–2: ἦ ῥα, καὶ ἐκ χειρὸς χεῖρα σπάσατ᾿ Ἀντινόοιο | ῥεῖα . . . See Heubeck et al. (1988) 149–50 (ad Od. 2.302 and 320).

[42] Galen, *De san. tuenda* 1.7.4–7, 16 Koch = 6.32–3 Kühn; Soranus' advice on cleansing the neonate is similar (*Gyn.* 2.14–15, 2.21–4 Burguière). There is more from Galen on swaddling at *De motu musculorum* 2.7, 4.451 Kühn, and *De causis morborum*, 7.27 Kühn. At *Hist. an.* 584b3–5 Aristotle spoke of weaknesses in a premature neonate, to be corrected by swaddling with wool.
  The connection between umbilicus and placenta had to be examined in order to establish legitimacy in the female line, see Hanson (1994a) 190–5.

[43] Soranus, *Gyn.* 2.31–5, 2.42–6 Burguière. Molding the infant through swaddling was also a Roman priority, see, for example, French (1987) 69–84, and Gourevitch (1995) 239–58.

Plato's Athenian that the infant be swaddled for two years, in the effort to shape it "like wax," so that its body be as straight as possible (*Laws* 789e). Soranus knew of those who swaddled for forty or sixty days, or even longer, but he advised a flexible approach that looked to the physical development of the individual child, loosing the swaddling clothes only when the infant body was no longer in danger of distortion. The right hand was to be freed first, so that it earlier received more exercise and became stronger than the left hand.

The infants of the *Iliad* were no doubt swaddled at birth, but, by the time of their appearance on the epic stage, they exhibited a freedom of movement unavailable to a swaddling. Hesiod's *Theogony* pictured Rhea giving Cronus a stone she had swaddled in place of the infant Zeus (485), with the wrappings an essential part of her deception. Swaddling was likewise an important motif in the Homeric *Hymn to Hermes* and a major source of the poem's humor. The day-old Hermes cuddled down into his swaddling bonds, as he lay in his cradle, in order to deceive Apollo, who wanted to learn what had happened to his missing cattle.[44] Despite his age, the prodigious godlet knew that swaddling clothes were essential elements in his disguise as a newborn, and they validated his claims that his concerns were not about cows, but for "sleep, milk of his mother's breast, having swaddling around his shoulders and hot baths" (267–8).

Cilissa of Aeschylus' *Choephori* maintained close ties to her nursling in later life, as did the wet-nurses of epic, Hera to Thetis and Eurycleia to Odysseus.[45] Her tale of the care she lavished on Orestes also shared much with Phoenix's narration of his care for the young Achilles, for not only were the two old family retainers performing multiple functions within their larger stories, but both emphasized their selfless toil on behalf of their charges.[46] A major difference between the two children, however, was that of age, for Cilissa was caring for a swaddled infant. Orestes screamed in the night, and she rushed to answer his call, "for the child still in swaddling clothes does not tell when he is hungry or thirsty, or a need to pee occupies him" (755–7). The intimate details that Cilissa related about the bellies of infants and her own double duties as nurse and laundress, because she misguessed Orestes' needs, underscored the age difference between her baby and the little boys of epic who were escorted to banquets of the

---

44 See *Hymn to Hermes* 151, 237, 301, 306, 388. The *Hymn* is dated to *c.* 600–550 BC – thus Schmid and Stählin (1929) 238 and Lesky (1966) 87.

45 For Cilissa, see Garvie (1986) 244 (ad 730–82). For Thetis and Eurycleia as wet-nurses, see *Il.* 24.59–60 and *Od.* 19.482.

46 See Garvie (1986) 243–4, for metatheatrical aspects of the Nurse's role, and 247–8 (ad 749–62) for textual uncertainties, although some may be attributable to "Aeschylus' deliberate intention of characterizing the Nurse as an ordinary person in a state of agitation and excitement."

men. Aeschylus surrounded Cilissa with a decidedly nursery atmosphere, and what classified Orestes as a mewling and puking swaddling were his limited capacities and activities.

TODDLERS' EFFORTS TO STAND AND WALK

Galen enthusiastically endorsed passive exercises for infants, beginning with bath and massage for the neonate. He credited nurses with devising three methods for rocking babies – in their arms, in cradles, and in swings – for such motions were suitable to those who were not yet able to move themselves.[47] While well aware that self-locomotion was possible only for the child as it began to crawl and walk, Galen cautioned against compelling a toddler to move itself prematurely, "lest the little legs be deformed." Soranus was even more preoccupied with the damaging effects that premature standing and walking might have on the legs of small children. He lashed out at Roman mothers who did not devote sufficient attention to child-rearing, as 'truly Greek' women did, but allowed their children to stand and walk before they were physically ready. Thus, a small child's legs became distorted, bowing outward, for the weight of its body was resting on tender limbs, and the ground, solid and hard because it was paved with stones, did not give way.[48] Soranus advised clothing that supported the child's back, whenever it insisted on sitting up; any means to prop up the young one was preferable to having the burden fall entirely on its soft frame. As the baby progressed to crawling and standing alone, Soranus would place the child by a wall, or set the toddler in a chair with wheels. He claimed that Romans attributed the bowing of the small child's legs to the cold waters that flowed beneath the city, an explanation that blamed no one.[49] He had, however, heard less charitable explanations, such as the fact that the women of Rome had intercourse too frequently, or did so when they were drunk – both with devastating consequences for a child's legs in later years. Neither Galen nor Soranus mentioned the advice of Plato's Athenian that the infant be swaddled until the age of two and carried until three, to preclude risk of bodily distortion (*Laws* 789e).

What is clear is that the child reared under Greek norms was not to toddle about and fall, learning from bruised knees and bumps acquired

---

[47] Galen, *De san. tuenda* 1.8.1–14, 18–19 Koch = 6.37–8 Kühn; similar provisions in Soranus, *Gyn.* 2.40, 2.52 Burguière.

[48] Soranus, *Gyn.* 2.43–4, 2.54–5 Burguière. For various reactions to this passage by modern scholars, see the summary in Hanson (1994b) 105.

[49] For a marked preference in obstetrics and pediatrics for explanations that avoided assignment of blame to any of the participants, see Hanson (1987) 589–602.

during early attempts to stand and walk; rather, parents and child-minders were to prevent experimentation until the time when the child was capable of approximating the more graceful movements of the adult. Precocious efforts at self-locomotion ran the risk of causing malformations in later life, whenever the awkward attempts of childhood were practiced repeatedly.

Hector's son Astyanax (his father Hector called him Skamandrios) was the center of the epic's attention for a brief moment when his parents met on the battlements of Troy, and when Hector reached out to pick up his child, the sight of his father's bronze helmet with its nodding plumes inspired terror in him.[50] He shrieked and cowered back into the arms of his nurse, for she had been carrying him. Although preoccupied with their own serious concerns, Hector and Andromache immediately turned to soothe their child's anxieties. In response to the crying, Hector doffed his helmet, the cause of Astyanax' fears, and portentously set it on the ground. His parents had apparently protected the child in the past from even the sight of war's gear, as was suggested not only by his terrified reaction, but also by Andromache's later description of the luxurious life the child's royal lineage afforded him in the days before Hector's death (22.500–4). Although still being carried, Astyanax was no longer a swaddling, and in Galen's terms was capable of deliberate response to what caused him pain. Astyanax was probably able to walk on his own, albeit tentatively, but he and his parents seem to have preferred that a nurse carry him.

Achilles invoked the image of a little girl, a *kourē nēpia*, at the beginning of Book 16 to describe Patroclus, when the latter returned from the sidelines of battle in tears over the Achaeans being wounded and dying in Achilles' absence.[51] The girl was running after her mother, clinging to her mother's dress and begging to be picked up and carried, as the woman was hurrying along. The petulance of the little girl was stressed by the fact that, although capable not only of walking but even of running, she preferred to be nestled in her mother's arms, as she had been in days past, and she demanded that it be so again. Not only did the simile reinforce the notion that epic's children were often carried after learning to walk, but Achilles' winged words, "Why are you crying, Patroclus?,"[52] recalled a mother's comforting question to her grieving infant, as well as to her adult child. The little girl's mother acceded to her child's wishes, stooping to pick her up, and in applying this simile to Patroclus, Achilles implied that his was the indulgent

---

[50] 6.392–495, especially 466–70.
[51] 16.5–10; for useful commentary on the scene, with earlier bibliography, see Janko (1992) 315–17 (ad 16.5 and 7–10).
[52] τίπτε δεδάκρυσαι, Πατρόκλεες, and see above, nn. 34–8.

parent's role.[53] The poet's foreshadowing of Patroclus' death, however, had already begun at the point when Achilles sent Patroclus out to question Nestor about the identity of the wounded man whom he was driving from the battlefield in his chariot (11.604). Nestor's plan that Patroclus borrow Achilles' armor so that the Trojans mistake him for his mighty friend was fully underway, and the sense of impending doom had been intensified by Zeus's pronouncement that Patroclus was to die by the hand of Hector (15.65–6). The image of the crying little girl and her concerned and obliging mother, anxious to quiet her daughter's tears, lent a surface innocence to the interchange between the two heroes. Still, the comparison of a warrior to a *kourē nēpia* had already been applied to Carian Nastes, "who went to war dressed in gold," though he was soon to be cut down by Achilles (2.872–5). Time would show that for Achilles and Patroclus to replicate the roles of indulgent mother and demanding little girl befitted neither hero. Patroclus' counsels were not for good, and Achilles would suffer mightily for having acceded to them.

TEETHING AND THE "FAT CUTS OF LAMB"

Galen associated the introduction of solid foods with dental development, adding that nurses should premasticate vegetables and meat before offering them to a child.[54] Nursing contracts from the Greek and Hellenized population of Roman Egypt often engaged the wet-nurse for a period of between two to three years, and it is likely that mothers who nursed their own children also suckled them for a similar time. Although Soranus expected teething to begin at about the seventh month, he suggested that a child be breastfed until its teeth were sufficiently developed for chewing, setting the usual age for weaning at eighteen months to two years.[55] Should the weaned child fall ill, however, he thought it best to return it to the breast. Both doctors considered milk the most suitable food for an infant, although Soranus did permit young children to drink a little of the diluted wine that Galen (and Aristotle) considered totally inappropriate for them.[56] In their opinion even a little wine was likely to cause diseases!

---

[53] Well stressed by Moulton (1977) 100.

[54] Galen, *De san. tuenda*, 1.10, 23 Koch = 6.47–8 Kühn. Of the forty wet-nursing contracts surveyed by Masciadri and Montevecchi (1984), twenty-eight preserved information on the duration of nursing, and twenty-two of the twenty-eight were for two to three years; for the evidence on prolonged nursing in the Roman period, see Frier (1994) 318–33.

[55] Soranus, *Gyn.* 2.49–56, 2.58–64 Burguière.

[56] Galen, *De san. tuenda* 1.10, 23–5 Koch = 6.47–54 Kühn, and Aristotle, *Pol.* 7, 1336a; Soranus' view at *Gyn.* 2.46–8, 2.55–8 Burguière.

Rather, Galen prescribed a diet of milk and daily baths with sweet warm waters, for these had the desirable effect of making a small child's body remain soft as long as possible and were the best means to promote progress in growth. Only when the child began schooling, according to Galen, should this regimen be abandoned. Teething itself, however, occupied neither Galen nor Soranus with the same intensity that it received in earlier medical and lay literature.

Hippocratics were not given, as Galen was, to quoting epic poetry, and the only line in the *Corpus* explicitly said to derive from "the poet" does not occur in our Homer.[57] Nor did Hippocratics direct the same attention to children as they did to adults, and more was said about the fetus than about the child.[58] The information that babies were swaddled in Hippocratic times, for example, derives not from directions for swaddling, but from a comparison between splinting a fractured thigh bone and the way "babies in their beds were swaddled" and from the observation that adult Scythians went flabby and squat as adults because they eschewed infant swaddling.[59] The concerns for the growing of deciduous teeth and exhibiting signs of puberty in the requisite periods that marked Solon's elegy on the ages of man were replicated in *Epidemics 6*, for this medical writer likewise thought it important to note whether eruption of teeth, growth of pubertal hair, and production of semen occurred earlier or later than appropriate.[60] The Hippocratic *Eight-Months' Child* (*De octimestri partu*) was primarily concerned with embryology, although the author did apply his own arithmology, consisting of hebdomads and tessarakontads, to newborns and children:

In fact, individual intelligence is clearly present in the body on its first day. For right after birth, *paidia* seem to laugh and to cry, sometimes even in sleep. Yet once they have grown older, they neither laugh nor cry of their own accord before forty days; nor, when they are touched or aroused, do they laugh, sooner than this very period of time has taken place. Their faculties are dulled by the abundance of mucous . . . Many other phenomena distinguish themselves in the body by sevens, such as the teeth falling out for children and other [teeth] growing in their place.[61]

---

[57] Hippocrates, *De articulis* 8, 4.98 Littré: ὡς δ' ὁπότ' ἀσπάσιον ἔαρ ἤλυθε βουσὶν ἕλιξιν.

[58] On the lack of pediatric material in the *Corpus Hippocraticum*, see Demand (1994) 141–6; Hummel (1999) begins her survey only with Aretaeus.

[59] Hippocrates, *De fracturis* 22, 3.492 Littré, and *De aere, aquis, locis* 20, 2.74 Littré.

[60] Hippocrates, *Epid.* 6.8.11, 5.348 Littré.

[61] Hippocrates, *De octimestri partu* 1.15–18, 82.2–15 Grensemann; Grensemann's ordering of the chapters is to be preferred over that of Littré (where this is chapter 9, 7.450–2). The author had earlier said that 'baby teeth' began to appear for the child at seven months, along with other, unspecified bodily changes (1.7, 78.20–80.2 Grensemann = 7.448 Littré).

The only pediatric treatise in the *Corpus Hippocraticum* was *Teething* (*De dentitione*), a small work, perhaps fragmentary, that divided its attention between teething and tonsillitis. It warned that children who experienced stormy times while cutting teeth bore this more easily if properly attended to.[62] The Hippocratic author of the embryological *Fleshes* (*De carnibus*) was also interested in dentition, because in this author's view teeth were similar to bones, although the latter were more dense and hard. Teeth developed not only as result of the milk consumed by the fetus *in utero*, but also from the milk drunk during suckling at the breast; teeth only became visible, however, after the child was born. This medical writer's account of dentition extended into the fourth period of seven years, when wisdom teeth appeared:

The first teeth fall out when there have been seven years of the first regimen [of milk]; in some cases this occurs earlier, if the children are being fed a regimen that is sickly – but in most cases when they are seven years old. The teeth that grow in afterwards grow old with the person, unless they are lost as the result of disease . . . A person reaches adulthood when he has acquired his definitive form, and this generally occurs between seven and fourteen years of age. In that time all the teeth, including the largest, are formed, once those that came into being from the nourishment in the uterus have fallen out . . . In the fourth seven-year period two more teeth are formed in many persons, and these are called the "more prudent" teeth.[63]

For Hippocratics dental development was an important indicator of a child's degree of maturity, and the process was characterized by a first growth and then loss in early childhood, followed by the second and permanent growth of teeth during the period that culminated in puberty. This discourse underscored the folly of first teething, for the child must grow teeth a second time before setting out on a straight path to adulthood. First teething did not result in permanent teeth and was a matter of concern only to mothers and nurses. As the deciduous teeth became fully developed, and even sloughed, the child was also beginning to achieve some mastery over his body. Similar patterns of dentition characterized the larger farm animals, and it seems likely that children's predictable dental development served as a clear indicator of increased physical maturity, signaling to medical writers

---

[62] Hippocrates, *De dentitione* 12, 8.544 Littré.
[63] Hippocrates, *De carnibus* 12–13, 8.598–602 Littré = 12–14 Deichgräber.

and men of the family alike that the small child was at last moving closer to mature form.[64]

The princelings Astyanax and Achilles had choice pieces of meat cut for them at the feasts of the men, while they sat perched on the knees of father or child-minder (9.487–9). Astyanax refused all food but the marrow or flesh of fattest sheep (22.500–1). The suitor Eurymachus also boasted that in the days before the war at Troy Odysseus had set him on his lap, fed him bits of roasted meat, and offered him drinks of wine.[65] These boys possessed at least a full set of first teeth when deemed ready to join feasts in the men's quarters, for they were able to chew the meat cut specially for them. They were of an age when they could be displayed to friends, visitors, and the sons of visitors, with whom they would associate in adult life – and, in the case of princelings, over whom they would rule one day. At the same time, the little boys were also learning proper behavior in the *andrōn*, exemplified by the men who brought them there. Eurymachus of the *Odyssey* did not apparently profit from such lessons, if, in fact, he had sat on Odysseus' knees. Andromache coupled Astyanax's activities at the men's feasts with supervised play among age-mates (22.502–4).

SOCIALIZATION OF PRINCES AND SUPERVISED PLAY

Galen thought that the increased physical development of those who reached their third or fourth year from birth required more vigorous exercises, such as the motions provided by vehicles and boats.[66] A seven-year-old was sufficiently developed to learn riding on horseback, and, when attending school and learning sports, frequent bathing was no longer salubrious. Plato's Athenian implied that the transition from babyhood to childhood was marked by the move from care by mother and nurses to that of the teacher, and this view became commonplace among later medical writers and moralists.[67] Prior to the time of training by exempla and positive

---

[64] A not dissimilar timetable existed for Hippocratics and contemporary lay authors for birthing, which distinguished the events of concern to men and consigned the hours of waiting and comforting the parturient to midwives and other females; see Hanson (1994a) 176–81.

[65] *Od.* 16.442–4; Heubeck and A. Hoekstra (1989) 284–5 (ad 438–44 and 445–7) judge this not only a reminiscence of the *Iliad* scenes, but also clear proof of the hypocrisy in the affection the "brazen-faced liar" Eurymachus claimed to feel for Telemachus.

[66] Galen, *De san. tuenda* 1.8.5–6, 18–19 Koch = 6.38 Kühn.

[67] Plato, *De legibus* 808e and e.g. Plutarch, *De liberis educandis* 7 = *Moralia* 4a–b. For a similar view from Soranus, see above, p. 189.

learning from seven years onward, inculcation of obedience remained of prime importance. Galen described the third year as one in which children began to separate into two groups – those amenable to discipline, who learned to love praise for its own sake, and those who resisted out of impudence:

[w]e sometimes see one of them hurt by a playmate, and . . . we see some of them take pity on him and help him, and others laugh at him, gloat over him, and, sometimes, join in and take part in hurting him. We also see some children rescue others from difficulties, and others push playmates into dangerous places, poke their eyes out or choke them. Some are reluctant to give away anything that they have in their hands, some are envious, some are not envious . . .[68]

Once again, the recommendations of the Athenian in Plato's *Laws* hovered in the background, unacknowledged as before. Constructive play was to be introduced to the three-year-old, followed by lessons in music and gymnastics, when the child turned seven.[69] Aristotle's prescriptions were similar, with supervised games that imitated the serious occupations of later life recommended for those between two and seven years, for such activities not only instilled discipline, but also provided strenuous exercises for their growing bodies; serious schooling began only at seven years. Because Aristotle thought the younger children would be raised in the home, his lawgiver banished indecent stories so that the young would neither hear nor see anything disgraceful or slavish.

According to Andromache, Astyanax attended banquets of the men when Hector was among the living and, under his father's tutelage, was enjoying the socialization deemed appropriate for scions of princely houses.[70] When tired from play, he went to sleep in his soft bed, once again cradled in the arms of a nurse. Much of Andromache's laments for the dead Hector fastened upon the losses her orphaned boy would subsequently endure, including a rude ejection from those same feasts by another child, now emboldened to drive out the orphan, since his own father yet lived. Phoenix's elaborate remembrance of the young Achilles magnified his own role in that upbringing; he was the one who made Achilles into the man he had become, like to the gods, and this cost Phoenix many labors.[71] Achilles would accompany only him to the banquets, whether in the town or within Peleus' palace, and sitting on his knees, he too tasted bits of meat

---

[68] Galen, *De moribus* 240 Mattock.
[69] Plato, *De legibus* 793e–794d; Aristotle, *Pol.* 7.15, 1336a–1337a.
[70] 22.500–4; cf. 24.726–7, where she feared Astyanax would not reach puberty.
[71] Repeated at 9.485 and 494–5; cf. also 9.491–2.

cut for him, sipped from Phoenix's wine cup, and at times regurgitated a bit, soiling Phoenix's shirt. Phoenix recalled no weeping and wailing from the young prince, only that the hero's early socialization came at his hands, much as had occurred for the young Astyanax on his father's lap.

Patroclus was also resident in Peleus' palace during Achilles' boyhood, if not his babyhood, and his ghost reminded Achilles of their closeness throughout these years, when he begged him for burial and eventual interment together.[72] Presumably Achilles' lessons from the centaur Cheiron either preceded Patroclus' arrival, or took place while Patroclus was resident, since Eurypylus assumed that Patroclus learned healing salves from what Cheiron had taught Achilles.[73] In recalling the episode that brought him to Peleus' palace, Patroclus' ghost explained that he killed a playfellow, when angered during a game of knuckle-bones, and although his actions were neither premeditated nor willed, his wrathful act resulted in his removal from his father's palace. Other boys at play in the *Iliad*'s similes likewise seem to have enjoyed their games away from the supervision of an adult. Further, the boys themselves gave no indication of worrying whether or not their actions were potentially dangerous for one of their number – not when building sand castles and knocking them down, not when teasing wasps in their nest, not when vainly beating a donkey to make it move.[74] These epic playfellows, presumably having arrived at their second hebdomad of life, were tentatively testing the adult world of agonistic confrontations, and only in the case of Patroclus did unsupervised games prove harmful. Patroclus' presence was thus a constant reminder of the consequences of childhood angers left unchecked.

By contrast, younger epic children seem to have been under constant supervision, and concerned parents arranged that nurses be succeeded by other child-minders, analogous to the *paedagogus* of later times, so that an adult presence was ever available to reinforce positive habits of mind and body. An older child might also serve as companion and adviser to a younger one. Greek pediatric theory and practice, as surveyed above, actively aimed to prevent infants and small children from experiencing prolonged frustration, lest angry responses become habitual. Parents and child-minders deliberately tried to remove that which aroused wrath whenever infants and children encountered something that did not suit them. Preserving

---

[72] 23.83–90, stressing that they had been reared together through forms of τρέφειν in lines 84 and 90.

[73] 11.830–1. Many subsequent writers imagined how Cheiron's lessons proceeded – one of the most humorous of which is Dio Chrysostom, *Oratio* 58; cf. also Ovid, *Ars amatoria* 1.11–17 and Juvenal, *Satire* 7.210–12.

[74] 15.362–4; 16.259–62; 11.558–62.

the softness of babyhood well into childhood postponed the testing of a child's capacity for control of self, even as discouraging premature strivings after physical attainments aimed at preventing acquisition of the bad habits that led to deformity in the adult. The pliability that this softness implied allowed responsible adults to view infancy and childhood as offering considerable opportunity for shaping and molding a child's body and mind.

Phoenix was by no means an impartial witness when he claimed that Peleus considered Achilles yet *nēpios* and in need of guidance, as he set out from Phthia. Like Nestor, and perhaps also Phoenix, Odysseus was present at the farewell, and he rehearsed a portion of that scene during his speech in Book 9. The embassy to Achilles began auspiciously, as Ajax, Odysseus, and Phoenix encountered Achilles before his tent, pleasantly strumming on his lyre. He welcomed them as dear friends, and the heroes feasted together. Odysseus preempted his fellows by speaking first. In the body of his speech Odysseus repeated the words that Agamemnon announced to the Achaean chieftains back in his tent, enumerating the splendid gifts he would now give Achilles, if only he would give up his *cholos*.[75] The lengthy introduction, however, was Odysseus' own, as he outlined the plight of Achilles' comrades and remembered Peleus' parting words back in Phthia, and so too the more brief peroration, in which Odysseus edited out Agamemnon's tactless demand that Achilles yield to him because he was more kingly, replacing this with another plea to Achilles that he rejoin the war effort. Should he do so, he might even kill Hector. Odysseus reminded Achilles what Peleus had said: the gods would give him strength, if they chose, but he was to restrain his proud passion in his breast, for kindly regard was the better way. He was to keep clear of quarrels, for then the Argives, both young and old, would honor him all the more. "That is what the old man said, but you have forgotten." Even as Nestor was pursuing his own agenda when recalling for Patroclus Menoetius' urging that he give Achilles good advice in Book 11, so too Odysseus here remembered the farewell scene selectively, tailoring it to speak directly to Achilles' anger at Agamemnon, an anger that began and festered within him only in the Achaean camp at Troy.

---

[75] Lines 9.264–99 of Odysseus' speech repeated Agamemon's words from 9.122–57, altering only the first-person verbs to third-person; Odysseus' introduction occupies lines 9.225–63, and the peroration, lines 9.300–6. In the text I have paraphrased the entire scene, although of greatest importance for my argument are Peleus' instructions to Achilles: τέκνον ἐμὸν κάρτος μὲν Ἀθηναίη τε καὶ Ἥρη | δώσουσ᾽ αἴ κ᾽ ἐθέλωσι, σὺ δὲ μεγαλήτορα θυμὸν | ἴσχειν ἐν στήθεσσι· φιλοφροσύνη γὰρ ἀμείνων· | ληγέμεναι δ᾽ ἔριδος κακομηχάνου, ὄφρά σε μᾶλλον | τίωσ᾽ Ἀργείων ἠμὲν νέοι ἠδὲ γέροντες. | ὡς ἐπέτελλ᾽ ὁ γέρων, σὺ δὲ λήθεαι . . . (9.254–9).

It seems likely, then, that Achilles acquired the habits of wrathful response for which he became famed largely on the battlefields of Troy, when *cholos* was useful in a fight to the death. By the tenth year of the war his wrath against Agamemnon could no longer be contained within his breast and it burst out in the quarrel of *Iliad* 1. The child-rearing practices imagined for epic, however, offer no encouragement to the notion that Achilles was allowed to practice anger at home.

CHAPTER 9

Reactive and objective attitudes: anger in Virgil's Aeneid and Hellenistic philosophy

Christopher Gill

REACTIVE AND OBJECTIVE ATTITUDES

In this chapter, I reexamine the much-discussed issue of the relationship between Hellenistic ideas about anger and Virgil's *Aeneid* by applying a distinction between types of emotional attitude that has been drawn in modern philosophy. My starting-point is a famous essay on "Freedom and Resentment" by P. F. Strawson (1974); despite its age and relatively modest length, this essay draws an important distinction which has not been much explored subsequently. One of the advantages of Strawson's discussion is that it helps us to see that the Stoic (and to a lesser extent Epicurean) approach to anger and other passions is more intelligible than is often supposed and is not simply an unrealistic anti-emotional view.

Strawson draws a distinction between two types of interpersonal reaction or attitude, based in each type on beliefs or judgments about what should count as appropriate behaviour in a given situation. The distinction is between "reactive" and "objective" attitudes. The criterion of a reactive attitude is that the other person is treated as an equal partner in interactive engagement with oneself. The other is also treated as a fully responsible agent in personal interaction and liable for praise or blame and other such reactions, including anger and resentment, on that basis. The reactive attitude is, on the face of it, the normal one; but there are certain types of relationship in which a different, "objective" attitude is more appropriate. Strawson cites the examples of the relationship of parent to child or psychotherapist to patient. This kind of relationship is unequal or asymmetrical; the leading or superior partner refrains from the kind of reactive attitude that would be appropriate for an equal partner in personal interaction. She also does not treat the other person (child or patient) as a fully responsible agent nor does she praise or blame or resent her accordingly. Her response is "objective" in the sense of being dispassionate (not subjectively involved) and also in the sense of referring to more objective factors and a wider framework of reference or worldview than the other partner is able to apply.

Strawson's distinction can help us to define different types of attitude that we find analyzed or advocated in ancient philosophy and portrayed in ancient literature and to correlate these with each other. In particular, it can help us to correlate the responses we find presented in Virgil's *Aeneid* with those promoted by leading philosophical movements of his day. In broad terms, I want to suggest that Stoicism and (to some extent) Epicureanism advocate the adoption of an "objective" attitude toward other people in general (not just children and the mentally ill). In Aristotle, by contrast, and in the kind of Aristotelianism familiar in the late Republic and early Empire,[1] the "reactive" attitude is assumed to be normal and valid. There is thus a rather rich intellectual background against which to locate the kinds of attitude we find in the *Aeneid*: and I will suggest that there is a comparably rich combination of objective and reactive attitudes within the poem. Strawson's distinction thus provides a new point of access to characterizing the ethical and psychological complexity that is widely seen as a special feature of Virgil's *Aeneid*.

ANCIENT PHILOSOPHICAL PERSPECTIVES ON ANGER

There are, for instance, some rather straightforward connections between Strawson's idea of reactive attitudes and Aristotle's account of emotions. Aristotle's definition of anger in *Rhetoric* 2, a much-cited text, brings out the main relevant features.

Let anger be defined as a desire, accompanied by pain, for revenge at what is taken to be an insult to oneself or those close to one, in a situation where insult is not appropriate . . . Every case of anger must be accompanied by a certain type of pleasure, namely that which derives from the hope of taking revenge.[2]

For Aristotle, a *pathos* (emotion) such as anger is a reaction, marked by pleasure or pain, based on a belief or set of beliefs. More precisely, it is based on a social judgment about how someone has acted in relation to yourself or to those who matter to you. The parties, yourself and the other

---

[1] On the distinction which can be drawn between (1) Aristotle's school-texts, (2) the kind of Peripatetic (Aristotelian) position reflected in Roman thinkers such as Cicero and Seneca, and (3) a kind of implicit "Aristotelianism" embodied in conventional thought, see Braund and Gill (1997) 6–8. However, in all three cases, reactive interpersonal attitudes are seen as valid; see further n. 7 below.

[2] Arist. *Rh.* 2.2.1378a30–2, b1–2. All translations are mine except where otherwise stated. The related definition in *De an.* 1.1.403a29–b3 combines a "physical" account, as "the boiling of the blood . . . around the heart," with a "dialectical" or "logical" one, as "the desire to return pain for pain."

person, are treated as responsible agents interacting with each other on the basis of social norms which are, in principle, recognizable by both parties. The alternatives to anger are either growing calm (a *pathos* which is also seen as having its basis in social judgments) or some other reactive attitude, such as friendship or enmity, which is analyzed in similar terms.[3]

There are also clear connections between Strawson's idea of reactive attitudes and the presentation of emotions in Homer's *Iliad* (a text whose relevance to the *Aeneid* is obvious). Some crucial points come out in one example, Ajax's appeal to Achilles to give up his anger in *Iliad* 9. Ajax, speaking to Achilles in third-personal form, says: "Achilles has made savage the great-hearted spirit in his breast, harsh man that he is, and gives no consideration to the friendship of his comrades" (9.628–30). He concludes by addressing Achilles directly and urging him to "make your spirit mild, and to have respect for your house in which are gathered those of the Greeks who wish to be most worthy of your care and most friends to you" (9.639–42). In his famous reply, Achilles responds: "Everything that you say seems to me acceptable; but my heart swells with anger [or bile] when I remember the disgraceful way Agamemnon treated me in the presence of the Greeks, as though I were some migrant without status" (9.645–8).

Aristotle cites the latter passage in his account of anger;[4] and this exchange between the two Homeric figures illustrates both Aristotle's analysis of emotion and Strawson's idea of reactive attitudes. Ajax and Achilles treat emotions such as "making your heart savage," "making your spirit mild," or having your heart "swelling with anger," as reactions based on social judgments. Those judgments are, in turn, based on what are seen as reasonable norms of interactive behavior toward others. This characterization applies both to the reactive attitude of anger and to the alternative reaction, of "making your spirit mild," which Ajax urges on Achilles.[5]

If we turn to the accounts of anger in the Hellenistic theories, Stoicism and Epicureanism, the contrast is striking. This is not wholly clear from the formal definitions of anger offered by the different schools. For instance, Seneca's Stoic definition may not seem very different from Aristotle's, while that found in the Epicurean Philodemus seems also to take its starting-point from an Aristotelian formulation.[6] But the differences in the wider

[3] See further, on Aristotle on anger and on his thinking on emotions and social relationships, Sherman (1997) ch. 2; M. R. Wright (1997) 169–73.

[4] Arist. *Rh*. 2.2.1378b34, citing *Il.* 9.648.

[5] See further, on the links between Homeric and Aristotelian thinking on emotions and on the interpretation of the Homeric lines cited, especially *Il.* 9.645–8, Gill (1996) 190–204.

[6] See Procopé (1998: 176–7), who cites a series of definitions given by Seneca (preserved by Lactantius, *De ira Dei* 17.13). Anger is (1) "a desire to avenge an injury," *cupiditas ulciscendae iniuriae* (orthodox

conceptual framework are huge. The most obvious one, and the one that has received the bulk of recent scholarly attention is this. For Strawson and Aristotle – and Homer – reactive attitudes represent what is, in principle, a valid and reasonable type of reaction. (Of course, there is room for argument about which reactive attitude counts as valid in any given case.) For the Stoics and, with rather more qualifications, the Epicureans, reactive attitudes as such, at least as normally understood, are unreasonable and unjustified. They represent a perversion or distortion of the ideal (or "natural") state of mind of *apatheia* (freedom from emotion) or *ataraxia* (freedom from disturbance). The aspect of these theories that has been most fully explored is that of the psychological models involved, and also the correlated conceptions of value. But those differences are related, in turn, to differing views of what count as valid forms of social relationships. All these differences can be further linked with divergent worldviews, more precisely, divergent views about how ethics is related to the study of nature.[7]

Much that is distinctive about the Stoic view comes out in this passage from Marcus Aurelius' *Meditations* (2.1), which is worth citing at length.

Say to yourself at dawn: I shall encounter meddling, ungrateful, insulting, deceitful, envious and unco-operative people. All this has happened to them because they do not know what is good and bad. But I have come to see the nature of the good – it is what is right – and of the bad – it is what is wrong, and the nature of the wrongdoer himself – he is my relative, not because he shares the same blood or seed but because he shares with me in mind and a portion of divinity. So I shall never be harmed by any of these people, because no one will involve me in anything wrong; nor can I become angry with any relative or hate him. We have come into existence to work together, like feet, hands, eyelids, or the rows of upper and lower teeth. So to work against each other is unnatural; and resenting and turning away from someone is to work against him.

Stoic); (2) "a desire to punish the person by whom you consider yourself unjustly damaged," *cupiditas puniendi eius a quo te inique putes laesum* (Posidonius); (3) "an agitation of the mind to harm someone who has harmed you or wanted to harm you," *incitatio animi ad nocendum ei qui nocuit aut nocere uoluit* (Epicurean, cf. Philodemus, *On Anger* 40.32–5; 41.32–6); (4) "the desire to pay back pain," *cupiditatem doloris reponendi* (Aristotle). See also, on the relationship between these theories of anger, Erler (1992) 113–22.

7 On the contrast between Aristotelian and Hellenistic (Stoic-Epicurean) theories of emotion, see, for concise treatments, Annas (1993) 53–66; Braund and Gill (1997), 5–15; more fully, Nussbaum (1994). For a major new study of the Hellenistic theories of emotion, including a reprint of Procopé (1993) on Epicurean thought and several chapters on Stoic passions, see Sihvola and Engberg-Pedersen (1998). On Seneca's theory of anger and its philosophical background, see Fillion-Lahille (1984). Important earlier studies of Stoic passions include Inwood (1985) ch. 5 and M. Frede (1986); a significant recent one is Sorabji (2000). On Hellenistic ethics and conceptions of nature, see Annas (1993) part 2. On anger specifically, and on philosophical and cultural strategies for its control, see Harris (2002), esp. chs. 6 and 15.

Evident here is the deliberate negation of conventional reactive attitudes and also part of the basis for this negation. Marcus begins by identifying the kind of behaviour that would, conventionally, give grounds for anger or hatred ("meddling, ungrateful, insulting . . . people"), and then spells out the reasons for not reacting in this way. One is that people who behave in this way do so out of ignorance of what is genuinely good, namely virtue, and bad, namely vice. Anyone who recognizes this truth knows that he cannot be harmed by anyone else, since the only real harm is moral error, which is a kind of harm you can only inflict on yourself. Also, Marcus identifies social ideals (the brotherhood of humankind, the idea of humanity as a single body, the shared possession of rationality) which he sees as counteracting anger or hatred. These are seen as normative, regulatory ideals, which underlie good forms of social relationship. These ideals hold good absolutely, unaffected by the interruption in friendship (in the conventional sense) that results from one person wronging another. To view one's relationships in this way is, in effect, to adopt a "cosmic perspective" on oneself and others. Another manifestation of this perspective, and one highly relevant to the *Aeneid*, is the recognition that all events form part of the seamless web of fate and are shaped by providential rationality. Elsewhere, Marcus links the kind of cosmic perspective that recognizes providential rationality (that does not "blame" fate) with the perspective that does not "blame" those who share the brotherhood of humankind (12.24, 26).[8]

Marcus is not a wholly orthodox Stoic; but this aspect of his thinking is confirmed by the more orthodox Epictetus. In *Discourses* 1.28, for instance, Epictetus argues that the appropriate response to Medea, and to her criminal wish to take vengeance on her husband by killing her children, is not anger but pity. It may seem, initially, as though Epictetus is reverting to a quasi-Aristotelian framework, in which pity, for instance, serves as a reactive alternative to anger. But this type of pity should be seen as an objective response to another's error, like Marcus' response of seeing someone in error as his cosmic brother. The moral drawn is that "whoever keeps clearly in mind [the core truths of Stoicism] will never be irritated with anyone, never be angry with anyone, will never criticize or blame or hate or take offence at anyone" (1.28.10).[9]

Earlier, I suggested that Strawson's distinction between reactive and objective attitudes could be connected with – and could help us to understand – the contrasting views of anger (and other emotions) in Aristotle and

---

[8] On Marcus, see further Gill (1997b) Introduction and Bibliography and (2000) 611–15 on social relations; also Hadot (1998).

[9] On Epictetus on Medea, see Long (1996) 277–80, (2002) 76–7; Dobbin (1998) 218–27.

in the Hellenistic philosophies. The main criterion of a reactive, as distinct from an objective, relationship is that one treats the other as a responsible agent with whom one interacts and to whom one responds according to mutually recognized norms. For Strawson, and also for Aristotle, being a responsible agent and being liable to praise and blame are closely linked. The Stoics, famously, hold a determinist worldview of a kind which holds (adult) humans to be rational – and therefore responsible – agents. But they sever, or at least attenuate, the linkage between responsibility and the reactive attitudes of praise and blame.[10] At the same time, as we see in Marcus and Epictetus, relationships (at least between non-wise people) are conceived in strongly asymmetrical terms, like Strawson's "objective" relationships. In effect, Marcus and Epictetus are treating other people as children or psychiatric patients. According to Stoic principles, you do not blame or get angry with or hate other (non-wise) people because you see them as not, or not yet, understanding the nature of good and bad, and as needing to be educated or "cured" until they do.[11] Human beings are seen as being fundamentally capable of achieving this understanding, rather than as being fundamentally capable of mutual interaction as responsible agents, as is normally assumed in conventional ethics.[12]

The Epicurean position on anger is more difficult to pin down. This is partly because of the inadequacy of our evidence: our fullest source, Philodemus, represents only one strand in a complex debate about the nature of Epicurus' true view of anger. Also, the Epicurean position seems sometimes to endorse and sometimes to reject the conventional, "reactive" view of anger which underlies Aristotle's account. I offer one possible way of interpreting the theory, while remaining conscious of the work that still needs to be done (if our evidence allows) to make sense of it.

The features of the theory that recall the conventional, reactive view are these. We hear of a distinction between "natural" and "empty" anger.[13] Also, we are told that natural anger involves the correct matching of response to situation: "it arises from insight into the state of the nature of things and from avoiding false opinion in calculating the disadvantages and in

---

[10] See further Bobzien (1998) 336–7, referring to this feature of Epictetus' thought and relating it to the background of orthodox Stoic thought about determinism and agency (chs. 6–7).

[11] Stoics such as Marcus and Epictetus do not assume that they are wise and that others are not; rather, that virtually all human beings are non-wise. But Stoics, whether teachers or not, are more aware than others of what wisdom would mean and of the need for all human beings to direct their lives toward gaining wisdom, and, to that degree, their relationship with non-Stoics is an unequal one, like that of psychotherapist to patient.

[12] See further, on Stoic thinking on agency, responsibility, and development, Inwood (1985) chs. 2–4, 6; also Gill (forthcoming).

[13] See Annas (1989) 147; Procopé (1998) 178–82.

punishing those who do harm."[14] Further, we are told that what produces gratitude, anger, or resentment is the "voluntary" nature of the acts, an idea which, as John Procopé has noted, is strongly reminiscent of Strawson's account of resentment as a reactive attitude.[15] On the other side, however, we find comments which run directly counter to the reactive view. Philodemus asserts: "Desiring to punish, as though it were something enjoyable, a desire that is coupled with great anger, is silly (*mataion*), and is characteristic of people who think that this is the greatest good and turn to it as though to something choiceworthy in itself."[16] Also, we learn that the wise person, even if he feels the need to punish someone or oppose an aggressor, does so without pleasure (in contrast to Aristotle's view about anger) and with reluctance. He goes toward punishment "as something most necessary, and what results is most unpleasant, as with drinking wormwood, and surgery"; if he reacts to aggression by opposition, he does so "gritting his teeth" (*dakōn*).[17] We are also told that the failure of the wise person to feel much anger, even when he seems to be harmed deliberately by someone, derives from his recognition that "nothing external is worth much."[18] Also, although Philodemus finds a role in Epicureanism for "natural anger," we learn from his essay about others, such as Nicasicrates, who see no room for it in a good Epicurean life.[19]

One way of interpreting these seemingly divergent indications is this. Anger is understood by Epicureans as a kind of natural defense mechanism, operative in animals as well as humans. Its function, in general, is that of responding to aggression, or preempting it, and so promoting security. To this extent, anger is a "natural," and, as most Epicureans suppose, ineradicable, response.[20] However, the way in which anger expresses itself is highly variable and depends on a person's overall structure of beliefs about values and on the way in which this informs her/his pattern of interpersonal relations. This leads to a further, and more complex, sense in which anger may be defined as "natural" rather than "empty."[21] For instance, most people

---

[14] Philodemus, *On Anger* 37.25, trans. Procopé (1998) 181.

[15] *On Anger* 46.28–35, Procopé (1998) 177, referring to Strawson (1974) 5.

[16] *On Anger* 42.22–34, trans. Annas (1989) 155.

[17] *On Anger* 44.20–2, trans. Annas (1989) 159; 40.32–41.8, trans. Procopé (1998) 180. Contrast Aristotle's view in *Rh.* 2.2, cited in n. 2 above.

[18] *On Anger* 42.12–14, trans. Annas (1989) 158.

[19] See further Fowler (1997) 24–30; Procopé (1998) 186–9.

[20] On a tendency to anger, like other emotions, as having a physiological basis, but also open to modification by education, see Lucr. 3.282–322. On its function, see Philodemus, *On Anger* 41.3–5, also Procopé (1993) 177. On the recognition of different senses of 'natural' by Epicureans, see Procopé (1998) 179–80.

[21] For this distinction, see Philodemus, *On Anger* 37; also Annas (1989) 147.

place excessive value on material possessions and social status, instead of seeing these as valuable only in so far as they produce freedom from pain and emotional disturbance. The "silly" desire to punish, "as though it were something enjoyable" or "choiceworthy in itself," derives from this kind of mistake. A reactive attitude which is, at most, a means to an end (to security) is taken to be an end in itself (a source of pleasure). Also, the recognition of the relative unimportance of wealth and status (we realize how little we need to achieve happiness[22]) alters our sense of what it means to be "harmed" by someone. Most of what is normally regarded as "harm" is treated by a wise person as something merely "external."

Several of the relevant points come out in this passage, which indicates the extent to which Epicureanism both does and does not validate reactive attitudes.

It is sufficient to show in general that the wise person will be susceptible to anger of a kind. But someone will say: "But if it is because of being harmed in intentional fashion that he gets angry, and he is harmed by someone to the highest degree, how will he not have a strong desire to pursue the person?" [In response], we will say that he will be alienated in the extreme from the person who inflicts much harm on him . . . and will hate him – that just follows (*touto gar akolouthon*) – but he does not experience great trouble. Nothing external is worth very much, since he is not even susceptible to great troubles in the presence of great pains, and much more is this so with anger.[23]

This passage indicates the extent to which anger at a deliberate attempt to harm is seen as being, even in the wise person, an instinctive and, in this sense, "natural" reaction. But it also indicates how the extent of, and grounds for, this reaction are drastically altered – and reduced – by a correct understanding of what happiness is and how it can be obtained. The overall effect is to underline the distance from the conventional, Aristotelian-type view of anger as a socially shaped reactive attitude.

However, there is another, and rather more complex, sense in which Epicureanism validates anger (in some sense) as a reactive attitude. It is a feature of Epicureanism that it emphasizes the role of forceful or frank interpersonal dialogue in (what we might call) "consciousness raising" and in persuading people to lead more Epicurean lives. Anger – or perhaps pseudo-anger – seems to have played a significant role in this process. This, for instance, is how Philodemus describes Epicurus' own practice: ". . . reproaching out of friendship all his acquaintances or most of them,

---

[22] For this point and its relevance to anger, see Annas (1989) 150, referring to Usener 469, RS 15.
[23] *On Anger* 41.28–42.14, trans. Annas (1989) 158–9.

frequently and intensely, and often abusively."[24] This behavior looked like anger. Hence, "even such a wise person as Epicurus gave some people the impression [of being angry]." In fact, however, he was "unangered" (*aorgētos*) and of a "completely opposite disposition" (*enantiotēn diathesin*) to the angry person.[25] How can this rather puzzling response be explained?[26] The point, presumably, is that Epicurus is not "angry" in the usual sense and on the usual reactive grounds; in this sense, he is "unangered." On the other hand, he is responding "out of friendship" with behavior that is marked by the same reactive intensity as anger. The motive, however, is not anger, but the desire to stimulate someone into leading a life shaped by true goals. This revisionist version of a reactive attitude has parallels with the Stoic response of trying to alter actions and attitudes by forceful persuasion. Vituperation (*psegein*) played a role in both Stoic and Epicurean therapeutic strategies.[27] Relatedly, and more generally, both Stoics and Epicureans rethink the whole question of what counts as an acceptable form of social and interpersonal relationship, in ways indicated earlier in connection with Marcus Aurelius.[28] But, whereas the Stoics think that this revision entails the complete "extirpation" of anger, the Epicureans allow at least the appearance of anger – as well as its ineradicable presence as an instinctive reaction – to remain part of a wise life.

HELLENISTIC PHILOSOPHY AND VIRGIL'S *AENEID*

How far can this contrast between reactive and objective approaches to anger help us to define the relationship between Virgil's *Aeneid* and its philosophical background? In particular, how far do the different kinds of alternatives to anger associated with these approaches figure in the poem? First, however, I highlight a rather pervasive – and questionable – feature of some previous discussions of the relationship between the *Aeneid* and its philosophical context. Scholars frequently note the divergent views of anger in the philosophical background of Virgil's age, above all the heated debate about the respective merits of the Stoic and Peripatetic (Aristotelian) views of anger that is so obvious in Cicero and, later, in Seneca.[29] They

---

[24] *On Anger* 35.18–40, trans. Procopé (1998) 177. On this side of Epicureanism, see esp. Nussbaum (1994) 117–27.

[25] *On Anger* 34.31–35.5; trans. Annas (1989) 163.

[26] See further on this question Annas (1989) 163–4; Fowler (1997) 28–9.

[27] Procopé (1998) 184–6.   [28] See further on this point Gill (1996) 391–5, on Marcus, n. 8 above.

[29] See, e.g., Cic. *Tusc.* 3.71–6; 4.37–47; Sen. *De ira* 1.9–10, 17; 3.3. See Putnam (1990) 13–18. See further Graver (2002) xv–xxiii and commentary on *Tusc.* 3.71–6; 4.37–47; also Cooper and Procopé (1995) 5–13.

note too that Philodemus' approach positions itself against that context of debate as well as that of controversy within the Epicurean school. Yet, when they turn to the *Aeneid* itself, there is a tendency to assume that the poem should be interpreted as expressing *a single* type of approach to anger. For instance, Galinsky (1988) and M. R. Wright (1997) see the poem as expressing a (broadly) Aristotelian, "reactive," view. Lyne (1983) and Putnam (1990), (1995) argue for a more Stoic view, in which reactive anger is presented negatively. Erler (1992) and Galinsky (1994) suggest that an Epicurean approach is most relevant.[30] But it is far from obvious that this is a reasonable expectation to hold about the *Aeneid*. We might, in this period, expect someone who has a philosophical position to have a single, determinate one, whether this is expressed in theory or in action. (However, we also need to bear in mind the rather generous view of what counts as a single philosophical position in the late Hellenistic and Roman periods.[31]) But it is far from clear that we should have the same expectations of an epic poem, particularly one in which there is a well-recognized fusion of influences, both literary and cultural, in other respects.[32]

Indeed, there are some rather obvious reasons for thinking that the poem combines a (roughly) Aristotelian approach to anger and a Stoic one, that is, precisely the two strands which are given such emphasis in, for instance, Cicero and Seneca. These are also strands which are, in different ways, easier to combine with the Roman-political dimension of the *Aeneid* than is an Epicurean approach.[33] I am not wholly persuaded by the case that the poem expresses an Epicurean approach, despite Virgil's supposed Epicurean associations. I think that the Epicurean view tends to be brought into the interpretation of the poem because it is seen as intermediate between the Aristotelian (reactive) and Stoic (objective) views, and hence seems to offer a way of accommodating the Stoic and Aristotelian strands within the poem. I think that the poem does – perhaps – provide a coherent synthesis of these two strands, but not in the form of an Epicurean approach.

But what form does this synthesis take? One suggestion, rather crude perhaps but not wholly implausible, might be that Virgil deploys different

---

[30] I give the positions of these discussions only in broad terms. For further scholarship on this topic, see Erler (1992) 105.

[31] On philosophy in action at this time, see Sedley (1997); on "eclecticism," see Dillon and Long (1988).

[32] For some parallel observations, see Fowler (1997) 30–4; Harris (2002) 216–17. Galinsky (2003) links the ambiguity of the poem with its reception of complex literary influences, notably Greek tragedy, itself a complex and problematizing genre.

[33] On the assimilation of Roman and Stoic thought-patterns on the reason–passion contrast, see Gill (1997a) 232–4. As indicated above, the central preoccupation of Epicurean thinking on anger seems to be that of correlating this emotion with the Epicurean value system, a project with little obvious relevance to the *Aeneid*.

kinds of approach in different parts of the poem, indeed, possibly, in different books. For instance, in Book 8, the characterization of the anger of the people of Argylla against Mezentius is, markedly, couched in Aristotelian, reactive terms. That anger is linked, by implication at least, with Hercules' anger against Cacus, and (more obliquely) with Augustus' assault against Antony and Cleopatra at Actium. Book 8 also introduces the Evander–Pallas theme, which is subsequently strongly linked with the motif of reactive anger.[34] So it is arguable that the whole of Book 8 is pervaded by a broadly uniform, reactive paradigm of anger, and one which provides a framework for the understanding of Aeneas' campaign against Turnus, inviting us to see this too in reactive terms. In Book 7, by contrast, the presentation of the onset of anger among the Italian people and leaders is couched in much more Stoic or objective mode. I have outlined elsewhere a Stoicizing literary pattern, found in Senecan tragedy as well as Virgilian epic, in which the surrender to passion generates a type of madness. I think that the onset of passionate anger in Turnus and Amata, as well as Dido's decline into passion-as-madness, are best explained by this pattern; and this same pattern is also evident in the outbreak of anger-warfare among the Italian people in Book 7.[35] The contrast between these two books can be seen as a more general one. For instance, Books 4 and 9 seem to be dominated by the passion-as-madness theme in ways that Books 10–11, for instance, are not. If this line of interpretation were pursued, we should, of course, need to find some larger explanation of the basis on which Virgil selects one or other mode of description in different parts of the poem, and we should need to consider whether these variations imply some larger, synthesizing or architectural vision.

However, this is not quite the line of thought I propose to pursue. Although this line of interpretation takes us further than the idea that the poem expresses a single (Aristotelian or Stoic) viewpoint, it still understates the complexity of Virgil's deployment of modes of representing anger. Part of what is omitted comes out if we examine one striking example of an alternative to anger, namely Aeneas' holding back from anger against Helen in Book 2 (567–633). That this scene represents a strongly Stoic view of anger has been underlined by Putnam (1990; 24–5, 35–9). But his discussion does

---

[34] See (reactive anger against Mezentius), *Aen.* 8.494, 501, cited below; (Hercules' anger) 219–20, 228–30; for the (parallel?) conflict of Actium, see 675–728; for Evander–Pallas, see 508–19, 560–83, and below; for Aeneas taking all this burden on his shoulders, 729–31.

[35] See Gill (1997a) esp. 228–30, 236–9; also *Aen.* 7.341–407, esp. 345–8, 373–7, 406 (Amata); 7.481–2, 519–30, 550, 580–5; 8.4–6 (Italian people).

not quite bring the combination in this passage of reactive, Aristotelian, and objective, Stoic, characterizations of anger. Aeneas narrates how he told himself: "yet I shall be praised for having put an end to a source of crime and taking justified retaliation, and there will be pleasure in satisfying my feelings and the shades of my ancestors with avenging flames" (*exstinxisse nefas tamen et sumpsisse merentis | laudabor poenas, animumque explesse iuuabit | ultricis flammae et cineres satiasse meorum*, 585–7). Aeneas' report of his desire for justified retaliation (*merentis . . . poenas*) and of the anticipated pleasure (*iuuabit*) in doing so evokes strongly the reactive pattern exemplified earlier in Aristotle (n. 2 above). This remains true although Aeneas also qualifies the credit he sees as coming from taking vengeance on a (mere) woman (583–4). However, Aeneas' own narrative comment and, still more, Venus' reported words characterize Aeneas' intention from an objective, Stoic, standpoint. Aeneas tells us that his own comment was made "with a frenzied mind" (*furiata mente*), and that his mother criticized his "uncontrolled anger" (*indomitas iras*), asking him "why are you frenzied?" (*quid furis?*, 588, 594–5). Most striking, however, and most evocative of the objective approach of, for instance, Marcus Aurelius, is what follows. Venus tells her son that neither Helen nor Paris are to be "blamed" (*culpatus*). She also shares with Aeneas the "cosmic perspective," stripping away his previous human blindness, and showing that the destruction of Troy is the work of the combined power of the gods (we can compare, in Stoic terms, the providential, inescapable nexus of fate). As in Marcus, the cosmic perspective is linked both with avoiding negative reactive attitudes such as anger and blame and with affirming positive ethical claims, such as acting as a Roman or, in this instance, as a father, son, and husband.[36]

It is worth trying to put this combination or "layering" of reactive and objective attitudes to anger in a rather larger context within the poem. In Book 4, I think that the predominant mode of description is Stoicizing and that Dido's state of mind, in particular, is best understood as a gradual descent into passion-as-madness (Gill [1997] 228–9). However, this context also includes some striking contrasts between reactive and objective modes. For instance, when Dido finds out about Aeneas' imminent departure, her intense speech to Aeneas deploys, and appeals to, a series of reactive attitudes, including blame or reproach, love, and pity, beginning with these words:

---

[36] See *Aen.* 2.589–92, 593–623, esp. 595–8, 601–3. See M. Ant. *Med.* 2.1, cited in text to n. 8 above, also, for example 6.44, coupling the cosmic perspective and localized duty: "As Antoninus, my city and fatherland is Rome; as a human being, it is the universe"; see further Gill (2000) 613–15.

> dissimulare etiam sperasti, perfide, tantum
> posse nefas tacitusque mea decedere terra?
> nec te noster amor nec te data dextera quondam
> nec moritura tenet crudeli funere Dido?
>
> (4.305–8)

Traitor, did you even hope to cover up so great a crime and silently get away from my land? Does nothing hold you here – neither our love nor your right hand given in pledge nor Dido, about to die in a cruel mode of death?

Aeneas' reply acknowledges that reciprocal acts of benefit or harm have moral weight ("I shall never deny what you deserve of me . . . [but] I never entered into a [marriage] agreement with you," *numquam . . . negabo promeritam . . . nec . . . in foedera ueni*, 334–5, 338–9). But his response is shaped, above all, by the motivational outcome of the "cosmic perspective" yielded by Mercury's message (265–82). It is this that makes Aeneas say that "this (Italy) is my love, this is my fatherland" (*hic amor, haec patria est*, 47), an assertion which is compatible with the claim, expressed in more conventionally emotional terms, that "I do not seek Italy of my own free will" (*Italiam non sponte sequor*, 361). Although the relationship between the orthodox Stoic conception of Fate and that of the *Aeneid* is, famously, complex, Virgil has gone very far in giving poetic expression to the idea that Fate, if knowable, could become a source of positive motivation, replacing other kinds of desire.[37] It is often felt that, in this encounter, Dido and Aeneas are, in effect, speaking in two different kinds of language or speaking past each other. The contrast between reactive and objective (or Aristotelian and Stoic) ways of thinking about motives can help to give conceptual content to this impression.

AENEAS AND ANGER – REACTIVE OR OBJECTIVE ATTITUDES?

The presentation of Aeneas' restraint of anger against Helen suggests that, although the *Aeneid* combines Aristotelian and Stoic approaches to anger, the Stoic, objective, view is given a more authoritative, privileged status. That impression is reinforced by the relationship just sketched between reactive and objective attitudes to passion more generally in Book 4. How far does this provide the basis for interpreting what is, undoubtedly, the most difficult body of material for this question, namely Aeneas' attitudes

---

[37] For an orthodox Stoic expression of this idea see Epict. *Diss.* 2.6.9, trans. Long and Sedley (1987) 58J: "Therefore Chrysippus was right to say: 'As long as the future is uncertain to me I always hold to the things which are better adapted to obtaining the things in accordance with nature [e.g. health, wealth, status] . . . But if I actually knew that I was fated now to be ill, I would even have an impulse to be ill. For my foot too, if it had intelligence, would have an impulse to get muddy.' "

during the Italian War (Books 8–12) and the place of anger and its restraint among those attitudes? Before turning to specific passages, it may be useful to identify several distinct, though related, issues bearing on this topic. One is that of the type or types of approach to anger (reactive or objective) that seem relevant to a given portrayal. Another is the question whether the attitude portrayed is presented in a positive or negative light. As already indicated, the presentation of anger and its alternatives in the *Aeneid* is complex, probably in both of these respects. But complexity is not the same as ambiguity. A further question is whether a given portrayal is not only complex but also ambiguous in its view of anger and in its narrative or authorial coloring.

It is useful also to hold in view the principal episodes bearing on this topic, and the interpretative questions that they raise. One is the range of types of anger displayed in Book 8; as noted earlier, these form a key part of the framework for gauging Aeneas' attitude to his campaign against the Italians. Another is Aeneas' response to Turnus' killing of Pallas in Book 10 and the start of Book 11. The third, and, of course, the most problematic, is Aeneas' outpouring (after initial restraint) of destructive anger against the Italian army, capital, and finally Turnus. It goes without saying that a crucial part of the framework for understanding this set of events is constituted by the representation of heroic anger (and its restraint) in the *Iliad* and *Odyssey*. My focus falls, however, on trying to identify the extent to which philosophical strands form part of the way in which anger and its alternatives are defined and colored in the *Aeneid*.

I noted earlier that in Book 8 the anger of the people of Argylla against Mezentius is presented in strongly reactive, "Aristotelian," terms, and that this is, significantly, juxtaposed to Aeneas' adoption of the project of war against Turnus and the Italians (8.470–540). However, this juxtaposition is combined with certain contrasts between the way that Evander, on the one hand, and Aeneas, on the other, characterize responses to wrongdoing. Evander, after outlining Mezentius' extreme wrongdoing ("unspeakable slaughter . . . the savage acts of the tyrant," *infandas caedes . . . facta tyranni | effera*), presents the Argyllans' response as that of intense, and justified, anger: "they are driven against the enemy by justified bitterness and Mezentius inflames them with well-deserved anger" (*quos iustus in hostem | fert dolor et merita accendit Mezentius ira*[38]). Aeneas' response is preceded by a divine sign from Venus, indicating that he should expect war

---

[38] *Aen.* 8.482–3, 500–1. The correlated phrase "with just fury," *furiis . . . iustis* (494) is rather more puzzling, given the typically negative connotations of *furiis*. It is also not altogether easy to gauge the force of the use of *furor*-terms in connection with Hercules (8.219, 228).

and armor to equip him for this war. As in Books 2 and 4, this intervention seems to introduce something close to the "cosmic perspective" of Stoicism, and to shape Aeneas' attitudes to the war and his opponents. Although his words register the view that Turnus and the Italians are in the wrong, in breaking the treaty and starting war, and that they should pay the penalty (*poenas*), this view is expressed without the kind of anger highlighted in Evander's speech.

> heu quantae miseris caedes Laurentibus instant!
> quas poenas mihi, Turne, dabis! quam multa sub undas
> scuta uirum galeasque et fortia corpora uolues,
> Thybri pater! poscant acies et foedera rumpant.
>
> (8.536–40)

Ah, how great is the slaughter that stands in wait for the poor Laurentine people! What a penalty you will pay to me, Turnus! How many are the shields, helmets, and brave bodies of fine men that you will turn over with your flow, father Tiber! So let them demand the clash of battle and break their treaties.

Aeneas' words seem, rather, to express the kind of detached "pity" (of a non-reactive kind) that is sometimes associated with the cosmic perspective in Marcus and Epictetus.

To this extent, this passage in Book 8 expresses the same kind of contrast (between reactive and non-reactive attitudes) that we saw in Books 2 and 4. However, there is a crucial difference in the context, which has a bearing on Aeneas' subsequent responses. In Books 2 and 4 the divine intervention is linked with drawing Aeneas away from a given situation, and from the people toward whom he is reacting (Helen and Dido). The positive ethical message, to protect his family or continue his mission, is distinct from the question of how to react toward those other people (Helen and Dido). In Book 8, however, the cosmic perspective directs Aeneas to engage more deeply with the interpersonal and communal situation in which he finds himself. The ethical message is to act against wrongdoing; is it also to have the reactive attitude of anger that normally accompanies such retaliation? That is not what Stoicism would require. In a passage on this question (*De ira* 1.12), Seneca rejects the idea that retributive action requires a reactive attitude:

"What," (one might ask) "doesn't the good person get angry if he sees his father murdered, his mother raped?" He will not get angry, but he will seek retaliation and defend them . . . If my father is being murdered, I shall defend him; if he is murdered, I will seek retaliation – because it is my duty (*oportet*) not because I feel hurt (*dolet*).

But the *Aeneid* does not have to adopt a uniformly Stoic line on anger. Is it possible that Virgil envisages some kind of combined or intermediate state of mind, in which the hero comes to feel that the cosmic perspective requires the kind of ethical engagement in which he not only acts against Turnus but also has (and is right to have) the correlated reactive attitudes?

One test case for this question is Aeneas' response to the death of Pallas in Book 10. Aeneas' actions here are clearly modeled on Achilles' intense responses to the killing of Patroclus in the *Iliad*: he mows down the enemy, takes four prisoners alive for human sacrifice, rejects suppliants (10.510–42). But is he angry? Translations such as Jackson Knight's famous Penguin Classics version sometimes suggest this, speaking of his "burning anger" (10.552) or saying that "his rage was the rage of . . . a black tornado" (10.604). The Latin is more neutral, or ambivalent. The phrases translated are *ardenti* ("burning") and *turbinis atri | more furens* ("raging like a dark whirlwind"). It is also said of Aeneas that "blazing . . . he drives on with the sword . . . seeking you, Turnus" (*ardens . . . agit ferro, te, Turne . . . | . . . quaerens*, 513–14). Terms such as *ardens* and *furens* can, certainly, carry connotations of intense emotion in the *Aeneid*, for instance in connection with the "mad," passionate responses of Euryalus or Turnus in Book 9 (342–3, 761–2). But in Book 10, the primary connotation seems to be that of rapid, quasi-instinctive action. Aeneas' state of mind as he does this is indicated in these words: "Pallas, Evander, everything comes before his very eyes – the table he first approached on that day as an incomer, the right hands given in pledge" (*Pallas, Euander, in ipsis | omnia sunt oculis, mensae quas aduena primas | tunc adiit, dextraeque datae*, 515–17). This reference to his awareness of his obligations might serve as an indication of the grounds of an Aristotelian type of reactive anger. But it could, equally, serve to convey obligations which, as in the Senecan passage just cited, can be met through action without the stimulus of the intense affective reactions stigmatized in Stoicism.

Similar questions are raised by the description of Aeneas' funeral for Pallas at the start of Book 11. Here, Aeneas seems to experience one reactive attitude at least, that of grief, which is, in Stoicism, just as much an irrational passion as anger ("thus he spoke crying," *sic ait inlacrimans*, 29; "with the tears welling up," *lacrimis . . . obortis*, 41).[39] However, this emotion is not linked with other interpersonal emotion such as love, hatred, or anger. Any connotations of passionate love or violent revenge are limited to the details

---

[39] For Stoic typologies of passions, see Long and Sedley (1987) 65 B and E; on grief (in Cicero and Seneca), see Erskine (1997); M. Wilson (1997).

of the funeral ritual.[40] At the end of the funeral, Aeneas' words express a kind of cosmic pathos rather than anger: "the same dreadful fates of war call us from here to other tears," *nos alias hinc ad lacrimas eadem horrida belli | fata uocant* (96–7). Similarly, Aeneas' speech of grief in 11.42–58 expresses the generalized pathos of the fact that *Fortuna* has deprived Pallas of a successful role in their project (42–4). It also focuses on the thought that Aeneas cannot now fulfil his undertakings to Evander (45–8, 55; cf. 10.515–17). It is left to Evander to articulate an unequivocally reactive response to Pallas' death, delivered as a message of obligation to Aeneas:

> . . . dextera . . . tua est, Turnum nato patrique
> . . . debere . . . meritis uacat hic tibi solus
> fortunaeque locus. non uitae gaudia quaero,
> nec fas, sed nato manis perferre sub imos.
>
> (11.178–81)

. . . your right hand . . . owes [the death of] Turnus to the son and his father. This is the only room that is left open for you to combine doing what is right and achieving success. I seek no joy in life – that would be wrong – but only to bring some joy to my son among the shades.

Evander's message conveys what are two central themes in an Aristotelian conception of anger (n. 2 above): the idea that anger constitutes desire for justified retaliation and that such retaliation brings pleasure, here, pleasure to Pallas' dead spirit.

Do these two episodes enable an answer to the question posed earlier? The answer is not fully determinate, and is less so, I think, than in the case of *Aeneid* 2 and 8, cited earlier. But these episodes in Books 10–11 allow, as a possible interpretation, that Aeneas understands his role as being that of fulfilling his obligations without – or without necessarily – having the reactive attitude of anger. The fact that, as in Book 8, the expression of a strongly reactive view is assigned to someone *other than* Aeneas (in fact, Evander, in both Books 8 and 11) suggests that there is a relatively systematic attempt to associate Aeneas with a more objective attitude, and to link this with his divinely given cosmic perspective.

However, if this is so, this renders even more difficult to understand the fact that in Book 12 Aeneas is shown, unequivocally, as displaying anger of a markedly reactive type. First, when Aeneas, unable to find his opponent Turnus, is suddenly wounded, "then indeed his anger rose up . . . he threw the reins off his anger" (*tum uero adsurgunt irae . . . irarumque omnis effundit*

---

[40] See, e.g., the Catullan imagery of 67–9 or the allusion to Dido in 74–5; also the victims for human sacrifice in 81–2.

habenas, 494, 499). His wrath is expressed in an indiscriminate attack on the Italians as a whole. The second response follows the pattern of reactive anger, though it is not identified explicitly as that. Aeneas decides to lay waste the capital of Latinus' kingdom in reciprocation for their broken truce and as the "source . . . of the criminal war" (*caput . . . belli nefandi* 569–73; cf. 580–2). Finally, we have the much-examined scene in which the sight of Pallas' sword-belt, now worn by Turnus, stimulates reactive anger in retaliation for Pallas' death:

> ille, oculis postquam saeui monimenta doloris
> exuuiasque hausit, furiis accensus et ira
> terribilis . . . "Pallas te hoc uulnere, Pallas
> immolat et poenam scelerato ex sanguine sumit."
> (12.945–7, 948–9)

When he drank in with his eyes the spoils, the reminders of savage grief, then he, inflamed with fury [or the Furies] and terrible in his anger [said] . . ."It is Pallas, Pallas, who sacrifices you with this wound and exacts retaliation from your criminal blood."

How can we correlate this feature of Book 12 with the pattern which seems to emerge elsewhere, in which, although we find both reactive and objective attitudes, higher status seems to be given to some version of the objective alternative to anger? I see two main possibilities, which answer, broadly, to the way that Aeneas' anger has been interpreted by scholars in this context.[41] One is that either Aeneas himself – or at least we, his readers – come to see his cosmically shaped mission as requiring not just the performance of appropriate actions but also the correlated reactive attitudes. The other is that a series of intense and exceptional pressures brings about a mode of response and set of actions that we – and Aeneas in a calmer hour – can recognize as falling short of what is elsewhere presented as the highest standard of attitude and action.

I am inclined to the latter reading and will shortly indicate reasons for doing so. But I am aware of the factors that lead other scholars to take a different view; and I think that this at least is a case where the *Aeneid* is not simply complex (in its psychological modes and its ethical coloring) but also ambiguous. As regards the status of Aeneas' actions in Book 12, the first two are presented as marking a deflection from Aeneas' settled policy of distinguishing between Turnus (as the person with whom he is in disagreement) and the Italians as a whole. This deflection is well marked

---

[41] But, for a crucial qualification of some current interpretations, see p. 226.

by narrative comments and by Aeneas himself;[42] and it is contrasted with Aeneas' earlier attempt to restrict generalized conflict and the associated emotions ("Why does this sudden conflict arise? Restrain your anger," *quaeue ista repens discordia surgit? | o cohibete iras!*, 313–14). It seems reasonable, then, to link Aeneas' non-standard behavior at this stage of the poem with his non-standardly reactive attitude. There is repeated emphasis on Aeneas' frustration at not being able to resolve the situation in the agreed way (by single combat with Turnus); the outburst of reactive anger at the Italians and the attack on their city express his exceptional response to that frustration. The fact that the attack is divinely prompted (by Venus, 554–6) is not coupled here with any move toward a wider, more cosmic, perspective or an associated objective attitude. Indeed, the apparent echo in Aeneas' words of Juno's highly reactive, and destructive, attitude to her opponents in Book 7 is a further sign of a deflection from the highest standards achieved by Aeneas elsewhere.[43]

The ethical status of Aeneas' final killing of Turnus (12.919–52) has been a matter for longstanding scholarly controversy. Does the killing, committed with passionate intensity, constitute a justified action accompanied by merited anger or a lapse from Aeneas' normally high standards of humanity and rationality? The scholarly debate is often formulated as being between Aristotelian (or perhaps Epicurean) and Stoic readings of the scene;[44] but I think that this is not the best way of specifying the possible interpretations. What would be needed, for consistency in Aeneas' pattern of reactions throughout the poem, would be that Aeneas, at this point, should come to recognize that his cosmically shaped mission requires not just retaliatory action but the associated reactive attitude, and that this recognition would be endorsed by the narrative framing (see p. 225 above). I think it is hard to claim that the passage meets these conditions. The preceding divine debate (12.791–842) prepares us for reconciliation and the renunciation of anger rather than a cosmic validation of reactive anger. Also, I think, the seemingly Aristotelian language in which, in the passage just cited, Aeneas expresses his sense of justified anger (*Pallas . . . Pallas | scelerato ex sanguine sumit*, 948–9), is undercut, rather than endorsed, by the Stoicizing narrative characterization of Aeneas' passionate state of mind: *furiis accensus et*

---

[42] For this policy, see *Aen.* 11.109–19 (coupled with a sense of generalized pathos and an absence of reactive attitudes, such as anger or bitterness, either directed against the Italians or Turnus), also 12.313–17. For indications of deflection from this policy, see 12.486–99, 554–60, 565–6.

[43] Cf. 12.569–73, esp. "I shall tear up," *eruam*, with 7.315–19, esp. "tear apart," *exscindere*; the related contrast with the fated outcome of events is signaled in both 12.503–4 (see also 12.791–842) and 7.313–14.

[44] See p. 217.

ira | terribilis, feruidus (946–7, 951). I have suggested elsewhere that this language, taken with Aeneas' self-distancing attribution of vengeance to Pallas, marks Aeneas' change of mind (in 940–4) as "akratic" or contrary to his better judgment. It aligns the passage to others, in this poem and elsewhere, in which, in a Stoicizing pattern, the surrender to passion is presented as falling short of what the person involved is, at his or her best, capable of achieving (Gill [1997a] 239–41).

One question that has not, I think, been much pursued is how we should understand the kind of response which Aeneas *might have given* to Turnus if he had not been swayed by the sight of Pallas' sword-belt in 941–4. Turnus, adopting a suppliant stance (931–2), invites the reactive attitude of pity (*miserere*, 933). Aeneas, we know, can react in this way, as he does with the dying Lausus ("pitying . . . pitiable boy," *miserans, miserande puer*, 10.823, 825). But he can also respond with a more generalized, even cosmic, "pity," which is closer to the response advocated by Stoics such as Epictetus and Marcus.[45] It is clear that Aeneas' wrath in Book 12 is partly patterned on that of Achilles in the later books of the *Iliad*. Achilles' wrath against Hector terminates in his positive response to Priam's supplication, in which a reactive attitude of pity is coupled with a more "cosmic" vision of shared human vulnerability to misfortune (24.486–551). The underlying presence of that paradigm, combined with earlier examples in which Aeneas responds with an objective attitude, informed by a cosmic perspective, may serve to suggest the kind of response which Aeneas, in this case, fails to give. A more immediate exemplar is the preceding divine dialogue in which Juno lays down her reactive anger and bitterness against the Trojans and reaches agreement with Jupiter about the future merger of the Trojan and Italian nations and cultures (12.791–842, esp. 800–2, 830–40). If this is the best way to interpret Aeneas' interrupted response, this supports further the view, taken here, that Aeneas' reactive response of anger in 12.945–9 is presented, at least by implication, as marking a deflection from the highest possible standard of attitude and action.

I am well aware that other scholars take an opposing view of this scene, and have grounds for doing so; nor have I framed this discussion to try to settle the interpretation of a text which is, perhaps ineluctably, both complex and ambiguous. What I have wanted to do is to sharpen our conceptual and critical means for defining this complexity by the distinction between reactive and objective attitudes and by linking this distinction with various ancient philosophical approaches. I am aware that this line of enquiry

[45] See the preceding discussion of *Aen.* 2.567–623, esp. 601–2; 8.537–40; 11.42–58; also 11.108–19.

could be taken much further, by a more systematic study of the language of emotion in Virgil's poem and of its cultural and conceptual background. I also recognize that the kind of interpretation offered here would make most sense for philosophically trained contemporary readers, though I think that for other readers too the poem constructs a framework for validating objective rather than reactive attitudes. Overall, I feel confident that the outcome of juxtaposing more closely the ancient philosophical debate about anger and Roman or later Greek representations of anger can only be instructive; and in the present chapter I have tried to take a further step in this direction.

CHAPTER 10

The angry poet and the angry gods: problems of theodicy in Lucan's epic of defeat

Elaine Fantham

Victrix causa deis placuit sed uicta . . . poetae. Despite a general assumption that Lucan kept the gods out of his epic, I would argue that he simply kept them out of engagement on the battlefield. If we are rightly curious about why he omitted divine causality from his opening enumeration of causes for the civil war, it is not long before his narrative provides portents in plenty to demonstrate divine anger to the Romans and to his readers. And the poet himself repeatedly reproaches the gods, but is far from consistent in his reproaches: at times he accuses them of active hostility to Roman liberty; on other occasions he seems only to blame them for inertia or indifference. Once, but only once, he will go so far as to assert that "they do not exist – or at least not for us," the Romans: *sunt nobis nulla profecto | numina* (7.445–6). But within ten lines he has corrected himself. The gods do exist: they are simply Epicurean gods "who do not care about mankind": *mortalia nulli | sunt curata deo* (454–5). Indeed Lucan ends the same outburst by holding them responsible for the Pompeian defeat, when he interprets the deified line of Caesars as the good republicans' revenge upon the Olympians – retaliation for purposive divine action.

And purposive divine action is the norm before and after the poet's self-generated crisis in the thick of battle. But Lucan's epic comes to us with a lot of baggage: the historiographical inheritance of Livy's teleology of empire, and its counterpart, the epic inheritance of Virgil's providential *fata*. Superficially in Virgil the best man/nation wins and the divine superstructure is merely retarded by the misguided Juno's obstruction, providing the necessary narrative deferral. Lucan's uncle Seneca believed in a providential Stoic deity, and might have been expected to find a level of interpretation of the Caesarian civil war which directed a higher kind of victory toward the just and proper side. And so he does, whenever he is focused on the moral victory of Cato, and his choice of death as liberty from Caesar. But Seneca's far fewer allusions to the events of the civil war at a communal, political, level[1] accept the triumph of might over right without attempting to explore the theological implications: compare the early *De ira* 2.2.3–4: *quis non contra Mari arma, contra Sullae proscriptionem concitatur? quis non Theodoto et Achillae et ipso puero non puerile auso facinus infestus est?* ("Who is not roused against the weapons of Marius, against Sulla's proscription? Who is not incensed against Theodotus and Achillas and the boy himself who dared an un-boyish crime?") Indeed his sense of human anger against tyrannical injustice is closely linked here to the power of song and imagery to stir men's indignation: *cantus nos nonnumquam et citata modulatio instigat Martiusque ille tubarum sonus; mouet mentes et atrox pictura et iustissimorum suppliciorum tristis aspectus* ("Singing sometimes stirs us and quickened rhythm and the familiar sound of Mars's trumpets. Our minds are affected by a shocking picture and by the gloomy sight of punishments even when they are just"). *Cantus* ("singing") and *modulatio* ("rhythm") evoke the form, and war and suffering the content, of epic, and Lucan, *ardens et concitatus* ("fiery and passionate," Quint. *Inst.* 10.1.90), is above all the epic poet of indignation. A major section of this chapter will explore the anger expressed by our poet and his republican protagonists, Cato and Pompey, against the gods for Caesar's victory. Against the extravagantly self-contradictory tirade at Pharsalus we can pit a whole range of explicit and implicit reproaches to the gods which mount in volume up to and around the death of their victim, Pompey.

And the victorious Caesar? On the one occasion when the gods are challenged by Caesar himself to vent their anger upon him, nothing happens. If success is confirmation of divine support, he has it until the last phase of the unfinished poem at Alexandria[2] and as history confirmed, for four years beyond.

I would like to start from some general implications of using divine retribution in historical narrative before treating in more detail Lucan's chief Augustan predecessors: Livy, his historiographical source, and Virgil, his epic antimodel. For Livy we now have the useful monograph of David Levene, *Religion in Livy*, to which I believe I can add some nuances relevant to my particular focus. For Virgil I will naturally be building on Feeney's splendid *Gods in Epic*, but also reconsidering ideas from Gordon Williams' unjustly neglected *Technique and Ideas in Virgil's Aeneid.*[3]

---

[1] For some Senecan discussions on the significance of Cato and his exemplary suicide cf. *Prou.* 2.9–12; 3.14; *Constant.* 1.3; 2.2–3; *Tranq.* 9.16; *Ep.* 14.2–13; 95.69–71; 98.8; 104.29–33. On the cause of Pompey and its survivors in Africa see *Ep.* 24.9; 71.8–10, also comment on individual republicans at *Ben.* 1.10.2; 2.20; 3.24; 5.17.2; 5.24.

[2] Here I am dissenting from the eloquent but to me unconvincing readings of Haffter (1957) 118–26; Masters (1992) 244–59; and John Henderson (1987) modified in Henderson (1998) 171–6.

[3] G. Williams (1983); Feeney (1991); Levene (1995).

After this opening section and a brief survey of explicit references to divine anger in Lucan, I want to consider how Lucan short-circuits the issue of justification through Roman guilt, and carries through the notion of divine support for Caesar even when it seems to be challenged by circumstance. In the third section I focus on the poet's own anger against divine jurisdiction for destroying liberty and its defenders: as a corollary we will have to judge whether the increasing prominence of a Caesarophiliac *Fortuna* is the poet's device to disengage the personal and collective gods above (*superi*) – and if so, how far he has succeeded. An epilogue returns to Caesar and advances some arguments for seeing him as the chosen instrument of divine punishment in Lucan's poem.

IRA DEORUM AND ITS ROLE IN HISTORIOGRAPHY AND EPIC BEFORE LUCAN

Discussion of divine anger is inevitably tied to the larger subject of divine justice. It will be useful, I think, to go back to the basic presuppositions behind human assumption of divine anger. In Homeric epic the gods are not judged: we can read their acts as just punishment or as self-interested, even arrogant, retaliation. Often mythology shows the gods as all-powerful, but behaving at best like kings, at worst like angry tyrants. Mortals are punished or metamorphosed by individual gods for competing or even comparing themselves to a god; they are treated like servants, disobedient or disloyal to their masters. The anger of a god, Apollo, opens the *Iliad* although its proclaimed and continuing theme is the anger of a human, Achilles. The anger of a god instigates tragic actions like the *Hippolytus* and *Trojan Women* of Euripides. In the *Iliad* the sins of the leaders are visited on the people: *quicquid delirant reges plectuntur Achiui* ("whatever folly the kings commit, the Achaeans pay for it").[4] In Euripides *anaitioi*, women and "innocent" non-combatants, suffer in divine punishment of a prince or a nation.

It seems that in classical Greek thought an increasing expectation of divine morality and justice cannot completely expel the older amoral reading of divine control. Anger is refined into the concept of retribution or righteous anger, yet not just the skeptic Euripides but even Herodotus, whose narrative generally represents victory and defeat as morally deserved divine dispensations, offers occasions when speakers read the gods collectively as jealous and destructive.[5]

---

[4] Hor. *Epistles* 1.2.; Parker (1996: ch. 8, 241–2) notes that the gods were expected to respond to the offenses of kings by causing suffering to their whole people.

[5] I am thinking of Solon's words in 1.32, where he warns Croesus of impending ruin by representing the gods (*to theion*) as both jealous and troublemaking.

But just as men in a community seek an explanation of the disease or bereavement of individuals, so the historian looks to divine action for an explanation of natural disasters like plague and flood, or the military defeats of societies.[6] If the gods are both all-powerful and just, then a defeated or ruined nation must have offended; or if no recent offense can be identified, the offense must have been incurred either by its individual leader or by a past generation.[7] Again the recording historian or poet will show a different attitude to the misfortunes of the enemy – for which it is easy to blame breaches of oath or treaty or other impious behavior – and to those of his own society. If a nation suffers a setback, it is relatively easy, as Parker notes, for that society to blame disaster on a ritual error, since it can then be cancelled out by ritual expiation.[8] Or there is the alternative, for both the society and its historians, of producing a scientific rather than a religious explanation, and blaming defeat on the incompetence of a commander. Given a relatively sophisticated society like classical Athens or Rome, its writers of history will prefer these scientific or tactical explanations for the defeats to their own people, and reserve for theodicy events set in the mythical past, or episodes that cannot be otherwise explained. But material and moral explanations can also be combined: this is how modern writers account for ecological disaster such as the dreadful floods of 1999 as caused by, for example, global warming, itself the product of the developed nations' misuse of the atmosphere.

Divine anger was so established by the time of Rome's first poets that it is a regular trope in Plautus and Terence. Besides actual *poena/-ae* ("punishments") there is no obvious equivalent of retribution,[9] but ideas of justice or propriety are invoked at, for example, *Rudens* 1146, *tibi hercle deos iratos esse oportet* ("the gods ought to be angry with you"). Most often divine anger is inferred from past misfortune, but it may instead be grounded in a moral judgment that some action ought to incur a future penalty.[10] The

---

[6] Here I am following the general argument of Parker (1996), ch. 8 and 9. But Parker (237–8) uses the contrast with Judaism and Old Testament narrative to bring out the relative willingness of the Greeks to see, for example, disease as sent in divine caprice.

[7] See Parker (1996) 201–2.   [8] Parker (1996) 271–8.

[9] *Indignatio*, righteous anger, which might have served the purpose, never conveys actual retribution, and is primarily the name of a rhetorical figure.

[10] Misfortune: (supposedly congenital) Plaut. *Mil.* 314, *quis magis dis inimicis natus quam te atque iratis*; *Mostell.* 564; cf. Augustus on the deformity of Claudius: Sen. *Apocol.* 11.3, *corpus eius dis iratis natum*; in reaction to a single calamity: Plaut. *Poen.* 452, 465, 645; Ter. *Phorm.* 74; judgmental statements: Plaut. *Curc.* 557 (the gods have been propitiated and so ought not to be angry with the speaker); and a nice combination of inference at Ter. *An.* 664, *mi deos [satis scio] iratos fuisse qui auscultauerim*, followed by the eavesdropper's curse, 666, *at tibi dignum factis exitium duint*. In *Amphitryo*, where gods are also scheming intriguers, their comments and curses at 392, 934 and 1022, *tibi Iuppiter dique omnes irati certo sint*, play ironically on the normal usage.

everyday invocation of angry gods in comedy will have its equivalent in the rhetoric of more formal genres.

So consider now the task of the Hellenistic or Roman historian: not just as a composer of tragic histories in which human offenses are shown to produce their downfall, but as a writer of the continuous history of his own nation from its humble origins. The work of a universal historian like Livy must follow his own society from a legendary age into a barely known early Republic before he reaches the periods when international warfare with Pyrrhus or Hannibal was documented by more or less contemporary Greeks. How will he handle religious causality? When will he invoke the anger of the gods, and when will he interpret events only on a political and military level? And is there a way he can have his scientific causation and still exploit the theme of divine anger and punishment? This topic has been handled most recently by David Levene, working from the previous assessments of Walsh[11] and Liebeschuetz.[12]

Levene constructs his study around four questions, of which the most important is: "what phenomena [can] be taken as indicative of divine intervention into human affairs and what [does] such intervention indicate?"[13] After reviewing the implications of the prodigies, auspices, and omens that Romans read as divine warnings or expressions of anger, he turns to the considerable variation in Livy's presentation of prodigy lists from one decade to another. His book is in fact constructed around finding explanations, often in terms of literary choice, for the omission or displacement of prodigy lists, and other forms of supernatural intervention.

But at the same time, Levene shows by close examination of the relevant texts how Livy avoids committing himself either to faith or to skepticism about the divine control of history, largely framing allusions to religion within citation of tradition or divergent reportage. In reviewing only the more limited passages in which Livy, and indeed Virgil and Lucan, allude to divine anger, I will rely more on Levene's second mode of analysis than his first, which seems to me more subjective. We will see that many of Livy's allusions to manifestations of divine anger are distanced by attributing them either to tradition or to specific sources, while others occur in speeches, and even in the speeches of suspect characters.

Straight theological explanation for "acts of god," natural disasters, and national defeat, are most common in Livy's first decade; of the twenty-two allusions to divine anger in the first pentad about two-thirds report events

---

[11] Walsh (1961) ch. 3, esp. 57 n. 3 and 68–9.   [12] Liebeschuetz (1967) and (1979).
[13] Modified from Levene (1995) 1.

as manifestations of divine anger; four are against individuals – the *praua religio* ("faulty religious observance") of Tullus Hostilius which led to his death by thunderbolt (1.31.8), the murderous impiety and pollution of the Penates by Tullia (1.48.7), the refusal of Latinius to obey a recurrent dream ordering him to warn the senate of a violation of the *Ludi Magni* (2.36.6), and the death of the blasphemer Annius.[14] But Levene notes that in 9.29.11 both the blinding of Appius Claudius and the extinction of the Potitius family are merely ascribed "by tradition" (*traditur*) to the wanton changing of ritual. Livy does not dispute this, but neither does he take responsibility for it.[15]

At the level of national misfortune, a plague is read as divine anger (3.6.5) and met with supplications to appease the gods in 3.7.8, as happens again after another plague in 7.2.4 and 3.3. In the latter case theatrical games are devised as "appeasements of divine anger" (*caelestis irae placamina*) but a Tiber flood shows "the gods [have] rejected the acts of appeasement" (*dis aspernantibus placamina irae*). In contrast to his straight narrative of divine retribution against Veii in Book 5,[16] Livy reports without endorsement a senatorial speech attributing a plague at Rome to the recent election of plebeian consular tribunes (5.14.4). On the other hand, references to divine anger at 13.6.11 and 13.9.10, as in 10.28.17, occur in the serious context of the ritual "self-sacrifice" of *deuotio*.[17]

In general Livy offers alongside genuine invocation of "divine anger" (*deorum irae*) a number of rhetorical uses: in an oath at 2.45.14, and as a figure or trope in speeches at 3.9.7; 5.11.16; 9.1.3 and 11; and 9.11.10. The last cases are surely to be discounted, since they come from Pontius the Samnite.[18]

---

[14] This instance (8.6.4) nicely illustrates the disclaiming of responsibility by referring to different sources; some *auctores* had a crash from heaven and others had Annius actually killed "whether the tales are true or invented as a fit representation of divine anger," *et uera esse, et apte ad repraesentandum iram deorum ficta.*

[15] 9.29.19, *traditur inde, dictu mirabile, et quod dimouendis statu suo sacris religionem facere posset . . . omnes intra annum cum stirpe exstinctos.*

[16] Compare the Veientine error in electing a king (5.1), the omens anticipating divine desertion in 5.15–16, and the references to *fata* framing the narrative of the city's capture in 5.19.1 and 22.8.

[17] Cf. 8.6.11, *placuit auerruncandae deum irae uictimas caedi*; 8.9.10, *sicut caelo missus piaculum deorum irae qui pestem ab suis auersam in hostes ferret*; 10.28.17 reports the younger Decius' repetition of his father's formula of *deuotio* to divert onto the enemy *caelestium inferorumque iras.* Besides the instance of divine retribution for Annius' sacrilege (8.6.4 above), 8.33.7 refers to public prayers *quae saepe deorum iras placant.*

[18] Pontius is at pains to argue that the gods have forgiven past Samnite offenses and are now acting with the Samnites against the Romans: cf. 9.1.3, *expiatum est quicquid ex foedere rupto irarum in nos caelestium fuit,* and 11.10, *nec moror quo minus in civitatem † oblectam † sponsione commissa* **iratis** *omnibus dis, quorum eluditur numen, redeant.*

Livy is understandably more restrained in alluding to divine anger during the prolonged phase of defeat and loss in the Hannibalic war narrative. While Trasimene and Cannae and their aftermath do indeed produce a number of references to religious offenses by the guilty commanders,[19] and to the attitudes of the gods, there is no literal report of divine anger. However, four successive speeches allude to the attitudes of the gods[20] before Fabius Pictor is sent to Delphi to find out "what kind of offerings can appease them" (*quibus precibus suppliciisque deos possent placare*, 22.57.5). But the few specific references to divine anger in these books all occur in speeches: a blasphemous speech by the disloyal Hirpini (23.42.4), an unconvincing speech by the deserters from Cannae (25.6.6), an honest enough speech by the Locrian envoys about the anger of Proserpina against Pleminius (29.18.10), and a brief witticism by Fabius Cunctator rejecting as plunder the gigantic Tarentine statues of their war gods (27.16.8): "Let them keep their angry gods!" And one might add from the fifth decade Perseus' dishonest exploitation of the concept when he accuses his brother of plotting the death of his father, Philip.[21] The only other event attributed to divine anger is the fate of Fulvius Flaccus (42.28.12), sent mad by Juno Lacinia after he plundered her roof-tiles to adorn his own Roman temple, where his offense has just been extensively denounced by "all without exception" (*uniuersi*) in the Roman senate. And it should be noted that such generally attributed speeches seem to be a favorite vehicle in Livy for allusions to the right relations between men and gods.

There is one occasion in our extant books when Livy seems to treat civil war as a manifestation of divine anger. He introduces the tale of the maid of Ardea in Book 4 with a comment comparing the internal "strife of factions" with "famine and plague and such other things as men attribute to divine anger as being the worst of public misfortunes" (4.9.3).[22] This reaction to civil conflict may serve as an indication of how Livy presented civil strife in the introduction to the *causae ciuilium armorum et initia* ("causes and beginnings of civil conflict") of the Caesarian civil war in the lost book 109.

---

[19] Note in particular Fabius' speech after Trasimene, 22.9.7: *quaeque piacula irae deum essent deos ipsos consulendos esse.*

[20] 22.49.7; 51.4; 53.11; 55.5. Note that in 54.8 Livy withdraws from his own narrative, which suggests that he may have offered a precedent for Lucan's famous refusal to narrate at 7.552–6. Here is Livy's counterpart: *itaque succumbam oneri neque adgrediar narrare quae edissertando minora uero faciam.*

[21] 40.10.2: but cf. Livy's own comment at 40.5.1.

[22] *frui namque pace optimo consilio cum populo Romano seruata per intestina arma non licuit, quorum causa atque initium traditur ex certamine factionis ortum, quae fuerunt eruntque pluribus populis exitio quam bella externa, quam fames morbiue, quaeque alia in deum iras uelut ultima publicorum malorum uertunt.* Note that the antecedent of *quae* is probably the explicit plural *arma* rather than a plural extrapolated from *factione*, but both are causally linked.

If we turn to Livy's contemporary Virgil, with epic's greater license for representation of divine action and motivation, the first sentence introduces Juno's anger as cause of Aeneas' sufferings: *saeuae memorem Iunonis ob iram* ("because of savage Juno's unforgiving anger," 1.4). Juno's anger will be responsible for more than the opening storm of the *Aeneid*, but her interventions, familiar material, are no index of the larger divine justice that prevails in the outcome. Instead I will look at Jupiter, who, as Feeney says, refrains from anger in Virgil's epic. So he does, but anger is part of his nature and function as ruler of gods and men.

Thus in the account of Hades we read how Jupiter wielded his thunderbolt to punish the blaspheming Salmoneus (6.585–94) and in his account of the forging of Jupiter's weapon of retribution Virgil includes both fear and anger, *fulgures terrificos sonitumque metumque . . . flammisque sequacibus iras* ("terrifying flashes and sound and fear and rage with pursuing flames," 8.431–2). Human fear of divine anger, like the subjects' fear of the angry tyrant, is the strongest demonstration of power, which is why *ira* forms the climax of Virgil's list here and elsewhere.

Three cities meet their doom in the *Aeneid*, if we include the doom of Carthage imaged at the end of Book 4 (669–71).[23] In Virgil's account of the fall of Troy divine anger dominates as the overwhelming causality. The Romans saw the justification of Troy's doom in Laomedon's original perjury and deception of the gods, but since the narrator of Troy's fall is the Trojan Aeneas, his reaction to the divine verdict is limited to his personal experience, and colored by his sense of injustice. From the moment when Panthus reports the departure of the gods from their altars (2.351–2), Aeneas' account is full of reproach: against Minerva who fails to save her priestess from rape: *heu nihil inuitis fas quemquam credere diuis!* ("Alas, in nothing may one trust the gods if they are unwilling," 402), lamenting the death of the just man Ripheus (*dis aliter uisum,* "the gods decided otherwise," 428), and quoting the climactic conclusion of Venus' apocalypse: *diuum inclementia, diuum | has euertit opes, sternitque a culmine Troiam* ("it is the gods, the relentless gods, that overturn these riches and topple Troy from her height," 602–3). *Inclementia* ("relentlessness") is a term of blame, and Aeneas' own report adds to this a note of destructive evil: the gods appear as *dirae facies, inimicaque Troiae | numina magna deum* ("terrible shapes, the mighty powers of the gods, hostile to Troy," 622–3). Even the epithet *dirae* ("terrible") evokes the dreadfulness of avenging furies who will be Jupiter's

---

[23] From the beginning of the *Aeneid* (1.20, *Tyrias olim quae uerteret arces*) Virgil has foreshadowed the fall of Carthage to Rome in the second century BC. Within Book 4 equally Dido's downfall is foreshadowed by sinister omens and prodigies (4.452–65).

last and nastiest servants in bringing the epic to a close.[24] Neither in Book 2 nor later will Virgil repeat his earlier acknowledgment of *Laomedontiae periuria Troiae*, "the broken oath of King Laomedon" that incurred this divine action.[25] In contrast, Aeneas' own family receives an act of divine forgiveness. Anchises argues that he is doomed, because Jupiter struck him down as an offender when he betrayed Venus' secret: *iampridem inuisus diuis et inutilis annos | demoror, ex quo me diuum pater atque hominum rex | fulminis adflauit uentis* ("Long hated by the gods and useless I have lingered ever since the father of the gods and king of men breathed on me with the winds of his thunderbolt," 2.647–9). But now, in response to his prayer, Jupiter sends his thunder again – as a favorable omen on the left, and when Virgil returns to Anchises in the next book he has become *cura deum* ("the gods' concern," 3.476).

Aeneas' narrative is filled with anger – of gods, and Greeks, of the dying Priam and Aeneas himself, to a degree we will not meet again until Juno's anger in Book 7 exploits the Fury (*Dira*) Allecto to enrage individuals and communities. But Virgil is too much of an artist to limit himself to an unambiguous code of *irae*. In Book 7 when Juno launches into her great speech of *indignatio* ("indignation"), her grievance is that she has not been allowed to sate her anger as Jupiter indulged Diana's angry destruction of Calydon (*concessit in iras | ipse deum genitor*, 305). But after Allecto spreads her infection it is human anger that takes over and dominates the books.[26]

It is as though divine anger subsides when it is absorbed by human combatants. In the early conflict of Book 10 Virgil offers the surprising contrast of pity for the futility of human anger shown not only by Juno for Turnus but by Hercules, Jupiter,[27] and all the gods: *di Iouis in tectis iram miserantur inanem | amborum* ("the gods in Jupiter's house pity the useless anger of both," 10.758–9). After the Latin defeat the multiple casualties of

---

[24] Cf. 12.845, *geminae pestes cognomine Dirae*, anticipated by the description of Celaeno in 3.211–15, *insulae Ionio in magno quas* **dira** *Celaeno | Harpyiaeque colunt aliae . . . | tristius haud illis monstrum, nec saeuior ulla | **pestis et ira deum**.

[25] This offense is Virgil's own explanation for Roman suffering in the civil war at *Georgics* 1.502; cf. Hor. *Odes* 3.3.27. Priam's grandfather Laomedon broke his promise to reward the gods Apollo and Neptune for constructing the walls of Troy.

[26] While most readers have resisted the claim of G. Williams (1983) that Virgil's gods are tropes for the motivation of human players, there is a much stronger case for reading Allecto in this way; see G. Williams (1983) 24: "by this stage the poet has enough confidence in the reader's ability to understand Allecto's actions as a trope so as to indulge in a figural expansion that brings the action of the Fury to the very border of allegory. For essentially this whole series of scenes is a figure, related to personification and allegory, designed to represent the way in which at times certain emotions seem almost to achieve an independent existence so that the same pattern of behavior springs up spontaneously in various places."

[27] Juno for Turnus 10.611–20; Hercules for Pallas and Jupiter's past grief for Sarpedon, 10.464–72.

this battle are read by Latinus, in the first explicit evocation of *ira deum*, as "divine anger" at his people's breach of the treaty with Aeneas: here indeed we might talk in Williams' terms of a trope, since divine anger appears as a gloss or an inference from the mention of "graves" (11.232–3):[28]

> fatalem Aenean manifesto numine ferri
> admonet ira deum tumulique ante ora recentes.

That Aeneas is summoned by fate, with clear divine intent, is the warning given by the anger of the gods and the fresh graves before his eyes.

Turnus duly answers in Latinus' terms, although he tries to reject this reading of the defeat: he promises single combat as a sort of *deuotio*, whether his death is needed to dispel divine anger, or as he would prefer, he will fight to win glory through valor.[29] Divine anger and its symbolism return with the implied rejection by Pallas Athene of the Latin women's supplication (11.477–81) and the relentless progress in Book 12 from the violated truce to the sack of Latinus' city – the third city to fall in the epic narrative – and death of Turnus. Feeney has pointed out how Virgil's authorial protests highlight the impropriety of anger in his gods and Jupiter's decision for war at the beginning and end of his epic: *tantaene animis caelestibus irae?* ("Can divine breasts rage so fiercely?" 1.11) and: *tantone placuit concurrere motu, | Iuppiter, aeterna gentes in pace futuras?* ("Was it your wish, Jupiter, that peoples that would live in everlasting peace should clash in such a huge upheaval?" 12.503–4).

This protest against divinely induced civil war[30] is perhaps the only explicit proof that the poet, or at least one aspect of his value system, shared the Stoic belief that anger was alien to the divine nature, in fact unworthy of the gods.[31] Yet the worst divine malice comes after Virgil's protest, and seems to answer his indignant question affirmatively, first with Jupiter's pleased recognition of his own angry nature in Juno (12.830–1):

> es germana Iouis Saturnique altera proles
> irarum tantos uoluis sub pectore fluctus.

You are the genuine sister of Jupiter, Saturn's other child, so huge are the waves of rage that surge beneath your breast.

---

[28] This is confirmed by the reported speech of Diomedes, 11.305: *bellum . . . cum gente deorum | inuictisque uiris gerimus.*

[29] 11.443–4, *nec Drances potius, siue haec est ira deorum | morte luat, siue uirtus et gloria, tollat.*

[30] "Civil war," because in the same phrase Virgil stresses the destined unity of Latins and Trojans.

[31] This is argued or even assumed not only by the Epicureans (cf. Lucretius 2.646–51; Cic. *Pis.* 59; *Nat. D.* 1.45; 3.91) but by the Stoics and by Cicero himself in *Nat. D.* 1.45; 2.70, 167; 3. 90–1 and *De officiis* 3.104, as it will be again by Seneca, for example *De ira* 2.27.

Anger, then, is Jupiter's own characteristic, and Ovid is not the only one to see anger as *Ioue digna* ("right for Jupiter").[32] Almost immediately after this admission comes the savage symbolism of the Dira (845, 865), sent by Jupiter to annihilate Turnus. In narrative terms, Turnus' collapse springs directly from his long-delayed recognition that the gods are against him. What paralyzes him with fear is not his adversary Aeneas, but divine anger: *di me terrent et Iuppiter hostis* ("What terrifies me is the gods and Jupiter's hostility," 895).

Much of this is only too familiar, but I have recalled it in order to contrast Virgil's representations of both divine and human anger with what Lucan will make of them. In Virgil there is certainly pity for those punished by the gods and protests from both speakers like Aeneas and the poet himself against divine actions. Human anger is shown in contrast as pitiable, largely harmful to the protagonists and ultimately futile. Only Aeneas as the man of destiny is allowed to succumb to anger without suffering for it; this may not be ethical justice but it is fated.

FROM VIRGIL TO LUCAN: THE GODS OFF-STAGE

Before considering the helpful treatment by Feeney (1991) of this aspect of the divine in Lucan, let me return for a moment to the more provocative comment of G. Williams (1983): "Lucan is . . . useful in showing one advantage the poet won from using a divine machinery. Lucan dispensed with gods in his epic: one result of this is a constant series of authorial invasions on [*sic*] the text to provide explanation, or rather, to ensure that the reader will view the particular events in the same way as the poet does."[33] He himself goes on to point out that Lucan will have found it advantageous "to enter his own text in person." I would go further. Lucan had always wanted to enter his own text, and when he does he often implicates the gods in his comments. He did not "dispense with" the gods, but constantly returns to their supposed responsibility for the vicissitudes of the narrative.

Feeney approaches the gods in Lucan through a preliminary discussion of historiography: he argues that characterful narration of divine actions is the irreducible line of demarcation between epic and history: on this he cites the verdict of Kroll, "epic achieves its characteristic effect through stunning and extraordinary displays of power to which the gods above all contribute."[34] After all, as Feeney reminds us, Caesar is confronted by a

---

[32] See *Met.* 1.166 with the comment of Feeney (1991) 199.   [33] G. Williams (1983) 17.
[34] Feeney (1991) 261, citing Kroll "Das Historische Epos" in *Sokrates* N.F. 4 (1916) 1–14 (not accessible to me).

reproachful fatherland (*Patria*) even before he takes the first hostile step of crossing the Rubicon: in reply, he affirms that he is following Fortune,[35] and soon after he guarantees his men divine support (*nec numina derunt*, 1.349). But it is true, and perhaps surprising, that Lucan has omitted the gods from his opening analysis of the human motives and causes for the war, shifting the divine causes to the end of Book 1 and beginning of Book 2.[36] This separation detaches from the horrors of civil war the offenses of the leaders and people of Rome which Lucan could have chosen to present explicitly as incurring divine punishment: there is, for example, no hint of the impiety of the preceding generation of civil wars. Why do the reminiscences of the aged survivor from the civil wars of Marius and Sulla include no declaration of Roman responsibility for the impious atrocities described?

No doubt these omissions are why Feeney (272) suggests that the opening statement of Book 2, *iamque irae patuere deum* ("And now the gods' anger was patent") is not enough, because "curiously, there is no explanation or description of the divine anger." And yet Lucan has set an expansive description of prodigies and Roman response to them in the last 185 lines of Book 1, prodigies introduced in terms of divine dispensation: *o facilis dare summa deos eademque tueri | difficiles!* ("O gods, so ready to bestow supremacy, so reluctant to preserve it!" 1.510–11).[37] Indeed this exclamation bears out two further points in Feeney's analysis: that Lucan seems to believe in the gods, continually addressing them and affecting to attribute to them motives and intention but that as poet he equally consistently has no access to "the operation of the divine" and "is radically uncertain of everything to do with their motives and meanings."[38]

In a useful survey of how varying Roman authors construed divine responsibility for the civil wars, Paul Jal[39] distinguished between texts which blame men for causing war through their impiety against the gods, and those which instead reproach the gods themselves for their passivity in the face of civil war. But it is not so simple or uniform: in discussing Lucan alone

---

[35] The apostrophe *te, Fortuna, sequor* (1.206) is more than a figure here; it sets up a rival deity: as Patria waves him back, Fortuna supposedly calls Caesar forward.

[36] Note, however, *inuida fatorum series* in 1.71 and the framing allusions to the amoral Fortuna (1.84 and 160).

[37] These prodigies were reserved by Virgil in *Georgics* 1.466 onwards for celestial grief at the death of Caesar. Did they occur at the moment of Caesar's invasion in Livy's narrative? We cannot infer anything from their omission from the Periocha of Book 109. They were probably in Livy, since they occur in Appian *B Ciu.* 2.36; however, they are not found in Dio or Plutarch's *Lives* of Caesar and Pompey.

[38] Feeney (1991) 274 and (quoted) 278.   [39] Jal (1962) 170–200.

Jal detected and isolated three or four different attitudes to the gods: that of Cato (normally a spokesman for the poet's belief) who claims his own reluctant participation will be a charge to level against the gods (2.288), and progressively more angry reactions in the poet's own voice. While Lucan at times depicts the gods as indifferent spectators at a gladiatorial show (*parque suum uidere dei*, "the gods saw their paired opponents," 6.3), his assumption of divine injustice becomes more frequent as he approaches the defeat of the Republic and its leader. Jal also notes accusations by the poet of divine jealousy and trickery.[40] It is worth pausing to examine two of Jal's passages more closely. In 4.243–5 Lucan is protesting at the resumption of hostilities in Spain after the brief *concordia* of fraternization between the armies:

> itur in omne nefas, et quae Fortuna deorum
> inuidia caeca bellorum in nocte tulisset
> fecit monstra fides.

I was happy to see that Susanna Braund (1992) and I read this in the same way: "They proceed to every guilt, and their loyalty commits horrors which if Fortune had inflicted them in battle's blind night would have been to the gods' discredit." This is surely right, rather than Jane Joyce's "to spite the gods," and is supported by other references to *inuidia*.[41] At 4.807–9 the poet is more explicit: Rome would have been blessed and had happy citizens "if the gods above had cared as much for our liberty as for revenge": *si libertatis superis tam cura placeret | quam uindicta placet*; only Tacitus would take this further in the opening of his *Histories*: *non esse dis curam securitatem nostram, esse ultionem* ("the gods are concerned not for our safety but for our punishment," 1.3). Yet neither in Lucan nor Tacitus are we told what Roman deeds the civil wars were sent to punish: are we to assume the vicious circle that these civil wars were merely punishment for earlier, less world-wide, civil wars?

There is no doubt that the anger of the gods which opens Lucan's second book is designed to echo Virgil's account of the fall of Troy in the fall of the free Roman Republic. This is why despite four or five allusions to divine anger in Book 1[42] Lucan holds back his statement of revelation until Book 2, "And now the gods' anger was patent." This is his equivalent of Venus' apocalypse, and is followed by explicit assumption of divine volition;

---

[40] This is implied by his report of Pompey's response to the pressure of Cicero 7.86, *ingemuit rector*.
[41] 2.35, *nullis defuit aris | inuidiam factura parens*.
[42] 1.510, *o faciles dare summa deos eademque tueri | difficiles*; 524, *superi . . . minaces*; 617, *atque iram superum raptis quaesiuit in extis*; 649, *quod cladis genus, o superi, qua peste paratis | saeuitiam?*

forty lines later, when Rome's fighting men beg the gods *date gentibus iras* (47), we should seriously consider translating this not just as "instill anger in the barbarians" but "give *your* anger to the barbarians." Let them attack Rome so that our fighting may be proper war, not civil war. Divine anger is reiterated at 2.85 in the strange phrase that describes the exiled Marius as *superum protectus ab ira*: he is not "protected from divine anger" but "protected *by* divine anger" – against Rome, so that he can begin its destruction.[43]

After establishing divine hostility to Rome in Books 1–2 Lucan returns to the gods only to display their indifference to sacrilege. Caesar's anger which opened the epic[44] returns when he reenters the narrative at 2.493[45] and dominates the action at Rome,[46] where he plunders the temple of Saturn scot-free, and at Massilia. Here, when his men hesitate to fell the trees of a grove sacred to unknown Gallic gods, Caesar like a modern Erysichthon seizes his axe and attacks a tree: *iam ne quis uestrum dubitet subuertere siluam | credite me fecisse nefas* ("Now none of you need hesitate to cut down the wood: believe that the guilt is mine!" 3.436–7).[47] When his men obey, the poet adds it is not because they no longer fear the supernatural powers, but they fear Caesar's anger more (*expensa superorum et Caesaris ira*, 3.439). Caesar's anger is more immediate. The Massilian youth are glad, hopeful that their gods will punish such impiety: *quis enim laesos impune putaret | esse deos?* ("Who would imagine that the gods are injured without taking revenge?" 3.447–8). But Caesar's success shows the limitations of the gods. Like Fortune they "leave the wicked unharmed and can only be angry with the unfortunate": *seruat multos fortuna nocentes, | et tantum miseris irasci numina possunt* (3.448–9).

Caesar's enjoyment of divine favor is confirmed more indirectly by Lucan's presentation of the mutiny of Book 5: the ringleaders boast that "for all the favor of the gods, Caesar will not be able to fight his war without his soldiers" (*licet omne deorum | obsequium speres, irato milite, Caesar, | pax erit*, 5.294–5). They believe their own fighting power outweighs the gods' support for Caesar: but he in turn quells their mutiny by his authority

---

[43] Compare Lucan's model, Sinon, in *Aen.* 2.257, *fatisque deum defensus iniquis.*

[44] At 1.146, 207, and 292.

[45] Cf. 2.493, *calida proclamat* (Bentley, kept by S-B: *prolatus* MSS) *ab ira.*

[46] 3.111, 133, 136, 142. On 3.111, *tamen exit in iram*, Shackleton Bailey (1982) 93 corrects Housman's interpretation and proposes *tamen exciet iram.* He argues that the anger must be Caesar's, and is "soundly historical." It seems that Caesar was most prone to violent anger when dealing with civilian (i.e. not military) opposition.

[47] Commentators have noted that Lucan models his narrative on Erysichthon's impiety in felling the sacred tree in Callimachus' *Hymn to Demeter.*

alone and nothing contradicts his own retort that the gods are indifferent to groundlings (5.341–2, 351–2).

Not speeches but events are the index of divine intent. Thus in Book 7 we can reject statements about the gods in the speeches of Pompey and Caesar alike. Both speeches are deception, whether of the audience or also of the speaker himself. Caesar invokes the gods, asserting that they will favor him for his clemency (7.311–15):

> di, quorum curas abduxit ab aethere tellus
> Romanusque labor, uincat quicumque necesse
> non putat in uictos saeuum destringere ferrum
> quique suos ciues, quod signa aduersa tulerunt
> non credit fecisse nefas.

Gods – your cares have been distracted from the ether by the earth and throes of Rome – make victorious the man who does not think it necessary to draw the savage sword against the conquered, who does not believe that fellow-citizens committed a crime because they bore opposing standards.

But Caesar's own behavior after the battle will give the lie to his pretence of earning divine support through clemency. Pompey too must appear confident when addressing his army, but Lucan's audience or readers have learned his reluctance to fight against his tactical judgment, and feel the hollowness of his claim that his own leadership is a guarantee of divine support: *non iratorum populis urbique deorum est | Pompeium seruare ducem* ("to preserve Pompey as leader is not the act of gods who are angered with the people and with Rome," 7.354–5). The hindsight of history betrays him, since every Roman knew he was not saved, and this speech itself ends in a pitiful contemplation of defeat. At this point I would like to move on beyond the passage I first cited, where outrage at Caesar's victory sent Lucan's narrative out of control, because we will learn more from the less familiar narrative presentation (*color*) and authorial comments that follow Pompey's flight to his death and beyond.

THE GODS, FORTUNA, AND POMPEY'S DEATH

It is the contradictions of 7.445–9 that lead Ahl to his judgment that "the Olympians have ceased to function and no longer wield any power in human affairs."[48] He is more accurate when he continues "the gods . . . have no dramatic role in the *Pharsalia*." But though the gods are not seen to

---

[48] Ahl (1976) ch. 8, here 281.

intervene in the action, Lucan continues throughout the epic to imply their active hostility as often as their harmful indifference. The passionate self-contradictions of Pharsalus permit no inference about the poet's fundamental beliefs, only that he is reexperiencing in the telling the moment when Roman lovers of republican *libertas* ("liberty") lost faith in the gods.

So why does Lucan continuously appeal to the gods, or for that matter to the semi-abstract Fortuna? It has often been suggested by readers who see 7.445–52 as a turning point that after Pharsalus Lucan turns away from the gods to hold arbitrary Fortuna[49] responsible for the increasingly unwelcome course of events, but there is reason to question this. Despite the poet's general overuse of apostrophe, we can detect a suggestive pattern in his appeals to the supernatural. In Book 7, certainly, he will invoke the gods only once again, as he contemplates the spreading of the civil war over the Roman world at 869–70, *o superi, liceat terras odisse nocentes | quid totum premitis, quid totum absoluitis orbem?* ("O gods above, permit us to hate the lands that are guilty. Why do you place the burden upon the entire world and so acquit it?") But this is a final and emphatic position. To determine Lucan's allocation of responsibility between the gods and Fortuna we need to examine two patterns: first the general context and role of Fortuna through the epic, and secondly the pattern of intensified appeals to, and comments on, both gods and Fortuna as Lucan approaches the death of Pompey.

From the beginning of *De bello ciuili* Lucan uses Fortuna in both an unmarked and a marked sense. Shackleton Bailey and other editors before him have tried to distinguish with a lower case unmarked *fortuna*, as in *fortuna loci* ("luck of position") or *fortuna belli* ("fortune of war") or *fortuna prior* ("former favor," 1.134–5); in contrast the Fortuna that favors Caesar or victimizes Pompey is capitalized. But anomalies soon challenge this neat division: compare (as printed in Shackleton Bailey's text) 1.109–11, *populique potentis . . . | non cepit fortuna duos* ("a mighty people's prosperity . . . was not enough for two men"), with 160–1, *opes nimias Fortuna mundo subacto | intulit* ("once the world had been subdued, Fortune introduced excessive wealth"). To avoid ambiguity, I will use only instances in which either (a) Fortuna is said authorially by Lucan to harm Pompey or help Caesar or (b) Fortuna's behavior is cited in parallel to that of the gods, as in 3.448–9 discussed above: *seruat multos Fortuna nocentes | et tantum miseris irasci*

---

[49] Fortuna / *Tyche* is particularly associated with short-term reversals, events that do not seem to fit into a teleological pattern or be adequately motivated by prior guilt or failure.

numina possunt ("often their good fortune guards the guilty and the gods can only be angry with the unlucky").

To confirm first that Lucan does not see Fortuna as a causality distinct from the gods, let me cite more examples of parallel comments. At 5.57–9 the poet apostrophizes Ptolemy as *non fidae gentis dignissime regno,* | *Fortunae, Ptolemaee, pudor, crimenque deorum* ("you, Ptolemy, well deserving power over an untrustworthy people, you, the shame of Fortune, a reproach against the gods"). At 7.205–6 Lucan grieves for the leaders: *o summos hominum, quorum Fortuna per orbem* | *signa dedit, quorum fatis caelum omne uacauit* ("O mightiest of men – your Fortune gave displays throughout the world, the entire sky was intent on your destiny!"). Fortuna and the gods, then, together provide the portents for the battle.

More often, however, Fortuna is involved in the fates of single individuals; above all of Caesar[50] and Pompey; indeed she tends to disappear from Lucan's narrative in parts of Books 3–6 where neither leader is involved in the action. As early as 2.727–8, "exhausted by his triumphs" she has "abandoned" Pompey (*lassata triumphis* | *desciuit Fortuna tuis*); at 3.169 Pompey's Fortuna has roused to warfare oriental allies "doomed to fall along with him"; at 3.394 Fortuna is "hastening to impose Caesar on the whole world." At Pharsalus itself Pompey realizes that the gods and fate have left him: *transisse deos Romanaque fata* ("he realized that the gods and Roman destiny had switched allegiance," 7.647) and Fortuna betrays him: *quamque fuit laeto per tres infida triumphos* | *tam misero Fortuna minor* ("fickle Fortune is as far beneath him in his days of misery as she was in his happy days of three triumphs," 685–6). In contrast Caesar sees both Fortuna and the gods on his side (*Fortunam superosque suos,* 796).

Why is this relevant to the question of anger? Because Pompey's downfall and fugitive state lead in Book 8 to an increasing stress on Fortuna's treatment of him;[51] and his death, with the defeat of liberty, drives Lucan to violent anger against both gods and Fortune. One would not attribute to the poet the pessimism of Pothinus' treacherous advice if Lucan had not himself spoken in the same terms: compare Pothinus' words *dat poenas laudata fides cum sustinet . . .* | *quos Fortuna premit. fatis accede deisque* | *et cole felices, miseros fuge* ("Loyalty, though praised, pays the cost when

---

[50] This is, of course, in keeping with Caesar's own stress on the power of Fortune: at *De bello ciuili* 3.10 the reported version of his own communication with the republicans invokes Fortuna three times at 3, 6, and 7. The biographical tradition concurs with Lucan in attributing to Caesar public claims to enjoy Fortune's favor.

[51] Fortune is mentioned either in narrative or speech at 8.21–2, 72, 95–6, 150, 271, 313, 334–5, 427; there are other unmarked references.

it supports the people Fortune crushes. Side with the fates and the gods. Court the fortunate and avoid the failures," 8.485–7) with Lucan's comment in 3.448–9 *seruat multos Fortuna nocentes | et tantum miseris irasci numina possunt* ("often Fortune guards the guilty and the gods can only be angry with the unlucky"). Lucan is angry with the gods and Fortune alike, as even his largely mild and acquiescent Pompey is angry, but this anger is itself a response to the belief that the gods/Fortuna have caused his ruin out of an unwarranted and unearned hostility. Lucan cries shame on Fortune and the gods in connection with Ptolemy's honors in 5.58–9[52] and repeats his denunciations to frame the death scene. Even while acknowledging that Pompey has been condemned by Fate[53] Lucan denounces gods and Fortune alike: *Septimius, qui pro superum pudor, arma satelles | regia gestabat . . .* ("Septimius who – shame on the gods above – carried the weapons of the king," 597–8); *quis non, Fortuna, putasset | parcere te populis . . .* ("Who would not have imagined that you were sparing the peoples, Fortune . . . ," 600–1); and *dedecus et numquam superum caritura pudore | fabula, Romanus regi sic paruit ensis* ("a dishonor and a story which will always shame the gods above – a Roman sword obeyed the king like this," 605–6). And Pompey himself dies "disdaining to present his bare head to Fortune" (*indignatus apertum | Fortunae praebere caput,* 615–16). Lucan has not made an end of these outcries, and if many more invoke Fortuna than the gods, he turns to them at least once more as responsible for this chain of indignities: *sit satis, o superi, quod non Cornelia fuso | crine iacet* ("O gods above, let it be enough that Cornelia does not lie with her hair loosened . . . ," 739–40). There is an important but problematic instance of such apparent anger against the gods in the extended description of the dead Pompey: "men who saw his mutilated head acknowledge that the reverend beauty of his holy body was preserved and his features angry with the gods; that the last moments of death had changed nothing of the man's demeanor and expression" (8.665–6). Suddenly we seem to have an extraordinary dissonance. If we are to follow the manuscripts, Pompey's nobility of appearance in death is combined with an *iratam . . . deis faciem* ("his features angry with the gods," 665). Yet Pompey himself seemed reconciled at the moment of death, when he addressed the gods and called himself happy; *sum tamen, o superi, felix nullique potestas | hoc auferre deo* ("Yet I am fortunate, o gods above, and no deity has the power to take this away from me," 630–1).

---

[52] *Et tibi . . . Fortunae, Ptolemaee pudor, crimenque deorum.*
[53] 8.567–9, *nisi fatorum leges . . . | damnatum leto traherent ad litora Magnum;* see also 575.

Here he denies that worldly ruin can destroy his inner happiness:[54] in the light of this and of the immediate context of 666, many editors have been unhappy with *iratamque deis faciem*. Housman after careful consideration of alternatives retained the MSS reading, but Shackleton Bailey (1982, 1997) has argued for and printed Francken's *placatamque deis*, which is translated by Susanna Braund as "reconciled with the gods."[55] If we see Pompey in his last speech as withholding just anger, the sense would be well conveyed by *placatam*: the dying man has actively controlled the anger he could properly have felt.

On the other hand, while *placatam* is consistent with Lucan's usage,[56] two further uses of *placare* in Book 8 could be used as arguments both for and against changing the text in 665. At 8.772, *si quis placare peremptum | forte uolet* ("if anyone should want to placate you in death") and again in the poet's own comment at 8.855–8, *quem non tumuli uenerabile saxum | . . . | auertet manesque tuos placare iubebit?* ("who will not be diverted by your grave's venerable rock . . . , not be compelled to placate your shade?"), men are expected to placate the dead Pompey's shade. Is he then still angry? With both men and gods? Caesar himself will urge his audience in Alexandria to placate the shade of Pompey (9.1092), and imagine how his forestalled reconciliation with his son-in-law could have enabled Pompey to pardon the gods in his defeat: *tum pace fideli | fecissem ut uictus posses ignoscere diuis* ("then in faithful peace I could have helped you in defeat forgive the gods," 9.1101–2). Is Caesar then acknowledging that the gods have been unjust? Logically his words seem to imply that Pompey's defeat (not just his murder) was unjust, but this is focalization through Pompey's eyes, not Caesar's own judgment.

Lucan does not return to the question of divine responsibility, except in passing, before the text of the epic comes to an end. There is no last word on the subject. So we must go back to the beginning and *uictrix causa deis placuit* ("the gods favored the conquered side," 1.128). What mattered in the civil war was victory, the index of divine intent, but in declaring the gods'

---

[54] This seems to be contradicted by Lucan's editorial judgment at 706–7 that Pompey was *felix nullo turbante deorum | et nullo parcente miser*. Has the poet already forgotten that he was using a higher concept of felicity in 630–1?

[55] Unfortunately Shackleton Bailey (1982) 99–100 repudiates *iratamque* without advancing any arguments for Francken's *placatam*. Contrast Joyce (1993): "his face still glared at the gods," and Widdows (1988), who adopts *inuictam*: "his mien was as ever solemn and seemly, that of a man who defied the gods." But Lucan elsewhere speaks of Pompey as *uictus*, and limits his use of *inuictus* to Caesar (5.324; 10.346); Cato, morally *inuictus*, (9.18); Antaeus, in an ironic anticipation of his defeat; and Rome (in a diplomatic speech 3.334). In contrast with Cato, Pompey is *uictus*.

[56] *Placare* is found ten times: cf. 2.173–4, *manes | placatos Catuli*, in the same sedes.

partisanship for Caesar and the Caesars the poet never brings this defeat of liberty together with a clear acknowledgement of Roman guilt: he thus continues angry with gods whose anger against Rome he seems neither to understand nor to forgive.

EPILOGUE: *IRA DEORUM / IOVIS IRA / CAESARIS IRA*

Besides the anger of the gods, the anger of one mortal leader, Caesar, is scarcely less prominent in the *De bello ciuili*. From his first introduction in the opening sequence of causes as *acer et indomitus quo spes quoque ira uocasset* ("fierce, indomitable, drawn wherever hope and indignation summoned," 1.146) through his comparison to the Libyan lion who *subsedit dubius, totam dum colligit iram* ("crouches in hesitation till he has concentrated all his rage," 207), Caesar accumulates anger, as in his reaction to Curio's speech at 1.292–3 *ipsi in bellum prono tantum tamen addidit irae,* | *accenditque ducem* ("though Caesar was already keen for war, he increased his rage and inflamed his leader"). It is anger that characterizes Caesar, and this anger is the momentum behind the conflict, returning in almost every scene where he appears: three times, for example, in one episode of Book 3, *magnam uictor in iram* | *uocibus accensus* ("by these words the victor was inflamed to mighty anger," 133), *dignum te Caesaris ira* | *nullus honor faciet* ("no office you hold will make you worthy of Caesar's anger," 136), and *nondum foribus cedente tribuno* | *acrior ira subit* ("when the tribune does not yet leave the doors, a fiercer anger comes over him," 142). No less than in Ovid's poetry of exile,[57] "Caesar's wrath" (*Caesaris ira*) is a force in its own right, given increasing prominence with Pharsalus and the book of Pompey's downfall.[58]

Caesar has only one rival for this claim; the dead Alexander, *terrarum fatale malum, fulmenque quod omnis* | *percuteret pariter populos* ("an evil deadly to the world, a thunderbolt that struck all nations equally," 10.34):[59] like Caesar, the thunderbolt-Alexander, initially driven by the

---

[57] For the phrase in this form and sedes cf. 8.134, 643, and 765. Ovid reports the anger of (Augustus) Caesar as *Caesaris ira* at *Tr.* 1.2.3 and 61; 1.3.85, etc., and relates Augustus' anger (and potential clemency) to that of his celestial counterpart in *Tr.* 2.33–40.

[58] Only in the climax of Pharsalus does Lucan go beyond *ira* to associate Caesar with actual battle rage – *rabies*; cf. 551, *hic furor hic rabies, hic sunt tua crimina Caesar,* and 557, *hic Caesar, rabies populis stimulusque furorum* | *... agmina circum* | *it uagus atque ignes animis flagrantibus addit.* This is followed by the unique comparison of Caesar with Mars (= Ares) at 567–71.

[59] There are more affinities than differences in Lucan's parallel portraits of Greek and Roman autocrats: cf. 1.153–6, *populosque pauentes* | *terruit...* | *... magnamque cadens magnamque reuertens* | *dat stragem late,* with 10.30, *fatis urgentibus actus* | *humana cum strage ruit...* and 34–5, *fulmenque quod omnes* | *percuteret pariter populos.*

fates (*fatis urgentibus actus* . . .) was also "removed by fate," this time acting to "avenge" or liberate the world (*terrarum uindice fato | raptus*, 10.21–2). Caesar too is fated to die in his prime, but until that time enacts divine anger against Rome.[60]

Should we not then make a further identification, between Caesar, the human thunderbolt (*qualiter expressum uentis per nubila fulmen*, 1.151, developed 152–6), and the traditional weapon of the angry Jupiter? Jupiter's bolts were the weapon of his *ira*; indeed, as we saw in Virgil's forge scene, *irae* were a vital ingredient of their manufacture.[61] There is already in the *Aeneid* an increasing focus on the anger of Jupiter alongside collective divine anger: hence Jupiter's own comment to Juno at *Aeneid* 12.830–1 that her anger proves her kinship to him; hence his reliance on the deadly Dira, *Dei ira* (literally, "god's anger"), to destroy Turnus. No doubt as a consequence of the establishment of Augustus' autocratic power, the anger of the collective gods is no longer active in Ovid's *Metamorphoses*: instead there are countless instances of the arbitrary anger of individual gods, but most prominent of all is the anger of Jupiter. As was noted above, Ovid introduces Jupiter possessed by this anger (*ingentes animo et dignas Ioue . . . iras*, "a mighty wrath worthy of Jupiter's soul," *Met.* 1.166) and exercising it to destroy the human race: in his epilogue Ovid will boast of his work of art as surviving even *Iouis iras* (15.871). This would surely be blasphemy if it were not a coded allusion to Augustus Caesar, parallel to more overt allusions in *Tristia* 2 and the poetry of exile.[62] But even without interpreting Lucan through Ovid, his text gives us the basis for a further claim: that Lucan in *De bello ciuili* is presenting his Caesar, and *Caesaris irae*, not just as analogue, but as the actual representative and embodiment of the divine anger which overthrew the Roman Republic and the liberty of its elite.

---

[60] For Caesar's death as fated in vengeance of his crimes see 7.595, *meruit fatis tam nobile letum*, and 9.17, *scelerum uindex in sancto pectore Bruti | sedit.*

[61] See *Aen.* 8.431–2, quoted above, and Ov. *Met.* 15.811–12, where Jupiter describes the celestial archives *quae neque concussum caeli neque fulminis iram | nec metuunt ullas tuta atque aeterna ruinas.*

[62] See Barchiesi (1997).

CHAPTER II

An ABC of epic ira: anger, beasts, and cannibalism

Susanna Braund and Giles Gilbert

E io, che di mirare stava inteso,
vidi genti fangose in quel pantano,
ignude tutte, con sembiante offeso.

    Queste si percotean, non pur con mano
ma con la testa e col petto e coi piedi,
troncandosi co' denti a brano a brano.

    Lo buon maestro disse: "Figlio, or vedi
l'anime di color cui vinse l'ira . . ."

And I, gazing intently, saw people muddied in
that slough, all naked, with indignant expressions.

    They kept striking each other, and not only with
hands, but with head and breast and feet, tearing
each other apart with their teeth, piece by piece.

    My kind master said: "Son, now behold the souls
of those whom anger vanquished . . ."

Dante *Inferno* canto 7.109–16 (tr. Durling)

BOY ACHILLES' DIET

Achilles is the classic angry warrior of antiquity. The story of the *Iliad* is the story of the wrath of Achilles. The parts of the *Iliad* most read in antiquity focus on Achilles' anger[1] and the emphasis on anger is reflected in the *Ilias Latina*, probably of Neronian date, which accords with the Greek original in making "anger" its first word: *iram pande mihi Pelidae, Diua, superbi* ("reveal to me the anger of the son of Peleus, goddess").[2] We know the specific cause of Achilles' anger in the *Iliad* – but could there be some

---

This chapter is jointly researched and written. It arises from the intersection of Susanna Morton Braund's interests in Roman anger with Giles Gilbert's 2001 Ph.D. dissertation (Royal Holloway, University of London) on the battle scenes in Roman epic, especially imperial epic.

[1] This is suggested by texts such as Horace *Epist.* 1.2.11–16 and Plutarch *Mor.* 19c–d, 26b–f, 28f–29a.

[2] On the *Ilias Latina*, whose author may be one Baebius Italicus, see entry in *OCD³*, positing a date of earlier than AD 68.

underlying disposition toward anger? There is the claim that his mother reared him on gall (*Iliad* 16.203), the starting-point for Ann Hanson's paper in this volume. Alternatively, consider Achilles' account of his early years as presented by Statius in his *Achilleid*. In response to questioning from Diomedes, Achilles delivers a seventy-line speech which begins (*Achil.* 2.96–102):

> dicor et in teneris et adhuc reptantibus annis,
> Thessalus ut rigido senior me monte recepit,
> non ullos ex more cibos hausisse nec almis
> uberibus satiasse famem, sed spissa leonum
> uiscera semianimisque lupae traxisse medullas.   100
> haec mihi prima Ceres, haec laeti munera Bacchi,
> sic dabat ille pater.

Even in my tender years when I was still crawling, when the Thessalian elder received me on his stark mountain, I am said to have devoured no usual foods and not to have satisfied my hunger at the nourishing breast, but to have torn the tough entrails of lions and the innards of a half-dead she-wolf. That was my first Ceres [= bread], that was the gift of joyful Bacchus, that was how that father of mine fed me.

Why does Statius specify this diet and in such a prominent position? The purpose of this diet is clearly to render Achilles fearless – and indeed Achilles immediately describes how under Chiron's teaching he came not to fear any aspect of the wilderness (102–5) and how he became hardy and strong (106–19). In particular, Chiron would not allow him to chase "unwarlike does or fearful lynxes" (*imbelles . . . dammas* or *timidas . . . lyncas*, 121–2) but confined him to the hunting of fierce animals (123–8):

> sed tristes turbare cubilibus ursos
> fulmineosque sues et sicubi maxima tigris
> aut seducta iugis fetae spelunca leaenae.   125
> ipse sedens uasto facta exspectabat in antro
> si sparsus nigro remearem sanguine; nec me
> ante nisi inspectis admisit ad oscula telis.

. . . but only to drive from their lairs the grim bears and the lightning-quick boars, or if anywhere there was an enormous tiger or the secret cave of a lioness with her cubs. Chiron himself, sitting in his huge cavern, was awaiting my exploits, if I returned spattered with dark blood. He did not welcome me with an embrace until he had inspected my weapons.

His training continued in every kind of weapon and warfare, as detailed in lines 129–53: "and no form of savage Mars passed me by" (*nec me ulla feri*

Mauortis imago | praeteriit, 130–1). His speech closes with a brief mention of his recreational activities (154–8) and his instruction in herbal medicine (159–62) and finally, the last item, his instruction in justice (163–4, "he implanted deep in my heart the precepts of sacred justice," *monitusque sacrae sub pectore fixit | iustitiae*).

> hactenus annorum, comites, elementa meorum
> et memini et meminisse iuuat: scit cetera mater.
>
> (166–7)

So much I remember of the training of my early years, my companions, and the memory is a good one. The rest my mother knows.

There, with the closure of Achilles' speech, the text of the *Achilleid* breaks off.

Clearly Chiron's education of Achilles is designed to prepare him for his short life of fighting. That is how the opening detail about Achilles' diet of wild animals – including wild animals still alive – should be read. Statius' representation of Achilles' diet is not an invention: other ancient sources make similar claims, specifying the innards of lions and marrows of boars and bears[3] and the marrows of lions and bears,[4] and a seventh-century Attic neck-amphora portrays Chiron bringing three live cubs to the infant Achilles.[5] The idea behind such a diet is clearly what James Frazer in *The Golden Bough* calls "homoeopathic magic" – that the diet provides the consumer with the animal's positive qualities, presumably fearlessness, fierceness, and invincibility, a belief which persists to this day in some cultures, for example, in the harvesting of bears' bile in China.[6] A fine example from a classical source is Herodotus' report of the Scythian custom whereby a young warrior drank the blood of his first victim.[7] The Statius passage is also discussed briefly by D. S. Robertson, who pays especial attention to Statius' adjective *semianimis* and argues for its relevance beyond being a piece of "macabre embroidery of the Silver Age" by connecting it

---

[3] Apollodorus, *Bibl.* 3.13.6: "Peleus brought the child to Chiron, who received him and fed him on the innards of lions and wild boar and the marrows of bears and named him Achilles, because he had not put his lips to the breast." That is, Apollodorus produces an etymology of ἀ (alpha privative) + χείλη.

[4] Scholia on Homer *Iliad* 16.37.

[5] *Corpus Vasorum Antiquorum*, Berlin, vol. i, plate v = *LIMC* "Achilles" plate 21.

[6] Frazer (1912) 138–68, for example 145–6, where he cites the Chinese belief that the gall-bladder is the seat of courage, resulting in the consumption of the bile of tigers and bears. This belief and practice is still extant in China where bears kept in small cages are farmed for their bile, which is extracted from their gall-bladders by the insertion of tubes through the abdomen.

[7] Herodotus 4.64.

with Pindar, *Nemean Odes* 3.43–9.[8] The efficacy of this diet is glanced at, though hardly spelled out explicitly, by Statius in the passage above where Achilles catalogues the kinds of prey Chiron made him hunt – and all this is, of course, a preparation for his martial skills in human combat. In this chapter we shall propose that Achilles' early diet may produce another manifestation in his character besides his fearlessness in fighting: a tendency towards aggression and anger. That is, the raw food of wild beasts may convey to him their raw energy in all its aspects, positive and negative.

ANGRY WARRIORS OF EPIC: THE SCOPE AND LIMITATIONS OF THIS STUDY

But before we return to Achilles, we will offer an analysis of the portrayals of angry warriors in Roman epic when they are facing battle and when they are actually in combat: the operation of *ira* on the battlefield. The most substantial body of evidence for this is provided not by direct descriptions of the warriors' behaviour but indirectly, by similes. These similes use precisely those fierce wild beasts that we have already met furnishing Achilles' food and his prey during his early years – lions and lionesses, tigers and tigresses, boars, wolves, and bulls. We shall subject these similes to detailed analysis for what they can reveal about the workings of epic anger. We shall also take a close look at two passages from Statius which portray the onset of anger in direct narrative: first, the fight between Tydeus and Polynices at the doors of the Adrastus' palace in Statius, *Thebaid* 1, where too we shall find imagery of wild beasts, and second, the description of the troops awaiting battle in *Thebaid* 8, where description of the warriors is intertwined with description of the war-horses. We hope that this analysis will advance the appreciation of such similes well beyond the prejudice evinced by Mozley, the Loeb translator of Statius, when he says "we get rather tired of the endless bulls and boars to which his heroes are compared" (1982: xviii).

We believe that this analysis will demonstrate that Agathe Thornton's thesis about *ira* in the *Aeneid* holds true for most of imperial Latin epic – namely that this concept takes its moral aspect from the context. Accordingly, we shall commence with a statement of Thornton's position. Then we

---

[8] Robertson (1940). Pindar, *Nem.* 3.43–9: "But fair-haired Achilles, while living in the home of Philyra would perform great deeds even as a child at play. He would often brandish in his hands the short javelin with steel tip and, as swift as the winds, battle wild lions to death and slay boars. From the age of six and forever after he would bring their gasping bodies to the Centaur, the son of Kronos." The detail "gasping" is especially significant, indicating that they are still alive, a point which becomes relevant later in this paper. See too Hanson n. 5 in this volume (ch. 8).

shall examine our main body of evidence – the portrayals of the process of anger in epic warriors, including the controlled arousal of anger, its main-tenance in battle, its passing out of control, and its fading. This material, most of which is furnished by similes, will demonstrate the full spectrum of moral loading of the *ira* of epic warriors, which bears out Thornton's view of its initial moral neutrality. Finally we shall examine the operation and morality of anger when it goes beyond limits. Throughout this discussion, we tend to leave the word *ira* in Latin. This is because the usual translation "anger" seems inadequate and likely to evoke unhelpful associations. In fact, the evidence gathered here suggests that a translation such as "rage" or, even better, because more neutral, "combativeness" is closer to the mark.

After this outline, it is useful to pause for a moment to indicate what this study is *not*. When we commenced work, we expected that our epic texts would yield up to us more or less detailed descriptions of the psychology of the warrior as he faced the prospect of fighting, descriptions which we intended to set alongside analysis of psychology and physiology of men in warfare in philosophical and medical treatises. We were disappointed. A thorough survey of the word *ira* in the Latin epics produced very little material related to this theme, although it did afford an opportunity to make an overview of the types of language associated with *ira* in the poems (which appears as Appendix 1 to this paper) – and doubtless the same applies to other related concepts, such as *dolor* ("resentment" or "hostility") and *furor* ("rage") and *animus* ("spirit"). A careful reading of Seneca's *De ira* along with a trawl through relevant sections of Cicero and Plutarch and medical writers brought to light nothing of relevance. Rather, our perusal of these authors, especially Seneca, revealed a focus almost exclusively upon the manifestations of anger in *domestic, civic* and *political* but not *military* contexts (and the little material that is relevant is discussed in Appendix 2). There is no dedicated discussion of the anger of the warrior.

At first, we were simply disappointed. Then we realized that this itself is significant. The question, why?, is a question we can pose to our own society, where too the representation of battle has usually been partial, filtered, and subject to taboos. Certainly the military historian John Keegan's book *The Face of Battle* (first edition, 1976) seems to have broken new ground with its unflinching description of the nature of the wounds sustained at the battle of the Somme. Perhaps for most of our ancient authors and their audiences anger on the battlefield was subject to the same kind of powerful taboo. Or perhaps it was an area beyond their experience and therefore of little interest. Or perhaps it was a subject too frightening to think about, because of the essential difference between domestic, civic, and political contexts on the one hand and military contexts on the other, where the constraints of "normal" life disappear. The phenomenon of anger and resentment that is so strong that it trumps the basic instinct for self-preservation is illustrated brilliantly by Virgil's portrayal of Aeneas' death wish at the sack of Troy in *Aeneid* 2, lines 314–17:

> arma amens capio; nec sat rationis in armis,
> sed glomerare manum bello et concurrere in arcem   315
> cum sociis ardent animi; furor iraque mentem
> praecipitant, pulchrumque mori succurrit in armis.

Frantically I grab weapons. There is not enough purpose in weapons, but my spirit is burning to muster a band to fight and to race with my comrades to the citadel. Rage and anger harry my mind and the thought comes to me that it is a fine thing to die under arms.

As Virgil demonstrates, when such feelings rage out of control, they can destroy everything. If Aeneas had had his way, he would have died fighting the Greek invaders and there would have been no story of Rome – and no Rome. Anger out of control in the context of battle can lead to total annihilation. Perhaps that is why our authors avoid facing up to the question of the warrior's anger.

THORNTON ON EPIC ANGER

After these preliminaries, we shall now address the central issue of the moral flavour of anger in Roman epic. Our starting point is Thornton's discussion of *ira* and *furor* which appears as Appendix A in her 1976 book *The Living Universe: Gods and Men in Virgil's Aeneid*, which we believe still provides a fundamentally valid interpretation of the *Aeneid*. In this appendix (pages 159–63), Thornton states that anger "was one of the most controversial subjects in the discussions on moral conduct in the first century BC" and she briefly reviews the Stoic and Peripatetic positions on anger. Moving on to the *Aeneid*, she rightly asserts that "*ira* is conceived as a necessary concomitant of or incentive to fighting in battle": "the close connection of 'anger' with *uirtus* shows its positive valuation." Her conclusion, after a brief review of the evidence, is that anger "is inherent in fighting and battle and . . . its moral evaluation depends on the specific situation in which it occurs. It is not in itself good or bad." Analysis of the whole situation in which anger arises is required to reach a view on its moral quality. Finally, she suggests that "the same problem of ethical valuation arises concerning *furor* and its cognates," a situation obscured by the antithesis set up by scholars between *pietas* ("right") and *furor* ("rage"). She concedes that the noun *furor* usually has negative connotations but argues that the verb *furere* is more complex. Denoting "a tremendous intensity of emotion, often accompanied by quick movements" the verb readily lends itself to battle contexts. Thornton argues that it describes fierce, frenzied, or zestful fighting, with no particular moral judgment. In her discussions of both *ira* and *furere* she makes reference to Hercules' conflict with Cacus in *Aeneid* 8 to demonstrate the possibility of a positive depiction of anger, that is, when anger has justice on its side.[9] Analysis of the evidence concerning the anger of the epic warrior bears out Thornton's view, as we shall now demonstrate.

THE ANGRY WARRIOR AS WILD BEAST: THE EVIDENCE

As stated above, we discovered that the most detailed and eloquent depictions of the workings and psychology of *ira* in epic warriors facing battle occur in similes, and these now supply the material for the central discussion in this chapter.[10] In our analysis, we have tried to use context and detail to form a judgment about the positive or negative flavour of the representation and have used this polarity to structure our discussion, presenting first the positive cases then the negative cases of *ira*.

A brief but classic case which demonstrates the positive aspect of *ira* in battle is Statius' description of Theseus at *Thebaid* 12.736–40 in which he is compared to "great lions" (*magnos . . . leones*) in contrast with "dogs and cowardly wolves" (*canesque | degeneresque lupos*), implicitly denoting his companions:

> taedet fugientibus uti
> Thesea, nec facilem dignatur dextra cruorem.
> cetera plebeio desaeuit sanguine uirtus.
> sic iuuat exanimis proiectaque praeda canesque
> degeneresque lupos: magnos alit ira leones.   740

[9] For Hercules' fight against Cacus as a reprise of Gigantomachic themes and as structurally parallel to Octavian's victory at Actium see Hardie (1986) 110–18. Thornton's point is borne out by the semi-allegorical portrayal of Mars with his retinue which includes *Ira* or *Irae* at, for example, Virgil, *Aen.* 12.33–6 and Silius, *Pun.* 4.436–9.

[10] The following analysis is not a complete survey of similes from battle scenes in Roman epic. We focus upon similes which feature the word *ira* and which seem to contribute to the psychologization of anger. Thus, for example, the comparison of Eteocles to a tigress upon awakening at *Theb.* 2.128–33 is not discussed because it simply states the fact of Eteocles'/the tigress's anger. See also Cairns n. 59 in this volume (ch. 1) .

Theseus disdains to take on the fugitives and his right hand scorns easy slaughter. The rest of the fighting-force expend their savagery on ordinary blood. Just like that dogs and cowardly wolves enjoy their prey half-dead and lying at their feet; great lions are fed by anger.

Theseus is here distinguished from the mass of the other warriors in his disdain to pursue fugitives: he seeks noble warriors as his opponents. His companions in the fighting are not thereby diminished so much as Theseus is enhanced in status. It is clear that his companions' *uirtus* (here translated "fighting-force" but more precisely "excellence" or "courage") and his own *ira* both result in slaughter. The difference is that Theseus' opponents are nobler and more resilient and challenging. In fact, we can press the details further to yield up something of central significance for an understanding of epic anger. The opponents whom Theseus disdains are already running away. He prefers nobler opponents, opponents who (we can infer) would stand their ground and require to be overcome in hand-to-hand combat. The association of *ira* with fighting at close quarters will emerge as crucial.

In this examination of the similes which represent *ira* as morally positive, we shall follow as closely as the material allows the sequence of battle. First, then, similes which describe the warrior preparing himself for combat.

The detail about close combat is present in our very first example, when Lucan compares Caesar to a lion immediately after he has addressed the personification of the city Roma at the Rubicon and declared his decision to cross the river (*Bellum Ciuile* 1.204–12):

> inde moras soluit belli tumidumque per amnem
> signa tulit propere; sicut squalentibus aruis   205
> aestiferae Libyes uiso leo comminus hoste
> subsedit dubius, totam dum colligit iram;
> mox, ubi se saeuae stimulauit uerbere caudae
> erexitque iubam et uasto graue murmur hiatu
> infremuit, tum, torta leuis si lancea Mauri   210
> haereat aut latum subeant uenabula pectus,
> per ferrum tanti securus uolneris exit.

> Then he broke the barriers of war and through the swollen river
> quickly took his standards. Just so in torrid Libya's
> barren fields the lion, on seeing his enemy at hand,
> crouches in hesitation till he has concentrated all his anger;
> next he goads himself with fiercely lashing tail,
> his mane is bristling, from his massive jaws
> deep he roars – then if a lance, hurled by a swift Moor,
> or hunting-spears pierce and stick in his broad chest, ignoring
> such a terrible wound he rushes onward, driving the weapon deeper.

Evidently the lion requires *ira* to face its enemies at close quarters (*comminus*). The point of the simile is Caesar's decision to go to war, which corresponds to the lion's heedlessness of any weapons that strike him once he has worked himself up for the combat. But what is especially interesting for our purposes is the description of the lion preparing himself for that state of high-energy impetuosity: just as Caesar initially hesitates at the sight and reprimand of Roma (just before this passage), so the lion "crouches in hesitation"; just as Caesar then alters his state of mind from fear and weakness by his assertive speech, so the lion is able to "concentrate all his anger." This he does by lashing his tail, by making his mane bristle and by roaring. Lucan explicitly describes this as self-willed (*se . . . stimulauit*), which suggests that the lion's (and thence Caesar's) alteration of state of mind is entirely under his control.

A similar case is the representation of Polynices as a bull at *Thebaid* 2.323–32:

> ueluti dux taurus amata
> ualle carens, pulsum solito quem gramine uictor
> iussit ab erepta longe mugire iuuenca,   325
> cum profugo placuere tori ceruixque recepto
> sanguine magna redit fractaeque in pectora quercus,
> bella cupit pastusque et capta armenta reposcit
> iam pede, iam cornu melior – pauet ipse reuersum
> uictor, et attoniti uix agnouere magistri: 330
> non alias tacita iuuenis Teumesius iras
> mente acuit.

Just like a bull leader who is missing his beloved valley, when he has been driven from his familiar pasture by a conqueror and told to low far away from his stolen heifer – though he is an exile he takes a delight in his muscles and his neck grows strong again with the blood restored and the oaks are shattered against his breast, he longs to fight and demands back the pastures and captured herds, already the better in his foot and his horn. The conqueror himself dreads his return and the astonished herdsmen barely recognize him. Not otherwise does the Teumesian young man sharpen the anger in his silent mind.

Although the prospect of fighting is not absolutely imminent, this bull is charging and preparing himself psychologically for conflict – and the sight is terrifying. Statius' picture of Polynices as a bull regaining his strength and harnessing his anger is indebted to two Virgilian intertexts,[11] the passage at *Georgics* 3.215–41 and *Aeneid* 12.101–6, our next passage here.

---

[11] For brief discussion see Hershkowitz (1998a) 272–5.

Turnus in *Aeneid* 12 is facing one-to-one combat more immediately than
Caesar or Polynices in the passages above. He has just put on his armour
and addressed a speech to his spear requesting that he may be allowed to
fell the "Phrygian eunuch" (*semiuiri Phrygis*) with the fancy hairdo, as he
styles Aeneas. Then comes the simile of the bull preparing itself for conflict
(*Aen.* 12.101–6):

> his agitur furiis totoque ardentis ab ore
> scintillae absistunt, oculis micat acribus ignis;
> mugitus ueluti cum prima in proelia taurus
> terrificos ciet atque irasci in cornua temptat,
> arboris obnixus trunco uentosque lacessit   105
> ictibus aut sparsa ad pugnam proludit harena.

Such a frenzy drives him. Fiery sparks shoot from his whole face and flame flashes
from his fierce eyes – just as when a bull before the battle begins unleashes a
terrifying bellowing and tries to channel anger into his horns by charging a tree-
trunk and provokes the winds with his strikes and paws the sand as a prelude to
the fight.

First we are given Turnus' symptomology of anger, his heightened emotional state (*furiis*) marked in his face and eyes.[12] Then we are told that the
bull makes a terrifying noise and hones his anger with practice fighting,
directed against trees and into the air and by pawing the sand. Here too
the preparation for battle is self-willed: the bull knows he is facing his "first
fight" (*prima . . . proelia*) and he readies himself for action, as the verb
temptat seems to indicate. As with Lucan's simile of Caesar as a lion above,
the arousal of anger includes noise and quick gestures and actions that will
inspire terror. That the simile performs the function of narrating Turnus'
psychological self-preparation is confirmed by how Virgil continues: he
passes immediately to Aeneas' self-preparation via the link "no less does
Aeneas . . ." (*Aen.* 12.107–9):

> nec minus interea maternis saeuus in armis
> Aeneas acuit Martem et se suscitat ira,
> oblato gaudens componi foedere bellum.

No less does Aeneas meanwhile, fierce in his mother's weapons, whet his War-spirit
and stir himself with anger, delighted that the war is settled by the treaty that has
been offered.

In Lucan it is the lion who goads himself; here it is Aeneas and by extrapo-
lation Turnus who "whets his War-spirit" (*acuit Martem*) and "stirs himself

---

[12] This can be closely paralleled in Seneca's *De ira*: 1.1.3–4; 3.4.1–2.

with anger" (*se suscitat ira*). Evidently anger or rage (again, the issue of the appropriate translation arises) is the necessary preliminary state of mind for warriors facing battle – and we suggest that Turnus' *furiis* (101) are the exact equivalent of Aeneas' *ira* (108) here.

The need for anger in order to enter the fighting is further illustrated in *Aeneid* 10 when Mezentius is surrounded by personal enemies. Although many of them have personal grudges against their former king, they do not have the courage to face him at close quarters. The simile renders the situation as a hunting scene when a wild boar is trapped between nets and hunting dogs, with the dogs afraid to attack the boar (*Aen.* 10.707–18):

> ac uelut ille canum morsu de montibus altis
> actus aper, multos Vesulus quem pinnifer annos
> defendit multosque palus Laurentia, silua
> pastus harundinea, postquam inter retia uentum est,   710
> substitit infremuitque ferox et inhorruit armos,
> nec cuiquam irasci propiusue accedere uirtus,
> sed iaculis tutisque procul clamoribus instant,
> haud aliter, iustae quibus est Mezentius irae,
> non ulli est animus stricto concurrere ferro;   715
> missilibus longe et uasto clamore lacessunt.
> ille autem impauidus partis cunctatur in omnis,
> dentibus infrendens et tergo decutit hastas.

And just as the boar, driven by the dogs' jaws from the high mountains, kept safe by pine-topped Vesulus for many years or for many years by the Laurentine marsh, feeding him on a forest of reeds, once he finds himself among the nets he stops and roars ferociously and bristles. No one has the courage to get angry or to come closer, but they all attack him from a distance with safe missiles and shouts. Just so, none of those that were justly angry towards Mezentius had the spirit to meet him with drawn sword. From a distance they provoke him with missiles and echoing shouting. But he fearlessly halts, turning in all directions, gnashing his teeth, and knocks the spears from his shield.

There are strong similarities with Lucan's lion here in the noise of the boar (*infremuit*) and his making himself look big and impressive (*inhorruit armos*). Line 712 is crucial and we shall return to it later: because the boar is so fierce, it would take a similar degree of anger to face him in close combat. Though their anger against Mezentius is justified because of past atrocities they have suffered, they cannot convert their legitimate anger from a civil context to a military context. Because they cannot rouse themselves adequately to fight with swords (*stricto concurrere ferro*), they have to be content to use javelins and to shout at him. In short, they lack the courage (*uirtus*) to get angry (*irasci*) and so to get close enough (*propius accedere*) for hand-to-hand fighting.

A further example of the necessity of anger for the warrior to face a fierce enemy close up is provided by Silius' simile in *Punica* 5 in which Mago, Hannibal's brother, sees his future son-in-law felled by the Roman Appius, whose actions in the preceding combat are clearly marked by *ira* (*uiolentas . . . iras*, "violent angers," 5.292; and *uires trux ira daret*, "fierce anger provided the strength," 5.299). In a simile which combines two classic wild animals, Mago is compared to a hungry lion watching a fierce bull preparing himself for action, with the bull rousing itself as in the passage from *Aeneid* 12 above (*Punica* 5.306–15):

> iamque aderat clipeumque uiri atque immania membra
> lustrabat uisu, propiorque a fronte coruscae
> lux galeae saeuas paulum tardauerat iras.
> haud secus e specula praeceps delatus opaca,
> subsidens campo summissos contrahit artus,   310
> cum uicina trucis conspexit cornua tauri
> quamuis longa fames stimulet leo; nunc ferus alta
> surgentes ceruice toros, nunc torua sub hirta
> lumina miratur fronte ac iam signa mouentem
> et sparsa pugnas meditantem spectat harena.   315

Now he approached and surveyed the shield and huge limbs of Appius. A closer view of the light that shone from the front of his gleaming helmet slowed down his savage anger for a little time. Just like this a lion that has raced down from his shady look-out crouches down on the plain and gathers his limbs beneath him when he sees nearby the horns of a fierce bull, however much his long hunger goads him on. The beast stares now at the muscles swelling on his high neck, now at the enraged eyes under the shaggy brow. He watches the bull now preparing for action and practicing his fight by pawing the sand.

What is particularly significant for our purposes is Silius' emphasis on the close physical proximity of the two combatants, in the simile and the "ground" (*propior*, "closer," 307; and *uicina*, "nearby," 311). Despite the lion's hunger, which urges him to attack, he is made to pause by the sight of the bull preparing himself for the fight. Again, fighting at close quarters clearly requires an extra concentration of physical and psychological resources.

Moving on through the sequence of battle, we also find animal similes which explicitly mention *ira* at later stages. For example, in *Thebaid* 8 during Tydeus' *aristeia*, Statius describes Tydeus as resembling a tigress exulting in the first blood she has drawn – *uelut primo tigris gauisa cruore | per totum cupit ire pecus* ("like a tigress delighting in her first blood and

eager to go through the whole herd," 8.474–5). He then pits Haemon against
Tydeus in what is inevitably a hopelessly imbalanced contest, at least once
Hercules, the champion of Haemon, has withdrawn in deference to Pallas,
the champion of Tydeus (*Theb.* 8.529–35):

> ille tamen nec stare loco nec comminus ire
> amplius aut uoltus audet perferre cruenti   530
> Tydeos; aegra animo uis ac fiducia cessit:
> qualis saetigeram Lucana cuspide frontem
> strictus aper, penitus cui non infossa cerebro
> uolnera, nec felix dextrae tenor, in latus iras
> frangit et expertae iam non uenit obuius hastae.   535

But he does not dare hold his ground any more or engage in close fighting or endure
the sight of murderous Tydeus. His mental powers grow faint and his confidence
has departed. He is like a boar that has been grazed on its bristly face by a Lucanian
javelin-point, when the wound has not penetrated deep into the brain and the aim
has not been true: he breaks the force of his side-swipes and does not attack the
now familiar spear.

Leaving on one side the meaning of *in latus iras frangit*,[13] what is important
for our purposes is that the boar is characterized as an animal typified by
its anger but which can have that anger broken by circumstances. Thus too
the warrior Haemon and the boar of the simile need *ira*. Once the force of
ira has been broken (*frangit*), strength and confidence are dissipated. Once
again, we see the crucial connection between *ira* and close combat.

   Another case where the warrior's *ira* is inadequate to his ambitions occurs
during the battle of Cannae in Book 10 of Silius' *Punica*. Toward the climax
of the narrative of the battle, one of the Roman commanders, Paulus, who
is seriously wounded, is given the opportunity to escape on horseback. He
refuses and chooses instead to die in battle. At this moment he is compared
to a wounded tigress (*Punica* 10.292–7):

> nec Paulus inultum
> quod superest de luce sinit; ceu uulnere tigris
> letifero cedens tandem proiectaque corpus
> luctatur morti et languentem pandit hiatum   295
> in uanos morsus, nec sufficientibus irae
> ictibus extrema lambit uenabula lingua.

And Paulus did not allow his last moments to pass unavenged. So a mortally
wounded tigress finally gives in and lies down for her struggle with death, opening

---

[13] The 1827 commentary of Amar and Lemaire compares Hor. *Odes* 3.22.7 of a boar *obliquum meditantis
ictum*, "practising its first side-long thrusts." The Loeb translation, "he lets the anger of his side-stroke
weaken," seems inaccurate but study of the entry for *latus* in *TLL* does not suggest any illuminating
analogues.

her feeble jaws for empty bites and with the tip of her tongue licking the spears with efforts that cannot match her anger.

The simile anticipates the description of Paulus' demise which follows: he manages to strike his first attacker, then looks around for Hannibal so that he can die gloriously at his hand, but at that point he is felled by a shower of weapons. Paulus' anger is clearly represented by Silius as a positive phenomenon. The fact that he dies with his *ira* unable to achieve its aims is ominous for the Roman cause in general.

One further case illustrates how *ira* is essential to a warrior under pressure. Toward the end of *Aeneid* 9, Turnus has been surrounded by Trojans who are forcing him to withdraw. Virgil compares him with a lion surrounded by hunters. Though the lion is terrified, yet his combination of *ira* and *uirtus* prevents him from turning his back and running away (*Aeneid* 9.791–8):

> acrius hoc Teucri clamore incumbere magno
> et glomerare manum, ceu saeuum turba leonem
> cum telis premit infensis: at territus ille,
> asper, acerba tuens, retro redit et neque terga
> ira dare aut uirtus patitur, nec tendere contra   795
> ille quidem hoc cupiens potis est per tela uirosque.
> haud aliter retro dubius uestigia Turnus
> improperata refert et mens exaestuat ira.

All the more fiercely the Teucrians crowd him with loud shouting and mass their ranks, as when a crowd corners a savage lion with their spears levelled. But the lion, terrified, dangerous, and glaring fiercely, backs away. His anger and his courage do not let him turn tail, but, much though he wants to, he is not able to charge the weapons and the men. In two minds just like this, Turnus steps backwards unhurriedly, his mind seething with anger.

Again we see that *ira*, in combination with *uirtus*, is essential to a warrior in facing his enemy at close quarters in a confrontation where loss of face is likely. The way that Virgil brackets *ira* with *uirtus* suggests that, in circumstances like this, the two mesh together to form the intrinsic backbone of the warrior mentality.

So far, the representation of angry epic warriors in similes as wild beasts has had positive connotations: the arousal of rage is essential to the warrior facing battle; it is part of his *uirtus* ("courage," "machismo"). But epic *ira* is not always positive. Turnus offers a classic case of anger running out of control and into an inexorable bloodthirsty rage earlier in *Aeneid* 9. Turnus has marched on the Trojan camp but the Trojans refuse to fight him. Turnus is then described as a wolf frustrated in its attempt to enter a sheepfold (*Aen.* 9.57–66):

>   huc turbidus atque huc
>   lustrat equo muros aditumque per auia quaerit
>   ac ueluti pleno lupus insidiatus ouili
>   cum fremit ad caulas, uentos perpessus et imbris,   60
>   nocte super media; tuti sub matribus agni
>   balatum exercent; ille asper et improbus ira
>   saeuit in absentis; collecta fatigat edendi
>   ex longo rabies et siccae sanguine fauces:
>   haud aliter Rutulo muros et castra tuenti   65
>   ignescunt irae, duris dolor ossibus ardet.

Here and there he rides wildly around the walls and seeks a way in where there is none, just like a wolf lying in wait outside a full sheepfold, when in the middle of the night he roars at the pens, enduring winds and rain. Safe beneath their mothers the lambs keep bleating. Fierce and reckless in his anger he rages at them, out of his reach. He is worn out by the fury for eating which has gathered for a long time and by his jaws, dry of blood. Even so the Rutulian's anger is on fire as he scans the walls and the camp and resentment is raging in his hard bones.

The pathos inherent in the detail of the bleating of the lambs as they shelter beneath their mothers determines a negative interpretation of Turnus' anger here. In contrast with the hungry lion in *Punica* 5, the wolf's hunger is expressed in hostile, emotive terms as "the fury for eating" (*edendi . . . rabies*). Moreover, whereas Silius pits a hungry lion against a bull, which promises a balanced contest, Virgil has his hungry wolf menace only defenceless lambs. Even the choice of a wolf makes Turnus ignoble, in the light of Statius' distinction between the noble lion and the (by implication) ignoble dogs and wolves at *Thebaid* 12.739–40 (above).

We find a similar phenomenon in the clash between Eteocles and Polynices in Book 11 of Statius' *Thebaid*, where the brothers are depicted as a pair of wild boars fighting savagely. The brothers, accompanied to the fight by the Furies, are already enmeshed in their duel. At 11.497–8 Statius steps up the intensity: "then truly angers are inflamed by greater goads: they decide to fight" (*tunc uero accensae stimulis maioribus irae:* | *arma placent*). The two brothers exchange blows and become entangled with one another (11.524–9), as the language reflects with the many elisions:

>   coeunt sine more, sine arte,
>   tantum animis iraque atque ignescentia cernunt   525
>   per galeas odia et uoltus rimantur acerbo
>   lumine: nil adeo mediae telluris, et enses
>   impliciti innexaeque manus, alternaque saeui
>   murmura ceu lituos rapiunt aut signa tubarum.

They engage without order, without skill, only with spirit and anger. Through their helmets they see blazing hatred and they rake each other's faces with pitiless gaze. There is no middle ground between them. Their swords are intertwined and their hands are interlocked. In their savagery they catch each other's grunts like bugles or trumpet-calls.

Then comes the simile of the clash of two wild boars, watched in silence by the hunter and his dogs (11.530–8):

> fulmineos ueluti praeceps cum comminus egit   530
> ira sues strictisque erexit tergora saetis:
> igne tremunt oculi, lunataque dentibus uncis
> ora sonant; spectat pugnas de rupe propinqua
> uenator pallens canibusque silentia suadet:
> sic auidi incurrunt; necdum letalia miscent   535
> uolnera, sed coeptus sanguis, facinusque peractum est.
> nec iam opus est Furiis: tantum mirantur et adstant
> laudantes, hominumque dolent plus posse furores.

As when headlong anger has driven lightning-swift boars into close combat and made their shaggy backs bristle, their eyes quiver with fire and their crescent mouths sound out with their curved tusks. From a nearby crag the anxious hunter watches the fight and tells his dogs to keep quiet. So, they attack eagerly and exchange wounds that are not yet fatal but blood is shed and the crime is committed. And there is no more need of Furies: they just stand and stare in delight – and they regret that human rage is more powerful than their own.

There are two points to the simile: the nature of the fight and the awe it inspires in the spectators. First, Statius emphasizes the fierceness of the fight. He specifies that the anger of the boars is *praeceps* ("headlong"), reflecting the fact that the duel has moved from its initial stages into a phase where the emotions are more raw and instinctual. The swiftness of the boars' movements is denoted well by *fulmineos* ("lightning-swift"). As with the lion at Lucan, *Bellum Ciuile* 1.208–10 and the boar at *Aeneid* 10.711, we find these boars enhance the terror of their appearance by raising their bristles, an effect increased by their looks of fire and by the noises they emit. Above all, Statius emphasizes that this fight involves the closest of close combat, with his picture of intertwined limbs and swords (527–8), which is reinforced in the simile with the word *comminus* (530), now familiar in these contexts. Such a close fight inevitably requires *ira* on the part of the combatants. This is hardly surprising given that the combatants are brothers, as Statius reminds us in the very next words, *fratris uterque* . . . (539). Their consanguinity presumably creates an additional psychological obstacle which has to be overcome. This of course explains Statius' choice of animals in this simile – this is a rare, perhaps unparalleled, case of conflict between two creatures of the same species.

The second point of connection between simile and ground is in the reaction of the spectators. The sheer ferocity of the conflict they are witnessing deprives both the hunter and his dogs in the simile and the Furies in the ground of any active role. That is, the duel between like-and-like is so intense that it is self-sufficient, requiring no intervention from outsiders. The negative moral implications of this fact are spelled out by Statius when he says "the crime is committed" (*facinus . . . peractum est*, 536) and interprets the lack of involvement of the Furies in terms of excessive human *furor*.

Finally, we might usefully observe that this simile provides the prelude to the denouement, in which Polynices first fatally wounds his brother and Eteocles falls but then manages to trick Polynices into approaching close enough to deliver a fatal wound, an exercise of "retributive anger" (*ultrices . . . iras*, 563). That is, the simile conveys the fierceness of an anger that is running out of control, with no holds barred, and it emphasizes the fatal consequences of this equilibrium of anger. Statius clearly conceptualizes this as a situation of two identical *irae* pitted against one another.

Finally, Statius provides pictures of the surfeit and passing of anger in two further similes. The first case occurs in the simile which compares Tydeus to a lion in *Thebaid* 2.[14] Tydeus is approaching completion of the task of killing the fifty men who had ambushed him. Despite his threatening words to his remaining victims, he feels feeble and exhausted (*Thebaid* 2.668–81):

> haec intonat; ast tamen illi
> membra negant, lassusque ferit praecordia sanguis.
> iam sublata manus cassos defertur in ictus   670
> tardatique gradus, clipeum nec sustinet umbo
> mutatum spoliis, gelidus cadit imber anhelo
> pectore, tum crines ardentiaque ora cruentis
> roribus et taetra morientum aspargine manant:
> ut leo qui campis longe custode fugato   675
> Massylas depastus oues ubi sanguine multo
> luxuriata fames ceruixque et tabe grauatae
> consedere iubae, mediis in caedibus adstat
> aeger, hians uictusque cibis; nec amplius irae
> crudescunt: tantum uacuis ferit aera malis   680
> molliaque eiecta delambit uellera lingua.

---

[14] On Tydeus as a lion here and in Book 8 (lines 593–6, n.b. *furor*), with the same lust for blood, see Vessey (1973) 225.

So he thunders. But his limbs say no and the tired blood strikes his heart. Now his raised arm falls in empty strikes and his steps are slow and his shield-arm cannot hold up his shield now altered by spoils. Cold sweat drenches his panting chest, and his hair and blazing face are dripping with bloody dew and the disgusting spattering of the dying. Just like a lion that has fed to satiety on Massylian sheep after driving the shepherd far from the meadows, when his hunger is sated by an abundance of blood and his neck and mane are stiff and congealed with gore, he stands there in the middle of the slaughter reeling, gaping and overcome by gorging. His anger rages no more. He just strikes the air with his empty jaws and lightly licks the soft wool with his lolling tongue.

Tydeus' *ira* has passed its peak. Again, this demonstrates the necessity for the arousal and maintenance of *ira* during close combat. Once *ira* has faded, the warrior is unable to maintain his momentum. One other significant feature of this episode is Pallas' intervention at this point to curb Tydeus' instinct to go to Thebes to vaunt his success: "now set a limit" (*iam pone modum*, 688), she advises him. This is a clear marker that Tydeus is prone to break the limits under the influence of anger and passion – a point to which we will return. For the moment, though, we should observe that on this occasion Pallas does manage to limit his *ira*.[15]

   The second case of the fading of anger occurs during the night-slaughter in *Thebaid* 10. Here, after massacring his unarmed, sleeping enemies until he is virtually wading through corpses, the augur Thiodamas experiences a palpable diminution of his anger. For this he is likened to a tigress whose rage is satisfied by the carnage she has wrought (10.286–95):

> iam tarda manus, iam debile ferrum
> et caligantes nimiis successibus irae.
> Caspia non aliter magnorum in strage iuuencum
> tigris, ubi immenso rabies placata cruore
> lassauitque genas et crasso sordida tabo   290
> confudit maculas, spectat sua facta doletque
> defecisse famem: uictus sic augur inerrat
> caedibus Aoniis; optet nunc bracchia centum
> centenasque in bella manus; iam taedet inanes
> exhaurire minas, hostemque adsurgere mallet.   295

Now his hand slows down, now his weapon weakens, and his anger dims from too much success. Exactly so a Caspian tigress looks at her deeds in a massacre of huge bullocks, when fury appeased by streams of blood has wearied her jaws and foully stained her stripes with clotted gore: she regrets her loss of appetite. Just so the augur wanders through the Aonian massacre, overcome. Now he would wish

---

[15] See Vessey (1973) 292.

for one hundred arms and one hundred hands to fight with. Now he dislikes to squander menaces in vain and he could wish the enemy would rise against him.

Taking the simile and its ground together, Statius here offers an equivalence between *irae* (287) and *rabies* ("fury," 289), an equivalence that again determines a negative reading of *ira*. In the case of both warrior and tigress, the discrepancy between mind and body is a matter for regret: the urge to continue killing is there but not the physical capacity. The simile also hints at an equivalence between anger and hunger, nicely captured in the Loeb's translation of *famem* as "appetite," to which we shall return later.

This investigation of the epic similes depicting the operation of warriors' *ira* through comparisons with wild beasts bears out Thornton's claim that the moral tenor of *ira* derives from its context. Broadly speaking, *ira* is depicted as a necessary requirement for the epic warrior as he prepares himself to face combat, and this is so whether *ira* is portrayed in a positive or negative light. More often than not, the warrior's *ira* is presented in a positive light. Especially at the initial stage, it appears that the warrior's anger is under his control: like a wild animal, he can stimulate himself to the necessary pitch to enter the fight. Epic *ira* is negative when it runs out of control, as in *Aeneid* 9 and *Thebaid* 11, significantly, in the latter case, not at the early stage of combat but toward its climax. Two texts present *ira* in a negative light as it fades and dissipates, when the warrior's desire to continue fighting beyond what is required is not matched by his physical capacity.

THE ROLE OF ANGER IN CLOSE COMBAT

One crucial aspect of the epic warrior's *ira* emerges from this investigation. Many of these texts indicate that *ira* is required for the most taxing kind of combat – fighting at close quarters. Three texts explicitly use the word *comminus* ("at close quarters": Lucan, *B.C.* 1.206; Statius, *Theb.* 8.529 and 11.530: the word is actually derived from *com-* = "together" and *manus* = "hand") while others imply or assume a context of hand-to-hand fighting. Other texts too, apart from the similes, bear out the close association of *ira* with hand-to-hand fighting: Virgil, *Aeneid.* 9.44, *ergo etsi conferre manum pudor iraque monstrat* ("so though honour and anger suggest hand-to-hand combat"); 11.688–90, *tum magis increscunt animis discordibus irae | et iam collecti Troes glomerantur eodem | et conferre manum et procurrere longius audent* ("then anger grows fiercer in their warring spirits and now the Trojans gather and swarm to the spot and dare to fight hand-to-hand and to make longer sallies"); Silius, *Punica* 1.515–16, *sic Poenus pressumque ira simul exigit ensem | qua capuli statuere morae* ("so spoke the Carthaginian and at the same time clutching his sword in anger he drove it home till the hilt stopped it"); 4.262–3, *surgit uiolentior ira | comminus* ("his anger became more violent as they closed"); 5.558–60, *pulchro Mauorte accensus in iram | et dignum sese ratus in certamina sacro | comminus ire uiro* ("he was aroused to anger by fine warfare and thought it matched his dignity to enter hand-to-hand combat with the fierce warrior"); 9.382, *capuloque tenus ferrum impulit ira* ("his anger drove in the sword up to the hilt"). Statius' simile of the diminution of the winds' *ira* when it finds no resistance at *Thebaid* 12.726–9, especially *uentorum uelut ira minor nisi silua furentes | impedit* ("just as the anger of the winds is weakened unless a forest impedes their rampage"), clearly participates in the same idea.

This representation of epic *ira* reflects an important difference between ancient warfare and modern warfare with its panoply of long-range, technological weapons. John Keegan, the military historian, in a chapter called "The Inhuman Face of War," remarks upon "the impersonalisation of battle," as follows:

Medieval soldiers not only saw their opponents at very close hand (the high-born among them indeed were very often acquainted with one another) but fought them face to face. The rhythm of the fighting and its duration were in consequence dictated by human limitations: a man gained ground on his opponent, scored a hit, felt his sword arm tire, knew he must win in the next five minutes or be done for; and *pari passu* the same rhythms imposed themselves on his opponent.[16]

By contrast:

direct, face-to-face, knock-down and drag-out violence is something which modern, middle-class Western man encounters rarely if at all in his everyday life.[17]

Keegan observes the gradual detachment from the act of killing by the class of men who direct battle. His speculation on the reasons for this resonates for the warriors of ancient epic:

For killing to be gentlemanly, it must take place between gentlemen; the rules of duelling were, indeed, specific on that point, and the laws of chivalry, though less exigent and exclusive, were equally insistent that the only feats of arms worth the name were those conducted between men of gentle birth, either one to one or in nearly (ideally in exactly) matched numbers. But every trend in warfare since the

---

[16] Keegan (1976) 281.
[17] Keegan (1976) 277. This separation from real violence is one of the themes of the recent movie, *Fight Club*.

end of the Middle Ages has been to make personal encounters on the battlefield between men of equal social status more and more difficult to arrange – drill, the most important military innovation of the sixteenth century, requiring that a man stay where put instead of wandering about looking for a worthy adversary, and smoke, the most obtrusive side-effect of musketry, making such a search improbably successful – and such encounters, even if possible of arrangement, less and less representable as "fair fight." For "fair fight" requires equality of skill. But firearms reduced skill-at-arms to an irrelevance – it was for this that the knight principally condemned them. The sword stroke, practised a thousand times, polished and refined and measured to pass unerringly beneath an opponent's parry, was beaten flat by a musket-shot.[18]

Epic *ira* fits into this same schema. And nowhere is this stated more explicitly than at *Aeneid* 10.104, where Virgil explicitly remarks that none of Mezentius' enemies has "the courage to get angry or to come closer" (*irasci propiusue accedere uirtus*). This line defines *uirtus* ("courage", "excellence," "manliness") in the context of battle as two equivalent or mutually implicated phenomena: "growing angry" and "approaching closer," demonstrating that *ira* is essential to the warrior's *uirtus*, above all for those facing hand to hand combat.

BATTLEFIELD ANGER WITHOUT SIMILES

As we remarked earlier, direct depictions of the arousal of anger in epic combat narratives are surprisingly rare. Statius, however, provides two such scenes and we shall close this central section by looking at these. The first is Tydeus' confrontation with Polynices at the door of Adrastus' palace at Argos in *Thebaid* 1. By way of introduction, we should observe that in the opening to his epic, Statius fixes upon Tydeus' excessively strong disposition towards *ira* in a remarkably prominent place. At *Thebaid* 1.41–2 he asks of his Muse:

> quem prius heroum, Clio, dabis? immodicum irae
> Tydea?

Which hero do you offer to me first, Clio? Tydeus, uncontrolled in his anger?

He proceeds to list the rest of the Seven Against Thebes (besides Polynices and Adrastus) in the sequence in which they will perish in the epic. Tydeus, however, he has taken out of sequence, ahead of Amphiaraus. This seems significant: Statius wishes to emphasize the negative manifestation of *ira* in the character of Tydeus.

---

[18] Keegan (1976) 279.

This is therefore an excellent preparation for the opening action of
the epic, following the preliminaries: Oedipus' invocation of the Fury
Tisiphone, the scene in Thebes, and the debate between Jupiter and Juno,
which closes with Jupiter's announcement, "That will be the cause of anger
and the rest I shall introduce in due sequence" (*hinc causae irarum, certo reli-
qua ordine ducam*, 1.302), namely, the clash between Polynices and Tydeus.
We are told that Adrastus had been forewarned that his future sons-in-law
were approaching, although he does not yet understand the warning – and
here we return for just a moment to the imagery of the similes (1.395–7):

> cui Phoebus generos – monstrum exitiabile dictu!   395
> mox adaperta fides – fato ducente canebat
> saetigerumque suem et fuluum aduentare leonem.

Phoebus under fate's guidance had revealed to him the arrival of his sons-in-
law – a fatal horror to tell, but soon its reliability was manifest – a bristly boar and
a tawny lion.

Polynices is forced to spend a horrific stormy night sheltering in the doorway
of Adrastus' palace. Tydeus is likewise caught in the storm and seeks the
same shelter. But neither of the two has the temperament to share the space,
a motif which recalls Don Fowler's invocation of anthropological material
in his essay on "Epicurean Anger," where he reports the absence of anger
among the Utku of Canada, who have some 35,000 square miles between
the two or three dozen of them.[19] This is what happens (*Theb.* 1.408–13):

> his uero ambobus rabiem fortuna cruentam
> adtulit: haud passi sociis defendere noctem
> culminibus, paulum alternis in uerba minasque   410
> cunctantur; mox ut iactis sermonibus irae
> intumuere satis, tum uero erectus uterque
> exsertare umeros nudamque lacessere pugnam.

Fortune affected both of these with a bloody fury: they could not endure warding
off the night under a shelter that was shared. For a while they delayed with an
exchange of threatening words, then when the taunts they had tossed had swollen
their anger enough, each one stood at full height, freed his shoulders, and offered
a challenge to naked combat.

The first stage here is *rabies* ("fury"): their uncontrolled reaction of indignation to being disturbed and challenged by the other. Then there is verbal
assault: the two hurl threats at one another. Statius explicitly tells us that

---

[19] Fowler (1997) 17.

this verbal exchange arouses their anger to the point where they start fighting physically. They do so without weapons (*nudam . . . pugnam*), wrestling for sole possession of the sheltered spot. The narrator says that they might have drawn their swords had not king Adrastus appeared, disturbed by the commotion (1.428–33):

> forsan et accinctos lateri – sic ira ferebat –
> nudassent enses, meliusque hostilibus armis
> lugendus fratri, iuuenis Thebane, iaceres,   430
> ni rex, insolitum clamorem et pectore ab alto
> stridentes gemitus noctis miratus in umbris,
> mouisset gressus . . .

Perhaps they would have unsheathed the swords that hung at their sides – that's what their anger was leading them towards – and you, young man of Thebes, would be lying better as the victim of an enemy's weapons, lamented by your brother, if the king had not come this way, amazed at the unusual noise and the groans dredged from deep in the chest in the shadows of the night . . .

Of course Statius must avoid them drawing their swords on one another as that could indeed spell the premature closure of his epic tale. But he explicitly marks their mood of anger with the phrase *sic ira ferebat*, a fine use of the imperfect tense, "that's what their anger was leading them toward," to underline the predominant feature of the encounter. And as Bonds observes, nowhere else in the epic does Polynices show the intensity of angry emotion that he displays in this fight with Tydeus until his final duel with his brother Eteocles in Book 11.[20]

What interests us especially here is the close correspondence between this description of the two sons-in-law working themselves into a psychological state in which they can fight as fiercely as possible and the representations in similes of animals working themselves up. Observe that Polynices and Tydeus, one wearing a lion-skin and the other a boar-skin (1.482–97: "under the feigned appearance of wild beasts," *uultu fallente ferarum*, 496), do not immediately leap into physical combat. There is a sequence of provocation which is verbal: they explicitly "delay" (*cunctantur*) over their "threatening words" (*uerba minasque*) and only after this preliminary "volley of insults" (*iactis sermonibus*) do they start to fight; that is, the exchange of angry words resembles the animals of the similes working themselves into fury, by their physical actions (lashing tail, feinting strokes in the air, pawing the ground, and especially roaring loudly). What is more, the effect of these preliminaries is to increase physical bulk or at least physical

---

[20] Bonds (1985) 227.

appearance: Statius says that their anger swells (*intumuere*) and that seems a most apposite word, because he next tells us that both of them stand at full height (*erectus*), just as the animals increase their impressiveness by making their hair stand up.[21] Finally, we should not neglect the noise of anger. Statius is explicit that Adrastus is disturbed by noise made by the men, the *clamor* and *gemitus*. This too connects closely with the similes of animals arousing their wrath in which noise plays a crucial role. In short, Adrastus' future sons-in-law could hardly resemble a boar and a lion more closely.[22] There is a really tight coherence between this episode and other epic treatments of angry warriors.

Finally in this section, we find a treatment of the mass psychology of warriors in *Thebaid* 8. Epic much more rarely offers representations of mass anger than of individual anger – probably genre is the most important factor here[23] – but even here, the author uses description of fierce and potentially terrifying animals to augment his representation of human *ira*. There is a difference here: the animals are not in a simile. After a strident invocation of the Muse Calliope – "But now battle summons me: supply new strength afresh, Calliope, and let a greater Apollo tune my lyre" (*sed iam bella uocant: alias noua suggere uires,* | *Calliope, maiorque chelyn mihi tendat Apollo, Theb.* 8.373–4) – Statius sets the scene (8.383–94):

> stat medius campis etiamnum cuspide sicca
> Bellipotens, iamque hos clipeum, iam uertit ad illos
> arma ciens, aboletque domos, conubia, natos.   385
> pellitur et patriae et, qui mente nouissimus exit,
> lucis amor; tenet in capulis hastisque paratas
> ira manus animusque ultra thoracas anhelus
> conatur, galeaeque tremunt horrore comarum.
> quid mirum caluisse uiros? flammantur in hostem   390
> cornipedes niueoque rigant sola putria nimbo,
> corpora ceu mixti dominis irasque sedentum
> induerint: sic frena terunt, sic proelia poscunt
> hinnitu tolluntque armos equitesque supinant.

---

[21] It also seems hard to resist the sexual implication of Statius' vocabulary here, perhaps particularly appropriate in this case of Adrastus' future sons-in-law, but found elsewhere in the *Thebaid* in a repeating pattern of the arousal and detumescence of powerful emotions, as Hershkowitz (1998a) sees, 252, n. 10 and 271–82.

[22] See Vessey (1973) 96: "their garb signifies all the bestial fury that is so soon to be unleashed. Apollo was right to term the two heroes lion and boar. It is not only their external vesture that is in question but their inner nature. The savagery of wild beasts is in possession of Polynices and Tydeus."

[23] Silius offers a few examples, e.g. *Punica* 6.317, *nec mens erat ulla sine ira*; 13.184, *aequarunt irae dextras*: 14.299, *par omnes simul ira rapit*. It is likely that historiography might supplement this gap.

In the middle of the plain the War-god stands with his spear-point still dry and he turns his shield against now these and now those, stirring up the fight and blotting out homes and marriages and children. He drives out love of country and love of the light, which leaves the mind last of all. Anger keeps their hands ready on the sword-hilts and the spears, the panting spirit is bursting out of its breastplates, and the helmets shake beneath their quivering plumes. It is not amazing that the heroes are hot for the fight – their horn-footed chargers are on fire against the enemy and bedew the crumbling soil with a white shower, as if their bodies were shared with their masters and they had put on the anger of their riders. That's how they champ at the bit, that's how they demand battle with their neighing and rear up and flip the horsemen backwards.

According to Statius, the prospect of battle wipes out all thought of the loyalties at the heart of life, even loyalty to life itself (cf. *Aen.* 2.314–17). But that is not to say that these warriors are out of control. On the contrary, they are highly focused. Their anger is not yet raging but explicitly holding their hands ready, with the pent-up energy well conveyed by their excited breathing (*animus... anhelus*), by their trembling (*tremunt*), and by the way their anger has communicated itself to their horses (*caluisse* and *flammantur* make clear the correspondence), so that their horses are foaming, champing at the bit, neighing, and rearing up in their enthusiasm. Although this is not presented as a simile, it serves the same purpose: the analogy between the waiting warriors and the horses is exact. To throw in a modern analogy, this picture of anger under control but about to be unleashed could be represented as the revving of Formula One cars as they await the signal for the start of the race.

ANGER, CONTEXT, AND APPROPRIATENESS

The evidence afforded by many of the passages discussed above suggests that *ira* is essential to the warrior facing combat at close quarters. *Ira* can be aroused and accessed for good effect and only constitutes a defect when it runs out of control.[24] Our close analysis bears out Thornton's views on the moral neutrality of epic *ira* and on the importance of context. Her emphasis

---

[24] Our focus here is almost wholly upon epic warriors, upon individuals acting on the battlefield. *Ira* plays a slightly different role when it becomes associated with military discipline on a larger scale. This is particularly evident in a strand of material in Silius' historical epic, *Punica*, which may after all reflect more closely the lived reality of legionary discipline familiar to any of the Roman elite with military experience. There is a series of episodes in *Punica* which focus upon the control of *ira* – his own and others' – by an idealized Roman commander. Fabius Maximus is the outstanding example, as in the incident in Book 7, for example 517, 564, 577–9. Similar is the character of Livius, who at 15.600, *patriae donauerat iram*, "gave up his anger for the sake of his country." Both are following the precedent set by Camillus (7.557–63). The control of anger in the aftermath of the fighting is also tackled by Silius, for example at 13.319–25, where Pan intervenes to dissipate Roman anger against the captured city of Capua, and in Book 14, where Marcellus represses the anger of his soldiers

upon context echoes the focus of the Peripatetics upon appropriateness with regard to anger. That view is hotly contested by the Stoics, who produce an absolute condemnation of anger. In Appendix 2 we outline the positions as articulated by the likes of Cicero and Seneca to the (not very great) extent that this material bears upon anger on the battlefield. The dichotomy articulated in the Hellenistic philosophical schools also underpins the constructions of anger offered by twentieth-century classical scholars. Nowhere do we see this more vividly than in interpretation of the end of the *Aeneid*.[25] Without reopening discussion of this matter here, we observe that the end of *Aeneid* 12 is open to debate precisely because of disagreement at the level of reception about whether or not Aeneas' very explicit anger – he is "inflamed by rage and terrifying in his anger" (*furiis accensus et ira* | *terribilis*, 12.946–7) – is appropriate.

IRA BEYOND THE BOUNDS: CANNIBALISM

We conclude this chapter with categorically the most horrific manifestation of anger on the battlefield: cannibalism. It occurs twice in our texts, in the aftermath to the battle of Lake Trasimene in Book 6 of *Punica*, and as the climax of *Thebaid* 8. In the first case, Silius adapts his narrative from Livy, who locates this incident in the aftermath to Cannae where he has a Roman soldier eating a Numidian, "anger turned into fury" (*in rabiem ira uersa*, Livy 22.51.9). Using the same word, *rabies*, to introduce the incident, Silius pauses to mark its horror (*Pun.* 6.41–53):

> iuxta cernere erat meritae sibi poscere carmen
> uirtutis sacram rabiem. Laeuinus ab alto
> Priuerno, uitis Latiae praesignis honore,
> exanimum Nasamona Tyren super ipse iacebat
> exanimis; non hasta uiro, non ensis; in artis   45
> abstulerat Fors arma; tamen certamine nudo
> inuenit Marti telum dolor. ore cruento
> pugnatum, ferrique uicem dens praebuit irae.
> iam lacerae nares foedataque lumina morsu,
> iam truncum raptis caput auribus, ipsaque diris   50
> frons depasta modis et sanguine abundat hiatus;
> nec satias donec mandentia linqueret ora
> spiritus et plenos rictus mors atra teneret.

and thus spares the city of Syracuse (14.666–73). Incidentally, Silius' language of *ira* is particularly rich – more so than any other of the epic poets, including Virgil. This, we suggest, would merit further investigation.

[25] For recent continuations of the debate that has now long raged see for example Galinsky (1994) and Putnam (1995) 201–45 and above all Christopher Gill's discussion in this volume.

Nearby could be seen a dreadful fury of courage that deserves to claim celebration in song. Laevinus from high Privernum, distinguished by the award of the Roman vine-staff, was lying on top of Tyres, a Nasamonian, both lifeless. The warrior had no spear, no sword. Chance had robbed him of his weapons in tough fighting. Yet in the unarmed struggle his resentment had found a weapon to fight with. He had battled with his bloody mouth and his teeth did the work of a weapon to gratify his anger. Already his nose was torn and the eyes defiled by his bite, already the ears were torn off and the head mutilated. Even the forehead was horribly gnawed and gaping wounds were streaming with blood. And Laevinus was not satisfied until the breath departed from his champing jaws and dark death took hold of his crammed mouth.

Silius makes explicit the role of *ira* in this incident at line 48 where he says that anger causes the substitution of tooth for weapon. The graphic and horrific detail of this example of "grim courage" (*tristis . . . uirtus*, 6.54) suggests that this is a case of *ira* rampantly out of moral control.

Our other example is even more graphic. The *aristeia* of Tydeus draws to a close when he is struck by a spear "charged with enormous anger," thrown by Melanippus: "Look! An enormous spear laden with anger and fate cuts through the breezes" (*ecce secat zephyros ingentem fraxinus iram | fortunamque ferens, Theb.* 8.716–17). Melanippus is terrified about having wounded Tydeus and would prefer not to claim responsibility, but his companions reveal his identity. Tydeus responds immediately by striking Melanippus, but is then removed to the edge of the battlefield by his companions. In the throes of death, he beseeches his friends to bring him Melanippus – specifically, Melanippus' head (*caput*), although for the moment it is possible to pass this over as an insignificant detail. Capaneus rushes off and returns with the still-breathing Melanippus. This is how Book 8 closes (751–66):

> erigitur Tydeus uoltuque occurrit et amens
> laetitiaque iraque, ut singultantia uidit
> ora trahique oculos seseque adgnouit in illo,
> imperat abscisum porgi, laeuaque receptum
> spectat atrox hostile caput, gliscitque tepentis   755
> lumina torua uidens et adhuc dubitantia figi.
> infelix contentus erat: plus exigit ultrix
> Tisiphone; iamque inflexo Tritonia patre
> uenerat et misero decus immortale ferebat
> atque illum effracti perfusum tabe cerebri   760
> aspicit et uiuo scelerantem sanguine fauces –
> nec comites auferre ualent –: stetit aspera Gorgon
> crinibus emissis rectique ante ora cerastae

uelauere deam; fugit auersata iacentem
nec prius astra subit quam mystica lampas et insons   765
Elisos multa purgauit lumina lympha.

Tydeus raises himself and looks him in the face. Crazed with exhilaration and
anger, when he saw them drag the gasping mouth and eyes and recognized himself
there, he orders them to cut off and hand to him his enemy's fierce head. He seizes
it in his left hand and gazes at it and he is elated to see it still warm with life and
the enraged eyes still resisting becoming fixed. The miserable man was content,
but avenging Tisiphone demands still more. And now Tritonia had appeased her
father and come and was carrying immortal glory to the wretched man – and then
she sees him drenched with the gore of the shattered brains and his jaws polluted
by living blood – and his companions cannot tear it away from him. The Gorgon
stood stiff with her snake-hair stretched out and the horned snakes rearing up
in front of her face shielded the goddess. With her face averted, she runs away
from him as he lies there and she does not enter heaven until the mystic lamp and
guiltless Elisos have cleansed her eyes with plenty of water.

Statius specifies that Tydeus' exultation and anger (marked by the Homeric-
style repeated enclitic *-que* in *laetitiaque iraque*) have here passed beyond
the bounds: his anger has transformed into madness and he is "crazed"
(*amens*, 751). At first, his anger was content with gazing upon the head of
Melanippus, but then we see the operation of anger-become-madness on
the battlefield, when the Fury Tisiphone, here marked by the etymologizing
epithet *ultrix*,[26] makes him go further and actually devour the living brains
of his killer and victim. This last act of insane anger deprives Tydeus of
the glory that Pallas was bringing him and extends his pollution even to
her. In other words, his anger on the battlefield apparently received divine
sanction when it extended to no more than gazing on the head of his enemy;
it is the Fury-driven act of eating the brains that deprives Tydeus of divine
approval and creates pollution.[27] The horror of this moment is captured on
the terracotta group from the pediment of the Temple of Pyrgi (first half
of the fifth century BCE), which represents Tydeus devouring the brains of
Melanippus with Pallas Athene looking on.[28] The moral loading is explicit.
For an apposite analogy, we need look no further than Juvenal's fifteenth
Satire. There, Juvenal condemns an Egyptian tribe for an act of cannibalism
perpetrated on a living victim, whose flesh is torn from him and eaten raw.
In his condemnation he represents anger and hunger as equivalent in the

---

[26] Punning on τίσις: see Hershkowitz (1998a) 264: Statius takes this from Virgil, *Aen.* 6.570–1.
[27] See Dominik (1994) 51.
[28] Temple at Pyrgi, Museo Villa Giulia, Rome.

Egyptian tribe's eyes: "these peoples who assimilate and identify anger and hunger" (*in quorum mente pares sunt | et similes ira atque fames*, 15.130–1).[29]

ABC: ANGER, BEASTS, AND CANNIBALISM

And so we have come full circle, back to the consumption of raw and living flesh that characterized Achilles' boyhood diet. In the case of Statius' Achilles, the diet of the raw and still-living flesh of fierce animals is represented as a positive and crucial element in his training as a warrior. The "homoeopathic magic" thus accessed functions to endow Achilles with the qualities of those beasts beyond all other warriors: he has the fearlessness and the capacity to arouse the anger which he needs to face any opponent imaginable and to fight with that opponent at close quarters. But we can also speculate that Achilles' diet may also hold a negative potential for the misuse of that anger, when it goes beyond bounds. After all, what his diet does not bestow is instruction in justice, a sense of right and wrong. That had to come separately, as Statius had Achilles point out at the end of his speech at *Achilleid* 2.163–4 (see above). Excessive anger is what characterizes Achilles in the *Iliad* – it leads to his withdrawal of his fighting services from the Greek army. And excessive anger is what characterizes Statius' Tydeus, the warrior who is introduced as *immodicum irae* (1.41), in the *Thebaid*. With *this* difference: *his* anger goes beyond that of Achilles and beyond the bounds of civilized society to manifest itself as eating raw the living brains of his enemy.

Achilles, of course, comes close to this when he articulates his threat against Hector in their duel. At *Iliad* 22.345–54 he expresses a wish to have the impetus to eat Hector raw, a wish he then modulates into an assertion that Hector will lie unburied for the dogs and birds (tr. Lattimore):[30]

> No more entreating of me, you dog, by knees or parents.
> I wish only that my spirit and fury would drive me
> to hack your meat away and eat it raw for the things that
> you have done to me. So there is no one who can hold the dogs off
> from your head, not if they bring here and set before me ten times
> and twenty times the ransom, and promise more in addition,
> not if Priam son of Dardanos should offer to weigh out

---

[29] John Henderson (1998) 234–8 at 235 sees Tydeus' cannibalistic savagery as "the worst that could be said on how people ought not to (tr)eat" and rightly links this incident with the fight between Polynices and Tydeus in Book 1 and the duel between the brothers in Book 11.

[30] This passage is reprised, virtually quoted, in *The Thin Red Line*, the recent and quite excellent movie treating in an unusually honest way the experience of soldiers in World War II.

your bulk in gold; not even so shall the lady your mother
who herself bore you lay you on the death-bed and mourn you:
no, but the dogs and the birds will have you all for their feasting.

Clearly, both the consumption of one's enemy's raw flesh and the leaving of
his body unburied are both offenses against *humanitas* ("humanity"). But
equally clearly, of the two, cannibalism is the worse offense. As Hans van
Wees says in his discussion of warriors and violence in Homer: "The range
of expressions of anger runs from ubiquitous 'scowling' at one's opponent,
via insulting, threatening, robbing, beating and wounding him, to killing
him and mutilating his corpse. In extreme fury one may wish to eat one's
enemy, but cannibalism remains in the realm of angry fantasy (IV.34–6;
XXII.346–7; XXIV.212–13)."[31] Achilles' anger does not extend as far as that
of Tydeus and, importantly, in the final book of the *Iliad* Achilles takes
the opportunity given him to modulate his anger with an element of self-
restraint (see Most's paper in this volume), whereas Tydeus' moment of
excess is also his moment of death.

Desires toward or acts of cannibalism on the battlefield may seem to
belong to the realm of fantasy. Yet the phenomenon features in doctors'
reports about soldiers who fought in Vietnam. In his 1994 book, *Achilles
in Vietnam: Combat Trauma and the Undoing of Character*, Jonathan Shay
devotes an entire chapter to the state of being "berserk." This refers to the
phenomenon of soldiers who perform amazing feats while in the grip of
a separate mental state caused typically by grief that has become anger at
the death of a close comrade. Such soldiers were called "berserkers" and, as
Shay points out, "Achilles is the prototype of the berserker."[32] Significantly
for our present study, the word "berserk" may be etymologically connected
with "bear." If this is so, and even if it is not but is widely believed to be so,
the word invites us to make a connection with the animal similes examined
in the central part of this paper. Shay lists the characteristics of the berserk
state, as follows:[33]

> Beastlike
> Godlike
> Socially disconnected
> Crazy, mad, insane
> Enraged
> Cruel, without restraint or discrimination
> Insatiable
> Devoid of fear

[31] van Wees (1992) 129.   [32] Shay (1994) 77.   [33] Shay (1994) 82.

> Inattentive to own safety
> Distractible
> Indiscriminate
> Reckless, feeling invulnerable
> Exalted, intoxicated, frenzied
> Cold, indifferent
> Insensible to pain
> Suspicious of friends

But what is specifically relevant to Achilles' fleeting desire and Tydeus' actual act of cannibalism is the following remark: "Clinicians working with combat veterans need to be aware that berserking may arouse a lust to eat the enemy. Even the remembered wish is extremely disturbing to veterans, and when it has been carried out, the ensuing post-traumatic stress disorder is particularly devastating and intractable."[34]

We can conclude, then, that Achilles' diet of raw and living flesh is integrally connected with his characteristic of "anger" and a highly appropriate form of training for a warrior who will have to face so much hand-to-hand fighting against opponents of the highest calibre. Achilles manages to restrain his anger from transforming into cannibalism, surely the closest possible form of close combat. Tydeus does not. When he is driven by Tisiphone in his death throes to eat raw and living flesh he has gone beyond what is appropriate for even the fiercest and angriest warrior. Anger has to have its limits.

APPENDIX I   CATEGORIES OF LANGUAGE USED IN EPIC DEPICTIONS OF *IRA*

(V = Virgil, *Aeneid*; VF = Valerius Flaccus; St = Statius, *Thebaid*; S = Silius Italicus; L = Lucan)

Anger is chiefly and fairly consistently represented as a powerful force that comes from the outside. Hence the language of: **goads/stimuli; arousal/swelling; disturbance.**

Verbs: *stimulauit Ira* (VF 5.137), *furore . . . exstimulat* (S 1.32–3), *spes addita suscitat iras* (V 10.263), *suscitat* (V 11.728), *se suscitat ira* (V 12.108), *increscunt animis discordibus irae* (V 9.688), *irae | intumuere satis* (St 1.412–13), *saeuae iamque altius irae | . . . surgunt* (V 10.813–14), *surgit uiolentior ira | comminus* (S 4.262–3), *adsurgunt irae* (V 12.499), *fodiant pectus in iras* (S 5.159), *turbato . . . uoltu* (L 3.356)
Participles: *immani concitus ira* (V 9.694), *concitus irae* (L 4.688), *arrectae stimulis haud mollibus irae* (V 11.452), *stimulis haud mollibus incutit iras* (V 11.728), *accensae stimulis maioribus irae* (St 11.497), *erectus* (St 1.412), *asper ab ira* (S 12.551), *caligantes nimis successibus irae* (St 10.287)

---

[34] Shay (1994) 219, n. 12, glossing the passage in *Thebaid* 8.

Nouns: *tantos . . . tumores* (S 15.689), *pari procurrunt agmina motu | irarum* (L 7.385–6)
Simile: snake *attollentem iras et caerula colla tumentem* (V 2.382)

An outside influence which often engenders anger in our texts is that of: **madness/frenzy.** (Doubtless searches around *furor* and *rabies* would generate more entries here.)
Verbs: *saeuit . . . ira* (V 7.461–2), *furens ira* (S 12.162)
Adjectives: *amens* (V 2.314; V 7.460; St 8.751 = cannibalism)

The pathology of anger is very often described in terms of: **heat, fire, and ignition.**
Verbs: *ardent animi* (V 2.315), *dolor . . . ardet* (V 9.66), *exarsere ignes animo* (V 2.575), *exarsit in iras* (V 7.445), *irae | hinc atque inde calent* (St 7.616), *ignescunt irae* (V 9.65–6), *urebat pectora flammis [irae]* (S 17.294), *ira accenderat* (S 4.270), *accendunt iras* (S 17.292), *succensere nefas patriae* (S 7.555), *ira coquit* (S 4.538), *scintillauitque cruentis | ira genis* (S 9.562), *mens exaestuat ira* (V 9.798), *fluctuat ira intus* (V 12.527), *iras aduersa fouent* (S 5.225)
Participles and (selected) adjectives: *feruidus ira* (V 9.736), *feruidus* (S 9.422), *feruentemque ira* (S 15.806), *ignifero mentes furiabat in iram | hortatu decorisque urebat pectora flammis* (S 17.293–4), *furiis accensus et ira | terribilis* (V 12.946–7), *accensae stimulis maioribus irae* (St 11.498), *accensa . . . ira* (S 4.642; S 5.105); *accensus in iram* (S 5.558), *succensa ira turbataque luctu* (S 1.169), *[animis iraque] ignescentia . . . odia* (St 11.525)
Nouns: *uirtutis stimulis irae calore* (L 7.100), cf. *ardor* (St 12.726)
Cf. simile of bull goading itself for fight: *agitur furiis totoque ardentis ab ore | scintillae absistunt, oculis micat acribus ignis* (V 12.101–2); simile of cauldron boiling (V 7.461–6) and bubbling over (S 5.603–6, indebted to V Book 7)

Hence it is that anger can be said to: **cool/fade/fall away/be broken.**
Cooling etc: *paulatim fugit ira ferox mentesque tepescunt* (L 4.284), *exciderunt irae* (St 7.801), *nec iam amplius irae | crudescunt* (simile of lion: St 2.679–80), *cassa . . . ira* (VF 6.556), *fracta . . . ira* (St 4.23), *iras | frangit* (St 8.534–5), *tremuere irae* (S 7.581), *paulatim atrocibus irae | languescunt animis* (S 13.324–5), anger diminishes without material to feed on: simile at St 12.728–9

Similarly, anger can disrupt **balance:**
praecipitare (V 2.317), *iram praecipitem* (L 4.267–8), *praeceps . . . ira* (simile of boars St 11.530–1)
and be put on like **clothing:**
induit iras | Hannibal (S 1.38), *irasque sedentum | induerint* (St 8.392)
and **steal over** someone:
subit ira (V 2.575; St 9.862 [*non*])

There are representations of an agent **rousing/unleashing their own anger:**
acuunt rumoribus iras [like a weapon?] (V 9.464), *acuunt stridoribus iras* (simile: bees) (V 12.590), cf. simile of bull *irasci in cornua temptat* (V 12.104), cf. stripping bare of weapons under anger's prompting: *nudassent enses* (St 1.429)

The role of **noise** in this activity is significant:

horrisonis ululatibus erigit iras (S 4.278), *iraque anhelatum proturbat pectore murmur* (S 5.605, cf. **breathing**), *iamque dolore furens ita secum immurmurat irae* (S 7.146), *tum feruidus acrem | ingentis clipei tonitru praenuntiat iram* (S 9.422–3), bull rousing self (simile V 12.103–4), *Mauors . . . intonat* (simile V 12.332)

Related to this are expressions where anger is given the **initiative** (nominative case) in the psychology: *extrema se colligit ira* (St 12.759), *tenet paratas | ira manus* (St 8.387–8 – whole passage is important), *telum ira facit* (V 7.508)

A combination of noise and anger taking the initiative is found in passages about **breathing:**

ira anhelat (S 10.131), *animusque ultra thoracas anhelus | conatur* (St 8.388–9), *iraque anhelatum proturbat pectore murmur* (S 5.605)

One recurrent idea suggested by the idea of anger as a (more or less) irresistible external force is that it **overwhelms/invades/fills**:

frenosque furentibus ira | laxat (L 7.124–5), *nec plura effari sinit ira* (S 2.242), *huic immittit atrox uiolentas Appius iras* (S 5.292), *non pertulit iram* (S 10.225), *non tulit hanc iram tantosque in corde tumores* (S 15.689), *iuuenis cui telum ingens accesserat ira* (S 16.62), *haud irae uacuus* (S 10.155). Cf. perhaps simile of wolf *improbus ira* (V 9.64). NB *mens impenetrabilis irae* (S 7.561) supplies the antithesis.

Hence it is hardly surprising that many of our texts focus on ideas of: **delaying/restraining** the onset or progress of anger:

Verbs: *saeuas paulum tardauerat iras* (S 5.308), *moratas a caede iras* (S 15.483–4), *o cohibite iras!* (V 12.314), *iras compesce* (S 7.330), *uulgumque arcebat ab ira* (S 10.616), *irasque coercet* (S 12.252), *iras euellere auebat* (S 14.183), *reuocata militis ira* (S 14.671), *irasque retentant* (VF 3.98), *fregit animos atque abstulit iras* (VF 6.284), cf. *quis iras | flexerit* (St 4.650–1); *Hannibal ad poenam lentae mandauerat irae* (S 1.451, especially sinister!) NB Fabius as *expers | irarum senior* (S 7.517), *patriae donauerat iram* (S 15.600)

Two loose ends: (1) anger **feeds:** *magnos alit ira leones* (in simile St 12.740) and (2) the force of anger is represented in term of **freshness**: *uiridissimus irae* (S 5.569)

APPENDIX 2   CONTEXTUALIZING EPIC *IRA* PHILOSOPHICALLY

A brief survey of the philosophical constructions of *ira* in the Roman reception of the Hellenistic schools may be valuable, particularly of how this material relates to anger on the battlefield, which is to say, hardly at all. On the one hand, there is the view based on what Aristotle says and articulated in Latin texts by Cicero's account of the Peripatetic view, which sees at least the possibility of overlap (if not identification) between concepts such as *pietas, uirtus*, and *ira* through the concept of appropriateness. This concept of appropriateness coheres closely with Thornton's view of the moral neutrality of anger considered on its own and of the necessity of studying the whole context in which anger is portrayed. On the other hand, there is the view inspired by the Stoics and, through some kind of

Christian back-reading, adopted by scholars such as Otis which asserts clearcut moral categories when it pits *ratio* and *iudicium* against the emotions (*affectus* or *impetus*) and sees a particular dichotomy between *ira* and *furor* on the one hand and *pietas* on the other. This is not to deny the strong Stoicizing flavour evident in these epics, not just that of Lucan; but, as Fantham (1997) argues in her analysis of hatred in the *Thebaid*, a reading simply in terms of Stoic systems neglects other important cultural factors that shape the ideas here.

Cicero expresses the fundamental disagreement between the Stoic and the Peripatetic views of anger at *Tusculan Disputations* 4.43:

quid? quod iidem Peripatetici perturbationes istas quas nos exstirpandas putamus non modo naturales esse dicunt sed etiam utiliter a natura datas; quorum est talis oratio. primum multis uerbis iracundiam laudant: cotem fortitudinis esse dicunt, multoque et in hostem et in improbum ciuem uehementiores iratorum impetus esse, leues autem ratiunculas eorum qui ita cogitarent: "proelium rectum est hoc fieri, conuenit dimicare pro legibus, pro libertate, pro patria": haec nullam habere uim nisi ira excanduerit fortitudo . . . uirum denique uideri negant qui irasci nesciat eamque quam lenitatem nos dicimus uitioso lentitudinis nomine appellant.

In particular, the phrase *cotem fortitudinis* is strikingly positive; the denigration of *ratiunculas* is designed to be withering; and the idea that only a man who can grow angry (*irasci*) truly deserves to be called a "man" (*uir*) strikes right to the core of Roman masculine identity. Perhaps he cites this view because it would be likely to incite disagreement, but nonetheless he does cite it and it does fit well with some of the epic material, above all, the passage from *Aeneid* 10 discussed above (pp. 260–1).

In his characterization of the Peripatetic view, Cicero is presumably thinking of passages such as this from Aristotle's *Nicomachean Ethics* (4.5.3 and 5–7, 1125b–1126a):

Now we praise a man who feels anger on the right grounds and against the right persons and also in the right manner and at the right moment and for the right length of time . . . The defect – call it a sort of lack of spirit – is blamed, because people who do not get angry at things at which it is right to be angry are considered foolish, and so are people who do not get angry in the right manner, at the right time and with the right people. It is thought that they do not feel or resent an injury and that if a man is never angry he will not stand up for himself; and it is considered servile to put up with an insult to oneself or to allow one's friends to be insulted. Excess is also possible in these ways, because one can be angry with the wrong people, for the wrong things, or more violently or more quickly or longer than is right.

The crucial element in Aristotle's formulation, as we see it, is the word *dei*, which he repeats in all these articulations of both the appropriate and the inappropriate aspects of anger. This not only coheres closely with Thornton's views of the impor-tance of context in the evaluation of epic anger, but also throws the emphasis upon the narrativization of any act of epic anger and the reception of any exhibition of epic anger.

On the other side, the fullest articulation of the (or at least a) Stoic view on anger is presumably that in Seneca's *De ira*. There can be no doubt of Seneca's monolithic negative opinion, starting with his opening definition of anger at *De ira* 1.1.1, where, in contrast with other *affectus*:

hic totus concitatus et in impetu doloris est, armorum sanguinis suppliciorum minime humana furens cupiditate, dum alteri noceat sui neglegens, in ipsa irruens tela et ultionis secum ultorem tracturae auidus.

This sentence expresses many of Seneca's central ideas which he develops in the treatise:

> that it is a disturbance that is thoroughly overwhelming;
> that it consists of impetuous action resulting from a feeling of resentment;
> that its characteristic arenas are weapons/warfare, blood/murder/torture, punishments;
> that it is intent on causing injury;
> that it is careless of the possibility of self-destruction.

What is immediately striking is that his description of anger applies well to the later, reckless, stages of *ira* as portrayed in our epic texts, but not at all to the opening phase when the warrior is working himself up to start fighting. Seneca's hostility becomes even clearer when he immediately proceeds to assimilate anger to madness (1.1.2): it is *breuem insaniam*, because *aeque . . . impotens sui est, decoris oblita, necessitudinum immemor, in quod coepit pertinax et intenta, rationi consiliisque praeclusa, uanis agitata causis . . .* (And throughout the work, Seneca constructs an antithesis between *ratio* or *iudicium* and *ira* [*passim*, e.g. 1.6.1; 1.15.1–3; 1.19.1–2; 1.19.5–8; 3.12.4; 3.29.2].) But what is still more striking about *De ira* is that Seneca is minimally concerned with anger in military contexts and maximally concerned with it as a phenomenon in civil life, which bears out William Harris' ideas ([2002] ch. 10, "Restraining the Angry Ruler," esp. 251; also Nussbaum [1994] 405) that *De ira* is essentially a political text designed for a readership that included the emperor, though of course it is actually addressed to Novatus. There is almost nothing about the warrior here. The role of anger in warfare occurs chiefly at the points where Seneca attempts to combat Aristotle's views on the usefulness of anger. His difficulties in doing so are betrayed by the fact that he returns to the attempt some seven times through the three books. This is not the place to analyze the material in detail, but a few brief examples follow.

So we find the objection that anger may be "useful" (*utilis*) vocalized at 1.7.1 (without a reference yet to Aristotle): *numquid, quamuis non sit naturalis ira, adsumenda est, quia utilis saepe fuit? extollit animos et incitat, nec quicquam sine illa magnificum in bello fortitudo gerit, nisi hinc flamma subdita est et hic stimulus peragitauit misitque in pericula audaces;* and again at 1.9.2, with a quotation from Aristotle (although we do not know the source): *"ira" inquit Aristoteles "necessaria est nec quicquam sine illa expugnari potest nisi illa implet animum et spiritum accendit; utendum autem illa est non ut duce sed ut milite."* Seneca attempts to resist this by asserting (1.9.2–4) that if anger listens to *ratio* it is no longer *ira* and if it cannot be controlled it is not helpful: *ita aut ira non est aut inutilis est.* That is, Seneca is entrapped by his view of anger as something "uncontrolled and uncontrollable" (*effrenatam indomitamque*). At 1.17.1 Seneca returns to these Aristotelian ideas: that some "passions serve as weapons" (*affectus . . . pro armis esse*). His opposition to this consists of the idea that anger cannot be set aside but takes over, which leads him to assert that reason (*ratio*) *ad res gerendas satis est per se ipsa.* In Book 3 Seneca returns to Aristotle's view of anger as *calcar . . . uirtutis: hac erepta inermem animum et ad conatus magnos pigrum inertemque fieri* (3.3.1). This time, Seneca resorts to a description (not the first) of the physical marks of anger, designed to provoke revulsion, in order to combat this view that anger consists of anything fine – hardly a convincing argument. One obvious response to the Aristotelian view of anger comes at 1.12.1–5, where Seneca answers another objection (attributed to Theophrastus), that a man should get angry if his father is murdered or his mother raped before his eyes. Seneca's response is that the action then taken should be inspired by *pietas*, not *ira*. Thus he states (1.12.5): *illud pulchrum dignumque pro parentibus, liberis, amicis, ciuibus prodire defensorem ipso officio ducente, uolentem, iudicantem, prouidentem, non impulsum et rabidum.* Thus Seneca is committed, almost irrationally it seems, to the view that anger is invariably negative and that if it can be construed positively it has ceased to be anger! We say "almost irrationally" because Seneca's view is actually more complex, convoluted, and confused than this summary suggests. Because he wants to hold out the possibility of the control of anger, he must also insist on the idea of warning signs at which the mind can act to resist anger (e.g. 1.8.1, *optimum est primum irritamentum irae protinus spernere ipsisque repugnare seminibus et dare operam ne incidamus in iram*) and on the possibility of bringing *ira* under control, although not until after its first overwhelming rush (e.g. 2.29.1, anger *graues habet impetus primos; desinet si expectat*; 2.2.1, *ira praeceptis fugatur*; 2.3.1, the mind is not *moueri* by passions but *permittere se*).

This glance at the central philosophical texts in this debate reveals the potential for morally loaded vocabulary in both directions. The rigid Stoic view whereby anger is rejected wholesale as an evil and self-destructive emotion is of only limited (but indeed occasional) relevance to the (extant) Roman epic tradition. Rather, the Aristotelian and Peripatetic view that anger can be appropriate and useful in certain circumstances and to certain degrees is more often applicable than not.

References

Abbreviations of journal titles correspond to those used in *L'Année Philologique*.

Adkins, A. W. H. (1969) "Threatening, abusing, and feeling angry in the Homeric poems," *JHS* 89: 7–21.
  (1972) *Moral Values and Political Behaviour in Ancient Greece*. London.
Ahl, F. M. (1976) *Lucan: an Introduction*. Ithaca, NY.
Alexiou, E. (1999) "Zur Darstellung der ὀργή in Plutarchs βίοι," *Philologus* 143: 101–13.
Allen, D. S. (2000) *The World of Prometheus: the Politics of Punishing in Democratic Athens*. Princeton, NJ.
Althoff, G. (1998) "*Ira regis*: prolegomena to a history of royal anger," in Rosenwein (1998), 59–74.
Anderson, G. (1984) *Ancient Fiction: the Novel in the Graeco-Roman World*. London and Sydney.
Anderson, W. S. (1964) "Anger in Juvenal and Seneca," *California Publications in Classical Philology* 19: 127–96.
Annas, J. (1989) "Epicurean emotions," *GRBS* 30: 145–64.
  (1993) *The Morality of Happiness*. Oxford.
Austin, N. (1999) "Anger and disease in Homer's *Iliad*," in *Euphrosyne: Studies in Ancient Epic and Its Legacy in Honor of Dimitris N. Maronitis*, ed. J. N. Kazazis and A. Rengakos. Stuttgart: 11–49.
Averill, J. R. (1990) "Inner feelings, the works of the flesh, the beast within, diseases of the mind, driving force, and putting on a show: six metaphors of emotion and their theoretical extensions," in *Metaphors in the History of Psychology*, ed. D. E. Leary. Cambridge: 104–32.
Axelrod, R. (1984) *The Evolution of Co-operation*. New York.
Bailey, F. G. (1983) *The Tactical Uses of Passion: an Essay on Power, Reason, and Reality*. Ithaca, NY.
Balot, R. K. (1998) "Foucault, Chariton, and the masculine self," *Helios* 25: 139–62.
Barbalet, J. M. (1998) *Emotion, Social Theory, and Social Structure: a Macrosociological Approach*. Cambridge.
Barchiesi, A. (1997) "Endgames: Ovid's *Metamorphoses* 15 and *Fasti* 6," in *Classical Closure*, ed. D. Roberts, F. Dunn, and D. Fowler. Princeton, NJ: 181–208.

Barkow, J. H., Cosmides, L., and Tooby, J. (eds.) (1992) *The Adapted Mind: Evolutionary Psychology and the Generation of Culture*. New York.

Barnes, J. (ed.) (1984) *The Complete Works of Aristotle* (2 vols.). Princeton.

Barton, R. E. (1998) " 'Zealous anger' and the renegotiation of aristocratic relationships in eleventh- and twelfth-century France," in Rosenwein (1998), 153–70.

Beattie, J. (1964) *Other Cultures: Aims, Methods, and Achievements in Social Anthropology*. London.

Beck, G. (1964) *Die Stellung des 24. Buches der Ilias in der alten Epentradition*. Diss. Tübingen.

Ben-Ze'ev, A. (2000) *The Subtlety of Emotions*. Cambridge, MA.

Berkowitz, L. (1990) "On the formation and regulation of anger and aggression," *American Psychologist* 45: 494–503.

Bethe, E. (1914) *Homer. Dichtung und Sage*, vol. 1: *Ilias*. Leipzig and Berlin.

Betz, H. D. (1982) "The formation of authoritative tradition in the Greek magical papyri," in Meyers and Sanders (1982), 161–70.

Biraud, M. (1985) "L'hypotexte homérique et les rôles amoureux de Callirhoé dans le roman de Chariton," in *Sémiologie de l'amour dans les civilisations méditerranéennes*, ed. A. Goursonnet. Paris: 21–7.

Birbaumer, N. (ed.) (1993) *The Structure of Emotions*. Toronto.

Blackburn, S. (1998). *Ruling Passions: a Theory of Practical Reasoning*. Oxford.

Blok, J. and Mason, P. (eds.) (1987) *Sexual Asymmetry: Studies in Ancient Society*. Amsterdam.

Blundell, M. W. (1989) *Helping Friends and Harming Enemies*. Cambridge.
  (1998) Review of Gill (1996), *CPh* 93: 75–82.

Blundell, S. (1995) *Women in Ancient Greece*. London.

Bobzien, S. (1998) *Determinism and Freedom in Stoic Philosophy*. Oxford.

Bonds, W. S. (1985) "Two Combats in the *Thebaid*," *TAPhA* 115: 225–35.

Bonner, C. (1950) *Studies in Magical Amulets Chiefly Graeco-Egyptian*, University of Michigan Studies, Humanistic Series 49. Ann Arbor.

Borgogno, A. (1971) "Menandro in Caritone," *RFIC* 99: 257–63.

Borod, J. C. (2000) *The Neuropsychology of Emotion*. Oxford.

Bowie, E. L. (1985) "The Greek novel," in *The Cambridge History of Classical Literature*, vol. 1: *Greek Literature*, ed. P. E. Easterling and B. M. W. Knox. Cambridge: 683–99.
  (forthcoming) "The chronology of the earlier Greek novels since B. E. Perry: revisions and precisions," to be published in *Ancient Narrative*.

Bradley, K. R. (1980) "Sexual regulations in wet-nursing contracts from Roman Egypt," *Klio* 62: 321–5.

Braund, S. M. (1992) *Lucan: Civil War*, tr. with introd. and notes. Oxford.
  (1997) "A passion unconsoled? Grief and anger in Juvenal *Satire* 13," in Braund and Gill (1997), 68–88.

Braund, S. M. and Gill, C. (eds.) (1997) *The Passions in Roman Thought and Literature*. Cambridge.

Bremer, J. M. (1991) "Exit Electra," *Gymnasium* 98: 325–42.

Bremmer, J. N. (1987) "The old women of ancient Greece," in Blok and Mason (1987), 191–215.

Bruce, V. and Young, A. (1998) *In the Eye of the Beholder: the Science of Face Perception.* Oxford.

Buckheit (1960) "Feigensymbolik im antiken Epigramm," *RhM* 103: 200–4.

Bührer-Thierry, G. (1998) " 'Just anger' or 'vengeful anger'? The punishment of blinding in the early medieval West," in Rosenwein (1998), 75–91.

Burguière, P., Gourevitch, D., and Malinas, Y. (eds.) (1990) *Soranos d'Ephèse. Maladies des Femmes*, vol. II. Paris.

Burkert, W. (1955) *Zum altgriechischen Mitleidsbegriff.* Diss. Erlangen.

  (1992) *The Orientalizing Revolution: Near Eastern Influence on Greek Culture in the Early Archaic Age*, tr. M. E. Pinder and W. Burkert. Cambridge, MA.

  (1996) *Creation of the Sacred: Tracks of Biology in Early Religions.* Cambridge, MA.

Buss, D. M. (1994) *The Evolution of Desire: Strategies of Human Mating.* New York.

  (2000) *The Dangerous Passion: Why Jealousy Is as Necessary as Love and Sex.* New York.

Butler, J. (1850) *Sermons upon Human Nature*, in *The Works.* Oxford.

Cairns, D. L. (1990) "Mixing with men and Nausicaa's *nemesis*," *CQ* 40: 263–6.

  (1993) *Aidōs: The Psychology and Ethics of Honour and Shame in Ancient Greek Literature.* Oxford.

  (1999) Review of Gill (1996), *Pegasus* 42: 30–3.

  (2001a) "Affronts and quarrels in the *Iliad*," in *Oxford Readings in Homer's Iliad*, ed. D. L. Cairns. Oxford: 203–19, revised from *Papers of the Leeds Latin Seminar* 7 (1993), 155–67.

  (2001b) "Anger and the veil in ancient Greece," *G&R* 48: 18–32.

  (2002) "The meaning of the veil in ancient Greek culture," in *Women's Dress in the Ancient Greek World*, ed. Ll. Llewellyn-Jones. London: 73–93.

Calhoun, C. and Solomon, R. (eds.) (1984) *What Is an Emotion? Classic Readings in Philosophical Psychology.* Oxford.

Carey, C. (1994) "Rhetorical Means of Persuasion," in *Persuasion: Greek Rhetoric in Action*, ed. I. Worthington. London: 26–45.

Carson, A. (1990) "Putting her in her place: woman, dirt, and desire," in *Before Sexuality: the Construction of Erotic Experience in the Ancient Greek World*, ed. D. M. Halperin, J. J. Winkler, and F. I. Zeitlin. Princeton, NJ: 135–69.

Carter, I. (1986) *The Quiet Athenian.* Oxford.

Carter, R. (1998) *Mapping the Mind.* Berkeley, Los Angeles, and London.

Casadio, V. (1970–72) "L'eleos nell'epica," *MCr* 5–7: 54–9.

Caswell, C. P. (1990) *A Study of Thumos in Early Greek Epic.* Leiden.

Cataudella, Q. (1927) "Riflessi virgiliani nel romanzo di Caritone," *Athenaeum* 5: 302–12.

Cauer, P. (1895) *Grundfragen der Homerkritik.* Leipzig.

Chantraine, P. (1968–80) *Dictionnaire étymologique de la langue grecque.* Paris.

  (1999) *Dictionnaire étymologique de la langue grecque: histoire des mots.* Paris.

Christ, M. (1998) *The Litigious Athenian.* Baltimore.

Clark, P. (1998) "Women, slaves, and the hierarchies of domestic violence: the family of St. Augustine," in *Women and Slaves in Greco-Roman Culture: Differential Equations*, ed. S. R. Joshel and S. Murnaghan. London and New York: 109–29.

Clarke, M. (1999) *Flesh and Spirit in the Songs of Homer: a Study of Words and Myths*. Oxford.

Cohen, D. (1991) *Law, Sexuality, and Society*. Cambridge.

Collart, P. (1930) "Une nouvelle tabella defixionis d'Egypte," *RPh* 56: 248–56.

Connors, C. (2002) "Chariton's Syracuse and its histories of empire," in *Space in the Ancient Novel*, ed. M. Paschalis and S. Frangoulidis. Ancient Narrative Suppl. 1. Groningen: 12–26.

Considine, P. (1966) "Some Homeric terms for anger," *AClass* 9: 15–25.

 (1986) "The etymology of *mēnis*," in *Studies in Honour of T. B. L. Webster*, vol. 1, ed. J. H. Betts, J. T. Hooker, and J. R. Green. Bristol: 53–64.

Cooper, J. M. (1996) "An Aristotelian theory of the emotions," in Rorty (1996), 238–57, reprinted in Cooper (1999), 406–23.

 (ed.) (1999) *Reason and Emotion: Essays on Ancient Moral Psychology and Ethical Theory*. Princeton, NJ.

Cooper, J. M. and Procopé, J. F. (eds.) (1995) *Seneca: Moral and Political Essays*, tr. with introd. and notes. Cambridge.

Cope, E. M. (1877) *The Rhetoric of Aristotle*, ed. J. E. Sandys, vol. II. Cambridge.

Corbato, C. (1968) "Da Menandro a Caritone: studi sulla genesi del romanzo greco e i suoi rapporti con la commedia nuova (1)," *Studi triestini sul teatro antico* 1: 5–44.

Couraud-Lalanne, S. (1998) "Récit d'un τέλος ἐρωτικόν: réflexions sur le statut des jeunes dans le roman de Chariton d'Aphrodisias," *REG* 111: 518–50.

Croiset, M. (1909) *Aristophanes and the Political Parties at Athens*. London.

Crotty, K. (1992) *The Poetics of Supplication*. Ithaca, NY.

Csapo, E. (1993) "Deep ambivalence: notes on a Greek cockfight parts I–IV," *Phoenix* 47: 1–28, 115–24.

Cueva, E. P. (2000) "The date of Chariton's *Chaereas and Callirhoe* revisited," *C&M* 51: 197–208.

Dalgleish, T. and Power, M. (eds.) (1999) *Handbook of Cognition and Emotion*. Chichester.

Damasio, A. R. (1994) *Descartes' Error: Emotion, Reason, and the Human Brain*. New York.

Darwin, C. (1872, repr. 1955) *The Expression of the Emotions in Man and Animals*. New York.

 (1998) *The Expression of the Emotions in Man and Animals*, 3rd edn., ed. P. Ekman. London.

Davies, M. and Stone, T. (1995) *Folk Psychology: the Theory of Mind Debate*. Oxford.

d'Avino, R. (1969) "La funzionalità di ὀνομάζω a la formula ἔπος τ' ἔφατ' ἔκ τ' ὀνόμαζε," in *Studia classica et orientalia Antonino Pagliaro oblata*, vol. II. Rome: 7–33.

Dawkins, R. (1989) *The Selfish Gene*, 2nd edn. Oxford.

Deichgräber, K. (ed.) (1935) *Hippokrates über Enstehung und Aufbau des menschlichen Körpers*. Leipzig and Berlin.

(1972) *Der letzte Gesang der Ilias*. Abh. d. Mainzer Akad. d. Wiss. u. Lit., Geistes- und sozialwiss. Klasse, Nr. 5. Mainz.

De Lacy, P. (ed.) (1977–84) *Galen: de Placitis Hippocratis et Platonis*, with tr. and comm. (3 vols.) Berlin.

Demand, N. (1994) *Birth, Death, and Motherhood in Classical Greece*. Baltimore and London.

Dennett, D. C. (1995) *Darwin's Dangerous Idea*. New York.

Descartes, R. (1985) *The Passions of the Soul*, in *The Philosophical Writings of Descartes*, tr. J. Cottingham, R. Stotthoff, and D. Murdoch, vol. 1. Cambridge.

de Sousa, R. (1987) *The Rationality of Emotion*. Cambridge, MA.

Detienne, M. and Vernant, J.-P. (1978) *Cunning Intelligence in Greek Culture and Society*, tr. J. Lloyd. Hassocks, Sussex and Atlantic Highlands, NJ.

Dickey, E. (1996) *Greek Forms of Address*. Oxford.

Dillon, J. and Long, A. A. (eds.) (1988) *The Question of "Eclecticism": Studies in Later Greek Philosophy*. Berkeley.

Dobbin, R. (1998) *Epictetus: Discourses Book I*, tr. with introd. and comm. Oxford.

Dominik, W. J. (1994) *The Mythic Voice of Statius*. Leiden.

Dover, K. J. (1974) *Greek Popular Morality in the Time of Plato and Aristotle*. Oxford.

(1978) *Greek Homosexuality*. London.

(1994) *Greek Popular Morality in the Time of Plato and Aristotle*, rev. edn. Indianapolis.

Durkheim, E. (1995) *The Elementary Forms of Religious Life*, tr. K. E. Fields. New York.

Edmonds, J. W. (1961) *The Fragments of Attic Comedy*. Leiden.

Edmunds, L. (1987) *Cleon, Knights, and Aristophanes' Politics*. New York.

Edwards, D. R. (1991) "Surviving the web of Roman power: religion and politics in the Acts of the Apostles, Josephus, and Chariton's *Chaereas and Callirhoe*," in *Images of Empire*, ed. L. Alexander. *Journal for the Study of the Old Testament* Supplement Series 122. Sheffield: 179–201.

(1996) *Religion and Power: Pagans, Jews, and Christians in the Greek East*. New York and Oxford.

Edwards, M. W. (1987) *Homer: Poet of the Iliad*. Baltimore and London.

(1991) *The Iliad: a Commentary*, ed. G. S. Kirk. Vol. 5: Books 17–20. Cambridge.

Egger, B. M. (1988) "Zu den Frauenrollen im griechischen Roman: die Frau als Heldin und Leserin," in *Groningen Colloquia on the Novel*, vol. 1, ed. H. Hofmann. Groningen: 33–66 = (in Eng. tr.) "The role of women in the Greek novel: woman as heroine and reader," in Swain (1999), 108–36.

(1990) "Women in the Greek novel: constructing the feminine." Unpublished Ph.D. dissertation, University of California, Irvine.

(1994a) "Looking at Chariton's Callirhoe," in *Greek Fiction: the Greek Novel in Context*, ed. J. R. Morgan and R. Stoneman. London and New York: 31–48.

(1994b) "Women and marriage in the Greek novels: the boundaries of romance," in *The Search for the Ancient Novel*, ed. J. Tatum. Baltimore and London: 260–80.

Eibl-Eibesfeldt, I. (1989) *Human Ethology*. New York.

Ekman, P. (1980) "Biological and cultural contributions to body and facial movement in the expression of emotions," in Rorty (1980), 73–101.

(ed.) (1982) *Emotion in the Human Face*, 2nd edn. Cambridge and Paris.

(1992a) *Telling Lies: Clues to Deceit in the Marketplace, Politics, and Marriage*. 2nd edn. New York.

(1992b) "An Argument for Basic Emotions," *Cognition and Emotion* 6: 169–200.

Ekman, P. and Davidson, R. (eds.) (1994) *The Nature of Emotion*. New York.

Ekman, P. and Friesen, W. V. (1969) "Non-verbal leakage and clues to deception," *Psychiatry* 32: 88–105.

Elderkin, G. W. (1936) "An Athenian maledictory inscription on lead," *Hesperia* 5: 43–9.

Elsom, H. E. (1992) "Callirhoe: displaying the phallic woman," in Richlin (1992): 212–30.

Elster, J. (1990) "Norms of revenge," *Ethics* 100: 862–85.

(1999a) *Alchemies of the Mind: Rationality and the Emotions*. Cambridge.

(1999b) *Strong Feelings: Emotion, Addiction, and Human Behavior*. Cambridge, MA.

Erbse, H. (ed.) (1969–88) *Scholia Graeca in Homeri Iliadem (scholia vetera)* (7 vols.). Berlin.

Erim, K. (1986) *Aphrodisias: City of Venus Aphrodite*. London.

Erler, M. (1992) "Der Zorn des Helden, Philodems 'De Ira' und Vergils Konzept des Zorns in der 'Aeneis,'" *GB* 18: 103–26.

Erskine, A. (1997) "Cicero and the expression of grief," in Braund and Gill (1997), 36–47.

Fantham, E. (1997) "'Envy and fear the begeter of hate': Statius' 'Thebaid' and the genesis of hatred," in *The Passions in Roman Thought and Literature*, ed. S. M. Braund and C. Gill. Cambridge: 185–212.

Faraone, C. A. (1989) "An accusation of magic in classical Athens (Ar. *Wasps* 946–48)," *TAPhA* 119: 149–61.

(1990) "Aphrodite's KESTOS and apples for Atalanta: aphrodisiacs in early Greek myth and ritual," *Phoenix* 44: 224–43.

(1991) "The agonistic context of early Greek binding spells," in Faraone and Obbink (1991), 3–32.

(1995) "The 'performative future' in three Hellenistic incantations and Theocritus' Second *Idyll*," *CPh* 90: 1–15.

(1996) "Taking the Nestor's cup inscription seriously: conditional curses and erotic magic in the earliest Greek hexameters," *CLAnt* 15: 77–112.

(1999) *Ancient Greek Love Magic*. Cambridge, MA.

Faraone, C. A. and Obbink, D. (eds.) (1991) *Magika Hiera: Ancient Greek Magic and Religion*. New York.

Feeney, D. (1991) *The Gods in Epic*. Oxford.

Fernandez-Galiano, M. (1992) Books 21–2, in *A Commentary on Homer's Odyssey*, vol. III: *Books xvii–xxiv*, ed. J. Russo, M. Fernandez-Galiano, and A. Heubeck. Oxford.

Fillion-Lahille, J. (1984) *Le De Ira de Sénèque et la philosophie stoïcienne des passions.* Paris.

Fischer, A. H., Manstead, A. S. R., and Rodriguez Mosquera, P. M. (1999) "The role of honour-related vs. individualistic values in conceptualising pride, shame, and anger: Spanish and Dutch cultural prototypes," *Cognition and Emotion* 13: 149–79.

Foley, H. P. (1994) *The Homeric Hymn to Demeter: Translation, Commentary, and Interpretive Essays.* Princeton, NJ.

Fortenbaugh, W. W. (1975) *Aristotle on Emotion.* London.

Foucault, M. (1978) *The History of Sexuality*, vol. 1: *An Introduction*, tr. R. Hurley. New York.

Fowler, D. P. (1997) "Epicurean anger," in Braund and Gill (1997), 16–35.

Foxhall, L. (1989) "Household, gender, and property in classical Athens," *CQ* 39: 22–44.

Frank, R. H. (1988) *Passions within Reason: the Strategic Role of the Emotions.* New York.

Frazer, J. (1912) *The Golden Bough Part V: Spirits of the Corn and of the Wild*, vol. 11, 3rd edn. London.

Frede, D. (1996) "Mixed feelings in Aristotle's *Rhetoric*," in Rorty (1996), 258–85.

Frede, M. (1986) "The Stoic doctrine of the affections of the soul," in *The Norms of Nature: Studies in Hellenistic Ethics*, ed. M. Schofield and G. Striker, Cambridge: 93–110.

French, V. (1987) "Midwives and maternity care in the Greco-Roman world," *Helios* 13: 69–84.

Friedrich, R. (1993) "Medea *apolis*: on Euripides' dramatization of the crisis of the polis," in *Tragedy, Comedy and the Polis*, ed. A. H. Sommerstein et al. Bari: 219–39.

Frier, B. W. (1994) "Natural fertility and family limitation in Roman marriage," *CPh* 89: 318–33.

Frisk, H. (1946) "*Mēnis*: zur Geschichte eines Begriffes," *Eranos* 44: 28–40.

Fusillo, M. (1989) *Il romanzo greco: polifonia ed eros.* Venice.

(1990) "Les conflits des émotions: un topos du roman grec érotique," *MH* 47: 201–21 = (in Eng. tr.) "The conflict of emotions: a *topos* in the Greek erotic novel," in Swain (1999), 60–82.

(1996) "Modern critical theories and the ancient novel," in Schmeling (1996), 277–305.

Galinsky, K. (1988) "The anger of Aeneas," *AJPh* 109: 321–48.

(1994) "How to be philosophical about the end of the *Aeneid*", *ICS* 19: 191–201.

(2003) "Greek tragedy and the *Aeneid*," in *Myth, History and Culture in Republican Rome: Studies in Honour of T. P. Wiseman*, ed. D. Braund and C. Gill. Exeter.

Gantz, T. (1993) *Early Greek Myth: a Guide to Literary and Artistic Sources.* Baltimore.

Garvie, A. F. (1986) *Aeschylus: Choephori.* Oxford.

Geddes, W. D. (1878) *The Problem of the Homeric Poems.* London.

Gill, C. (1996) *Personality in Greek Epic, Tragedy, and Philosophy: the Self in Dialogue.* Oxford.

(1997a) "Passion as madness in Roman poetry," in Braund and Gill (1997), 213–41.

(ed.) (1997b) *Marcus Aurelius: Meditations*, tr. R. Hard. Ware, Hertfordshire.

(2000) "Stoic writers of the imperial period," in *The Cambridge History of Greek and Roman Political Thought*, ed. C. J. Rowe and M. Schofield. Cambridge: 597–615.

(forthcoming) *The Structured Self in Hellenistic and Roman Thought*. Oxford.

Goffman, E. (1967) *Interaction Ritual: Essays on Face-to-Face Behavior*. New York.

Golden, M. (1990) *Children and Childhood in Classical Athens*. Baltimore and London.

Goldhill, S. (1994) "Representing democracy: women at the Great Dionysia," in *Ritual, Finance and Politics. Athenian Democratic Accounts Presented to David Lewis*, ed. R. Osborne and S. Hornblower. Oxford: 347–69.

(1995) *Foucault's Virginity: Ancient Erotic Fiction and the History of Sexuality*. Cambridge.

Goldie, P. (2000) *The Emotions. A Philosophical Explanation*. Oxford.

Goold, G. P. (ed.) (1995) *Chariton: Callirhoe*. Loeb Classical Library 481. Cambridge, MA and London.

Gordon, R. (1987) *The Structure of Emotions: Investigations in Cognitive Psychology*. Cambridge.

Gourevitch, D. (1995) "Comment rendre à sa véritable nature le petit monstre humain?," in *Ancient Medicine in Its Socio-Cultural Context*, ed. P. J. van der Eijk, H. F. J. Horstmanshoff, and P. H. Schrivers. Amsterdam and Atlanta.

Graf, F. (1991) "Prayer in magical and religious ritual," in Faraone and Obbink (1991), 188–213.

Grafton, A. T., Most, G. W., and Zetzel, J. E. G. (eds.) (1985) *F. A. Wolf: Prolegomena to Homer 1795*. Princeton, NJ.

Grastyán, E. (1986 [orig. 1974]) "Human Emotion and Motivation" (Part 1: "Emotion"), *The New Encyclopedia Britannica*, vol. XVIII. Chicago: 347–65.

Graver, M. (2002) *Cicero on the Emotions: Tusculan Disputations 3 and 4*. Chicago.

Grensemann, H. (ed.) (1968) *Hippocratis: De octimestri partu, De septimestri partu, spurium*. Berlin.

Griffin, J. (1978) "The divine audience and the religion of the *Iliad*," *CQ* 28: 1–22.

(1980) *Homer on Life and Death*. Oxford.

Griffiths, P. E. (1997) *What Emotions Really Are: the Problem of Psychological Categories*. Chicago.

Grimaldi, W. (ed.) (1988) *Aristotle Rhetoric II: a Commentary*. New York.

Gurney, O. R. and Finkelstein, J. J. (1957) *The Sultantepe Tablets*. London.

Hadot, P. (1998) *The Inner Citadel: the Meditations of Marcus Aurelius*, tr. M. Chase. Cambridge, MA.

Haffter, H. (1957) "Dem zwanken Zünglein lauschend wachte Caesar dort," *MH* 14: 118–26.

Halperin, D. M., Winkler, J. J., and Zeitlin, F. I. (eds.) (1990) *Before Sexuality: the Construction of Erotic Experience in the Ancient Greek World*. Princeton, NJ.

Hamilton, R. (1992) *Choes and Anthesteria*. Ann Arbor.

Hansen, M. H. (1975), *Eisangelia: The Sovereignty of the People's Court in Athens in the 4th Century B.C. and the Impeachment of Generals and Politicians.* Odense.

(1980) "Athenian nomothesia in the Fourth Century B.C. and Demosthenes' speech against Leptines," *C&M* 32: 87–104.

(1983) *The Athenian Ecclesia: a Collection of Articles 1976–83.* Copenhagen.

(1987) *The Athenian Assembly in the Age of Demosthenes.* Oxford.

(1989a) *The Athenian Ecclesia II: a Collection of Articles 1983–89.* Copenhagen.

(1989b) "Solonian democracy in fourth-century Athens," *C&M* 40: 71–100.

(1989c) "Demos, ekklesia and dikasterion: a reply to Martin Ostwald and Josiah Ober," *C&M* 40: 101–6.

(1989d) "On the importance of institutions in an analysis of Athenian democracy," *C&M* 40: 107–14.

(1991) *The Athenian Democracy in the Age of Demosthenes: Structure, Principles, and Ideology.* Oxford.

Hanson, A. E. (1987) "The eighth-month child: obsit omen," *BHM* 61: 589–602.

(1990) "The medical writers' woman," in Halperin, Winkler, and Zeitlin (1990), 309–37.

(1994a) "A division of labor: roles for men in Greek and Roman births," *Thamyris* 1: 157–202.

(1994b) "Obstetrics in the *Hippocratic corpus* and Soranus," *Forum* 4: 93–110.

Hanson, A. E. and Green, M. H. (1994) "Soranus, *methodicorum princeps*," *ANRW* 37.2: 968–1075.

Hardie, P. R. (1986) *Virgil's Aeneid: Cosmos and Imperium.* Oxford.

Harré, R. (ed.) (1986) *The Social Construction of Emotions.* Oxford.

Harré, R. and Parrott, W. (eds.) (1996) *The Emotions: Social, Cultural and Biological Dimensions.* London.

Harris, W. V. (1997) "Saving the *phainomena*: a note on Aristotle's definition of anger," *CQ* 47: 452–4.

(2002) *Restraining Rage: the Ideology of Anger Control in Classical Antiquity.* Cambridge, MA.

Harrison, A. R. W. (1971) *The Law of Athens*, vol. II. Oxford.

Haynes, K. (2003) *Fashioning the Feminine in the Greek Novel.* London and New York.

Heald, S. (1989) *Controlling Anger: the Sociology of Gisu Violence.* Manchester.

Heiberg, J. L. (1927) "Geisteskrankheiten im klassischen Altertum," *Allgemeine Zeitschrift für Psychiatrie* 86: 1–44.

Heiden, B. (1996) "The three movements of the *Iliad*," *GRBS* 37: 5–22.

(2000) "Major systems of thematic resonance in the *Iliad*," *SO* 75: 34–55.

Heilman, K. M. and Satz, P. (eds.) (1983) *Neurophysiology of Human Emotion.* New York.

Heiserman, A. (1977) *The Novel before the Novel: Essays and Discussions about the Beginnings of Prose Fiction in the West.* Chicago and London.

Henderson, J. [Jeffrey] (1991a) *The Maculate Muse.* New York and Oxford.

(1991b) "Women and the Athenian dramatic festivals," *TAPhA* 121: 133–47.

Henderson, J. [John] (1987) "Lucan: the word at war," in *Ramus* 16 = *The Imperial Muse*, ed. A. J. Boyle. Bendigo, Australia: 122–64, modified in Henderson (1998), 165–211.

(1998) *Fighting for Rome: Poets and Caesars, History and Civil War.* Cambridge.

Herman, G. (1995) "Honour, revenge and the state in fourth-century Athens," in *Die athenische Demokratie im 4. Jahrhundert v. Chr.: Vollendung oder Verfall einer Verfassungsform?*, ed. W. Eder. Stuttgart: 43–60.

Hershkowitz, D. (1998a) *The Madness of Epic: Reading Insanity from Homer to Statius.* Oxford.

(1998b) *Valerius Flaccus' Argonautica: Abbreviated Voyages in Silver Latin Epic.* Oxford.

Herwegen, O. (1912) *Das Mitleid in der griechischen Philosophie bis auf die Stoa.* Diss. Bonn.

Heubeck, A., West, S., and Hainsworth, J. B. (1988) *A Commentary on Homer's Odyssey*, vol. I. Oxford.

Heubeck, A. and Hoekstra, A. (1989) *A Commentary on Homer's Odyssey*, vol. II. Oxford.

Heusch, C. (1997) *Die Achilles-Ethopoiie des Codex Salmasius: Untersuchungen zu einer spätlateinischen Versdeklamation.* Studien zur Geschichte und Kultur des Altertums. I. Reihe, n.F. 12. Paderborn.

Hillman, J. (1992 [orig. 1960]) *Emotion: a Comprehensive Phenomenology of Theories and their Meanings for Therapy.* Evanston, IL.

Hjort, M. and Laver, S. (eds.) (1997) *Emotion and the Arts.* Oxford.

Hobbes, T. (1966) *Of Human Nature*, in *The English Works*, ed. W. Molesworth. Aalen.

Hochschild, A. R. (1975) "The sociology of feeling and emotion: selected possibilities," in *Another Voice: Feminist Perspectives on Social Life and Social Science*, ed. M. Millman and R. Moss Kanter. Garden City, NY: 280–307.

Holoka, J. P. (1983) ' "Looking darkly (ὑπόδρα ἰδών): reflections on status and decorum in Homer," *TAPhA* 113: 1–16.

Holst-Warhaft, G. (1992) *Dangerous Voices: Women's Laments and Greek Literature.* London.

Hopfner, T. (1938) "Ein neues *Thumokatochon*: Über die sonstigen *Thumokatocha, Katochoi, Hypotaktika* und *Phimotika* der griechischen Zauberpapyri in ihrem Verhältnis zu den Fluchtafeln," *ArchOrient* 10: 128–48.

Horder, J. (1992) *Provocation and Responsibility.* Oxford.

Hornsby, J. (1997) *Simple Mindedness.* Cambridge, MA.

Hume, D. (1978) *A Treatise of Human Nature*, ed. L. A. Selby-Bigge, 2nd edn., ed. P. H. Nidditch. Oxford.

Hummel, C. (1999) *Das Kind und seine Krankheiten in der griechischen Medizin.* Frankfurt, Berlin, and New York.

Humphreys, S. C. (1983) "The evolution of legal process in ancient Attica," in *Tria Corda: Scritti in onore di Arnaldo Momigliano*, ed. E. Gabba. Como, Italy: 220–40.

(1985) "Law as Discourse," *History and Anthropology* 1: 241–64.

(1989) "Family Quarrels (Dem. 39–40)," *JHS* 109: 182–4.

Hunter, R. (1994) "History and historicity in the romance of Chariton," *ANRW* 11.37.2: 1055–86.

Hunter, V. (1994) *Policing Athens*. Princeton, NJ.

Hupka, R. B., Zaleski, Z., Otto, J., Reidl, L., and Tarabrina, N. V. (1996) "Anger, envy, fear, and jealousy as felt in the body," *Cross-cultural Research* 30: 243–64.

Inwood, B. (1985) *Ethics and Human Action in Early Stoicism*. Oxford.

Irmscher, J. (1950) *Götterzorn bei Homer*. Leipzig.

Jal, P. (1962) "Les dieux dans les guerres civiles," *REL* 40: 170–200.

James, W. (1884) "What is an emotion?," *Mind* 9: 188–205.

(1890) *The Principles of Psychology*. New York.

Janko, R. (1992) *The Iliad: a Commentary*, vol. IV. Cambridge.

Janson, W. (1987) *Women without Men: Gender and Marginality in an Algerian Town*. Leiden.

Jenkins, J. M., Oatley, K., and Stein, N. L. (eds.) (1998) *Human Emotions: A Reader*. Oxford.

Johnson, M. (1987) *The Body in the Mind: the Bodily Basis of Meaning, Imagination, and Reason*. Chicago.

Johnston, S. I. (1995) "The song of the iunx: magic and rhetoric in *Pythian* 4," *TAPhA* 125: 177–206.

Jordan, D. R. (1975) "A curse from a well in the Athenian Agora," *ZPE* 19: 245–8.

(1985) "*Defixiones* from a well near the southwest corner of the Athenian Agora," *Hesperia* 54: 205–55.

(1991) "Choliambs for Mary in a papyrus phylactery," *HThR* 84: 343–6.

Joyce, J. W. (1993) *Pharsalia: Lucan*, tr. with introd. Ithaca, NY.

Kagarow, E. G. (1929) *Griechische Fluchtafeln*, Eos Suppl. 4. Leopoli.

Kaimio, M. (1995) "How to manage in the male world: the strategies of the heroine in Chariton's novel," *AAntHung* 36: 119–32.

(1996) "How to enjoy a Greek novel: Chariton guiding his audience," *Arctos* 30: 49–73.

Kassell, R. (ed.) (1976) *Aristotelis ars rhetorica*. Berlin.

Keegan, J. (1976) *The Face of Battle*. London.

Kendon, A. (1977) *Studies in the Behavior of Social Interaction*. Bloomington, IN.

Kenny, A. (1963) *Action, Emotion and Will*. London.

Kerrigan, J. (1996) *Revenge Tragedy*. Oxford.

Kim, J. (1996) *Philosophy of Mind*. Boulder, CO.

(2000) *The Pity of Achilles. Oral Style and the Unity of the Iliad*. Lanham, MD, Boulder, CO, New York, and Oxford.

King, K. C. (1987) *Achilles: Paradigm of the War Hero from Homer to the Middle Ages*. Berkeley.

Kirk, G. S. (1962) *The Songs of Homer*. Cambridge.

Kluge, A. (1996) *Learning Processes with a Deadly Outcome*, tr. C. Pavsek. Durham, NC.

Knox, B. M. W. (1977) "The *Medea* of Euripides," *Yale Classical Studies* 25: 193–225, reprinted in (1979) *Word and Action. Essays on the Ancient Theater*. Baltimore and London: 295–322.

Koch, K. (ed.) (1923) *Galen: De sanitate tuenda, De alimentorum facultatibus, De bonis malisque sucis, De victu attenuante, De ptisana*. Leipzig and Berlin.

Konstan, D. (1985) "The Politics of Aristophanes' *Wasps*," *TAPhA* 115: 27–46.

  (1994) *Sexual Symmetry: Love in the Ancient Novel and Related Genres*. Princeton, NJ.

  (1997) *Friendship in the Classical World*. Cambridge.

  (1999) "Pity and self-pity," *Electronic Antiquity* 5: 2.

  (2001) *Pity Transformed*. London.

Kotansky, R. (1991a) "Incantations and prayers for salvation on inscribed Greek amulets," in Faraone and Obbink (1991), 110–11.

  (1991b) "Magic in the court of the governor of Arabia," *ZPE* 88: 41–60.

  (1991c) "An Inscribed Copper Amulet from 'Evron," *'Atiqot* 20: 81–7.

Kövecses, Z. (2000) *Metaphor and Emotion: Language, Culture, and Body in Human Feeling*. Cambridge.

Kristeva, J. (1989) *Black Sun: Depression and Melancholia*, tr. L. S. Roudiez. New York.

Kühn, C. G. (ed.) (1821–33) *Galen: Opera omnia* (20 vols.). Leipzig.

Kurke, L. (1997) "Sex, politics, and discursive conflict in archaic Greece," *ClAnt* 16: 106–50.

Lachmann, K. (1847, 1865, 1874) *Betrachtungen über Homers Ilias* 1st, 2nd, and 3rd edns. Berlin.

Lakoff, G. and Johnson, M. (1980) *Metaphors We Live By*. Chicago.

Lakoff, G. and Kövecses, Z. (1987) "The cognitive model of anger inherent in American English," in *Cultural Models in Language and Thought*, ed. D. Holland and N. Quinn. Cambridge: 195–221.

Lane, R. D. and Nadel, L. (eds.) (1999) *Cognitive Neuroscience of Emotion*. Oxford.

  (eds.) (2000) *Cognitive Neuroscience of Emotion*. New York.

Laplace, M. (1980) "Les légendes troyennes dans le 'roman' de Chariton, *Chairéas et Callirhoé*," *REG* 93: 83–125.

Latacz, J. (1995) *Achilleus. Wandlungen eines europäischen Heldenbilde*. Lectio Teubneriana 3. Stuttgart.

Lateiner, D. (1995) *Sardonic Smile: Nonverbal Behavior in Homeric Epic*. Ann Arbor.

Lazarus, R. S. (1991) *Emotion and Adaptation*. New York.

Lazarus, R. S., Kanner, A. D., and Folkman, S. (1980) "Emotions: a cognitive-phenomenological analysis," in *Emotion: Theory, Research, and Experience*, vol. 1: *Theories of Emotion*, ed. R. Plutchik and H. Kellerman. New York: 189–217.

LeDoux, J. (1996) *The Emotional Brain: the Mysterious Underpinnings of Emotional Life*. New York.

  (1998) *The Emotional Brain: the Mysterious Underpinnings of Emotional Life*. London.

Leighton, St. R. (1996) "Aristotle and the emotions," in Rorty (1996), 206–37.

Lendon, J. E. (2000) "Homeric vengeance and the outbreak of Greek wars," in van Wees (2000), 1–30.

Lesky, A. (1953) "Homer 1. Fortsetzung," *Anzeiger für die Altertumswissenschaft* 6: 129–50.

  (1966) *A History of Greek Literature*. New York.

Levene, D. (1995) *Religion in Livy*. Oxford.

Lewis, M. and Haviland, J. M. (eds.) (1993) *Handbook of Emotions*. New York.

  (eds.) (2000) *Handbook of Emotions*, 2nd edn. New York and London.

Lewis, T., Amini, F., and Lannon, R. (2000) *A General Theory of Love*. New York.

Liddell, H. G. and Scott, R. (1940) *A Greek–English Lexicon*, 9th edn., revised by H. Stuart Jones. Oxford.

Liebeschuetz, J. H. W. G. (1967) "The religious position of Livy's history," *JRS* 57: 45–55.

  (1979) *Continuity and Change in Roman Religion*. Oxford.

Littman, R. J. (1990) *Kinship and Politics in Athens 600–400 B.C.* New York.

Littré, E. (ed.) (1839–61) *Hippocrates. Opera omnia* (10 vols.). Paris.

Liviabella Furiani, P. (1989) "Di donna in donna: elementi 'femministi' nel romanzo greco d'amore," in Liviabella Furiani and Scarcella (1989), 43–106.

Liviabella Furiani, P. and Scarcella, A. M. (eds.) (1989) *Piccolo mondo antico: le donne, gli amori, i costumi, il mondo reale nel romanzo antico*. Naples.

Lloyd, M. (1987) "Homer on poetry: two passages in the *Odyssey*," *Eranos* 85: 85–90.

Lloyd-Jones, H. (1990) "Erinyes, Semnai Theai, Eumenides," in *"Owls to Athens": Essays on Classical Subjects Presented to Sir Kenneth Dover*, ed. E. M. Craik. Oxford: 203–11.

Lobel, E. and Page, D. (1955) *Poetarum Lesbiorum fragmenta*. Oxford.

Lofberg, G. (1917) *Sycophancy in Athens*. Menasha, WI.

Long, A. A. (1970) "Morals and values in Homer," *JHS* 90: 121–39.

  (1996) *Stoic Studies*. Cambridge.

  (2002) *Epictetus: a Stoic and Socratic Guide to Life*. Oxford.

Long, A. A. and Sedley, D. N. (1987) *The Hellenistic Philosophers* (2 vols.). Cambridge.

Lorenz, K. (1996 [orig. 1966]) *On Aggression*, new edn. London.

Lutz, C. A. (1988) *Unnatural Emotions: Everyday Sentiments on a Micronesian Atoll and Their Challenge to Western Theory*. Chicago and London.

Lyne, R. O. A. M. (1983) "Vergil and the politics of war," *CQ* 33: 188–203.

MacDowell, D. M. (ed.) (1971) *Aristophanes, Wasps, with Introduction and Commentary*. Oxford.

  (1971, repr. 1995) *Aristophanes and Athens: an Introduction to the Plays*. Oxford.

  (1978) *The Law in Classical Athens*. Ithaca.

Macleod, C. W. (1982a) "Politics and the *Oresteia*," *JHS* 102: 124–44.

  (ed.) (1982b) *Homer. Iliad Book XXIV*. Cambridge.

Malten, L. (1961) *Die Sprache des menschlichen Antlitzes im frühen Griechentum*. Berlin.

Manakidou, F. (1998) "χόλος, μῆνις, νεῖκος, in den Argonautika des Apollonios Rhodios," *Philologus* 142: 241–60.

Mansfeld, J. (1971) *The Pseudo-Hippocratic tract* Περὶ ἑβδομάδων *ch. I–II and Greek Philosophy*. Assen.

Masciadri, M. M. and Montevecchi, O. (eds.) (1984) *I contratti di baliatico*.

Masters, J. (1992) *Poetry and Civil War in Lucan's Bellum Civile*. Cambridge.

Matsumoto, D. (1990) "Cultural similarities and differences in display rules," *Motivation and Emotion* 14: 195–214.

Mattock, J. N. (1972) "The Arabic epitome of Galen's book Περὶ ἠθῶν," in *Islamic Philosophy and the Classical Tradition: Essays Presented by His Friends and Pupils to Richard Walzer on his Seventieth Birthday*, eds. S. M. Stern, A. Hourani, and V. Brown. Columbia, SC: 235–60.

Mauch, M. (1997) *Senecas Frauenbild in den philosophischen Schriften*. Frankfurt.

Meyers, B. F. and Sanders, E. P. (eds.) (1982) *Self-Definition in the Greco-Roman World*, Jewish and Christian Self-Definition 3. Philadelphia.

Michelini, A. (1994) "Political themes in Euripides' *Suppliants*," *AJPh* 115: 219–52.

Milhaven, J. G. (1989) *Good Anger*. Kansas City.

Miller, G. (2000) *The Mating Mind: How Sexual Choice Shaped the Evolution of Human Nature*. London.

Miller, W. I. (1993) *Humiliation and Other Essays on Honor, Social Discomfort, and Violence*. Ithaca, NY.

Monsacré, H. (1984) *Les larmes d'Achille. Le héros, la femme et la souffrance dans la poésie d'Homère*. Paris.

Montague, H. (1992) "Sweet and pleasant passion: female and male fantasy in ancient romance novels," in Richlin (1992), 231–49.

Morris, D. (1977) *Manwatching: a Field Guide to Human Behaviour*. London.

Mossman, J. (1995) *Wild Justice: a Study of Euripides' Hecuba*. Oxford.

Most, G. W. (1989) "The stranger's stratagem: self-disclosure and self-sufficiency in Greek culture," *JHS* 109: 114–33.

(1993) "Die früheste erhaltene griechische Dichterallegorese," *RhM* N.F. 136: 209–12.

Moulton, C. (1977) *Similes in the Homeric Poems*. Göttingen.

Mouterde, R. (1930) *Le glaive de Dardanus: objets et inscriptions magiques de Syrie*, Mélanges de l' Université Saint-Josephe 15.3. Beirut.

Mozley, J. H. (ed.) (1982) *Statius*. Loeb Classical Library. Cambridge, MA and London.

Mueller, M. (1984) *The Iliad*. London.

Muellner, L. C. (1996) *The Anger of Achilles: Mēnis in Greek Epic*. Ithaca, NY.

Müller, C. W. (1976) "Chariton von Aphrodisias und die Theorie des Romans in der Antike," *A&A* 22: 115–36.

Müller, H. M. (1980) *Erotische Motive in der griechischen Dichtung bis auf Euripides*. Hamburg.

Nagy, G. (1979) *The Best of the Achaeans: Concepts of the Hero in Archaic Greek Poetry*. Baltimore.

North, H. (1966) *Sophrosyne: Self-Knowledge and Self-Restraint in Greek Literature*. Cornell Studies in Classical Philology 35. Ithaca, NY.

Nussbaum, M. C. (1994) *The Therapy of Desire: Theory and Practice in Hellenistic Ethics*. Princeton, NJ.

(1996) "Aristotle on emotions and rational persuasion," in Rorty (1996), 303–23.

(2001) *Upheavals of Thought*. Cambridge.

Nutton, V. (ed.) (1979). *Galen: De praecognitione*, with tr. and comm. Berlin.

(1995) "Galen *ad multos annos*," *Dynamis* 15: 25–39.

Oakley, J. (1992) *Morality and the Emotions*. London.

Oatley, K. (1992) *The Best Laid Schemes: the Psychology of the Emotions*. Cambridge.

Oatley, K., Jenkins, J. M., and Stein, N. L. (1998) "Functions of emotions in society and in the individual," in Jenkins, Oatley, and Stein (1998), 239–44.

Oatley, K. and Johnson-Laird, P. N. (1998) "The communicative theory of emotions," in Jenkins, Oatley, and Stein (1998), 84–97.

Ober, J. (1989a), *Mass and Elite in Democratic Athens: Rhetoric, Ideology, and the Power of the People*. Princeton, NJ.

(1989b) "The nature of Athenian democracy: review of *The Athenian Assembly in the Age of Demosthenes* by Mogens Herman Hansen, Oxford and New York: Basil Blackwell. 1987," *CPh* 84: 322–34.

O'Hear, A. (ed.) (1998) *Current Issues in Philosophy of Mind*. Oxford.

Olson, S. D. (1996) "Politics and poetry in Aristophanes' *Wasps*," *TAPhA* 126: 129–50.

Osborne, R. (1990) "Vexatious litigation in classical Athens: sykophancy and the sykophant," in *Nomos: Essays in Athenian Law, Politics, and Society*, ed. P. Cartledge, P. Millett, and S. Todd. Cambridge: 82–102.

O'Sullivan, J. N. (1995) *Xenophon of Ephesus: His Compositional Technique and the Birth of the Novel*. Untersuchungen zur antiken Literatur und Geschichte 44. Berlin and New York.

Padel, R. (1992) *In and Out of the Mind: Greek Images of the Tragic Self*. Princeton, NJ.

Panksepp, J. (1998) *Affective Neuroscience*. New York.

Papanikolaou, A. D. (1973) *Chariton-Studien: Untersuchungen zur Sprache und Chronologie der griechischen Romane*. Hypomnemata 37. Göttingen.

Parker, R. C. T. (1996) *Miasma: Pollution and Purification in Early Greek Religion*. Oxford.

Pedrick, V. (1982) "Supplication in the Iliad and the Odyssey," *TAPhA* 112: 125–40.

Peppmüller, R. (1876) *Commentar des vierundzwanzigsten Buches der Ilias*. Berlin.

Perkins, J. (1995) *The Suffering Self: Pain and Narrative Representation in the Early Christian Era*. London and New York.

Philippides, S. (1988) "Lovers' fate: narrator's providence in *Chaereas and Callirhoe*," in *The Greek Novel AD 1–1985*, ed. R. Beaton. Beckenham: 182–9.

Pinker, S. (1997) *How the Mind Works*. New York.

Planalp, S. (1999) *Communicating Emotion: Social, Moral, and Cultural Processes*. Cambridge.

Platts, M. (1991) *Moral Realities: an Essay in Philosophical Psychology*. London.

Plutchik, R. (1980) *Emotion: a Psychoevolutionary Synthesis*. New York.

(1994) *The Psychology and Biology of Emotion*. New York.

Plutchik, R. and Kellerman, H. (eds.) (1986) *Emotion: Theory, Research, and Experience*, vol. III: *Biological Foundations of Emotion*. New York.

Power, M. and Dalgleish, T. (1997) *Cognition and Emotion. From Order to Disorder*. Hove, East Sussex.

Preisendanz, K. (1972) "Fluchtafel (Defixion)," *RAC* 8: 1–29.

Procopé, J. (1998 [orig. 1993]) "Epicureans on anger," in Sihvola and Engberg-Pedersen (1998), 171–96, reprinted from *Philanthropia kai Eusebeia: Festschrift für Albrecht Dihle zum 70. Geburtstag*, ed. G. Most, H. Petersmann, and A. M. Ritter. Göttingen (1993): 363–86.

Putnam, M. (1990) "Anger, blindness, and insight in Virgil's *Aeneid*," in *The Poetics of Therapy*, ed. M. C. Nussbaum. Edmonton, Alberta = *Apeiron* 23.4: 7–40.

(1995), *Virgil's Aeneid: Interpretation and Influence*. Chapel Hill, NC and London.

Rawls, J. (1973) *A Theory of Justice*. Oxford.

Reardon, B. P. (1982) "Theme, structure and narrative in Chariton," *YClS* 27: 1–27, reprinted in Swain (1999), 163–88.

(ed.) (1989) *Collected Ancient Greek Novels*. Berkeley, Los Angeles, and London.

(1991) *The Form of Greek Romance*. Princeton, NJ.

(1996) "Chariton," in Schmeling (1996), 309–35.

Reckford, K. J. (1977) "Catharsis and dream interpretation in Aristophanes' Wasps," *TAPhA* 107: 283–312.

Redfield, J. M. (1975) *Nature and Culture in the Iliad: the Tragedy of Hector*. Chicago.

(1982) "Notes on the Greek Wedding," *Arethusa* 15: 181–201.

Reichl, M. (1994) *Fernbeziehungen in der Ilias*. Tübingen.

Reiner, E. (1966) "La magie babylonienne," in *Le monde du sorcier. Sources Orientales* 7. Paris: 67–98.

Reynolds, J. (1982) *Aphrodisias and Rome. Journal of Roman Studies* Monographs 1. London.

Richardson, N. J. (ed.) (1974) *The Homeric Hymn to Demeter*. Oxford.

(1993) *The Iliad: a Commentary*, vol. VI. Cambridge.

Richlin, A. (ed.) (1992) *Pornography and Representation in Greece and Rome*. New York and Oxford.

Ridley, M. (1996) *The Origins of Virtue*. London.

Riess, E. (1896) "Pliny and Magic," *AJPh* 17: 77–83.

Robertson, D. S. (1940) "The Food of Achilles," *CR* 54: 177–80.

Robertson, G. I. C. (1999) "The Eyes of Achilleus: *Iliad* 1. 200," *Phoenix* 53: 1–7.

Robiano, P. (1984) "La notion de *Tyché* chez Chariton et chez Héliodore," *REG* 97: 543–9.

Rohdich, H. (1987) "Ein Gleichnis der Odyssee," *AuA* 33: 45–52.

Roisman, H. (1984) *Loyalty in Early Greek Epic and Tragedy*. Königstein.

Rolls, E. T. (1999) *The Brain and Emotion*. Oxford.

Roncali, R. (1991) "Zelotypia/daimon in Caritone," *QS* 17 (34): 183–6.

Rorty, A. O. (ed.) (1980) *Explaining Emotions*. Berkeley and Los Angeles.

(ed.) (1996) *Essays on Aristotle's Rhetoric*. Berkeley and Los Angeles.

Rosaldo, M. Z. (1980) *Knowledge and Passion: Ilongot Notions of Self and Social Life.* Cambridge.

(1984) "Toward an anthropology of self and feeling," in Shweder and LeVine (1984), 137–57.

Rosenwein, Barbara H. (ed.) (1998) *Anger's Past: the Social Uses of an Emotion in the Middle Ages.* Ithaca, NY.

(2002) "Worrying about emotions in history," *AHR* 107: 821–45.

Ross, W. D. (1959) *Aristoteles Ars Rhetorica.* Oxford.

Ruiz Montero, C. (1989) "Caritón de Afrodisias y el mundo real," in Liviabella Furiani and Scarcella (1989), 107–49.

Russell, J. A. (1991) "Culture and the categorization of emotions," *Psychological Bulletin* 110: 426–50.

Russell, J. A., Fernandez-Dols, J.-M., Manstead, A., and Wellenkamp, J. (eds.) (1995) *Everyday Conceptions of Emotion: an Introduction to the Psychology, Anthropology and Linguistics of Emotion.* Dordrecht, Netherlands.

Sartre, J.-P. (1962) *Sketch for a Theory of the Emotions,* tr. P. Mairet. London.

Saunders, T. J. (1991) *Plato's Penal Code. Tradition, Controversy and Reform in Greek Penology.* Oxford.

Scheil, V. (1921) "Catalogue de la collection Eugene Tisserant," *Revue d'Assyriologie et d'Archéologie Orientale* 18: 21–7.

Scherer, K. R. and Ekman, P. (1984) *Approaches to Emotion.* Hillsdale, NJ.

Scherer, K. R., Schorr, A., and Johnstone, T. (eds.) (2001) *Appraisal Theories of Emotions: Theories, Methods, Research.* New York.

Schlesier, R. (1993) "Mixtures of masks: maenads as tragic models," in *The Masks of Dionysos,* ed. T. H. Carpenter and C. A. Faraone. Ithaca, NY: 89–114.

Schmeling, G. L. (1974) *Chariton.* Twayne's World Authors Series 295. New York.

(ed.) (1996) *The Novel in the Ancient World.* Mnemosyne Suppl. 159. Leiden, New York, and Cologne.

Schmid, W. and Stählin, A. (1929) *Geschichte der griechischen Literatur.* Munich.

Schmitt, A. (1990) *Selbständigkeit und Abhängigkeit menschlichen Handelns bei Homer: Untersuchungen zur Psychologie Homers.* Abh. Ak. Wiss. Lit. Mainz, geistes- u. sozialwiss. Kl. 1990.5. Stuttgart.

Schoek, H. (1966) *Envy.* Indianapolis, IN.

Scott, M. (1979) "Pity and pathos in Homer," *AClass* 22: 1–14.

Scurlock, J. (1989–90) "Was there a 'love-hungry' *Entu*-priestess named Etirtum?," *AOF* 36: 107–12.

Sealey, R. (1982) "On the Athenian concept of law," *CJ* 27: 298–302.

(1987) *The Athenian Republic: Democracy or Rule of Law?* University Park, PA.

(1990) *Women and Law in Classical Greece.* Chapel Hill, NC.

Sedley, D. (1997) "The ethics of Brutus and Cassius," *JRS* 87: 41–53.

Shackleton Bailey, D. R. (1982) "On Lucan," *PCPhS* 28: 91–100.

(1997) *Lucanus; de Bello Civili.* Stuttgart and Leipzig.

Shay, J. (1994) *Achilles in Vietnam: Combat Trauma and the Undoing of Character.* New York.

(2000) "Killing rage: *physis* or *nomos* – or both?' " in van Wees (2000), 31–56.

Sherman, N. (1997) *Making a Necessity of Virtue: Aristotle and Kant on Virtue.* Cambridge.

Shweder, R. A. and LeVine, R. A. (eds.) (1984) *Culture Theory: Essays on Mind, Self, and Emotion.* Cambridge.

Sihvola, J. and Engberg-Pedersen, T. (eds.) (1998) *The Emotions in Hellenistic Philosophy*, New Synthese Historical Library 46. Dordrecht.

Simon, B. (1988) *Tragic Drama and the Family: Psychoanalytic Studies from Aeschylus to Beckett.* New Haven and London.

Slatkin, L. M. (1986) "The wrath of Thetis," *TAPhA* 116: 1–24.

Smith, A. (1976) *The Theory of Moral Sentiments*, ed. D. D. Raphael and A. L. Macfie. Oxford.

Smith, M. (1984) "The eighth book of Moses and how it grew (*P.Leid.* J 395)," *Atti del XVIII congresso internazionale di papirologia.* Naples: 683–93.

Smith, W. D. (1966) "Physiology in the Homeric Poems," *TAPhA* 97: 547–56.

Solomon, R. (1993) *The Passions. Emotions and the Meaning of Life.* Indianapolis, IN.

Solomon, R. C. (1984) "Getting angry: the Jamesian theory of emotion in anthropology," in Shweder and LeVine (1984), 238–54.

Sommers, S. (1988) "Understanding emotions: some interdisciplinary considerations," in *Emotion and Social Change: towards a New Psychohistory*, ed. C. Z. and P. N. Stearns. New York and London: 23–38.

Sorabji, R. (1999) "Aspasius on emotion," in *Aspasius: the Earliest Extant Commentary on Aristotle's Ethics*, ed. A. Alberti and R. W. Sharples. Berlin: 96–106.

(2000) *Emotion and Peace of Mind: from Stoic Agitation to Christian Temptation.* Oxford.

Sowa, C. A. (1984) *Traditional Themes and the Homeric Hymns.* Chicago.

Spelman, E. V. (1989) "Anger and insubordination," in *Women, Knowledge and Reality: Explorations in Feminist Philosophy*, ed. A. Garry and M. Pearsall. Boston: 263–73.

Spengel, L. (1867) *Aristoteles Ars Rhetorica.* Leipzig.

Stocker, M. (with E. Hegeman) (1996) *Valuing Emotions.* Cambridge.

Strawson, P. F. (1974) *Freedom and Resentment and Other Essays.* London.

Striker, G. (1996) "Emotions in context: Aristotle's treatment of the passions in the *Rhetoric* and his moral psychology," in Rorty (1996), 286–302.

Swain, S. (ed.) (1999) *Oxford Readings in the Greek Novel.* Oxford.

Szabó, Á. (1956) "Achilleus, der tragische Held der Ilias," *AAntHung* 4: 55–108.

Taberner, P. V. (1985) *Aphrodisiacs: the Science and the Myth.* Philadelphia.

Tafrate, R. C. (1995) "Evaluation of treatment strategies for adult anger disorders," in *Anger Disorders: Definition, Diagnosis, and Treatment*, ed. H. Kassinove. Washington, DC: 109–29.

Taillardat, J. (1962) *Les images d'Aristophane: Etudes de langue et style.* Paris.

Taplin, O. (1972) "Aeschylean silences and silences in Aeschylus," *HSPh* 76: 57–97.

(1992) *Homeric Soundings. The Shaping of the Iliad.* Oxford.

Tavris, C. (1989) *Anger: The Misunderstood Emotion.* Rev. edn. New York.

Taylor, G. (1985) *Pride, Shame and Guilt. Emotions of Self-Assessment.* Oxford.

Thornton, A. (1976) *The Living Universe: Gods and Men in Virgil's Aeneid*. Mnemosyne Suppl. 46. Leiden.

(1984) *Homer's Iliad: Its Composition and the Motif of Supplication*. Hypomnemata 81. Göttingen.

Todd, S. (1993, repr. 1995) *The Shape of Athenian Law*. Oxford.

Toohey, P. (1999) "Dangerous ways to fall in love: Chariton 1.1.5–10 and VI.9.4," *Maia* 51: 259–75.

Treggiari, S. (1991) *Roman Marriage: Iusti coniuges from the Time of Cicero to the Time of Ulpian*. Oxford.

Trevett, J. (1992) *Apollodorus the Son of Pasion*. Oxford.

Tritle, L. (2000) *From Melos to My Lai: War and Survival*. London.

Trivers, R. (1971, repr. 1994) "The evolution of reciprocal altruism," in *Quarterly Review of Biology* 46 (1971), 35–57, reprinted in *Ethics*, ed. P. Singer. Oxford: 78–88.

(1985) *Social Evolution*. Menlo Park, CA.

Urmson, J. O. (1973) "Aristotle's doctrine of the mean," *American Philosophical Quarterly* 10: 223–30, reprinted in Rorty (1980), 157–70.

Vaio, J. (1971) "Aristophanes' *Wasps*: the relevance of the final scenes," *GRBS* 12: 335–51.

van der Valk, M. (ed.) (1971–87) *Eustathius: Commentarii ad Homeri Iliadem pertinentes ad fidem codicis Laurentiani editi*. Leiden.

Van Steen, G. (1998) "Destined to be? Tyche in Chariton's *Chaereas and Callirhoe* and in the Byzantine romance of *Kallimachos and Chrysorroi*," *AC* 67: 203–11.

van Wees, H. (1992) *Status Warriors: War, Violence, and Society in Homer and History*. Amsterdam.

(ed.) (2000) *War and Violence in Ancient Greece*. London.

Vessey, D. (1973) *Statius and the Thebaid*. Cambridge.

Veyne, P. (1993) *Sénèque: Lettres à Lucilius*. Paris.

Vico, G. B. (1948) *The New Science*, tr. from the 3rd edn. (1744) by T. G. Bergin and M. H. Fisch. Ithaca, NY.

Volkmann, R. (1874) *Geschichte und Kritik der Wolfschen Prolegomena*. Leipzig.

Von der Mühll, P. (1952) *Kritisches Hypomnema zur Ilias*. Schweizerische Beiträge zur Altertumswissenschaft 4. Basel.

von Staden, H. (ed.) (1989) *Herophilus: the Art of Medicine in Early Alexandria*. Cambridge.

Wallace, R. (1994) "Private lives and public enemies: freedom of thought in classical Athens," in *Athenian Identity and Civic Ideology*, ed. A. Boegehold and A. Scafuro. Baltimore: 127–55.

Walsh, P. G. (1961) *Livy: His Historical Aims and Methods*. Cambridge.

Watkins, C. (1977a) "A propos de *mēnis*," *BSL* 72: 193–9.

(1977b) "On μῆνις," *Indo-European Studies* 3: 686–722.

Wenkebach, E. and Pfaff, F. (eds.) (1956) *Galen: In Hippocratis Epidemiorum VI commentaria*. Leipzig.

West, M. L. (ed.) (1972) *Iambi et elegi graeci ante Alexandrum cantati*, vol. II. Oxford.

White, St. D. (1998) "The politics of anger," in Rosenwein (1998), 127–52.

Widdows, P. (1988) *Lucan's Civil War, Translated into English Verse*. Bloomington, IN.

Wiersma, S. (1990) "The ancient Greek novel and its heroines: a female paradox," *Mnemosyne* 43: 109–23.

Wierzbicka, A. (1992) *Semantics, Culture and Cognition: Universal Human Concepts in Culture-Specific Configurations*. New York.

(1999) *Emotions across Languages and Cultures: Diversity and Universals*. Cambridge.

Wilamowitz-Moellendorff, U. von (1916) *Die Ilias und Homer*. Berlin.

Williams, B. (1973) *Problems of the Self*. Cambridge.

(1993) *Shame and Necessity*. Berkeley.

Williams, G. (1983) *Technique and Ideas in Virgil's Aeneid*. New Haven, CT.

Wilson, M. (1997) "The subjugation of grief in Seneca's *Epistles*," in Braund and Gill (1997), 48–67.

Wilson, E. O. (1998) *Consilience: the Unity of Knowledge*. London.

Winkler, J. J. (1990a) *The Constraints of Desire: the Anthropology of Sex and Gender in Ancient Greece*. New York.

(1990b) "Laying down the law: the oversight of men's sexual behavior in classical Athens," in *Before Sexuality*, ed. D. Halperin, J. Winkler, and F. Zeitlin. Princeton, NJ: 45–71.

(1991) "The constraints of eros," in Faraone and Obbink (1991), 214–43.

Winnington-Ingram, R. P. (1948) "Clytemnestra and the vote of Athena," *JHS* 68: 130–47 = (with some changes) Winnington-Ingram (1983), 101–31.

(1983) *Studies in Aeschylus*. Cambridge.

Wißmann, J. (1997) *Motivation und Schmähung: Feigheit in der Ilias und in der griechischen Tragödie*. Stuttgart.

Wittgenstein, L. (1967) *Philosophische Untersuchungen*. 2nd edn. with Eng. trans. by G. E. M. Anscombe. Oxford.

Wolf, C. (1983) *Kassandra*. Darmstadt and Neuwied.

Wollheim, R. (1999) *On the Emotions*. New Haven, CT.

Wright, M. R. (1997) "*Ferox uirtus*: anger in Virgil's *Aeneid*," in Braund and Gill (1997), 169–84.

Wright, R. (1995) *The Moral Animal: Evolutionary Psychology and Everyday Life*. London.

Yamagata, N. (1994) *Homeric Morality*. Mnemosyne Suppl. 131. Leiden, New York, and Cologne.

Zahn-Waxler, C., Cummings, E. M., and Iannotti, R. (eds.) (1986) *Altruism and Aggression: Biological and Social Origins*. Cambridge.

Zanker, G. (1987) *Realism in Alexandrian Poetry: a Literature and Its Audience*. London.

Zeitlin, F. I. (1990) "Playing the other: theater, theatricality, and the feminine in Greek drama," in *Nothing to Do with Dionysus? Athenian Drama in Its Social Context*, ed. J. J. Winkler and F. I. Zeitlin. Princeton, NJ: 63–96.

Index of passages cited

Aeschines (1.1–2) 81
(3.197) 77

Aeschylus (*Cho.* 755–7) 197
(*PV* 381–2) 89

Antiphon (5.69, 71, 91) 76
(5.71–2) 126

Apollodorus (*Bibliotheca* 3.13.6) 190

Aristophanes (*Aves* 442) 93
(*Eq.* 259) 92
(*Lys.* 463–5) 132
(*Nub.* 713) 93
(*Pax* 1351) 92
(*Plut.* 706–8) 92
(*Vesp.* 145) 88
(160) 89
(243) 83
(297) 89
(302) 89
(383) 83
(407) 89
(436) 88
(511) 88
(548–630) 84
(549) 84
(552–5) 84
(574–5) 84
(808) 89
(877) 83
(883–4) 83
(1071–88) 83
(1107–11) 83
(1114–16) 95
(1115) 89
(1121) 89
(1343) 89
(1367) 88
(1379) 89

Aristotle (*De an.* 1.1.403a16–b2) 105
(1.1.403a30) 80
(*Eth. Nic.* 2.5.1105b21–3) 111
(2.6.1107a8–11) 119
(2.7.1108a4–6) 119
(3.8.1117a5–15) 119
(4.5.1125b29) 120
(4.5.3 and 5–7, 1125b–1126a) 283
(7.6.1149a25–b27) 128–9
(8.5.1157b28–32) 111
(*Pol.* 1.5.1260a13) 136
(5.8.1312b25–34) 102
(*Rh.* 1.10–11) 103
(1.11.1370a27–34) 100
(1.11.1370b29) 81
(2.1.1378a1) 81
(2.1.1378a20–3) 100
(2.1.1378a21–2) 111
(2.2–11) 103
(2.2.1378a30–2) 17, 79, 176
(2.2.1378a30–2, b1–2) 209
(2.2.1378a31) 123
(2.2.1378a31–2) 26
(2.2.1378a31–3) 100
(2.2.1378a34–5) 110
(2.2.1378b1–2) 103
(2.2.1378b1–9) 101
(2.2.1378b2) 81
(2.2.1378b6–7) 27
(2.2.1378b10–11) 108
(2.2.1378b14) 102
(2.2.1378b18–19) 108
(2.2.1378b23–5) 109
(2.2.1378b25–6) 112
(2.2.1378b28) 112
(2.2.1378b34–1379a6) 112
(2.2.1379a4–5) 117
(2.2.1379a11) 113
(2.2.1379a29–32) 109
(2.2.1379a36–1379b2) 112
(2.2.1379b1–2) 102

(2.2.1379b11–13) 112
(2.2.1379b17–19) 109
(2.2.1379b24–6) 113
(2.2.1379b29–31) 113
(2.3.1380a8–12) 106
(2.3.1380a15–18) 119
(2.3.1380a21–3) 119
(2.3.1380a22–3) 109
(2.3.1380a33) 109
(2.3.1380a34) 81
(2.3.1380a34–5) 110
(2.3.1380b2–5) 113
(2.3.1380b16–18) 106
(2.4.1380b35–1381a1) 110
(2.4.1381a1–3) 110
(2.4.1381a5–6) 110
(2.4.1381b33) 110
(2.4.1382a1–2) 110
(2.4.1382a2) 102
(2.4.1382a4–7) 110
(2.4.1382a7–8) 111
(2.4.1382a8) 110
(2.4.1382a9–11) 102
(2.4.1382a12–13) 102
(2.4.1382a14–15) 110
(2.5.1382a21–2) 101, 114
(2.5.1382a27–30) 114
(2.5.1382a32–3) 114
(2.5.1382b8–9) 114
(2.5.1382b15–19) 114
(2.5.1382b21–2) 80
(2.5.1383a22–5) 114
(2.5.1383a32–1383b3) 114
(2.6.1383b13–15) 115
(2.6.1384a9–11) 115
(2.6.1384a23) 115
(2.7.1385a17–19) 115
(2.8.1385b13–14) 101
(2.8.1385b13–16) 57, 116
(2.9.1386b9–12) 116
(2.9.1386b18–19) 116
(2.9.1386b19–20) 116
(2.10.1387b22–4) 116
(2.10.1387b23–4) 116
(2.11.1388a30–3) 116
(2.11.1388a33–6) 116
(2.11.1388b23–7) 117
(*Top.* 4.5.125b28–34) 103
(4.6.127b26–32) 103

Marcus Aurelius (*Med.* 2.1) 211
(12.24, 26) 212

Chariton (1.1.3) 174, 175
(1.2.1) 164

(1.2.2) 164
(1.2.3) 164
(1.2.5) 164
(1.2.6) 164
(1.3.4) 164
(1.3.6) 175, 179
(1.4.10) 164
(1.4.12) 164, 169
(1.5.4–6.1) 171
(1.8.4) 176
(1.11.2) 179
(1.14.7) 176
(2.2) 182
(2.2.6) 176
(2.2.7) 176
(2.4.4–5) 169
(2.5.8) 179
(2.9–11) 180
(2.9.3–4) 178
(2.11.1) 177
(3.8.7) 177
(3.10.5) 177
(3.10.7) 177
(5.4.13) 179
(5.8.5–6) 182
(6.3.2) 170
(6.3.8) 169
(6.5.8) 136, 179
(6.7.9) 179
(7.1.3–11) 172
(7.1.6) 173
(7.1.8) 172, 173–4, 175
(7.4.9) 173
(7.6.1) 173
(7.6.11) 179
(8.1.3) 166, 171
(8.6.8) 175

Cicero (*Tusc.* 4.43) 283

Dante (*Inferno* 7.109–16) 250

Demosthenes (18.278) 126
(21.42, 43) 77
(21.112) 81
(21.123) 76
(21.123–4) 127
(36.9) 81
(36.26–7) 93
(37.2) 81

Epictetus (*Diss.* 1.28.10) 212

Euripides (*El.* 1204) 86
(*Hec.* 1118–9) 142

Euripides (*cont.*)
(*Heracl.* 970–4) 80
(*Hipp.* 1078–9) 60
(*Ion* 1026) 80
(*Med.* 407–9) 140–1

Galen (*De moribus* 239 Mattock) 192
(240 Mattock) 204
(*De plac. Hipp. et Plat.* 3.3.2–5) 187
(3.3.7) 187
(*De propriorum animi cuiuslibet affectuum dignotione et curatione* 5.2 De Boer) 124
(8.1 De Boer) 135
(*De san. tuenda* 1.8.1–14) 198
(1.8.25) 192

Herodotus (4.162.5) 132
(4.205) 132

Hesiod (*Op.* 304) 78, 94
(*Theog.* 485) 197
(594) 94

Hippocrates (*Aer.* 5.13) 82
(*Carn.* 12–13) 202
(*Mul.* 1–3.12.8) 82
(1–3.57.5–6) 82
(*De octimestri partu* 1.15–18) 201

Homer (*Il.* 1.1–2) 50
(1.34–42) 64
(1.55–6) 63
(1.80–3) 31, 186
(1.101–5) 41
(1.103–4) 22, 42
(1.148) 43, 47
(1.188–91) 47
(1.192) 21
(1.207) 22
(1.223) 21
(1.243–4) 21
(1.244) 29
(1.247) 31
(1.282) 22
(1.356) 113
(1.414–18) 64
(1.419–20) 64
(1.426–7) 64
(2.195) 25
(2.196) 117
(2.223) 38
(2.239–42) 47
(2.241–2) 25, 26
(2.245) 43
(2.378) 24

(2.872–5) 200
(3.216–20) 46
(3.217) 46
(3.220) 46
(4.22–4) 44, 45
(4.23–4) 29
(4.34–6) 279
(4.35–6) 25
(4.36) 25
(4.168) 30
(4.178) 25
(4.349) 43
(4.349–50) 43
(4.356–7) 43
(4.391) 26, 38
(4.411) 43
(4.506) 35
(4.507–8) 34
(5.177–8) 31, 32
(5.251) 43
(5.561–3) 56
(5.610–12) 56
(5.677–82) 61
(5.757) 38
(5.872) 38
(5.888) 43
(6.325) 37
(6.325–31) 46
(6.329–30) 37
(6.407) 65
(6.431) 65
(6.442) 65
(6.450) 65
(6.484) 65
(8.190–7) 35
(8.198) 35
(8.459–60) 29
(8.459–61) 44, 45
(9.163–4) 65
(9.198) 44, 66
(9.247–8) 65
(9.254–9) 73
(9.302) 65
(9.356–63) 66
(9.427–9) 66
(9.436) 21
(9.439–41) 190
(9.487–9) 203
(9.497) 66
(9.516) 24
(9.523) 26
(9.556–65) 47
(9.574–6) 47
(9.581–3) 47
(9.588) 47

(9.618–19) 66
(9.628–30) 210
(9.629) 66
(9.630–1) 66
(9.632) 66
(9.639–42) 210
(9.645–8) 210
(9.648) 113
(9.650–3) 66
(9.678) 25
(9.679) 22
(10.446) 43
(11.403) 23
(11.598–601) 66
(11.604) 67, 200
(11.609–10) 66
(11.611–15) 66
(11.649) 35
(11.656) 67
(11.830–2) 186
(12.230) 43
(12.466) 42
(12.782–9) 188
(13.15–16) 61
(13.121–2) 36
(13.292–3) 35, 38
(13.460) 31
(14.82) 43
(14.82–103) 43
(14.111) 30
(14.197–210) 154
(14.214–17) 154
(14.336) 38
(14.367) 24
(14.584–5) 26
(15.13) 43
(15.65–6) 200
(15.69–71) 38
(15.85–101) 45
(15.100–4) 44, 45
(15.101–3) 45
(15.184–99) 22
(15.185–95) 34
(15.186) 23
(15.211) 23, 34
(15.227) 34
(15.607) 42
(16.2–4) 67
(16.5–10) 199–200
(16.5–11) 67–8
(16.30–5) 188
(16.33–5) 68
(16.50–63) 68
(16.64–70) 68
(16.97–100) 69

(16.124–9) 68
(16.203) 185, 251
(16.386) 31
(16.544–7) 35
(16.546) 36
(16.585) 24
(17.14) 31
(17.90) 23
(17.91–5) 34
(17.141) 43
(17.169) 43
(17.254–5) 36
(17.346–8) 56
(17.352–3) 56
(18.33–4) 69
(18.34) 61
(18.71–3) 194
(18.98–9) 61
(18.98–121) 69
(18.251) 187
(18.284) 25, 43
(18.318–22) 25
(19.16–18) 42
(19.182) 38
(19.183) 24
(19.199–214) 70
(19.301–2) 59
(19.326–7) 190
(20.252–5) 130
(20.428–9) 43
(21.77) 61
(21.99–113) 69
(21.134–5) 70
(21.136) 24
(21.273–83) 69
(21.552) 23
(22.37) 70
(22.59) 70
(22.82) 70
(22.98) 23
(22.260) 43
(22.271–2) 70
(22.291–3) 46
(22.344) 43
(22.345–54) 278–9
(22.346–7) 279
(22.500–1) 203
(22.500–4) 199
(22.502–4) 203
(23.391) 30
(23.473–81) 37
(23.492–4) 36–7
(23.534) 71
(23.548) 71
(24.23) 71

Homer (*cont.*)
(24.44) 71
(24.53) 38
(24.113–14) 29
(24.113–16) 71
(24.134–5) 29
(24.134–6) 195
(24.156–8) 61
(24.174) 71
(24.207) 71
(24.212–13) 279
(24.301) 71
(24.309) 71
(24.332) 71
(24.369) 23
(24.462–4) 38
(24.486–7) 71
(24.486–551) 227
(24.503–6) 71
(24.511–12) 71
(24.516) 72
(24.559) 43
(24.559–70) 72
(24.568) 74
(24.582–6) 186
(24.628–33) 72
(24.650–5) 72
(24.669–70) 72
(24.686–8) 72
(24.723–45) 60

Homer (*Od.* 2.312–15) 196
(4.661–2) 42
(8.490) 60
(8.517–20) 60
(8.521–31) 59
(9.14–15) 60
(16.377) 31
(17.14) 31
(20.18) 187
(22.489) 38

Homeric Hymn to Demeter (203–4) 79

Homeric Hymn to Hermes (267–8)
  197

Horace (*Epist.* 1.2) 231

Isaeus (3.48) 81

Isocrates (1.21) 127
(15.315) 93

Juvenal (15.130–1) 278

Livy (1.31.8) 234
(1.48.7) 234
(2.45.14) 234
(3.3) 234
(3.6.5) 234
(3.7.8) 234
(3.9.7) 234
(4.9.3) 235
(5.11.16) 234
(5.14.4) 234
(7.2.4) 234
(9.1.3) 234
(9.1.11) 234
(9.11.10) 234
(10.28.17) 234
(13.6.11) 234
(13.9.10) 234
(22.51.9) 275
(22.57.5) 235
(23.42.4) 235
(25.6.6) 235
(27.16.8) 235
(29.18.10) 235
(42.28.12) 235

Lucan (1.109–11) 244
(1.128) 247
(1.134–5) 244
(1.146) 248
(1.151) 249
(1.152–6) 249
(1.160–1) 244
(1.204–12) 257
(1.206) 268
(1.207) 248
(1.208–10) 265
(1.292–3) 248
(1.349) 240
(1.510–11) 240
(2.1) 240
(2.47) 242
(2.85) 242
(2.288) 241
(2.493) 242
(2.727–8) 245
(3.133) 248
(3.136) 248
(3.142) 248
(3.169) 245
(3.394) 245
(3.436–7) 242
(3.439) 242
(3.447–8) 242
(3.448–9) 242, 244–5, 246
(4.243–5) 241

(4.807–9) 241
(5.57–9) 245
(5.58–9) 246
(5.294–5) 242
(5.341–2) 243
(5.351–2) 243
(6.3) 241
(7.205–6) 245
(7.311–15) 243
(7.354–5) 243
(7.445–6) 229
(7.445–9) 243
(7.445–52) 244
(7.454–5) 229
(7.647) 245
(7.685–6) 245
(7.796) 245
(7.869–70) 244
(8.485–7) 245–6
(8.597–8) 246
(8.600–1) 246
(8.605–6) 246
(8.615–16) 246
(8.630–1) 246
(8.665–6) 246
(8.739–40) 246
(8.772) 247
(8.855–8) 247
(9.1092) 247
(9.1101–2) 247
(10.21–2) 249
(10.34) 248

Luke (6:36) 62

Lysias (3.39) 81
(16.20) 81

Matthew (5:7) 62

Ovid (*Met.* 1.166) 249
(15.871) 249

Philodemus (*De ira* 34.31–35.5) 216
(35.18–40) 215–16
(40.32–41.8) 214
(41.28–42.14) 215
(42.22–34) 214
(44.20–2) 214

Pindar (*Nem.* 3.43–9) 253
(*Pyth.* 9.43) 82

Plato (*Ap.* 35a) 78
(*Leg.* 789e) 197, 198

(790c–791a) 193
(792a) 193
(*Phdr.* 267c–d) 127
(*Resp.* 439e) 95
(440a) 96
(441a7) 192
(455d–457d) 132
(552c–e) 97

Plautus (*Rud.* 1146) 232

Plutarch (*Coniugalia praecepta* 2, 3, 39
  [*Mor.* 139e, 143e]) 137
(*De cohibenda ira* 8 [*Mor.* 457ab])
  137

Quintilian (*Inst.* 10.1.90) 230

Seneca (*Clem.* 1.5.5–6) 180–1
(*De ira* 1.1.1) 284
(1.1.2) 284
(1.7.1) 284
(1.8.1) 285
(1.9.2) 284–5
(1.9.2–4) 285
(1.12) 222
(1.12.1–5) 285
(1.16.7) 130
(1.17.1) 285
(1.20.3) 136, 180
(2.2.1) 285
(2.2.3–4) 230
(2.3.1) 285
(2.29.1) 285
(3.3.1) 285

Silius Italicus (1.515–16) 269
(4.262–3) 269
(5.306–15) 261
(5.558–60) 269
(6.41–53) 275–6
(6.54) 276
(9.382) 269
(10.292–7) 262–3

Solon (frag. 27 West) 189

Sophocles (*Ant.* 354–5) 98
(*El.* 983, 997–8) 86
(*OC* 229–33) 79
(*Trach.* 552–3) 86
(1062–3) 86
(1075) 86

Soranus (*Gyn.* 2.31–5) 196

Statius (*Achil.* 2.96–102) 251
(2.102–5) 251
(2.106–19) 251
(2.121–2) 251
(2.123–8) 251
(2.129–53) 251–2
(2.130–1) 251–2
(2.154–8) 252
(2.159–62) 252
(2.163–4) 252, 278
(2.166–7) 252
(*Theb.* 1.41) 278
(1.41–2) 270
(1.302) 271
(1.395–7) 271
(1.408–13) 271
(1.428–33) 272
(1.482–97) 272–3
(2.323–32) 258
(2.668–81) 266–7
(2.688) 267
(8.373–4) 273
(8.383–94) 273–4
(8.474–5) 261–2
(8.529) 268
(8.529–35) 262
(8.716–17) 276
(8.751–66) 276
(10.286–95) 267–8
(11.497–8) 264
(11.524–9) 264–5
(11.530–8) 265
(11.536) 266
(11.539) 265
(11.563) 266
(12.726–9) 269
(12.736–40) 256–7
(12.739–40) 264

Tacitus (*Hist.* 1.3) 241

Virgil (*Aen.* 1.3, 5) 167
(1.4) 236
(1.11) 238
(2.314–17) 255, 274
(2.351–2) 236
(2.402) 236
(2.428) 236
(2.567–633) 218
(2.583–4) 219
(2.585–7) 219
(2.588) 219
(2.594–5) 219
(2.602–3) 236
(2.622–3) 236

(2.647–9) 237
(3.476) 237
(4.47) 220
(4.265–82) 220
(4.305–8) 220
(4.338–9) 220
(4.361) 220
(4.669–71) 236
(5.292) 261
(5.299) 261
(6.585–94) 236
(7.305) 237
(8.431–2) 236
(8.470–540) 221
(8.482–3) 221
(8.500–1) 221
(8.536–40) 222
(9.44) 268
(9.57–66) 264
(9.342–3) 223
(9.688–90) 268–9
(9.761–2) 223
(9.791–8) 263
(10.104) 270
(10.410–42) 223
(10.513–14) 223
(10.515–17) 223, 224
(10.552) 223
(10.604) 223
(10.707–18) 260
(10.711) 265
(10.758–9) 237
(10.823) 227
(10.825) 227
(11.29) 223
(11.41) 223
(11.42–4) 224
(11.42–58) 224
(11.45–8) 224
(11.55) 224
(11.96–7) 224
(11.178–81) 224
(11.232–3) 238
(11.477–81) 238
(12.101–6) 259
(12.107–9) 259
(12.313–14) 226
(12.494) 224–5
(12.499) 224–5
(12.503–4) 238
(12.569–73) 225
(12.580–2) 225
(12.791–842) 226, 227
(12.800–2) 227
(12.830–1) 238, 249

(12.830–40) 227
(12.845) 239
(12.865) 239
(12.895) 239
(12.919–52) 226
(12.931–2) 227
(12.933) 227
(12.940–4) 227
(12.941–4) 227
(12.945–7) 225

(12.945–9) 227
(12.946–7) 227, 275
(12.948–9) 225, 226
(12.951) 227
(*G*. 3.215–41) 258

Xenophon (*Hell*. 5.3.5–6) 119
(5.3.7) 119
(*Oec*. 19.17–19) 91
(19.19) 88

Index of proper names

Achaean/Achaeans 36, 43, 130
  Achilles' withdrawal from 185, 199
  and Apollo's *nemesis* 34–5
  camp 206
  chieftains 206
  wall 42
Achilles 28, 29, 44, 130, 195
  anger of 3, 8, 22–32, 42, 43, 44, 125, 161, 167,
    185–6, 187–8, 210, 227, 231
  Chaereas compared to 174
  childhood 9, 190, 197, 203, 204–5, 206–7,
    250–3, 278–80
  encounter with Aeneas 130
  evolution of 5, 50–75 *passim*
  and Patroclus 194, 199–200
  quarrel with Agamemnon 22, 24, 42,
    46–7, 48
  and quarrel of Ajax and Idomeneus 36, 37
Actium 218
Adkins, Arthur 23, 29–30, 78
Adrastus 253, 270–2, 273
Adrestus 55
Aeneas 9, 31–2, 55, 236–7, 238, 239
  anger of 3, 167, 220–7
  combat with Turnus 259–60
  departure from Carthage 219–20
  and Helen 219
  in the *Iliad* 130
  at sack of Troy 255
  victim of Juno's anger 236
Aeschines 76, 81, 126
Aeschylus 48, 86, 178, 197–8
Agamemnon 43
  anger of 22, 29, 30, 31–2, 41, 54, 72
  death of 142
  killing of Adrestus 55
  presiding over case of Hecuba 142
  quarrel with Achilles 5, 24, 42, 47, 48,
    50–1, 52, 62–3, 64, 66, 69, 113, 185–6,
    207
  restitution to Achilles 65, 73, 206

Agenor 23
Ahl, Frederick 243
Aigeus 141
Ajax (Oiliades) 36, 37
Ajax (Telamonius) 56, 66, 124, 182, 206, 210
Alcmene 80, 131
Alexander the Great 248
Alexandria 230, 247
Allecto 237
Allen, Danielle 118, 122, 178
Althoff, Gerd 118
Amata 218
Amini, Fari 105
Amphiaraus 270
Amyntor 131
Anatolius 189
Anchises 236–7
Andromache 65, 195, 199, 203, 204
Annius 234
Antigone 140
Antinous 195–6
Antiphon 76, 85, 126, 159
Antony, Mark 160, 218
Aphrodite 54, 173, 175, 195
  angered by Chaereas 166–7, 171
  attacked by Callirhoe 176, 177, 179
  in the *Dios apatē* 154, 155
  feast of 164
Apollo 34–5, 41, 54, 63–4, 80
  anger of 231
  and Hermes 197
  and murder of Clytemnestra 142
  pursuit of Cyrene 82
Appius 261
Arabia 159–60
Aradus 166, 173
Ardea 235
Ares 42, 54
Argives 206
Argos 270
Argylla 218, 221

Ariadne 134
Aristophanes 6, 94, 97
  Wasps 5, 83, 84, 88–9, 95, 118, 161
  Wealth 92
Aristotle 6, 63–4, 127, 128–9, 159, 162
  definition of anger 3, 4–5, 6, 17–18, 19, 25,
    26–8, 39, 79, 80, 100–20 *passim*, 122, 123,
    138, 176, 209–11, 213, 215, 217–19, 224, 226,
    282
  definition of pity 57–8
  on emotions 2
  on plot unity 53
  on raising children 191, 193, 200, 204
  and "reactive" attitude 209, 213–14
  on usefulness of anger 283, 284
  on women 136, 139
Artaxates 169, 179
Artaxerxes 166, 172
Artemis 195–7
Assyrian 155–7, 158, 162
Astyanax (Skamandrios) 65, 199, 203,
  204–5
Athena (Pallas)
  and Achilles 22, 47, 64
  anger of 71
  champion of Tydeus 262, 267, 277
  and the Erinyes 131
  in guise of Mentor 196
  rejection of Latin women's supplication
    238
  restraint of 44
  see also Minerva
Athens/Athenian 5–6, 76–98 *passim*, 113, 119,
  120, 123, 232
  control of anger 126, 128
  law courts 4, 147, 161
  magical spells 145, 148–9
  and Medea 141
  and *orgē* 178
  Plato's Athenian 193, 197, 198, 203
  women 137, 139
Attica/Attic 126, 131, 141, 145, 190
Augustus 218, 249
Aurelius, Marcus 211–13, 216, 219, 222,
  227
  on anger 123, 130
Axelrod, Robert 15

Babylon 136, 179, 182
Balot, Ryan 175
Barbalet, J. M. 99
Barton, Richard 118
Bdelykleon 88
Bellerophon 124
Ben Ze'ev, Aaron 106

Bion the Borysthenite 129
Bitinna 133–4
Black Sea 145
Blundell, Sue 85
Bonds, W. S. 272
Braund, Susanna 3, 27, 241, 247
Briseis 53, 59, 64, 65
Bührer-Thierry, G. 118

Cacus 218, 256
Caesar, Julius 160, 229–30, 235, 259
  anger of 9, 242–3, 248–9
  crossing the Rubicon 239, 257–8, 259
  favored by *Fortuna* 231, 244–8
Cairns, Douglas 3
Calchas 41–2, 186
Calliope 273
Callirhoe 7, 136, 164–84 *passim*
Callisthenes 159
Cambyses 124
Canada 271
Cannae 235, 262, 275
Cannon, Walter 105
Capaneus 276
Carthage 236
Cato Uticensis 229–30, 240–1
Catullus 54, 134
Chaereas 7, 164–84 *passim*
Chariton 7, 136, 163–83 *passim*
Cheiron 186, 205
  Chiron 251–3
China 252
Chryseis 43, 53, 63, 64
Chryses 63, 72
Chrysippus 131
  definition of pity 57, 58
Cicero, Marcus Tullius 129, 254
  Tusculan Disputations 129, 283
  on gender roles and anger 136, 137, 139
  view of anger 129, 136, 137, 216, 217, 275,
    282, 283
Cicero, Quintus Tullius 129
Cilissa 197–8
Claudius, Appius 234
Clement of Alexandria 189
Cleon 92, 110
Cleopatra 160, 218
Clytemnestra 85, 86, 178
  anger of 131
  murder of 142, 143
Cooper, John 111
Corinth 171
Creusa 80, 85
Cronus 197
Curio 248

Cyprus/Cyprian 146, 147, 152
Cyrene (nymph) 82
Cyrene (place name) 132

Darwin, Charles 1, 12, 45, 104
Deianira 85, 86, 131, 159
Delphi 235
Demeter 48
Demodocus 59–60
Demosthenes 5, 77, 81, 88, 93, 126
    prosecution of Meidias 76–7, 127
Dennett, Daniel 15
Descartes, René 2, 16, 104
Dido 218, 219–20, 222
Diomedes 30, 43, 172, 251
Dione 195
Dionysius 169–82 *passim*
Dioscuri 142
Dioskourides of Samos 10
Dolon 43
Duchenne, Guillaume 45

Egypt/Egyptian 166, 172, 173
    and cannibalism 277–8
    magical spells 146, 150, 152
    Roman Egypt 191, 200
Ekman, Paul 12, 45, 105
Electra 142–3
Eleusis 82
Elster, Jon 115, 118, 122
English language 121
    American English 18, 20, 25
    anger terminology 18, 23, 24, 25–6, 27, 29,
        108, 111
Epictetus 130, 212–13, 222, 227
Epicurus 2, 129, 213, 216
Erinyes 131
Erler, Michael 217
Eros 164, 170
Erysichthon 242
Eteocles 264, 266, 272
Euripides 7, 231
    and women's anger 139, 140–1, 143
    Electra 86, 142
    Hecuba 133
    Ion 80
    Hippolytus 60
    Medea 86, 140–1, 178
Euryalus 223
Eurycleia 130, 197
Eurymachus 195, 203
Eurypylus 205
Eurystheus 80
Eustathius 185
Evander 218, 221, 222, 224

Fabius Cunctator 235
Fabius Pictor 235
Fantham, Elaine 283
Faraone, Christopher 178
Feeney, Denis 230, 236, 238, 239–40
Flaccus, Fulvius 235
Flavians 9
Folkman, S. 104
Fortuna 9, 224, 231, 244–6
Foucault, Michel 90–2
Fowler, Don 12, 271
Foxhall, Lin 85
Francken, C. M. 247
Frank, Robert 15–16, 19
Frazer, James 252
French language 121
Freud, Sigmund 16

Galen 4, 8, 124
    *On the Diagnosis and Care of the Passions of
        the Soul* 129, 135
Galinsky, Karl 217
Gantz, T. 154
Gastron 133
Gilbert, Giles 27
Gill, Christopher 3, 219, 227
Glauce 141
Glaucon 95
Glaucus 35
Goffman, Erving 40, 48
Goldhill, Simon 131
Grastyán, Endre 104–5

Hades 34, 236
Haemon 262
Hannibal 233, 235, 261, 263
Hanson, Ann 251
Harris, William 3, 284
Hector 23, 46, 56, 206
    Achilles' anger at 5, 50, 52–3,
        62–3, 70, 73, 194–5, 227,
        278
    and Andromache 65, 195, 199
    anger of 42, 46, 187
    assault on Greek camp 66
    and Hera's *nemesis* 35
    killing of Patroclus 43, 69, 200
    mourned by Andromache 60, 204
    pity of 61, 65
    treatment of corpse 71, 72, 186
Hecuba 71, 86, 130, 141–2, 195
Helen 46, 54, 139
    and Aeneas 218, 219, 220, 222
Henderson, Jeffrey 89, 93, 131
Hephaestus 188

Hera 197
  and Achilles 63
  anger of 35, 44, 71
  assault on Artemis 195
  and the *Dios apatē* 44, 54, 154, 155, 160
  see also Juno
Heracles 131–2
  Hercules 218, 237, 256, 262
Herculaneum 129
Hercules
  see Heracles
Hermes 23, 158, 197
Hermocrates 171
Herodas 6, 133, 134
Herodotus 79, 231, 252
  anger in 124, 126, 132
  and women 6, 132
Hesiod
  Theogony 197
  Works and Days 78, 94, 95, 97
Hipponax 161
Hirpini 235
Holoka, James 43, 44
Homer/Homeric 20–49 *passim*, 50–75 *passim*
  and anger 3, 5, 6, 7, 78, 177
  anger terminology 4, 5, 122
  children in 8, 190, 194
  Dios apatē 155–6, 162
  gods in 231
  and heroic code 174
  Iliad 117, 167–8, 211
  in medical texts 187, 201
  and women's anger 130–1
  violence in 279
Horace 54, 134
Hostilius, Tullus 234
Housman, A. E. 247
Hume, David 2
Hunter, Virginia 85

Ida, Mount 44
Idomeneus 35, 36, 37
Inuit 1, 12
Iolaus 80
Ion 80
Ionia/Ionian 169
Ischomachos 91
Ishtar 155
Isocrates 93, 126
Italy/Italian 218, 221–2, 225, 227
Ithaca/Ithacan 195–6

Jackson Knight, W. F. 223
Jal, Paul 240, 241
James, William 106, 121

Jason 86, 141
Jocasta 140
Jordan, David 147, 150
Joyce, Jane 241
Juno 271
  anger of 167, 226, 227, 229, 236, 237, 238
  Juno Lacinia 235
  pity of 237
  see also Hera
Jupiter 9, 237–9, 271
  anger of 236–7, 249
  see also Zeus
Juvenal 130, 277

Kanner, A. D. 104
Keegan, John 254, 269
Kim, Jinyo 51
Kluge, Alexander 74
Konstan, David 3, 17, 59, 116, 169, 182
Kövecses, Zoltán 13, 18, 20, 22, 25, 27
Kroll, W. 239

Lakoff, George 13, 18, 20, 25, 27
Lannon, Richard 105
Laomedon 236
Latinius 234
Latinus 225, 238
Lausus 227
Lazarus, Richard 104
LeDoux, Joseph 106
Leocritus 195
Leontios 95–6
Lesky, Albin 52
Levene, David 230, 233, 234
Lewis, Thomas 105
Libya/Libyan 248
Liebeschuetz, J. H. W. G. 233
Littman, R. J. 84
Livy 9, 230, 233, 235, 275
Locri/Locrian 235
Lucan 9, 229–49 *passim*, 265, 268, 283
  portrayal of Caesar 9, 257–8, 259, 260
Lucian 135
Lucullus 159
Lutz, Catherine 122
Lycaon 69, 70
Lyne, R. O. A. M. 217
Lysias 76, 77
Lysistrata 132

Mago 261
Mansfeld, Jaap 189
Maori 1
Marius 240, 241, 242
Massilia 242

Medea 85, 86, 131, 140–1, 142, 178
Meidias 76, 77, 127
Melanippus 276–7
Meleager 47, 66
Menander 7, 125, 168
Menelaus 23, 36, 37, 55–7, 60
Menoetius 188, 206
Meriones 35
Mesopotamia/Mesopotamian 153, 156, 157
Metrotime 134
Mezentius 218, 221, 260, 270
Miletus 165, 176
Minerva 236
Mithridates 170
Most, Glenn 279
Mozley, J. H. 253
Muellner, L. C. 11, 17, 33, 78
Myrmidons 36, 68, 185, 187–8

Neaera 133
Neoptolemus 190
Nereids 194
Nestor 22, 65, 66–7, 188, 200, 206
Nicasicrates 214
Novatus 284
Numidia/Numidian 275
Nussbaum, Martha 3, 284

Oatley, Keith 107
Oceanus 154
Octavian 160
Odysseus 23, 70, 73, 141, 197
    anger of 27–43, 54
    delayed by Calypso and Circe 177
    and Demodocus 59–60
    in embassy to Achilles 65–6, 206
    and Helen 46
    hindered by wrath of Poseidon 167
    and the suitors 187, 196, 203
Oedipus 271
Olympus/Olympians 45, 194, 229
Opora 92
Orestes 142, 143, 197–8
Osborne, Robin 87
Otis, Brooks 282
Ovid 239, 248, 249

Palatine 191
Pallas 218
    death of 221, 223–4, 225, 227
Panaetius 130
Pandora 94
Panthus 236
Paris (Alexander) 37, 46, 47, 219
Parker, Robert 232

Patroclus 187–8, 206
    Achilles' pity for 5, 62–3, 66–70
    death of 36, 42, 43, 53, 59, 194, 223
    ghost of 190, 205
    taking Achilles' place 52, 185, 199–200
Paulus 262–3
Peleus 188, 190, 204–5, 206
    and Achilles 68, 71, 73–4
Penates 234
Periander of Corinth 171
Perseus 235
Persia/Persians 83
    Athenian defeat of 161
    and Herodotus 132
    King Artaxerxes 166, 169, 173, 179
    Queen Statira 183
Petronius 134
Pharnaces 170
Pharsalus 9, 230, 244, 245, 248
Pheretime 132
Philip 235
Philippines 121
Philo Judaeus 189
Philodemus of Gadara 137, 139
    De ira 125, 129, 136
    on Epicurus 215
    on punishment 214
    view of anger 210, 213
    and women's anger 7, 130, 137, 139
Philokleon 83–4, 88–9
Phoenicia/Phoenician 166
Phoenix 47, 65–6, 131, 190
    care for boy Achilles 197, 204–5, 206
Phthia 190, 206
Pindar 82, 253
Plato 2, 6, 8, 94
    Apology 78
    on emotions 2
    Laws 193, 195–7
    Phaedrus 127
    on raising children 191, 193, 195–7, 198,
        203
    Republic 95–6, 97, 132–3, 192
Plautus 232
Pleminius 235
Plutarch 254
    Coniugalia praecepta 172, 176
    Peri aorgēsias 129
    and Stoicism 129
    and women's anger 7, 135, 137
Polybius 126
Polycharmus 172, 173, 175
Polydamas 187
Polydorus 141
Polymestor 141–2

Polyneices 140, 258–9
  fight with Eteocles 264, 266
  fight with Tydeus 253, 270, 272
Pompey 229, 230
  address to his troops 243
  death of 9, 244–7, 248
Pontius the Samnite 234
Poseidon 22, 34, 71
Posidonius 189
Pothinus 245
Potitii 234
Preisendanz 150, 151
Priam 5, 23, 31
  anger of 237
  embassy to Achilles 43, 53, 62–3, 71–2, 74, 130,
    186, 227
Procopé, John 214
Proserpina 235
Ptolemy 245, 246
Putnam, Michael 217, 218
Pylos 196
Pyrgi 277
Pyrrhus 233
Pythagoras 135

Reckford, Kenneth 89
Rhea 197
Ripheus 236
Robertson, D. S. 252
Roma 257–8
Rosaldo, Michele 122
Rosenwein, Barbara 1
Rubicon 240, 257
Rusticus 124

Salmoneus 236
Sappho 125
Sarpedon 36
Saturn 242
Schlesier, R. 86
Scythians 201, 252
Semonides of Amorgos 130
Seneca 122, 129
  belief in deity 229
  De clementia 180
  De ira 136, 180, 222, 254, 284–5
  tragedy 218
  view of anger 210, 217, 223, 275
Shackleton Bailey, D. R. 244, 247
Shay, Jonathan 279
Sicily 145
Silius Italicus 9, 264
  Punica 261, 262–3, 269, 274, 275–6
Skyros 190
Smith, Adam 1, 34

Socrates 78, 91, 95–6, 97, 127, 132, 192
Solomon 99, 103, 104
Solon 83, 126, 189, 201
Somme 254
Sophocles 79, 86, 98, 124, 139–40
  Electra 7, 142
Sorabji, Richard 3
Soranus 189, 191, 193, 196–7, 198
  on teething 200–1
Sotion 129
Spain 241
Spelman, Elizabeth 138
Statira 183
Statius 9
  Achilleid 251–2, 278
  Thebaid 256, 258, 261, 264–6, 268, 269,
    270–4, 278
Stocker, Michael 120
Strawson, P. F. 8, 106, 208–11, 212–13, 214
Sulla 240–1
Synesius 131
Syracuse 164, 168, 175, 179, 182
Syria 148

Tacitus 241
Tarentum/Tarentine 235
Tecmessa 140
Telemachus 31–2, 190, 195–6
Terence 232
Tethys 154
Theano 135, 136
Thebes/Theban 26, 38, 267, 271
Themis 45
Theognis 79
Theophrastus 162, 285
Thersites 34, 47, 54
Theseus 256–7
Thetis 29, 68, 188, 197
  comforting Achilles 64, 194
Thornton, Agathe 253–83 *passim*
Thrace 141
Thrasymachus 127
Thucydides 126
Tiber 234
Tisiphone 271, 277, 280
Todd, Stephen 87
Trasimene 235, 275
Trivers, Robert 15, 19
Troy/Trojans 50–75 *passim*, 174, 194, 195, 203,
    206
  Achilles' anger at 5, 186
  in the *Aeneid* 263
  battlements of 199
  fall of 35, 141, 219, 236, 255, 256
  fighting against Achaeans 185, 188, 200

Troy/Trojans (*cont.*)
  and the gods 160
  Phoenix sent to 190
  plain of 130
  proposed departure from 43, 66
  victims of Juno's anger 227
Tullia 234
Turnus 218, 225
  anger of 218, 223, 259–60, 263–4
  breaking of treaty 222–4
  death of 225–6, 227, 237–8, 239, 249
  killing of Pallas 221
Trygaios 92
Tyche 166, 176
Tydeus 9, 26, 38
  anger of 266–7, 278, 279–85
  aristeia of 261–2
  cannibalism of 276–7, 280
  fight with Polyneices 253, 270, 272
Tyre 172, 173

Uganda 121
Utku 12, 271

van Wees, Hans 279
Veii 234
Venus 219, 221, 226, 236–7, 241
Veyne, Paul 122
Vico, Giambattista 75
Vietnam 279
Virgil 54, 229, 258

Aeneid 167, 236–9, 255, 259, 260–3, 264, 268, 270
  divine retribution in 9, 230, 236–9
  and Hellenistic philosophy 8, 208–28 *passim*
  and *ira* 9, 255–75 *passim*
  influence on Chariton 167

Walsh, Patrick 233
White, Stephen 118
Wierzbicka, Anna 13, 122
Williams, Gordon 230, 237, 238, 239
Wittgenstein, Ludwig 20
Wolf, Christa 54
Wolf, Friedrich 51
Wright, M. R. 217

Xanthippe 132
Xenophon (of Athens) 91, 92, 119, 132
Xenophon (of Ephesus) 163

Zeno of Citium 129
Zeus 89, 131, 143, 200
  anger of 194–5
  and the *Dios apatē* 44–5, 158, 159, 160
  and Hera 35, 44, 54
  as an infant 197
  and Poseidon 23, 34
  pity for Priam 71, 186
  and Thetis 29, 64
  see also Jupiter

Index of topics

achos 21, 29, 56
affectus 283, 284
aidōs 41, 43, 49
  and Hector 65, 70
altruism 15–16
amulets, magical 144–5, 151–60, 162
analgēsia 128
Analysts 50
anger
  of Achilles 50–75 *passim*, 174, 210, 227,
    250–3, 278
  Achilles' control of 72, 74, 186, 206,
    279
  Aristotle's definition 4–5, 6, 17–18, 39, 79,
    100–20 *passim*, 123, 209–11
  of Caesar 248–9
  in children 8, 185–207 *passim*
  control of 6, 7, 44, 117–18, 123–4, 125–30,
    172–3, 179–81, 187
  divine 31–2, 71, 167, 229–49 *passim*
  Epicurean view 208–28 *passim*
  in Greek epic 20–49 *passim*, 50–75 *passim*
  in Greek novel 164–84 *passim*
  in oratory 76–98 *passim*
  in Roman epic 229–49 *passim*,
    285 *passim*
  Stoic view 208–28 *passim*
  of women 130–43, 176–84
  see also rage
animals
  as diet for Achilles 250–3, 278–80
  in similes 55, 248, 285 *passim*
  and women's anger 180
animus 254
annoyance 29, 35
  as alternative to anger 123
  in babies 192
  see also irritation
anxiety 23, 68
aorgēsia 128
apatheia 129, 211

Aristotelianism *see* Peripatetic philosophy
arrogance 109, 116
ataraxia 211
auspices 233

battle scenes
  in Homer 54–6, 200
  in Roman epic 250–85 *passim*
  see also epic poetry
beasts *see* animals
bee/drone imagery 94–7
benevolence 115
brephos 188–9

cannibalism 9, 130, 275–80
chalepainein 23–4, 31, 122, 137
charis 115
chōesthai 21, 24, 29, 33
  distinguished from *kotos* 31
  and facial expressions 43
  and honor 35
  and *nemesis* 38
  and the self 39
  translation of 30
cholē 152–3, 154–5, 160
cholos/cholousthai 4, 8, 21, 24–33
  of Achilles 125, 185–6, 194, 206–7
  of Electra 143
  and enemies 39
  in Herodotus 132
  in Homer 122
  in magical spells 154
  and *nemesis* 38
  and *orgē* 123, 125
  and pity 56, 62
Christianity
  post-Christian philosophy 85
  view of anger 17, 283
civil war 229–49 *passim*
cognitive accounts of anger 6, 18, 19–20, 104,
  107, 138

cold, as metaphor for emotions 146, 148, 149–50,
    151, 153, 281
    see also heat
comedy
    Greek 83–98 *passim*, 132, 168
    Roman 232–3
comminus 258, 265, 268–9
compassion 74
    of Achilles 51, 52, 63, 70, 71
    see also pity
competition 7, 113, 115, 117, 118
    and magical spells 144, 145–51, 159
confidence 114
constructionism 13
container, as metaphor for anger 18, 25, 31
contempt 43, 108, 109, 116, 117
cruelty 69, 134
curses *see defixiones*

deception 154, 236, 243
defixiones 145–53, 159
delegitimization, of women's anger 137–9, 143
democracy 83, 85, 118
depression 124
determinism, cultural 11–12, 17
devotio 234, 238
disgust 12
dishonor 35–6, 47, 118
distress 58, 63

eleos/eleeo
    and Aristotle 57
    in Homer 56–62, 65, 70, 71
embarrassment 123
embassy to Achilles 65–6, 73, 185, 206
emulation *see* rivalrousness
enmity *see* hatred
envy 116, 119, 164
epēreasmos 102, 108
epic poetry 2, 3, 4–5, 8–10
    Greek 20–49 *passim*, 50–75 *passim*, 210, 231
    influence on Chariton 167–8, 174
    Roman 167–8, 216–28, 229–49 *passim*, 285
        passim
Epicurean philosophy 2, 8, 208–28 *passim*
    on anger in women 136, 139–43
    view of gods 229
eros 90–2, 122, 125, 140, 161
evil 57
evolution 14, 16–20
expressions, facial 12–13, 29, 42–5
eye contact 41–2

fate 220, 246, 249
fear 109, 114, 116, 117, 119

fertility 82
figs, as metaphor for anger/lust 89, 90–3
fire, as metaphor for anger 18, 22, 25, 281
friendship 210, 212, 215–16
frustration 23, 29, 30, 226
furor/furere 254, 255–6

gender roles
    in expressing anger 5–8, 13, 130–43, 176,
        177–84
    in Hesiod 94
    and magical spells 155–6, 159–62
    and *orgē* 94, 97–8
    and punishment 85–7, 89
    and sexual desire 139
    see also women
graphē 83
grief 28, 29–30, 223–4
    see also mourning
guile 79, 87
guilt 15, 61, 231

hatred
    in Aristotle 102, 109, 110–11, 114, 120, 210
    in babies 192
    distinguished from anger 6
    and facial expressions 43
    and grief 223
    and Stoic philosophy 212, 213
heat, as metaphor for anger/passion 80–2, 83, 87,
    161, 281
    see also cold
Hellenistic philosophy
    on anger in women 136–7
    ideas about anger 8–9, 129, 208–28 *passim*,
        275, 282–5
    see also Stoic philosophy, Epicurean
        philosophy, Peripatetic philosophy
heroic code 65, 174
heterosexuality 92
historiography
    Greek 59
    Latin 233–5, 239, 273
homosexuality 90–1, 92, 93
honor 120
    and Achilles 206
    in Aristotle 112, 113, 117
    competition over 84
    connection with anger 6, 27, 35, 41
    and veiling 48
hostility 102, 109, 244, 254
hubris/hubrizo 108–9, 112, 113, 164, 166

inclementia 236
indignatio 237

indignation 34, 35–6, 116, 117, 230, 237
insolence 109
insults 40
inuidia 241
ira/irasci
  of Caesar 248–9
  and depression 124
  divine 9, 234, 236, 237–8, 240, 242, 248–9
  elimination of 123, 125
  of epic warriors 9–10, 285 *passim*
  and Pompey 246–7
  in Seneca 122
  translation of 253
iracundia 122, 129
irascibility 128
irritation 123, 143, 176

jealousy 164, 231, 241

katadesmoi *see defixiones*
kataphronēsis 108, 117
kentron as symbol of anger 89, 95
kestos himas 154–6
kotos 24, 30–1, 33

law courts 76–98 *passim*, 118
  and anger 126–8, 161
  and magical spells 146–7, 158–9
  trial of Chaereas 170–1
  see also oratory
love
  in Aristotle 110, 111, 117
  and Callirhoe 169–71, 177, 181, 183, 184
  in Greek novels 182
  and grief 223
lupē 124, 164

madness 124, 132, 178, 219, 281
magic 144–62 *passim*, 252, 278
melancholia 124
mēnis 4, 31–3, 122
  of Achilles 50–1, 125
  and *nemesis* 38
  and *timē* 39
menos/meneainein 22, 42
misein 109, 111
misogamy 130
misogyny 130
mortality 57
mourning 28, 60
  for Hector 72
  for Patroclus 59, 69
  see also grief
murder 40, 140
  Chaereas acquitted of 165

of Clytemnestra 142
distinguished from punishment 86
and Medea 212
of Patroclus 70
Patroclus' murder of playfellow 190, 205
of Pompey 245–7

nemesan 116, 122
nemesis 4, 21, 24, 33–8
  and the self 39
  and *timē* 43, 49
nēpion/nēpios 190, 196, 199–200, 206
nous 145, 161

"objective" attitudes 8, 208–28 *passim*
ochthein 22–3, 43
offense 35, 39, 47
oikteiro/oikto- 62, 68, 72, 74
oligoria 58, 63, 108
omens 233
oratory
  Athenian 76–98 *passim*, 118, 126–8
  and magical spells 145
orgao 82
orgē 21, 122–9
  in Aristotle 25, 26–7, 120
  of Chaereas 164–5, 169
  in classical Athens 5–6, 76–98 *passim*
  restraint of 145–62 *passim*
  sexual aspect 178
orgilotēs 128
orgizomai 148–50, 164, 166
outrage 43

paidion 188–90
pain
  in Aristotle 100–1, 102, 110–11, 114, 209
  in babies 192, 199
  and pity 116
pais 189, 191
pathos 58
  in Aristotle 100–11, 209–10
  and Chaereas 170–1
  in women 137
Peripatetic philosophy 2, 8, 208–28 *passim*
  approval of anger 138, 275, 282–5
  definition of anger 4–5, 6, 17–18, 39, 79, 100–20 *passim*, 123, 209–11
  and "reactive" attitude 209
philein/philia 110, 111
phthonos 164
physiological basis of emotions 2, 4, 6, 12, 104–7
pietas 256, 282–3, 285

pity
  of Achilles 5, 50–75 *passim*
  of Aeneas 222, 227
  in Aristotle 57–8, 116, 117, 212
  Christian view 62, 73–4
  Chrysippus' definition 57–8
  in oratory 77, 78
  self-pity 5, 58–60
  for those punished 239
  see also compassion
plague 234
Platonic philosophy 2, 138
  post-Platonic philosophy 85
pleasure
  in Aristotle 100–1, 110–11, 209
  in babies 192
  and punishment 214, 215
plot unity of Homeric poems
  51–4
praos/praotēs 80, 128
prodigies 233
psuchē 145–6, 152, 161
punishment 15
  of Chaereas 171
  divine 231, 233, 239, 240, 241
  in Epicureanism 214, 215
  and pity 57
  of slaves 134

rabies 268, 271
rage 106, 254
  of Achilles 70, 73–4
  in babies 192
  of Chaereas 164, 165, 167, 168, 172, 173,
    175
  of Electra 143
  and murder 62
  and pity 74
  in tragedy 140
  women's 6, 132
  see also anger
rationality 26, 212, 226
  "irrational" anger 28
  see also reason
"reactive" attitudes 8, 208–28 *passim*
reason 95, 180, 181, 187
  see also rationality
reciprocity
  and punishment 79, 90
  role in anger 4, 43, 47
  and *timē* 49
religion, Roman 233–5
remorse 171
resentment 34, 164, 254, 255
  and pity 62

retaliation 25, 44
  and Aeneas 219, 226
  of Hecuba 142
  and *kotos* 31
  for loss of comrade 27, 28
  and silence 48
  of slaves 139
  see also revenge
retribution
  in Aristotle 109
  divine 9, 230, 231, 232
  against the gods 229
revenge 74, 123
  Achilles' desire for 79, 186
  and Aeneas 219, 223, 227
  in Aristotle 101, 102, 109, 111, 128
  in babies 194
  of Chaereas 172
  of Electra 142
  and the Erinyes 131
  and facial expressions 43
  against the gods 229
  of Hecuba 142
  of Medea 140–1, 212
  and punishment 40
  for slight 6, 18
  and suffering 61
  see also retaliation
rivalrousness 116–17
romance, Greek 59, 136, 163–83 *passim*

satire, Roman 277
scapegoats 88
self-pity *see* pity
sexual desire 7, 18–19, 88
  and gender roles 139
  and heat metaphors 82
  and magical spells 144, 161
  in Plato 95–6
  and sycophancy 89, 90–3
shame
  in Aristotle 113, 115, 117
  and revenge 123
  and sycophancy 93
skuzesthai 24, 29, 33
  and facial expressions 44
  and *nemesis* 38
slaves/slavery 119, 125
  and Trojan women 141
  and women 133–4, 139
slight
  in Aristotle 100–20 *passim*
  as cause of anger 6
social status 64
  and anger 6, 79

in Aristotle 112–14, 119
on the battlefield 270
and Epicureanism 215
and magical spells 154–5, 160
socialization of princes 203–6
sōphrosunē 173, 174
spite 102, 108
stereotypes
    of the elderly 138
    of women 6–7, 8, 130, 133–8, 179–81
Stoic philosophy 2, 8, 208–28 *passim*
    and deity 229
    and Hippocratic corpus 189
    view of anger 17, 117, 129–30, 161, 238, 275,
        282–5
suffering
    of Achilles 63–4, 65, 66, 69, 73
    in Aristotle 109
    caused by Achilles 50
    of Chaereas 166, 175
    in the *Iliad* 62–3
    mental 124
    of Odysseus 60
    and pity 57–8, 61, 116
suicide 165, 173, 175, 182
swaddling of infants 8, 191, 196–8
swelling, as metaphor for emotions 161, 178, 273,
    280
sycophancy 87–94
sympathy 142

teething 8, 200–3
threats 40, 43, 194
thumokatocha 144–62 *passim*
thumos/thumousthai 21, 24, 89
    in Aristotle 128–9
    Deianira's lack of 131
    in Herodotus 132

and *orgē* 123, 125
and pity 56
restraint of 7, 73–4, 144–62 *passim*
sexual aspect 178
in women 132
timē 22, 23
    and anger 30, 31, 34, 39–41, 47
    in Aristotle 113
    connection to *cholos* 27
    and facial expressions 43
    and *mēnis* 39
    and social interaction 49
    and veiling 48
tragedy
    and divine punishment 231
    Senecan 218
    women in 7, 86–7, 89, 131–2, 139–43,
        178

unfaithfulness 133, 164

valorization of anger 83–6, 94, 97
veiling, as result of anger 48
vengeance *see* revenge
verbal "cut-off" 48
virtus 255, 257, 261, 263, 270, 282
visual "cut-off" 45–6, 49

withdrawal 46–8, 49
    of Achilles 51, 52, 64
women
    expression of anger 6–7, 85–7, 130–43
    and magical spells 155–6, 159–62
    in tragedy 7, 86–7, 89, 131–2, 139–43, 178
wrath *see* anger

zēlos 116
zēlotupia 164, 166